KENKA BANCHO
Otome

1

LOVE'S BATTLE ROYALE

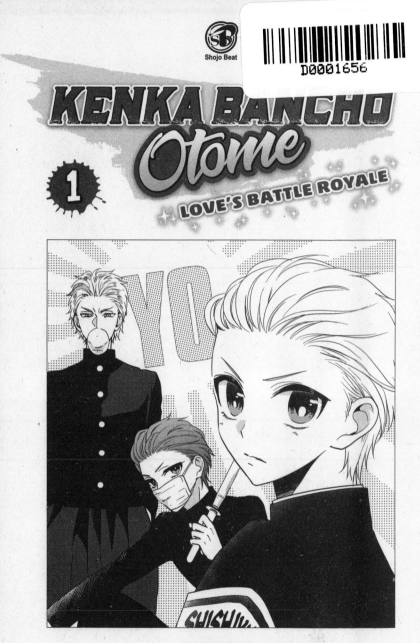

STORY & ART BY
CHIE SHIMADA

Original concept by Spike Chunsoft
Video game developed by Red Entertainment

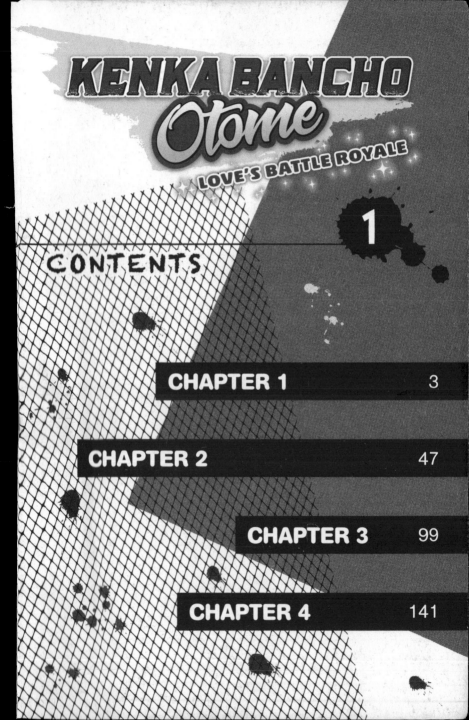

KENKA BANCHO Otome
LOVE'S BATTLE ROYALE

1

CONTENTS

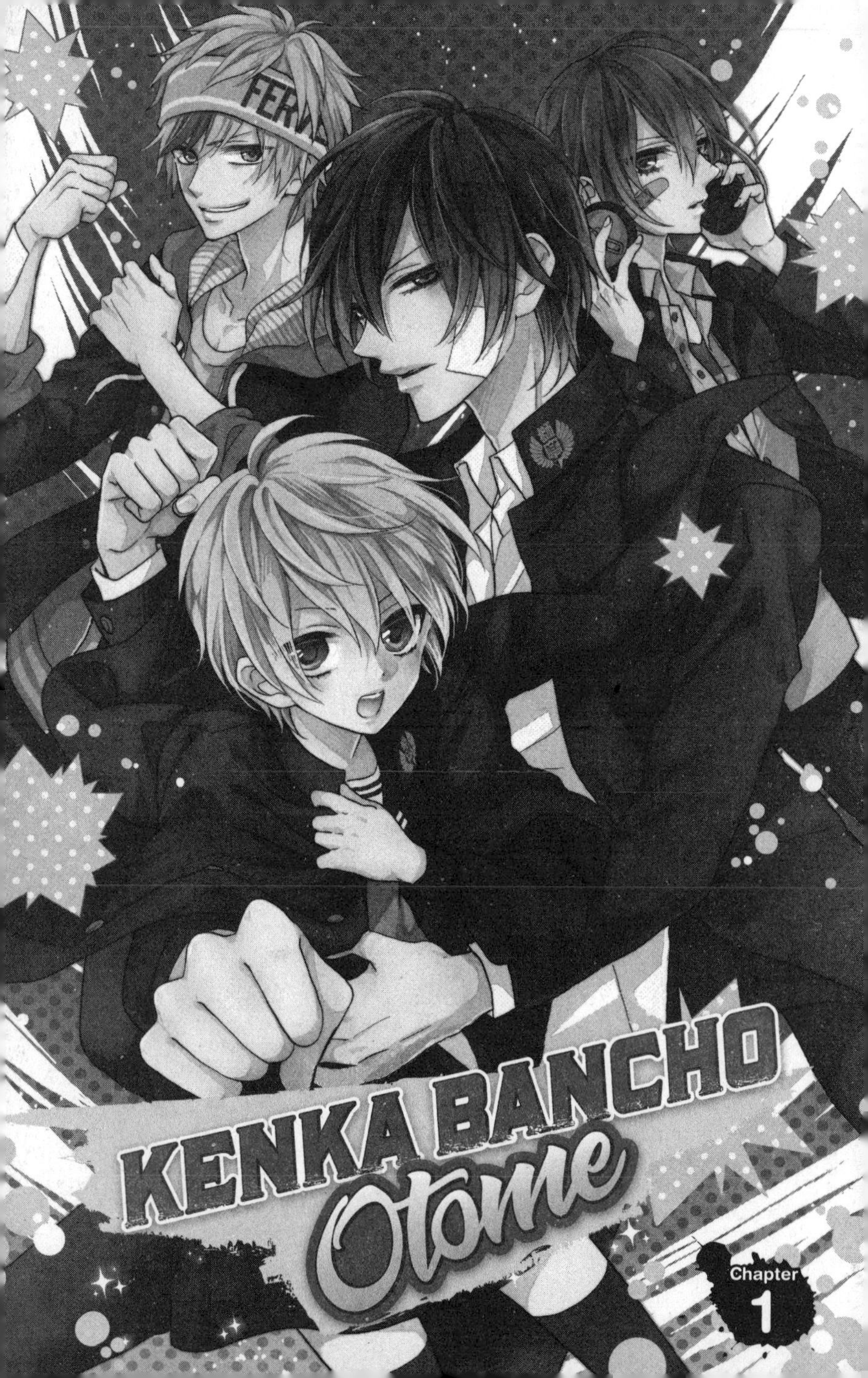
FERV
KENKA BANCHO
Otome
Chapter
1

HELLO!

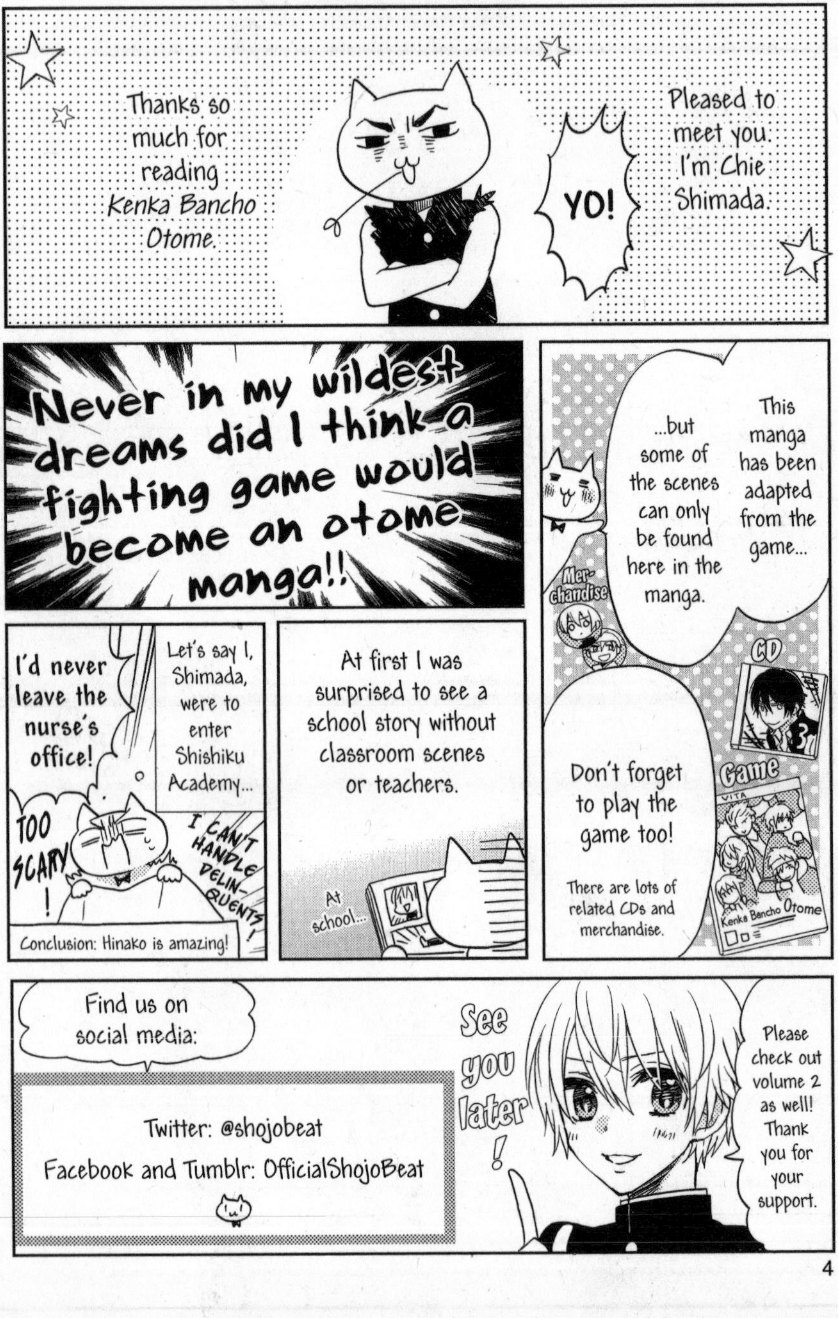

Pleased to meet you. I'm Chie Shimada.
YO!
Thanks so much for reading Kenka Bancho Otome.
This manga has been adapted from the game...
...but some of the scenes can only be found here in the manga.
Mer-chandise
CD
Game
VITA
Kenka Bancho Otome
Don't forget to play the game too!
There are lots of related CDs and merchandise.
Never in my wildest dreams did I think a fighting game would become an otome manga!!
At first I was surprised to see a school story without classroom scenes or teachers.
At school...
Let's say I, Shimada, were to enter Shishiku Academy...
I'd never leave the nurse's office!
I CAN'T HANDLE DELIN-QUENTS!
TOO SCARY!
Conclusion: Hinako is amazing!
Please check out volume 2 as well! Thank you for your support.
See you later!
Find us on social media:
Twitter: @shojobeat
Facebook and Tumblr: OfficialShojoBeat

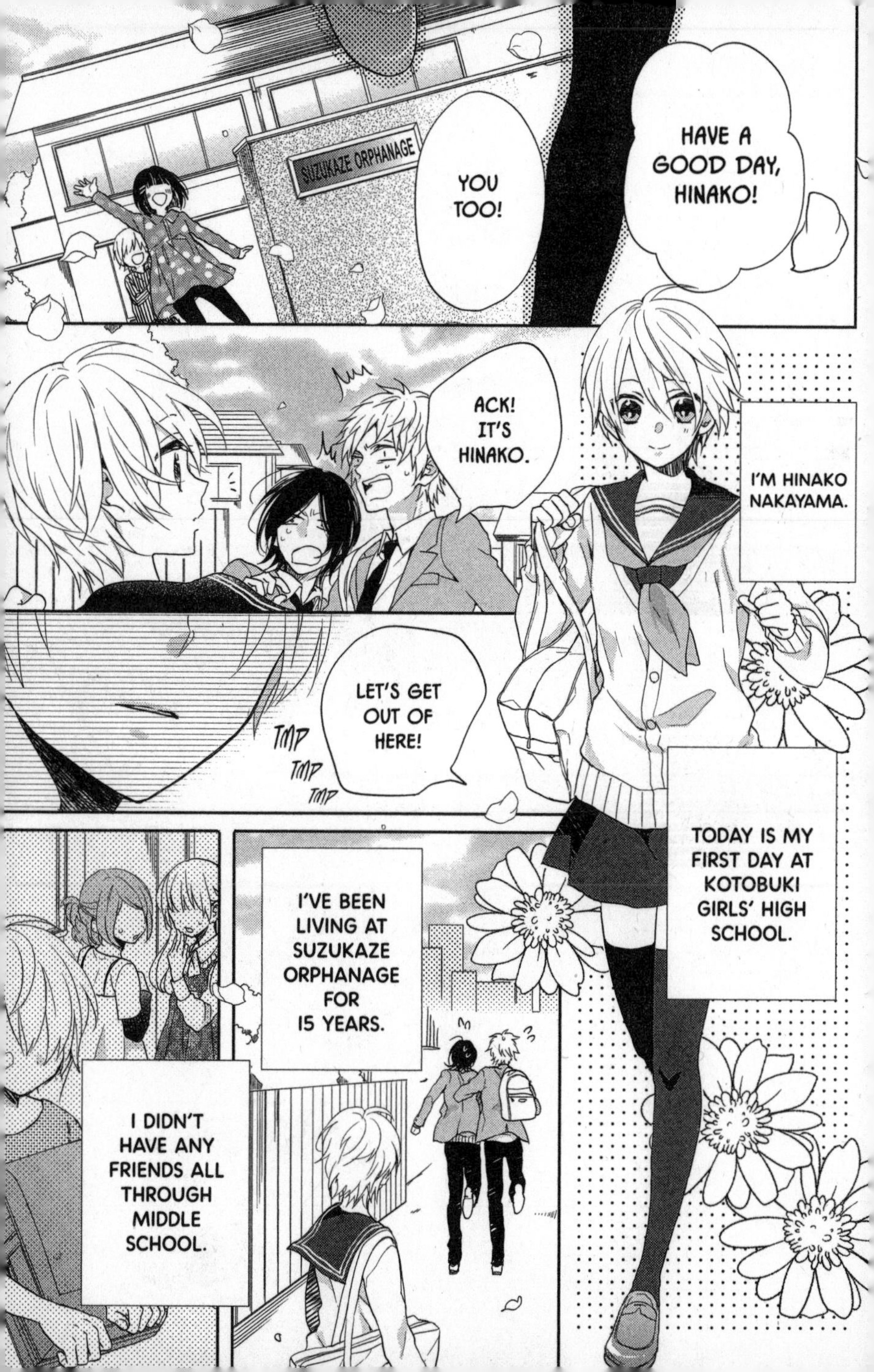
HAVE A GOOD DAY, HINAKO!
YOU TOO!
SUZUKAZE ORPHANAGE
I'M HINAKO NAKAYAMA.
TODAY IS MY FIRST DAY AT KOTOBUKI GIRLS' HIGH SCHOOL.
ACK! IT'S HINAKO.
LET'S GET OUT OF HERE!
TMP TMP TMP
I'VE BEEN LIVING AT SUZUKAZE ORPHANAGE FOR 15 YEARS.
I DIDN'T HAVE ANY FRIENDS ALL THROUGH MIDDLE SCHOOL.

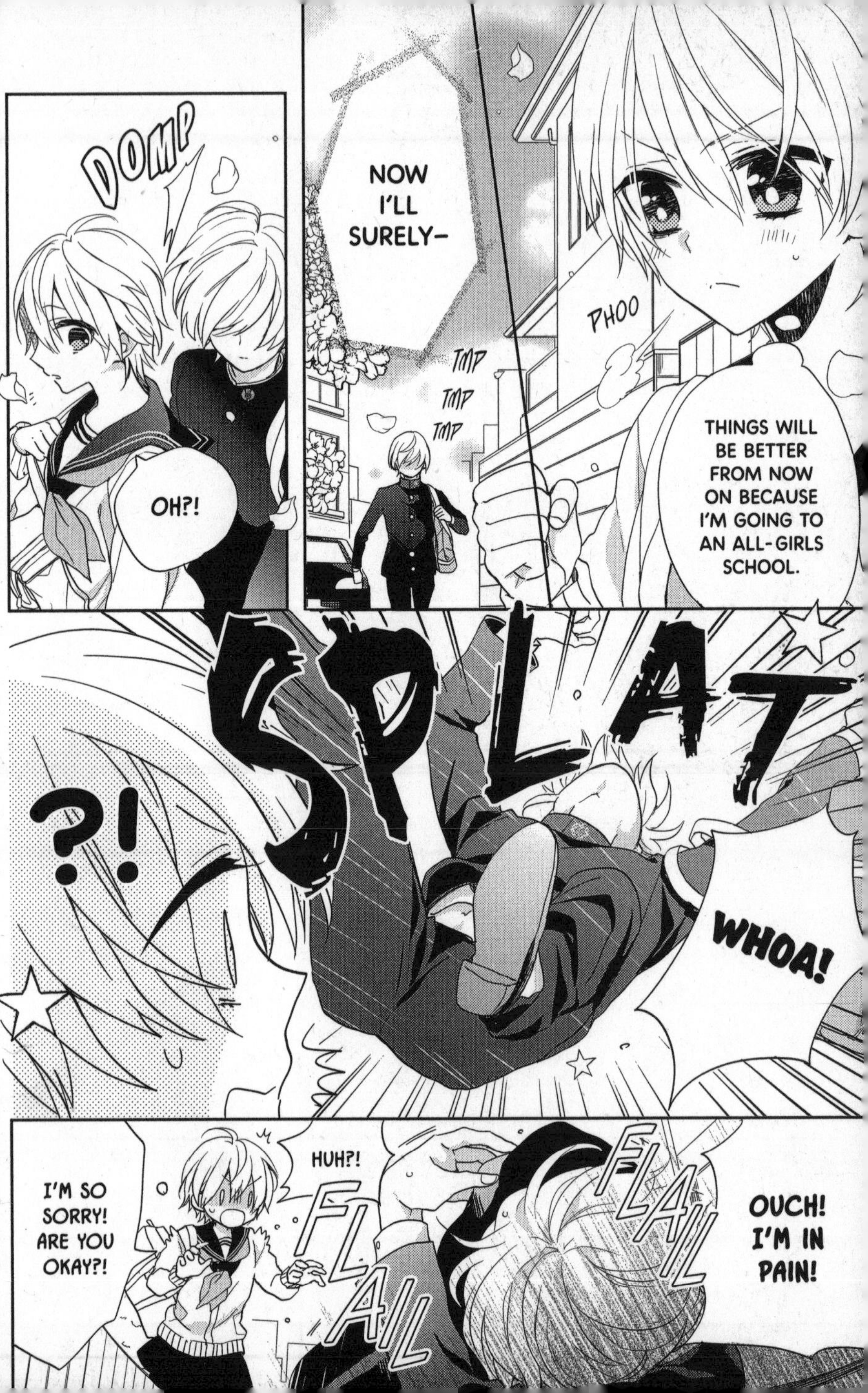
PHOO
THINGS WILL BE BETTER FROM NOW ON BECAUSE I'M GOING TO AN ALL-GIRLS SCHOOL.
NOW I'LL SURELY–
TMP
TMP
TMP
DOMP
OH?!
SPLAT
WHOA!
?!
OUCH! I'M IN PAIN!
FLAIL
FLAIL
HUH?!
I'M SO SORRY! ARE YOU OKAY?!

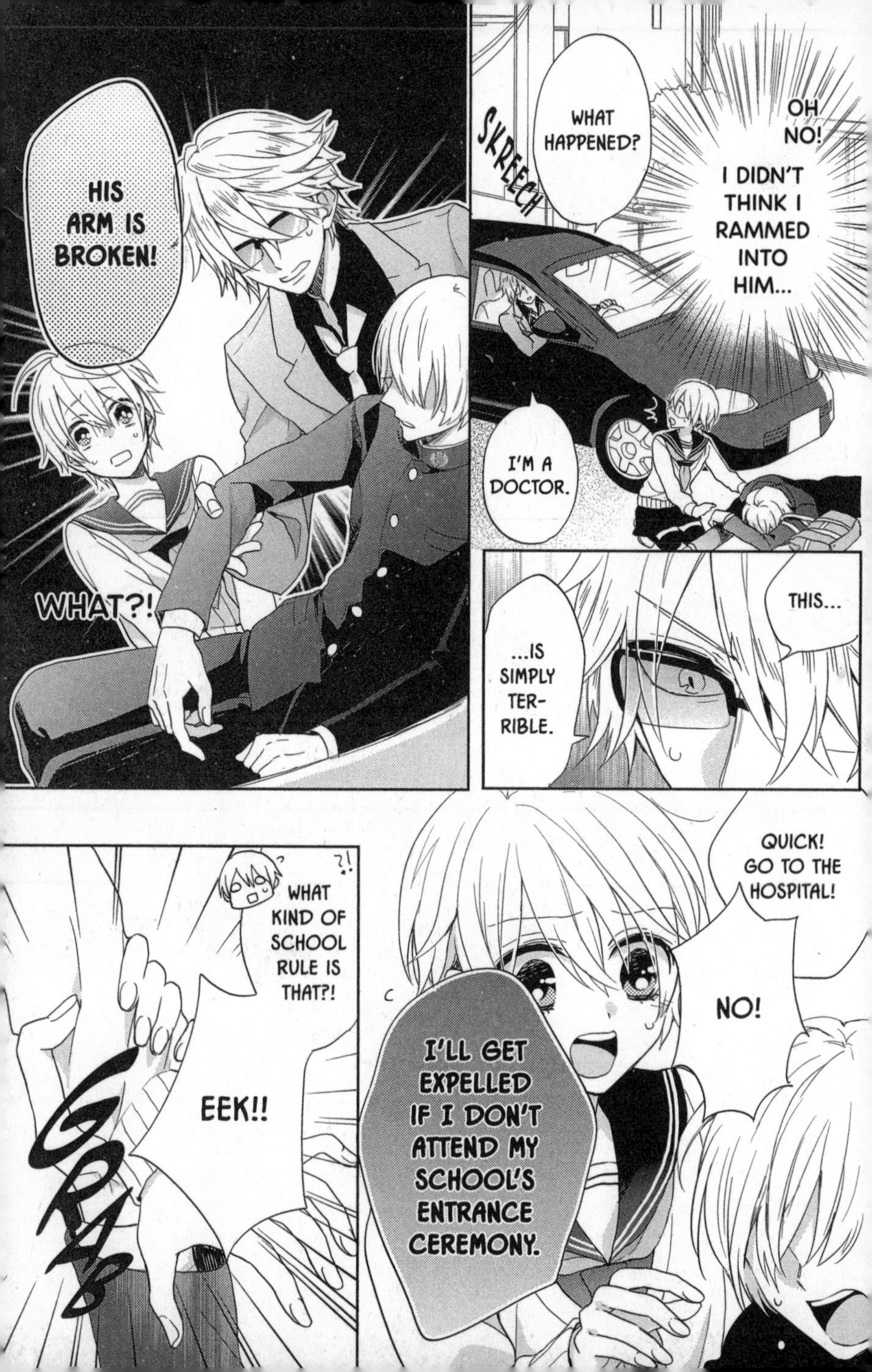
OH NO!
I DIDN'T THINK I RAMMED INTO HIM...
WHAT HAPPENED?
SKREECH
I'M A DOCTOR.
THIS...
...IS SIMPLY TERRIBLE.
HIS ARM IS BROKEN!
WHAT?!
QUICK! GO TO THE HOSPITAL!
NO!
I'LL GET EXPELLED IF I DON'T ATTEND MY SCHOOL'S ENTRANCE CEREMONY.
?!
WHAT KIND OF SCHOOL RULE IS THAT?!
EEK!!
GRAB

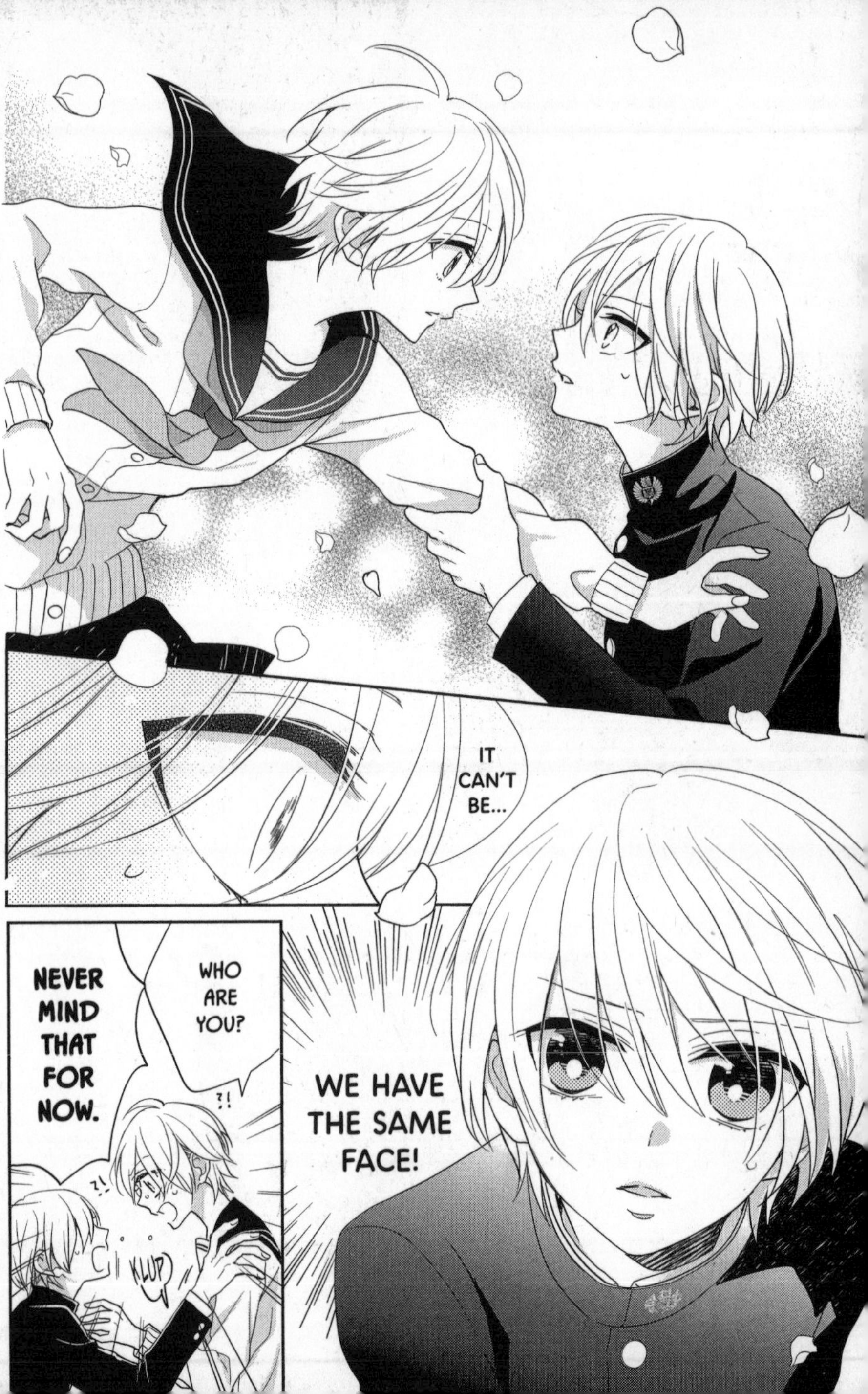
IT CAN'T BE...
WE HAVE THE SAME FACE!
WHO ARE YOU?
NEVER MIND THAT FOR NOW.
?!
?!
KLUP

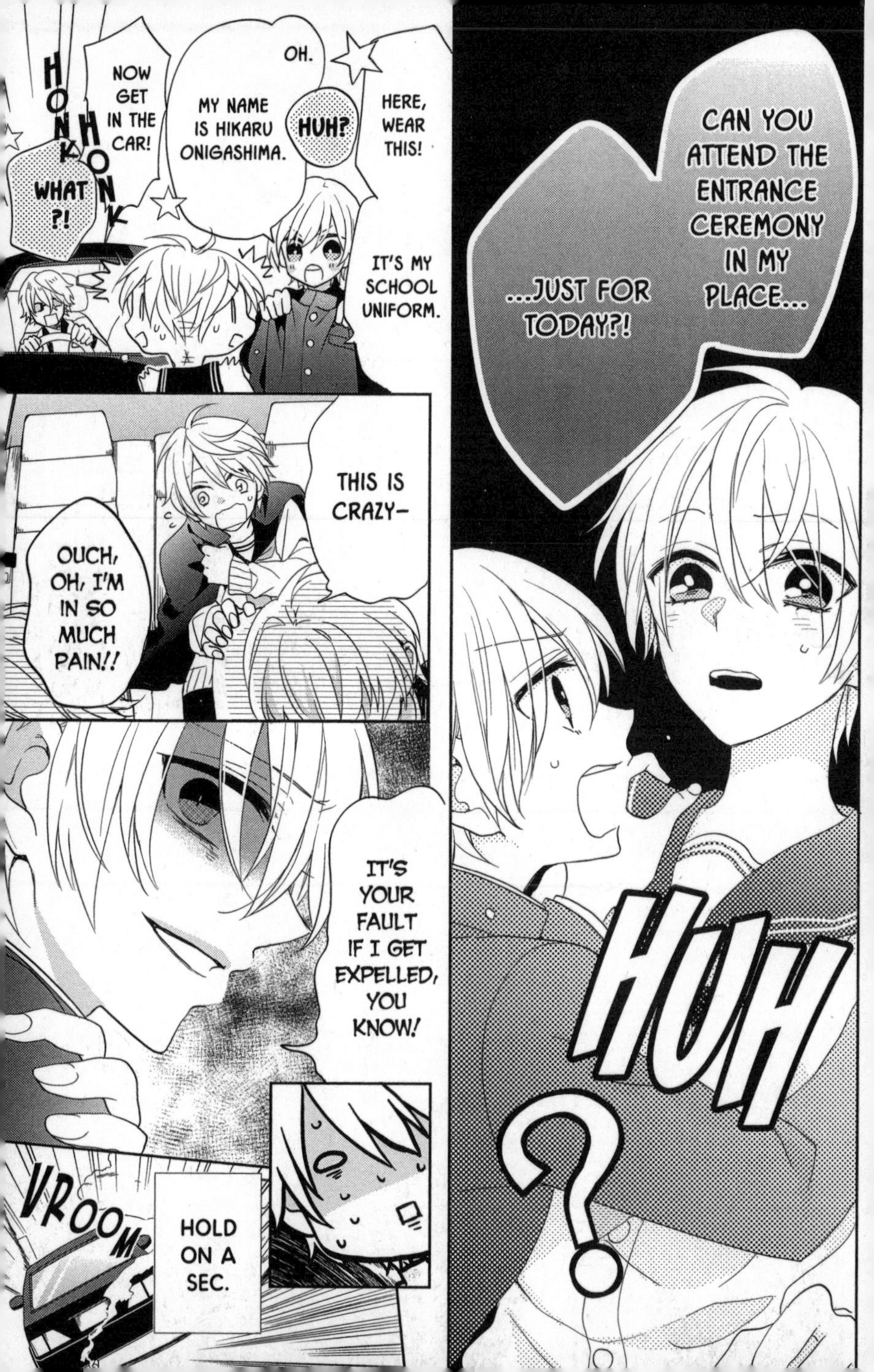
CAN YOU ATTEND THE ENTRANCE CEREMONY IN MY PLACE...
...JUST FOR TODAY?!
HUH?
OH.
HERE, WEAR THIS!
MY NAME IS HIKARU ONIGASHIMA.
HUH?
NOW GET IN THE CAR!
HONK HONK
WHAT?!
IT'S MY SCHOOL UNIFORM.
THIS IS CRAZY–
OUCH, OH, I'M IN SO MUCH PAIN!!
IT'S YOUR FAULT IF I GET EXPELLED, YOU KNOW!
HOLD ON A SEC.
VROOM

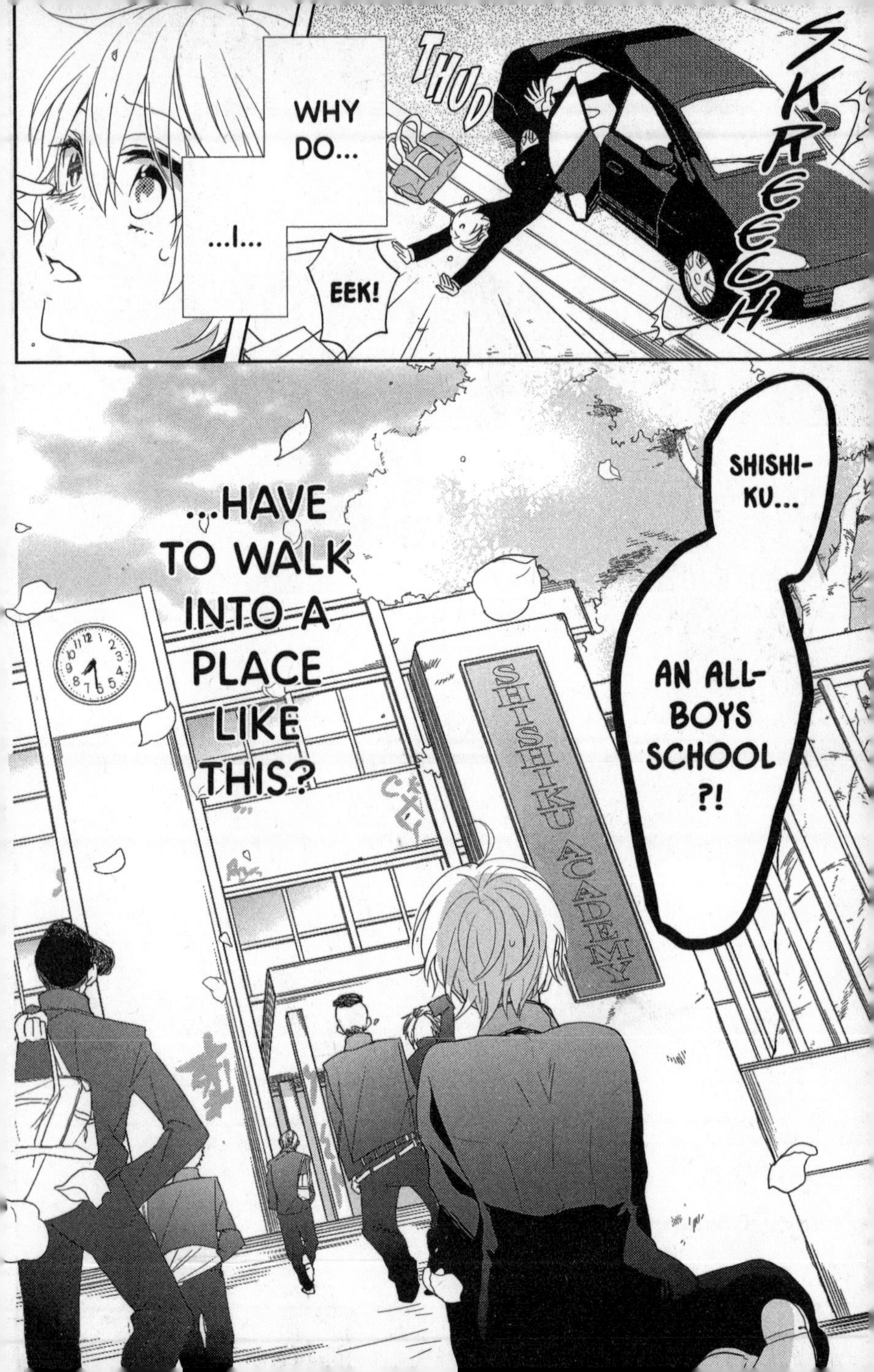
SKREECH
THUD
WHY DO...
...I...
EEK!
SHISHI-KU...
AN ALL-BOYS SCHOOL ?!
...HAVE TO WALK INTO A PLACE LIKE THIS?
SHISHIKU ACADEMY

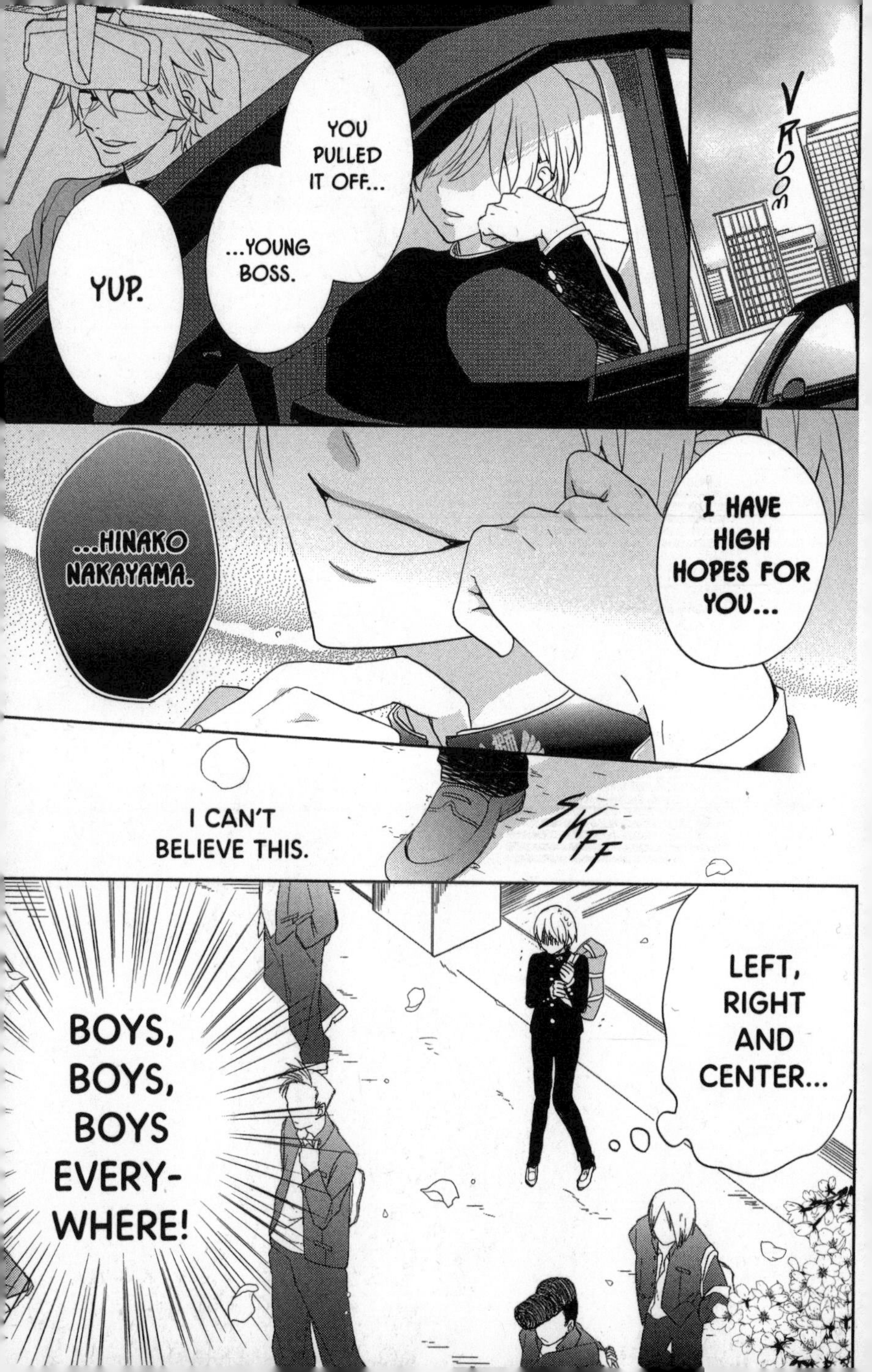
VROOM
YOU PULLED IT OFF...
...YOUNG BOSS.
YUP.
I HAVE HIGH HOPES FOR YOU...
...HINAKO NAKAYAMA.
SKFF
I CAN'T BELIEVE THIS.
LEFT, RIGHT AND CENTER...
BOYS, BOYS, BOYS EVERY-WHERE!

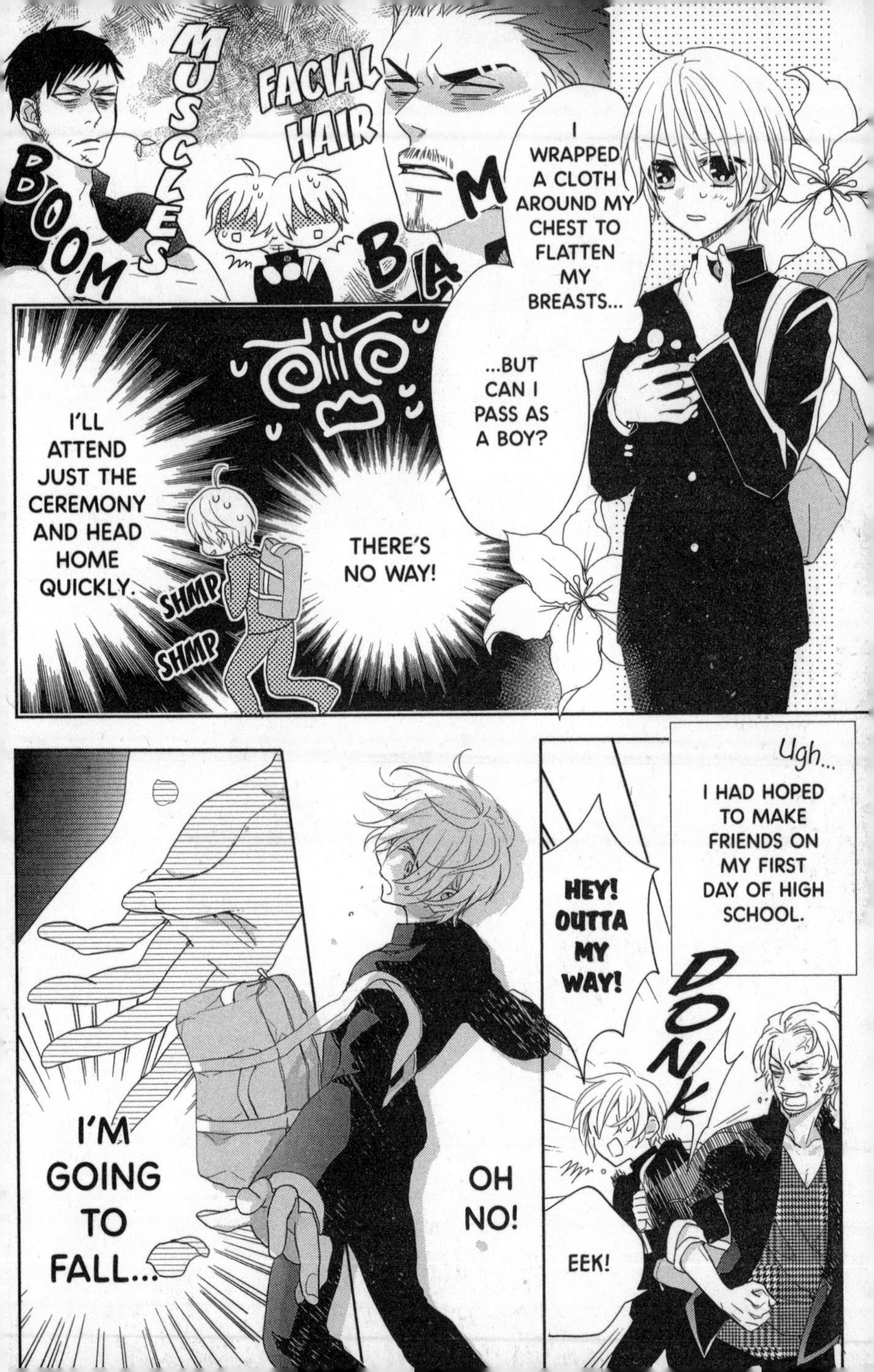
I WRAPPED A CLOTH AROUND MY CHEST TO FLATTEN MY BREASTS...
...BUT CAN I PASS AS A BOY?
BOOM
MUSCLES
FACIAL HAIR
BAM
THERE'S NO WAY!
I'LL ATTEND JUST THE CEREMONY AND HEAD HOME QUICKLY.
SHMP
SHMP
Ugh...
I HAD HOPED TO MAKE FRIENDS ON MY FIRST DAY OF HIGH SCHOOL.
HEY! OUTTA MY WAY!
DONK
EEK!
OH NO!
I'M GOING TO FALL...

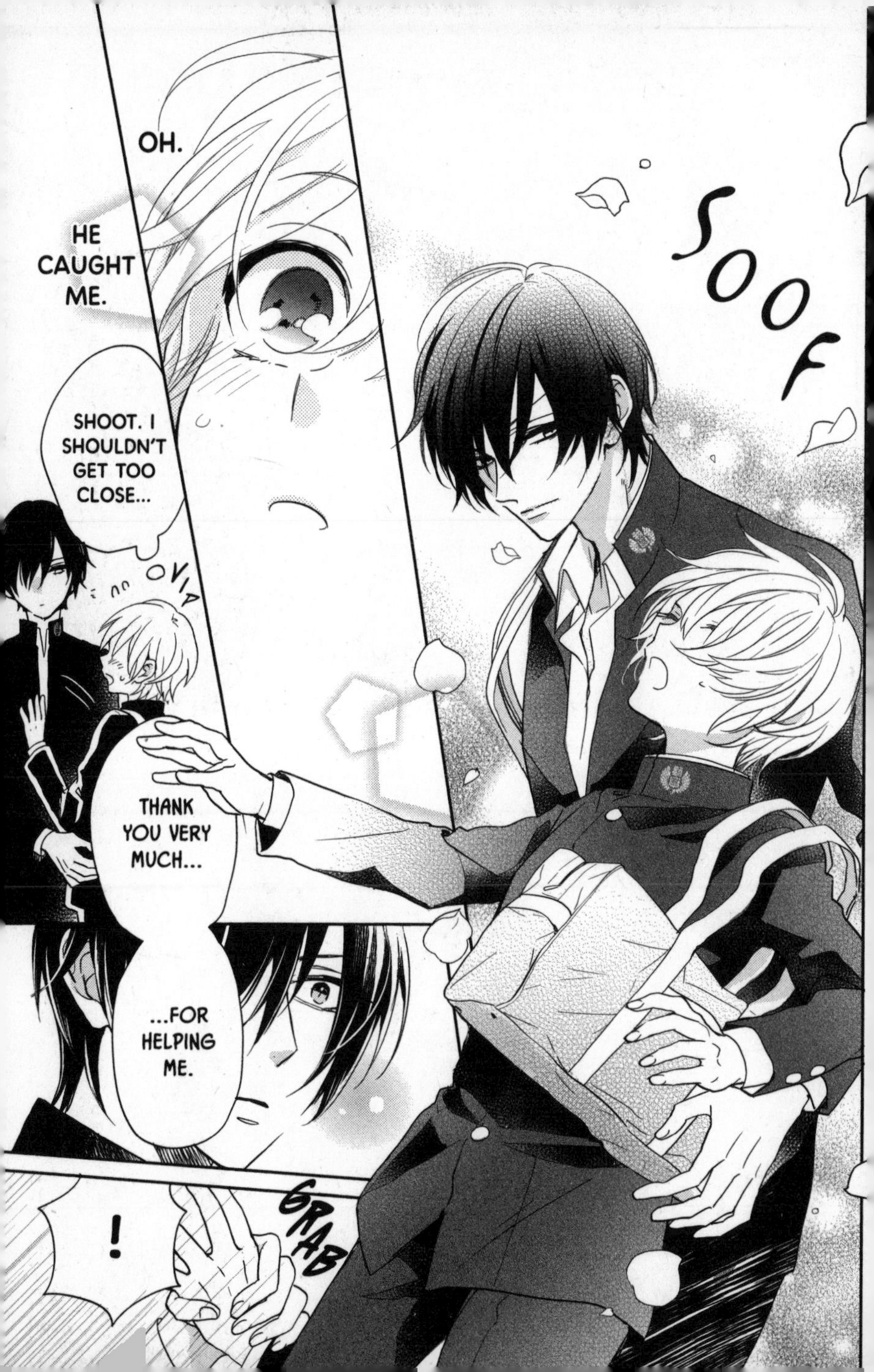
SOOF
OH.
HE CAUGHT ME.
SHOOT. I SHOULDN'T GET TOO CLOSE...
THANK YOU VERY MUCH...
...FOR HELPING ME.
GRAB
!

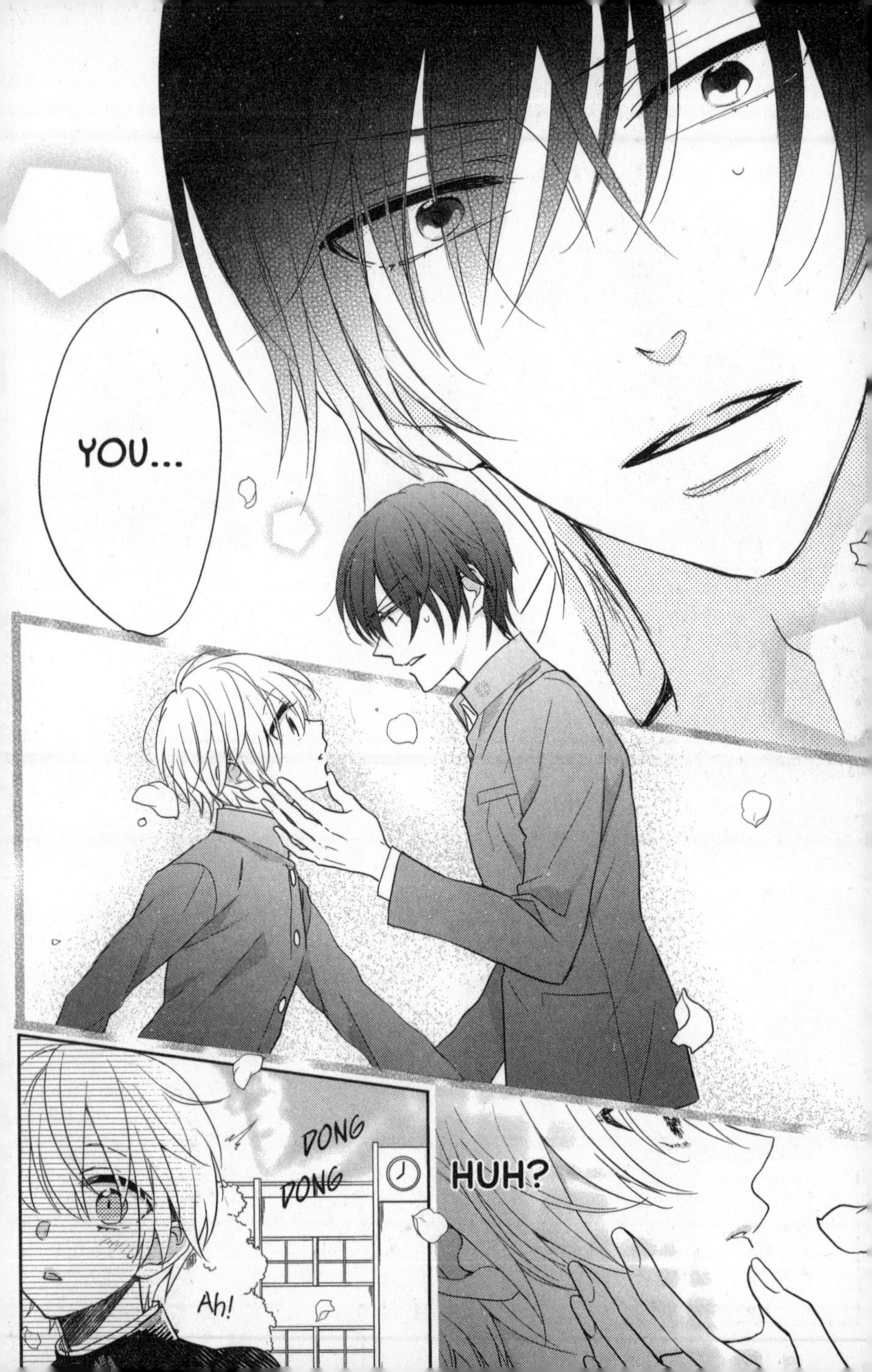
YOU...
HUH?
DONG DONG
Ah!

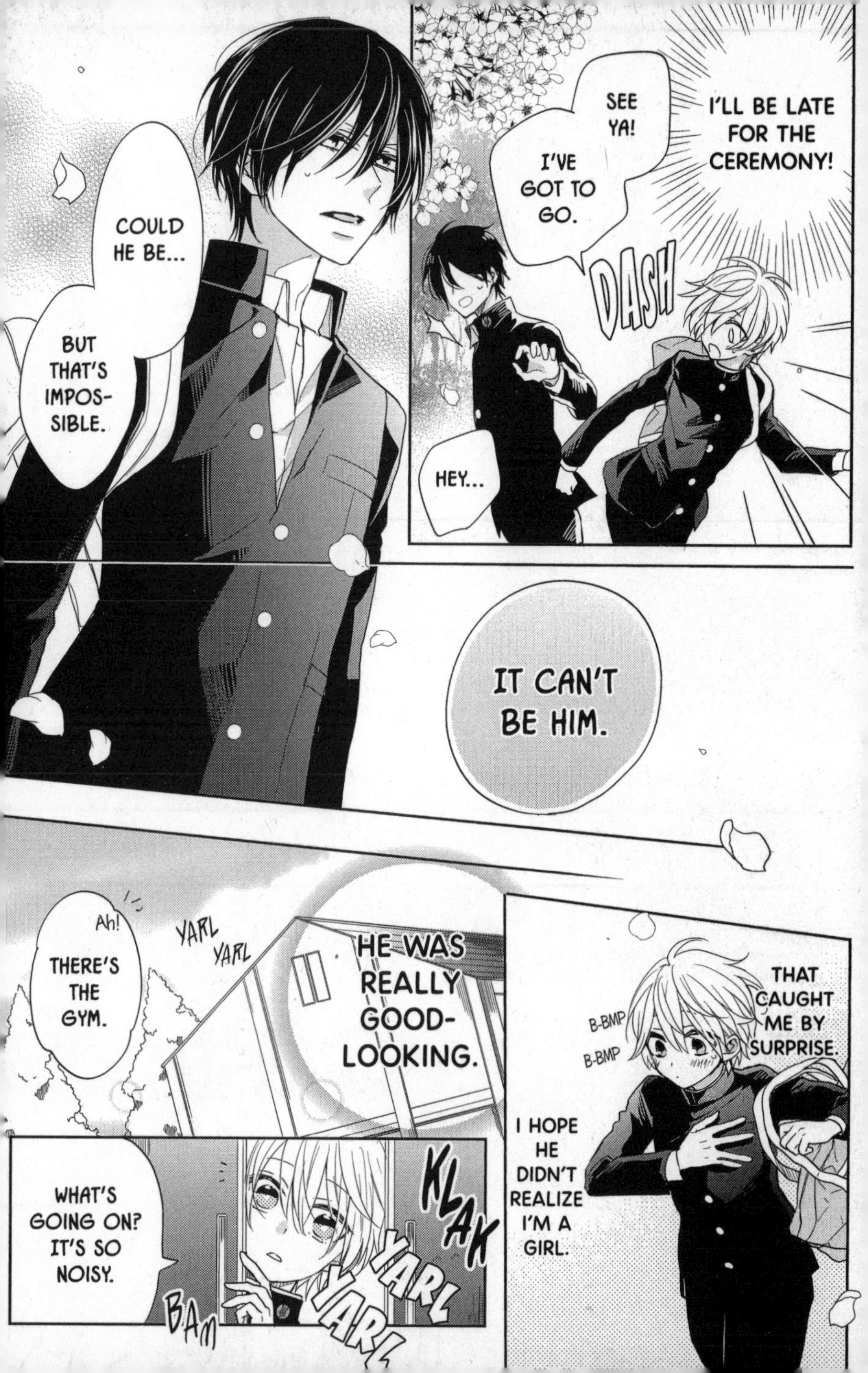
I'LL BE LATE FOR THE CEREMONY!
SEE YA!
I'VE GOT TO GO.
DASH
HEY...
COULD HE BE...
BUT THAT'S IMPOSSIBLE.
IT CAN'T BE HIM.
THAT CAUGHT ME BY SURPRISE.
B-BMP
B-BMP
I HOPE HE DIDN'T REALIZE I'M A GIRL.
HE WAS REALLY GOOD-LOOKING.
YARL
YARL
Ah!
THERE'S THE GYM.
KLAK
YARL
YARL
WHAT'S GOING ON? IT'S SO NOISY.
BAM

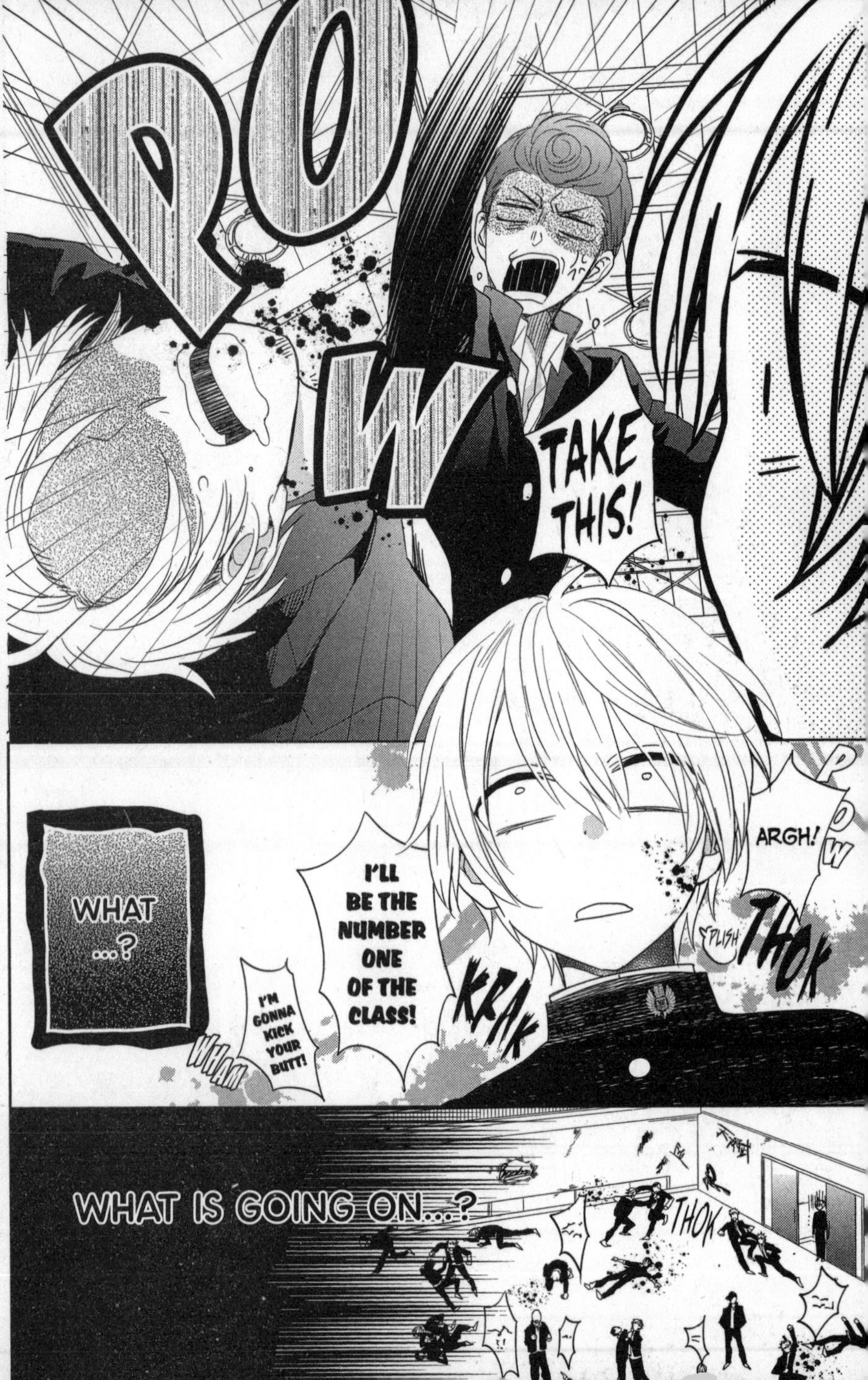
POW
TAKE THIS!
POW
ARGH!
THOK
SPLISH
KRAK
I'LL BE THE NUMBER ONE OF THE CLASS!
I'M GONNA KICK YOUR BUTT!
WHAM
WHAT ...?
THOK
WHAT IS GOING ON...?

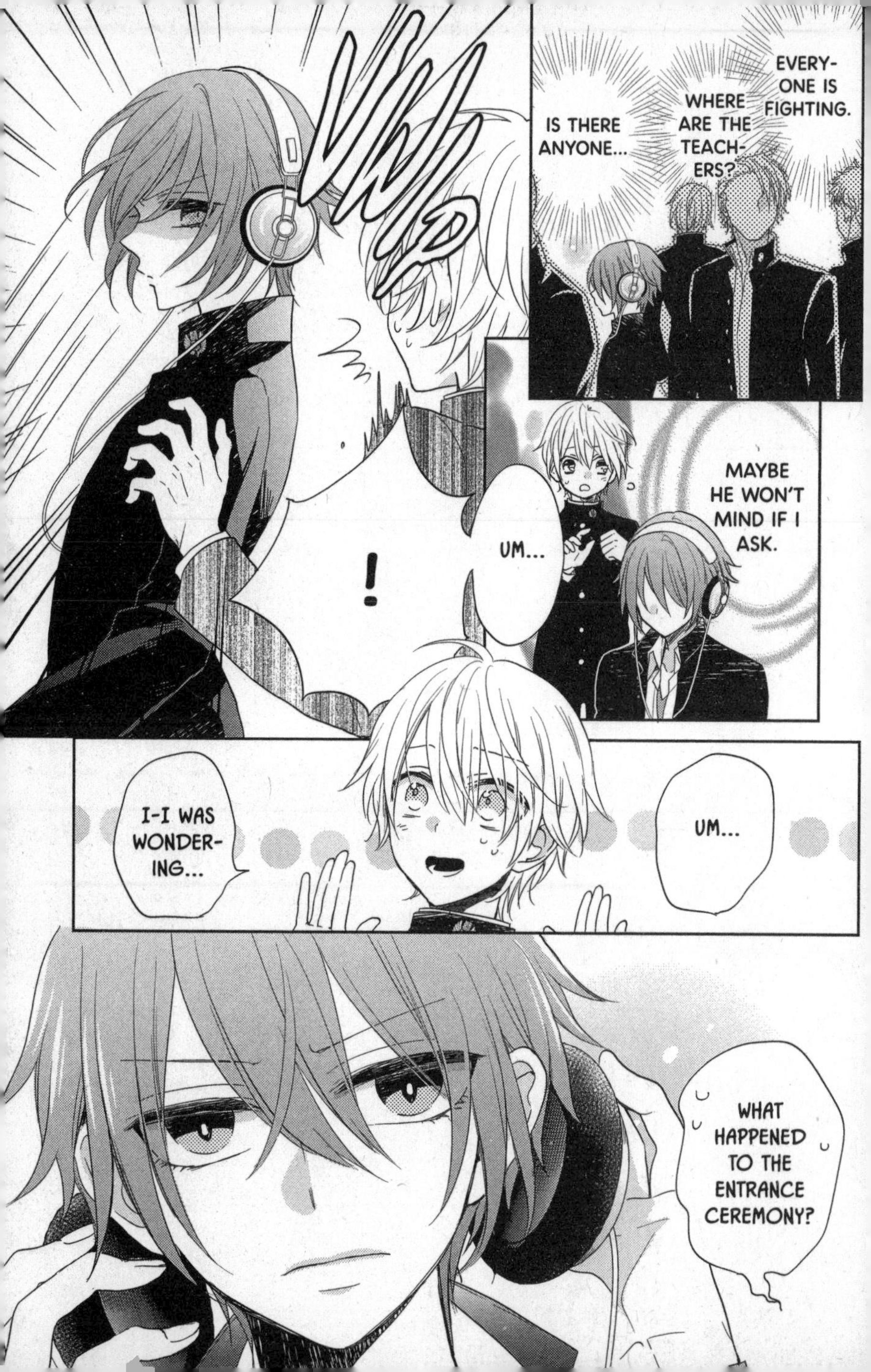
EVERY-ONE IS FIGHTING.
WHERE ARE THE TEACH-ERS?
IS THERE ANYONE...
MAYBE HE WON'T MIND IF I ASK.
UM...
!
UM...
I-I WAS WONDER-ING...
WHAT HAPPENED TO THE ENTRANCE CEREMONY?

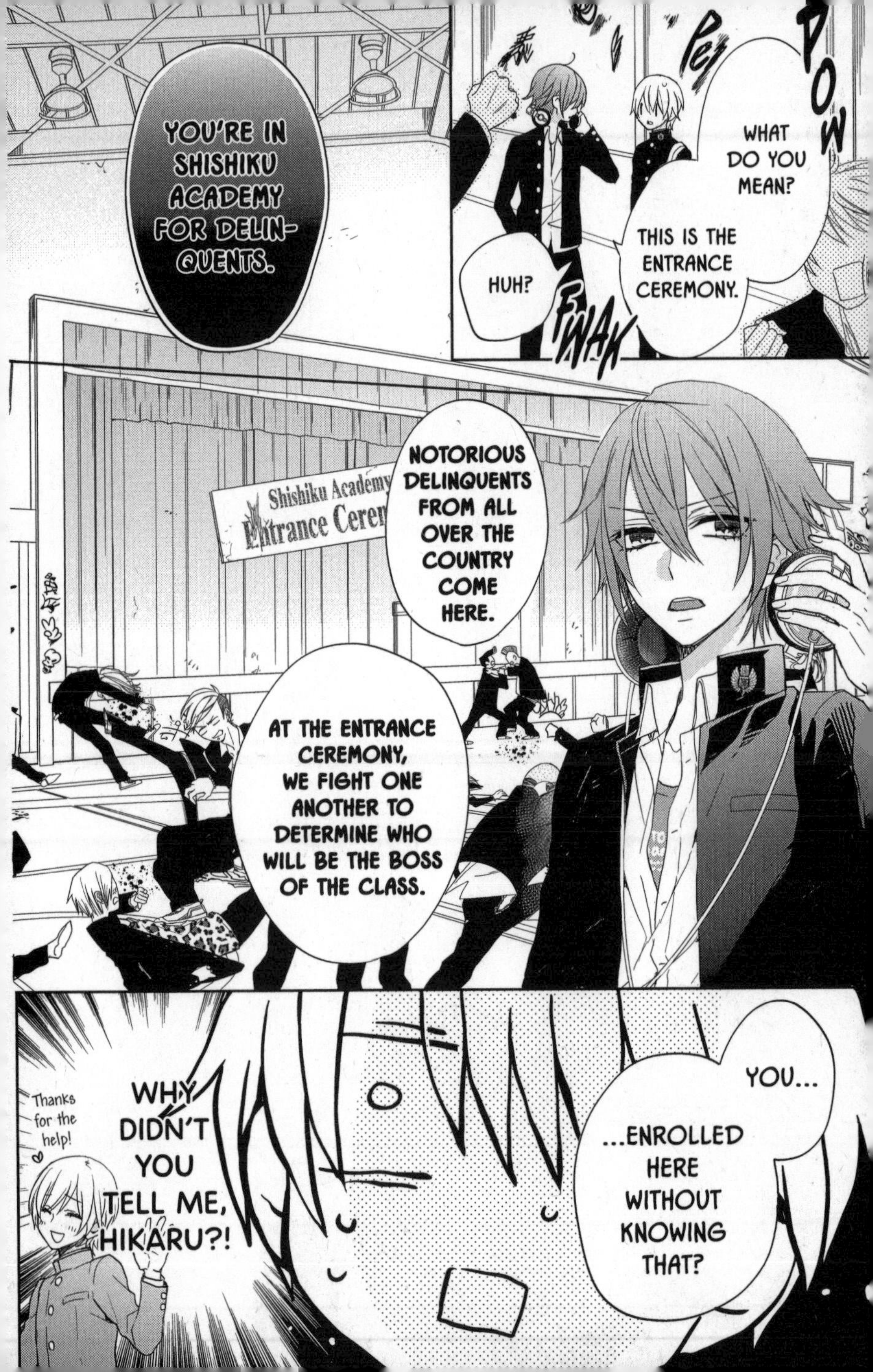
POW
Pe!
WHAT DO YOU MEAN?
THIS IS THE ENTRANCE CEREMONY.
HUH?
FWAK
YOU'RE IN SHISHIKU ACADEMY FOR DELIN-QUENTS.
NOTORIOUS DELINQUENTS FROM ALL OVER THE COUNTRY COME HERE.
Shishiku Academy
Entrance Cere
AT THE ENTRANCE CEREMONY, WE FIGHT ONE ANOTHER TO DETERMINE WHO WILL BE THE BOSS OF THE CLASS.
YOU...
...ENROLLED HERE WITHOUT KNOWING THAT?
WHY DIDN'T YOU TELL ME, HIKARU?!
Thanks for the help!

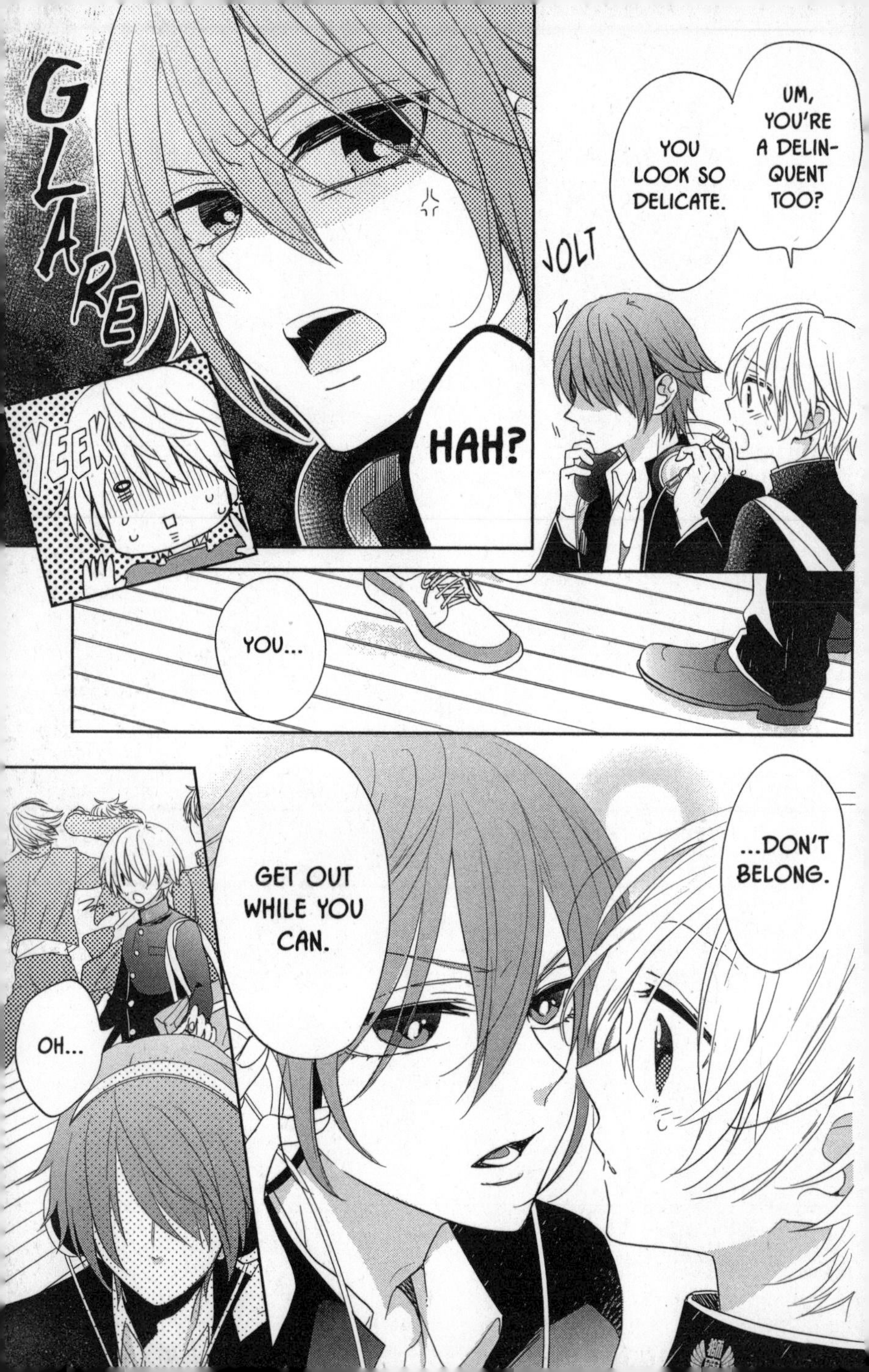
UM, YOU'RE A DELIN-QUENT TOO?
YOU LOOK SO DELICATE.
JOLT
HAH?
GLARE
YEEK
YOU...
...DON'T BELONG.
GET OUT WHILE YOU CAN.
OH...

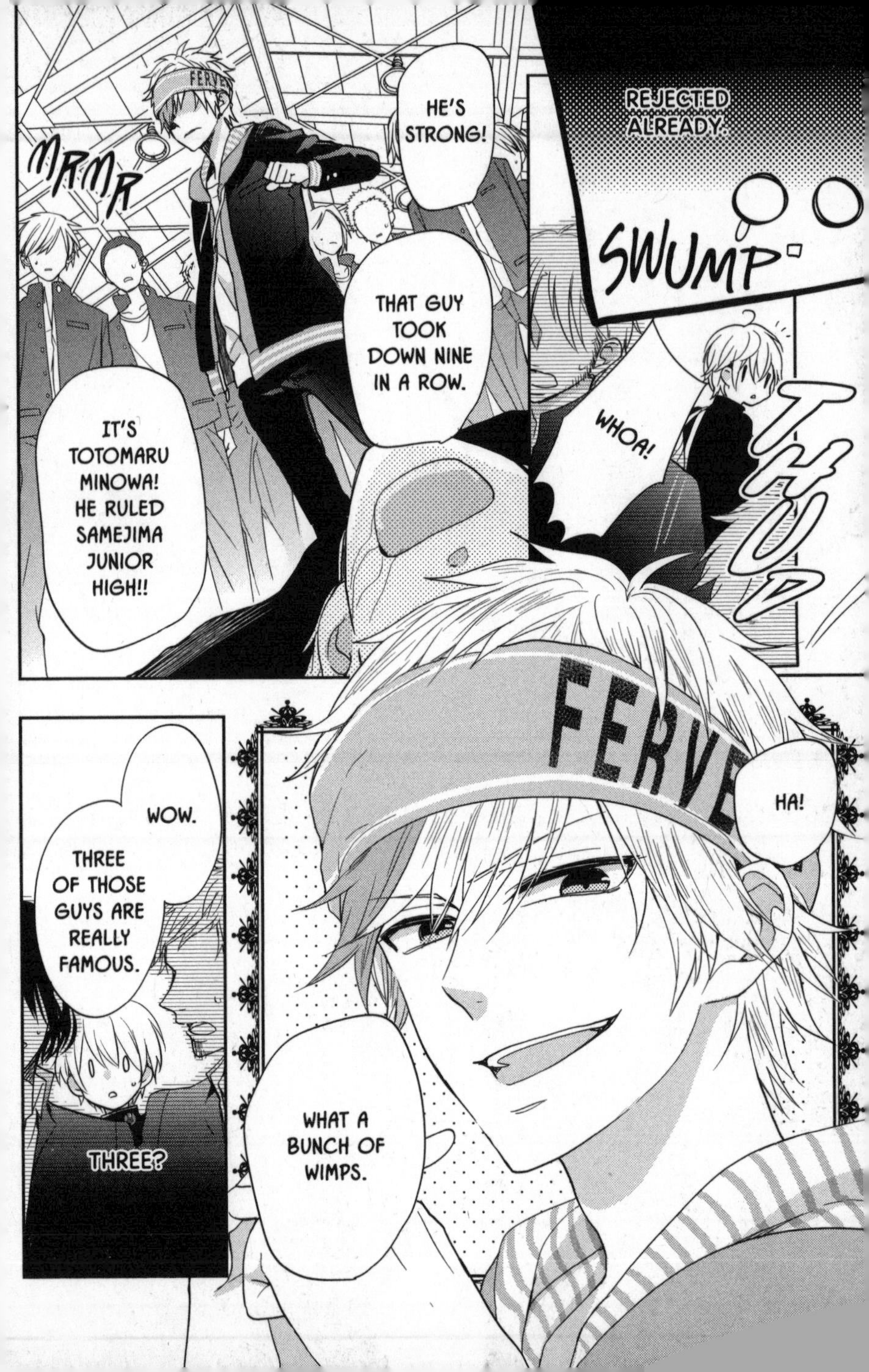
REJECTED ALREADY
SWUMP
WHOA!
THUD
HE'S STRONG!
MRMR
THAT GUY TOOK DOWN NINE IN A ROW.
IT'S TOTOMARU MINOWA! HE RULED SAMEJIMA JUNIOR HIGH!!
HA!
WHAT A BUNCH OF WIMPS.
WOW.
THREE OF THOSE GUYS ARE REALLY FAMOUS.
THREE?

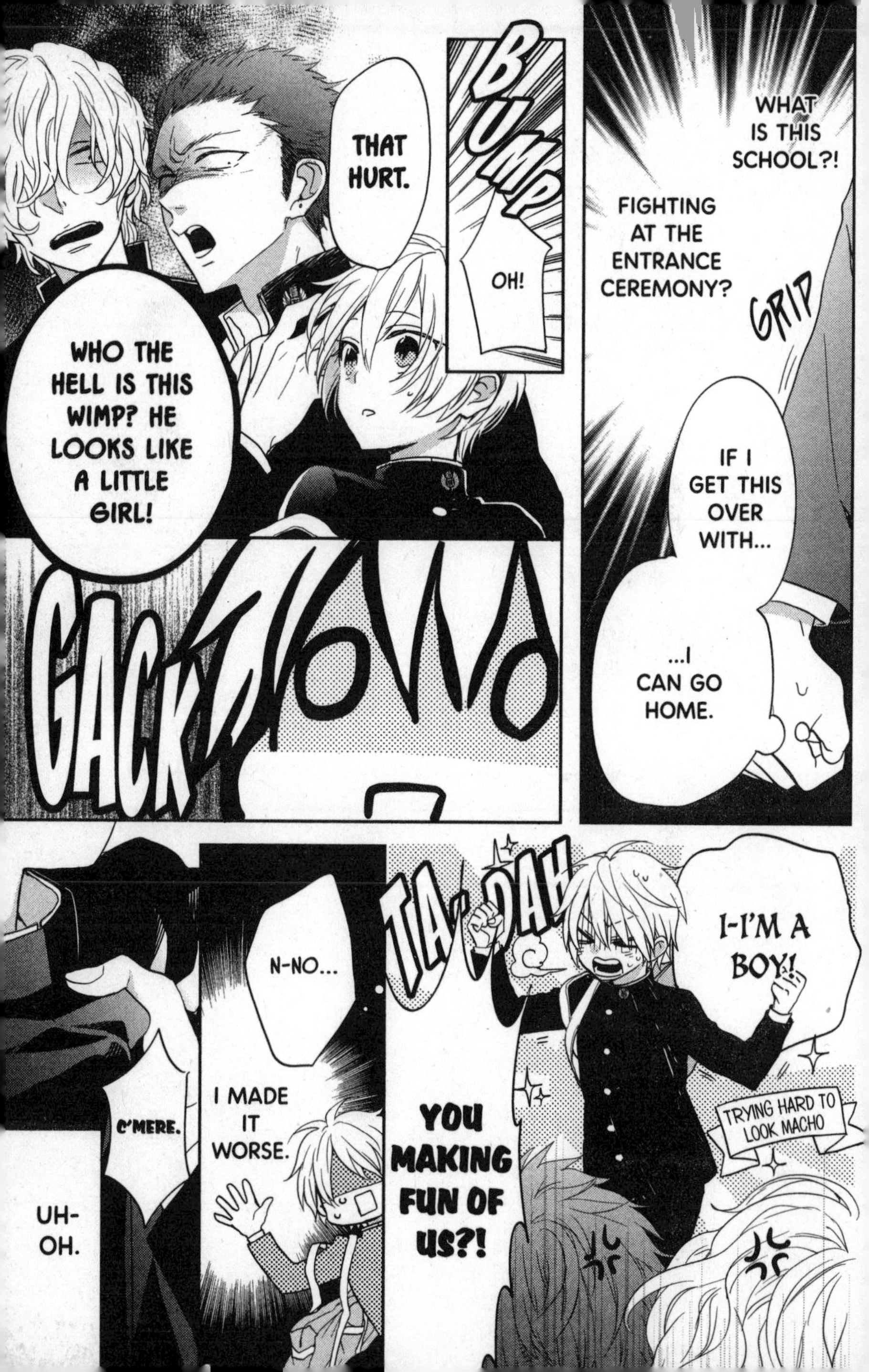
WHAT IS THIS SCHOOL?!
FIGHTING AT THE ENTRANCE CEREMONY?
GRIP
IF I GET THIS OVER WITH...
...I CAN GO HOME.
BUMP
THAT HURT.
OH!
WHO THE HELL IS THIS WIMP? HE LOOKS LIKE A LITTLE GIRL!
GACK
I-I'M A BOY!
TA-DAH
TRYING HARD TO LOOK MACHO
YOU MAKING FUN OF US?!
N-NO...
I MADE IT WORSE.
C'MERE.
UH-OH.

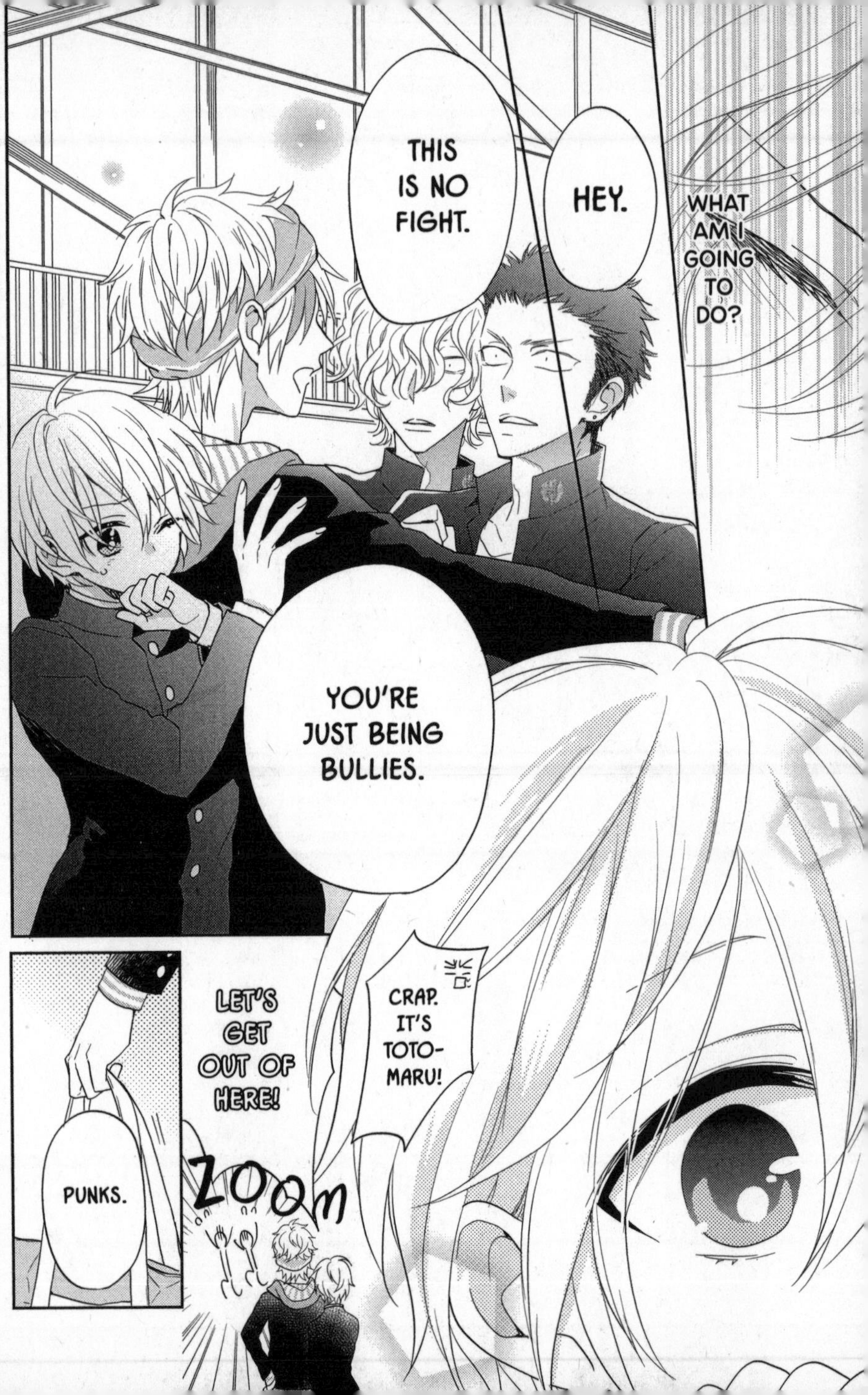
WHAT AM I GOING TO DO?
HEY.
THIS IS NO FIGHT.
YOU'RE JUST BEING BULLIES.
CRAP. IT'S TOTO-MARU!
LET'S GET OUT OF HERE!
ZOOM
PUNKS.

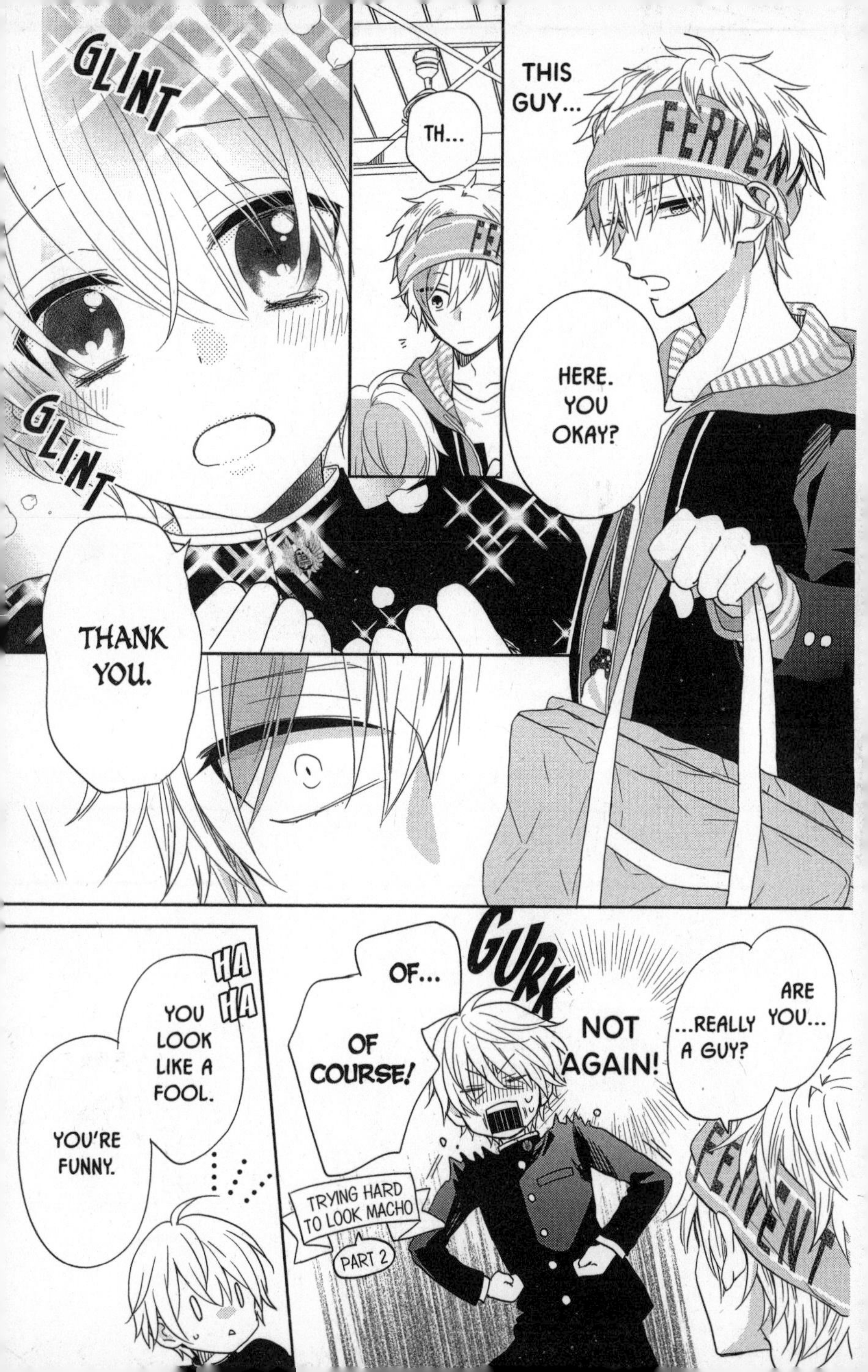
THIS GUY...
FERVENT
HERE. YOU OKAY?
FE
TH...
GLINT
GLINT
THANK YOU.
ARE YOU... ...REALLY A GUY?
FERVENT
GURK
NOT AGAIN!
OF... OF COURSE!
TRYING HARD TO LOOK MACHO
PART 2
HA HA
YOU LOOK LIKE A FOOL.
YOU'RE FUNNY.

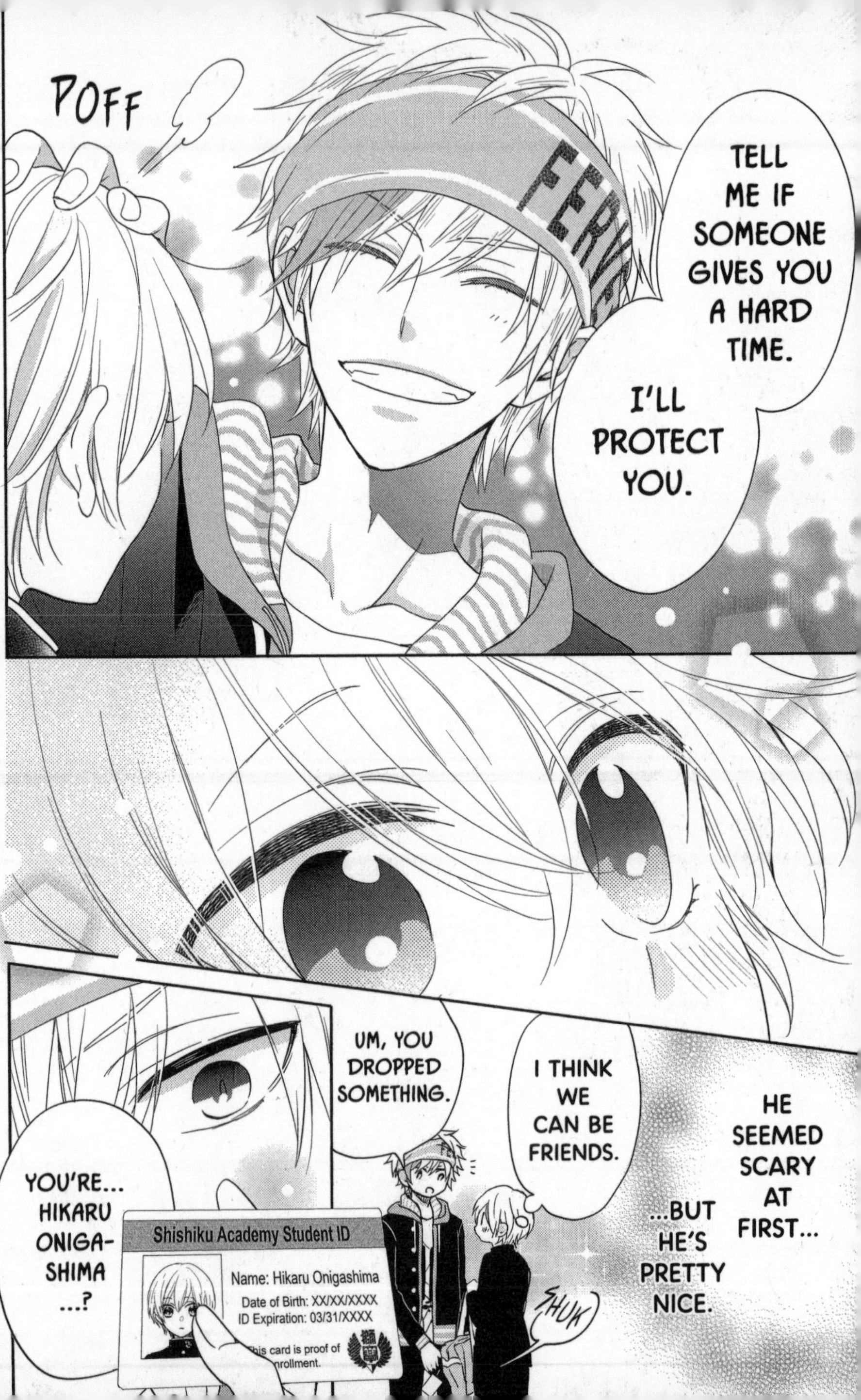
TELL ME IF SOMEONE GIVES YOU A HARD TIME.
I'LL PROTECT YOU.
POFF
HE SEEMED SCARY AT FIRST...
...BUT HE'S PRETTY NICE.
I THINK WE CAN BE FRIENDS.
UM, YOU DROPPED SOMETHING.
SHUK
YOU'RE... HIKARU ONIGA-SHIMA ...?
Shishiku Academy Student ID
Name: Hikaru Onigashima
Date of Birth: XX/XX/XXXX
ID Expiration: 03/31/XXXX
This card is proof of enrollment.

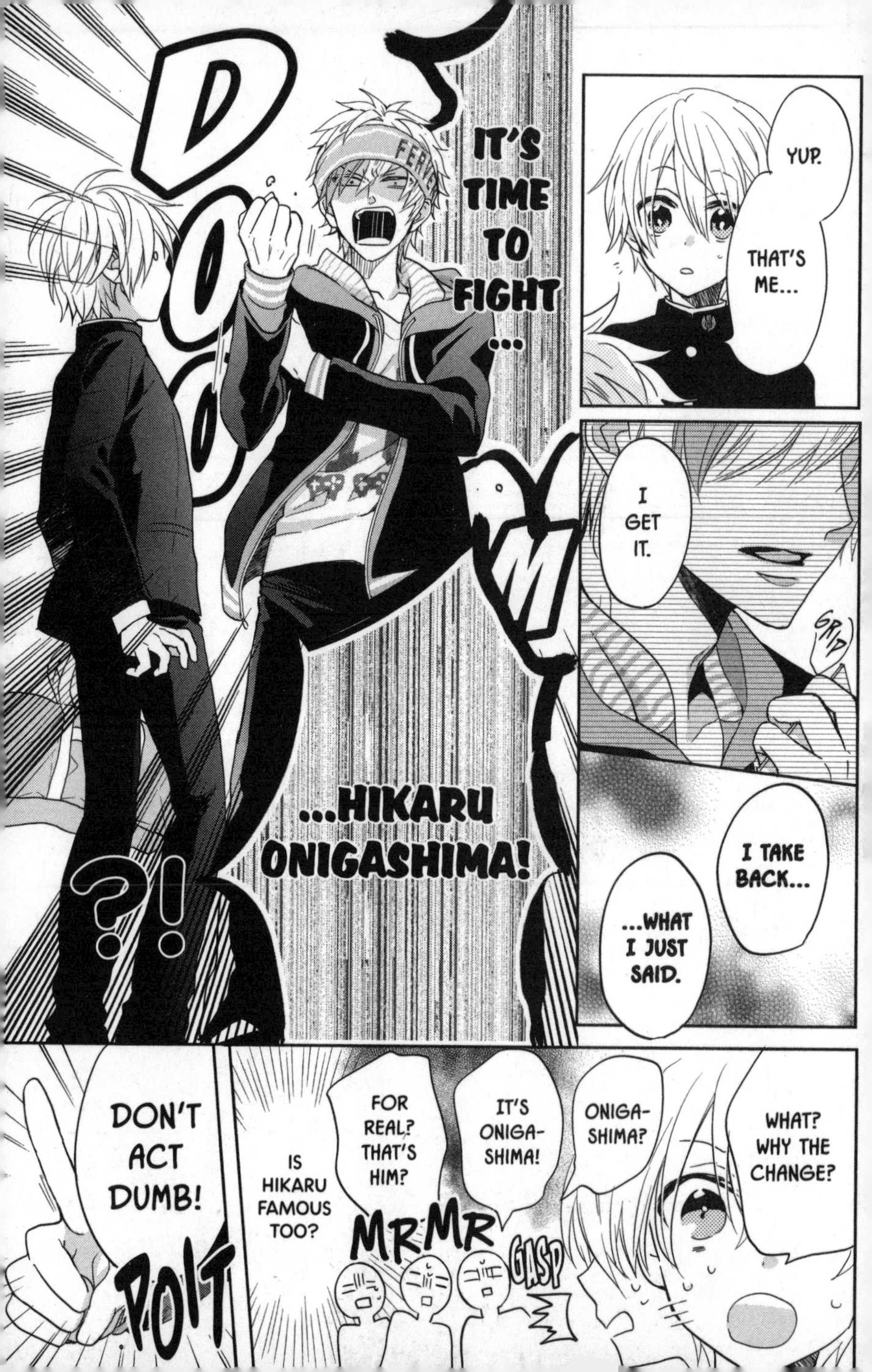
YUP.
THAT'S ME...
I GET IT.
GRIP
I TAKE BACK...
...WHAT I JUST SAID.
DOOOM
IT'S TIME TO FIGHT...
...HIKARU ONIGASHIMA!
?!
WHAT? WHY THE CHANGE?
ONIGA-SHIMA?
IT'S ONIGA-SHIMA!
FOR REAL? THAT'S HIM?
IS HIKARU FAMOUS TOO?
MR MR
GASP
DON'T ACT DUMB!
POIT

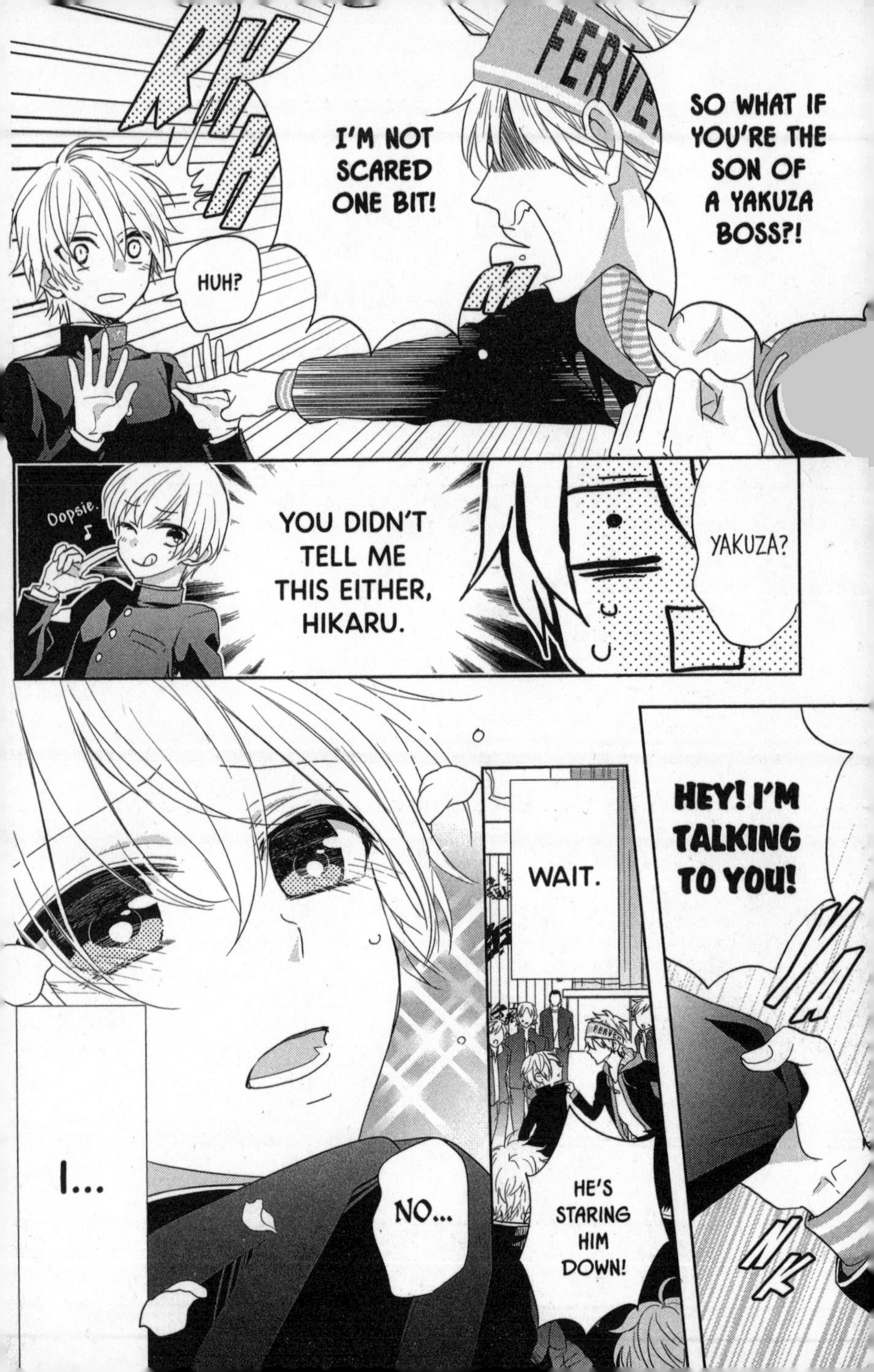
SO WHAT IF YOU'RE THE SON OF A YAKUZA BOSS?!
I'M NOT SCARED ONE BIT!
HUH?
YAKUZA?
YOU DIDN'T TELL ME THIS EITHER, HIKARU.
Oopsie.
HEY! I'M TALKING TO YOU!
WAIT.
HE'S STARING HIM DOWN!
NO...
I...

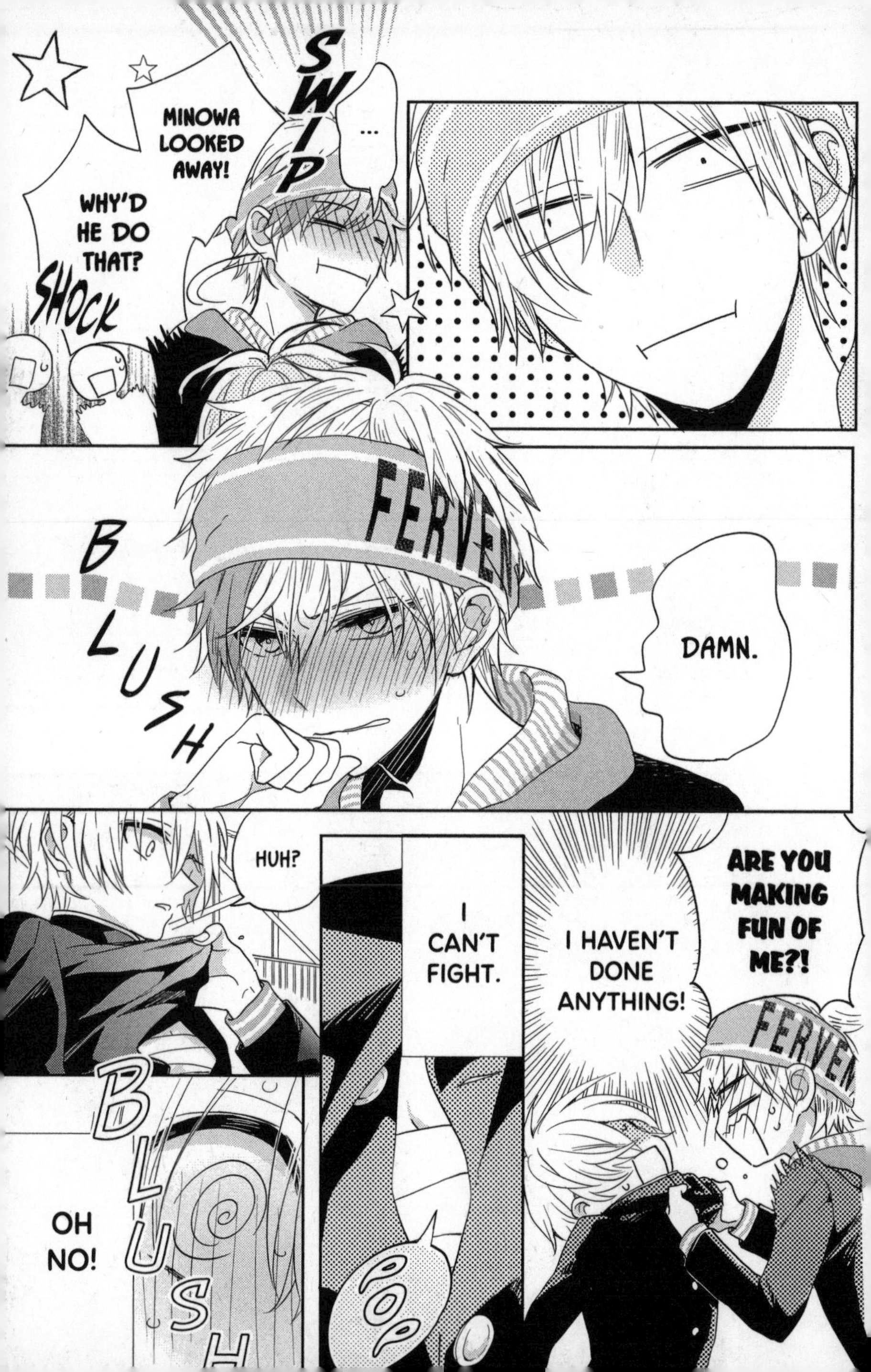
SWIP
...
MINOWA LOOKED AWAY!
WHY'D HE DO THAT?
SHOCK
DAMN.
BLUSH
ARE YOU MAKING FUN OF ME?!
I HAVEN'T DONE ANYTHING!
I CAN'T FIGHT.
POP
HUH?
BLUSH
OH NO!

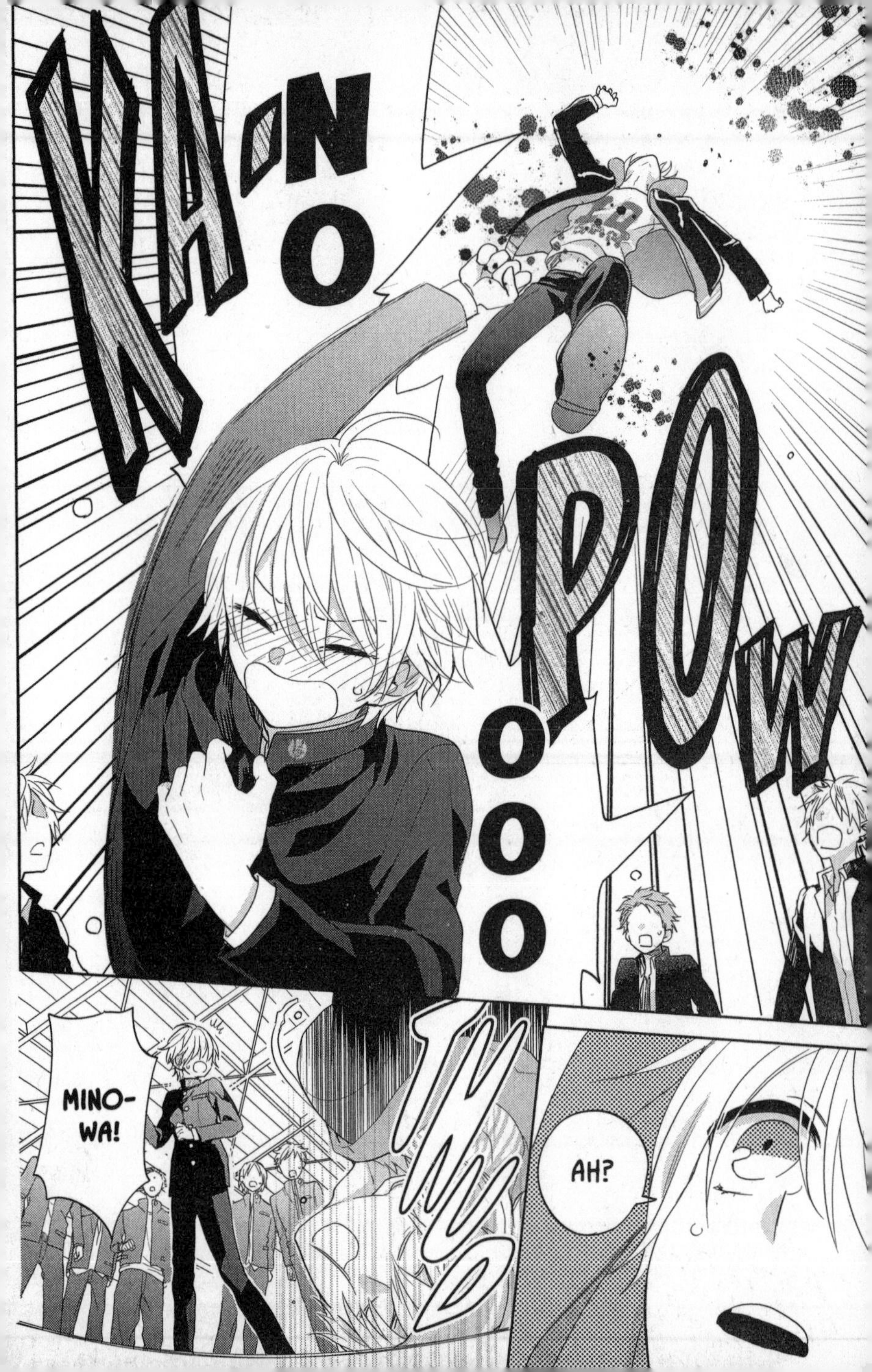
POW
KA
AH?
MINO-
WA!

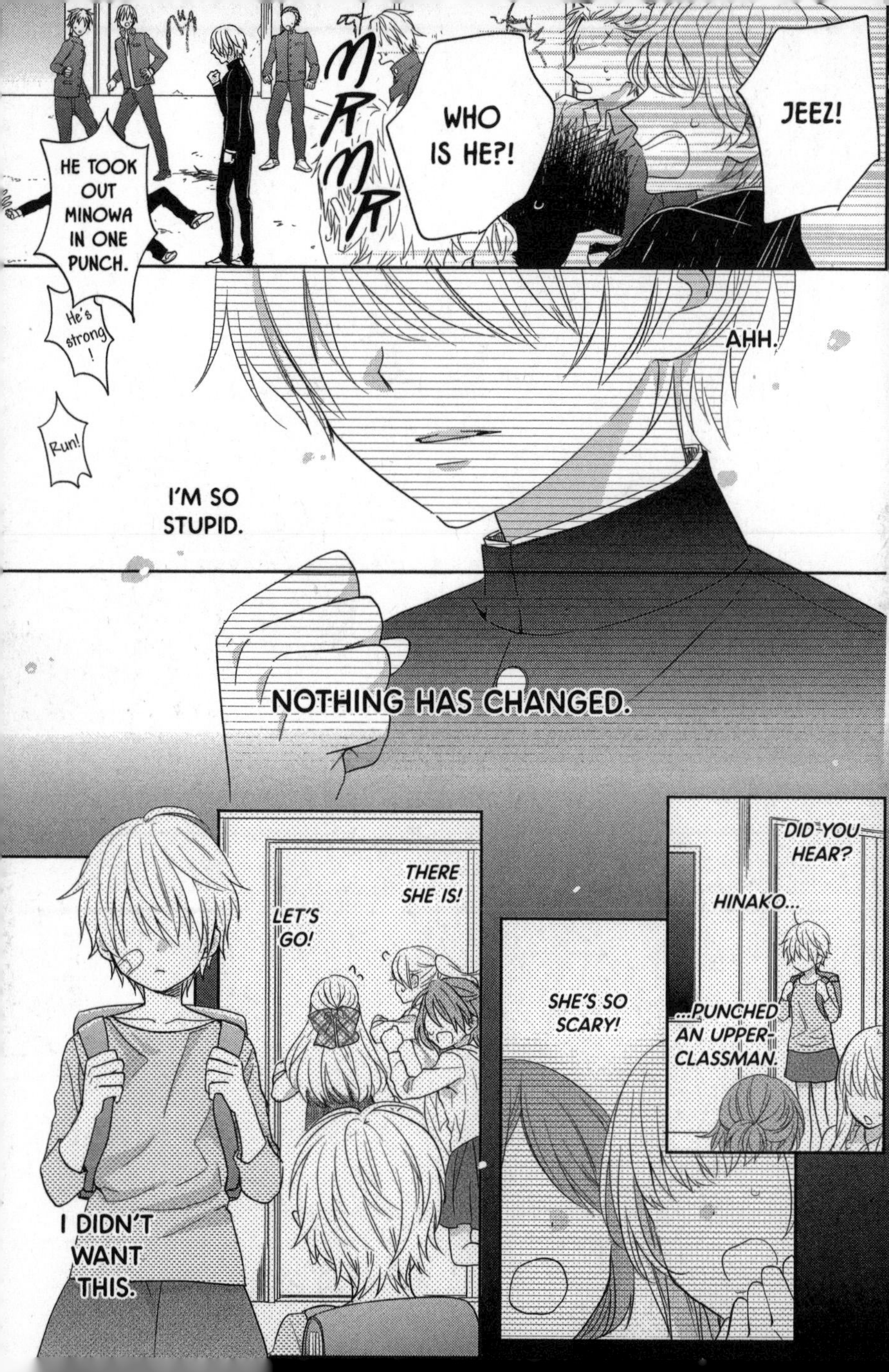
JEEZ!
WHO IS HE?!
MRMR
HE TOOK OUT MINOWA IN ONE PUNCH.
He's strong!
Run!
AHH.
I'M SO STUPID.
NOTHING HAS CHANGED.
DID YOU HEAR?
HINAKO...
...PUNCHED AN UPPER-CLASSMAN.
SHE'S SO SCARY!
THERE SHE IS!
LET'S GO!
I DIDN'T WANT THIS.

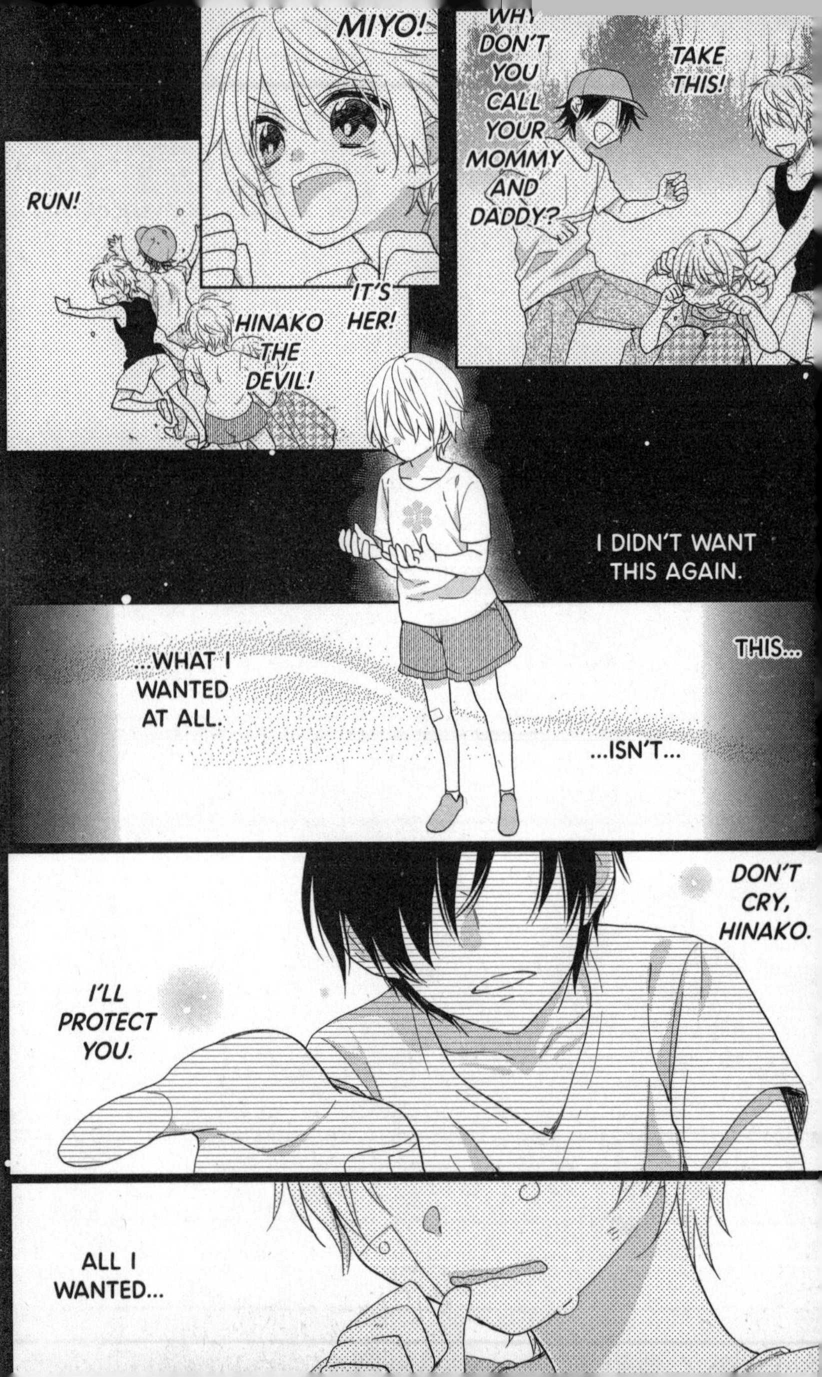
TAKE THIS!
WHY DON'T YOU CALL YOUR MOMMY AND DADDY?
MIYO!
IT'S HER!
HINAKO THE DEVIL!
RUN!
I DIDN'T WANT THIS AGAIN.
THIS...
...ISN'T...
...WHAT I WANTED AT ALL.
DON'T CRY, HINAKO.
I'LL PROTECT YOU.
ALL I WANTED...

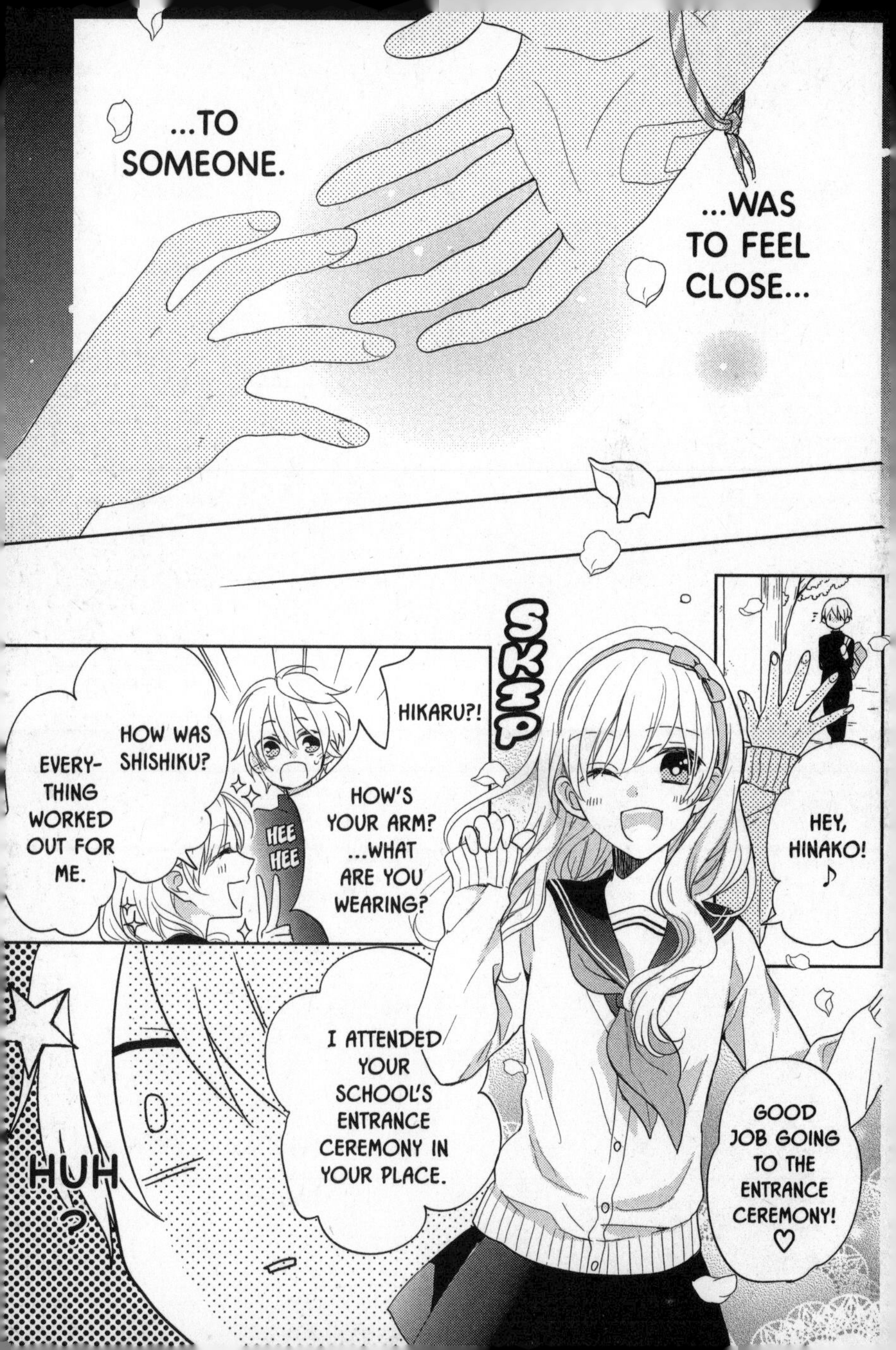
...WAS TO FEEL CLOSE...
...TO SOMEONE.
HEY, HINAKO! ♪
SKIP
HIKARU?!
HOW'S YOUR ARM? ...WHAT ARE YOU WEARING?
HEE HEE
HOW WAS SHISHIKU?
EVERY-THING WORKED OUT FOR ME.
GOOD JOB GOING TO THE ENTRANCE CEREMONY! ♡
I ATTENDED YOUR SCHOOL'S ENTRANCE CEREMONY IN YOUR PLACE.
HUH?

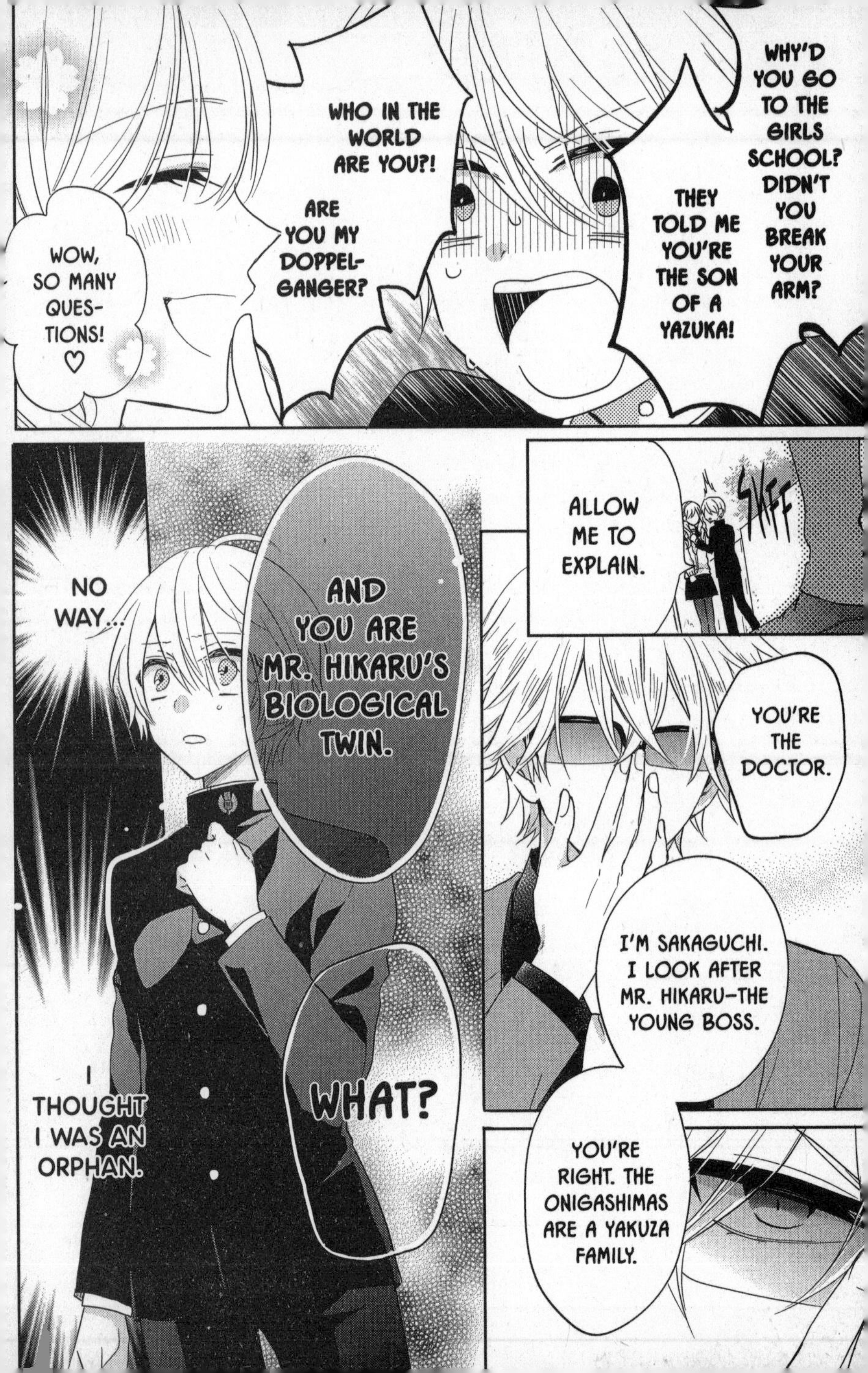
WHY'D YOU GO TO THE GIRLS SCHOOL? DIDN'T YOU BREAK YOUR ARM?
THEY TOLD ME YOU'RE THE SON OF A YAZUKA!
WHO IN THE WORLD ARE YOU?!
ARE YOU MY DOPPEL-GANGER?
WOW, SO MANY QUES-TIONS! ♡
ALLOW ME TO EXPLAIN.
YOU'RE THE DOCTOR.
I'M SAKAGUCHI. I LOOK AFTER MR. HIKARU—THE YOUNG BOSS.
YOU'RE RIGHT. THE ONIGASHIMAS ARE A YAKUZA FAMILY.
AND YOU ARE MR. HIKARU'S BIOLOGICAL TWIN.
NO WAY...
WHAT?
I THOUGHT I WAS AN ORPHAN.

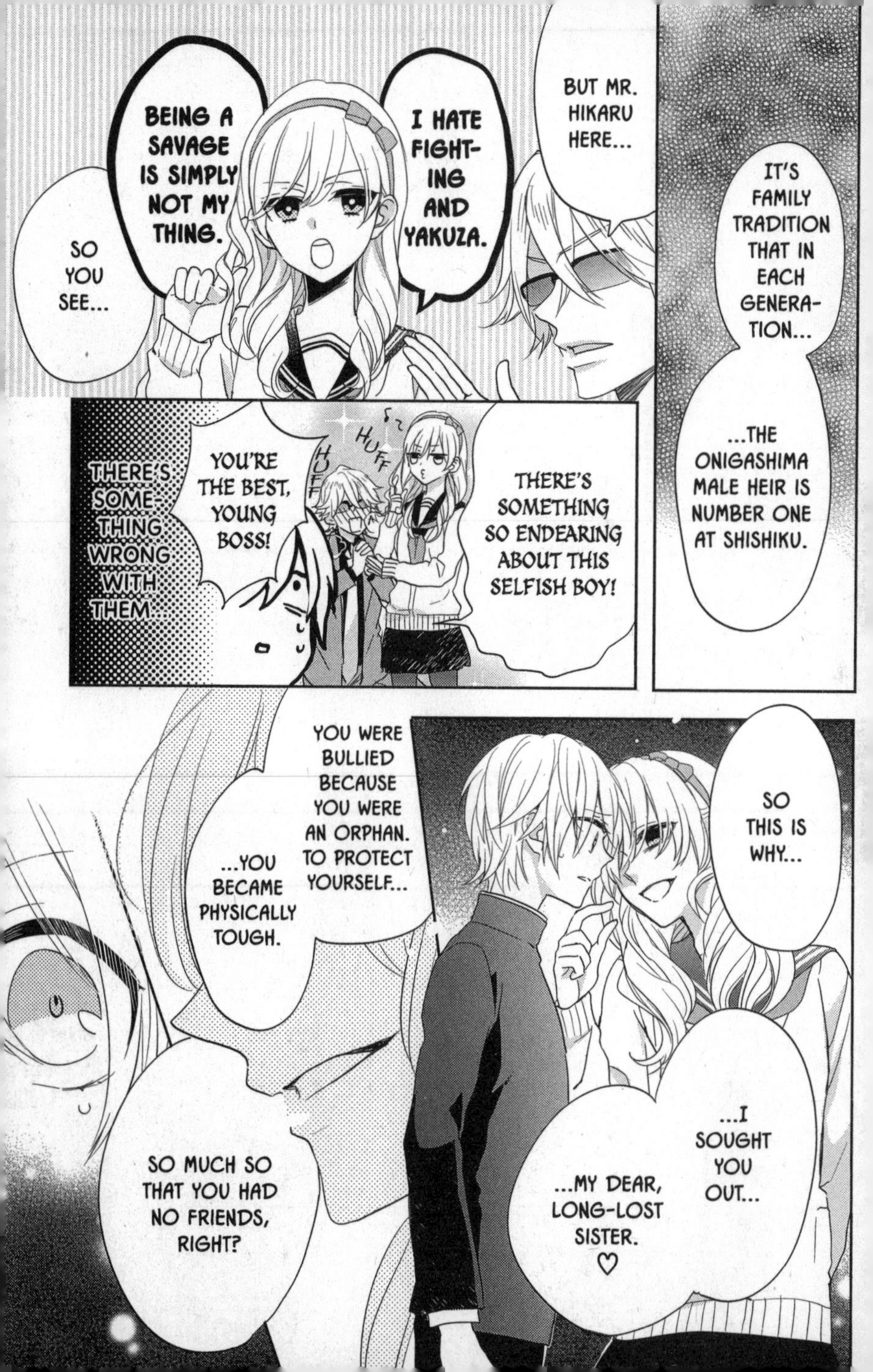
IT'S FAMILY TRADITION THAT IN EACH GENERATION...
...THE ONIGASHIMA MALE HEIR IS NUMBER ONE AT SHISHIKU.
BUT MR. HIKARU HERE...
I HATE FIGHTING AND YAKUZA.
BEING A SAVAGE IS SIMPLY NOT MY THING.
SO YOU SEE...
THERE'S SOMETHING SO ENDEARING ABOUT THIS SELFISH BOY!
HUFF
HUFF
YOU'RE THE BEST, YOUNG BOSS!
THERE'S SOMETHING WRONG WITH THEM...
SO THIS IS WHY...
...I SOUGHT YOU OUT...
...MY DEAR, LONG-LOST SISTER. ♡
YOU WERE BULLIED BECAUSE YOU WERE AN ORPHAN. TO PROTECT YOURSELF...
...YOU BECAME PHYSICALLY TOUGH.
SO MUCH SO THAT YOU HAD NO FRIENDS, RIGHT?

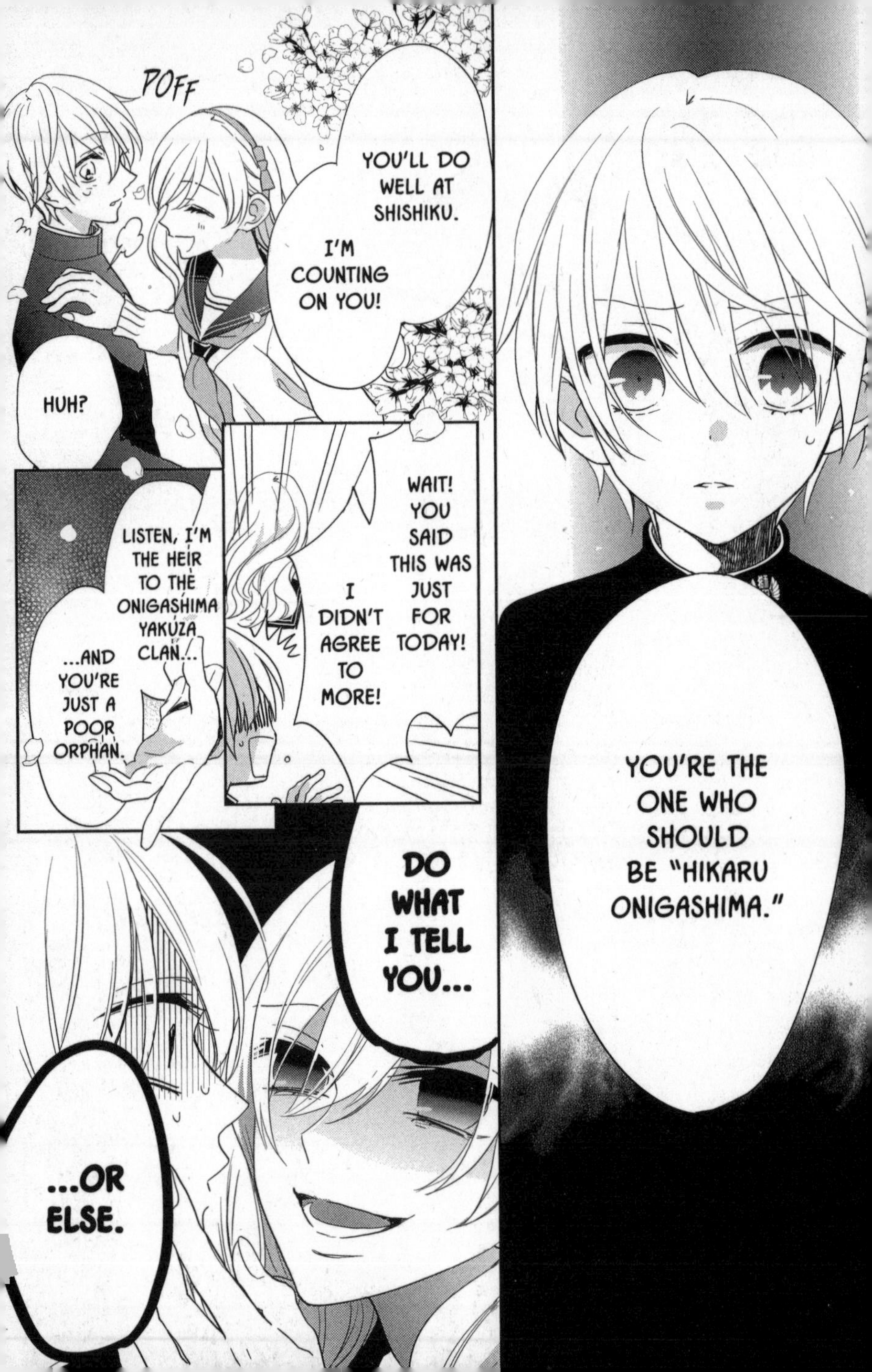
YOU'RE THE ONE WHO SHOULD BE "HIKARU ONIGASHIMA."
YOU'LL DO WELL AT SHISHIKU.
I'M COUNTING ON YOU!
POFF
HUH?
WAIT! YOU SAID THIS WAS JUST FOR TODAY!
I DIDN'T AGREE TO MORE!
LISTEN, I'M THE HEIR TO THE ONIGASHIMA YAKUZA CLAN...
...AND YOU'RE JUST A POOR ORPHAN.
DO WHAT I TELL YOU...
...OR ELSE.

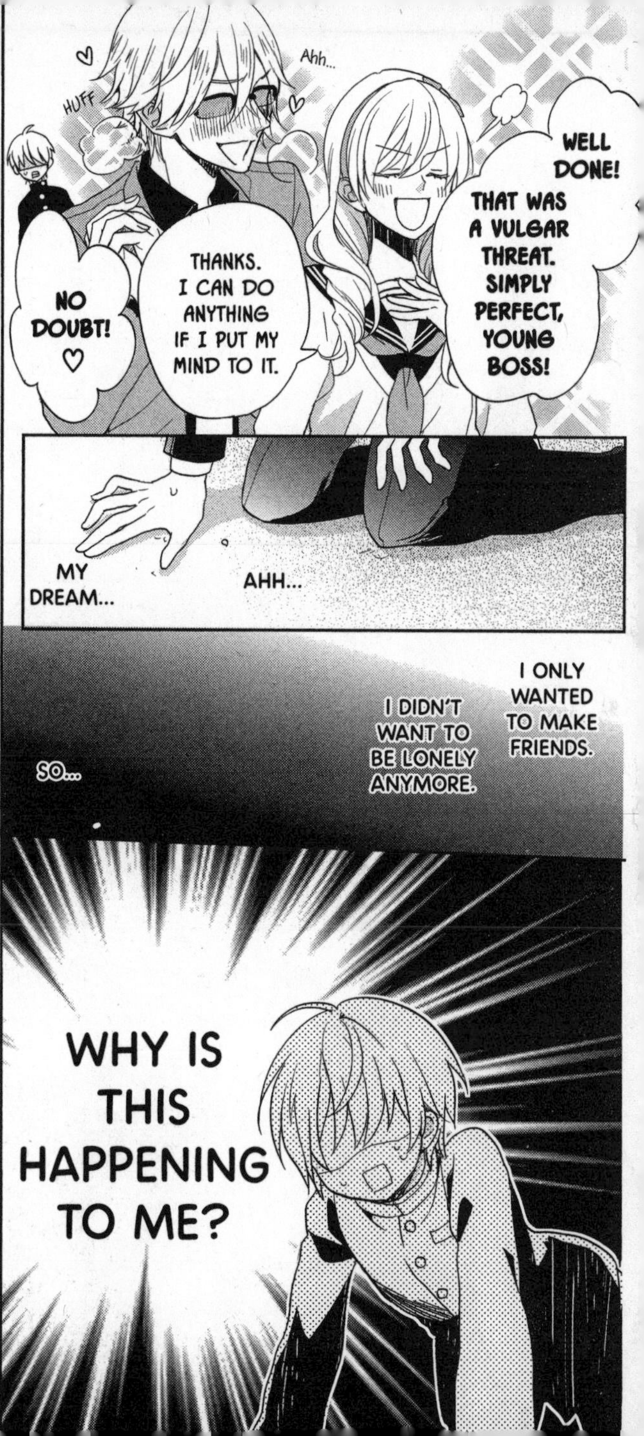
WELL DONE! THAT WAS A VULGAR THREAT. SIMPLY PERFECT, YOUNG BOSS!
Ahh...
THANKS. I CAN DO ANYTHING IF I PUT MY MIND TO IT.
HUFF
NO DOUBT! ♡
AHH...
MY DREAM...
I ONLY WANTED TO MAKE FRIENDS.
I DIDN'T WANT TO BE LONELY ANYMORE.
SO...
WHY IS THIS HAPPENING TO ME?

FIRST-YEAR, VIOLET CLASS

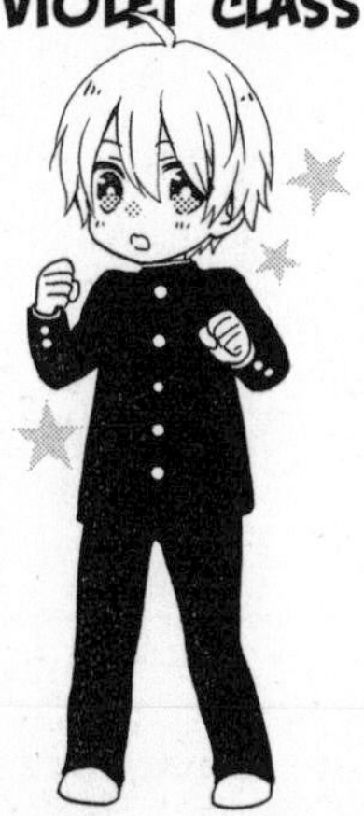

HINAKO NAKAYAMA
(FEMALE)

Height: 5'2"
Weight: 104 pounds
Blood Type: ?
Birthday: ?
Skill: Mixed Martial Arts

She has the sudden misfortune of attending a boys' school for delinquents in Hikaru's stead! I love the way she faces this challenge in her own special way. Go for it, Hinako! You're the strongest heroine (physically) ever!!

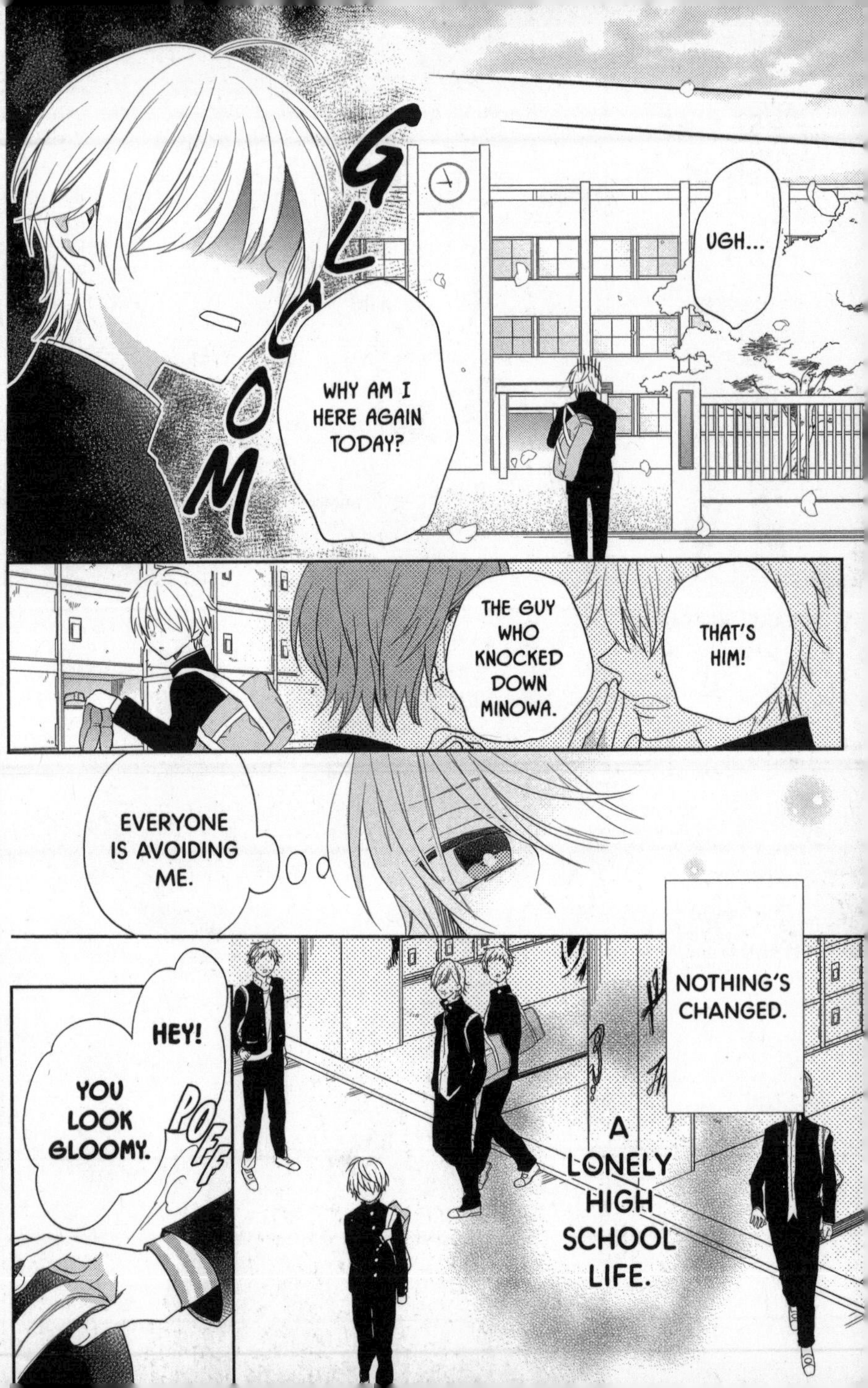
UGH...
GLOOM
WHY AM I HERE AGAIN TODAY?
THAT'S HIM!
THE GUY WHO KNOCKED DOWN MINOWA.
EVERYONE IS AVOIDING ME.
NOTHING'S CHANGED.
A LONELY HIGH SCHOOL LIFE.
HEY!
YOU LOOK GLOOMY.
POFF

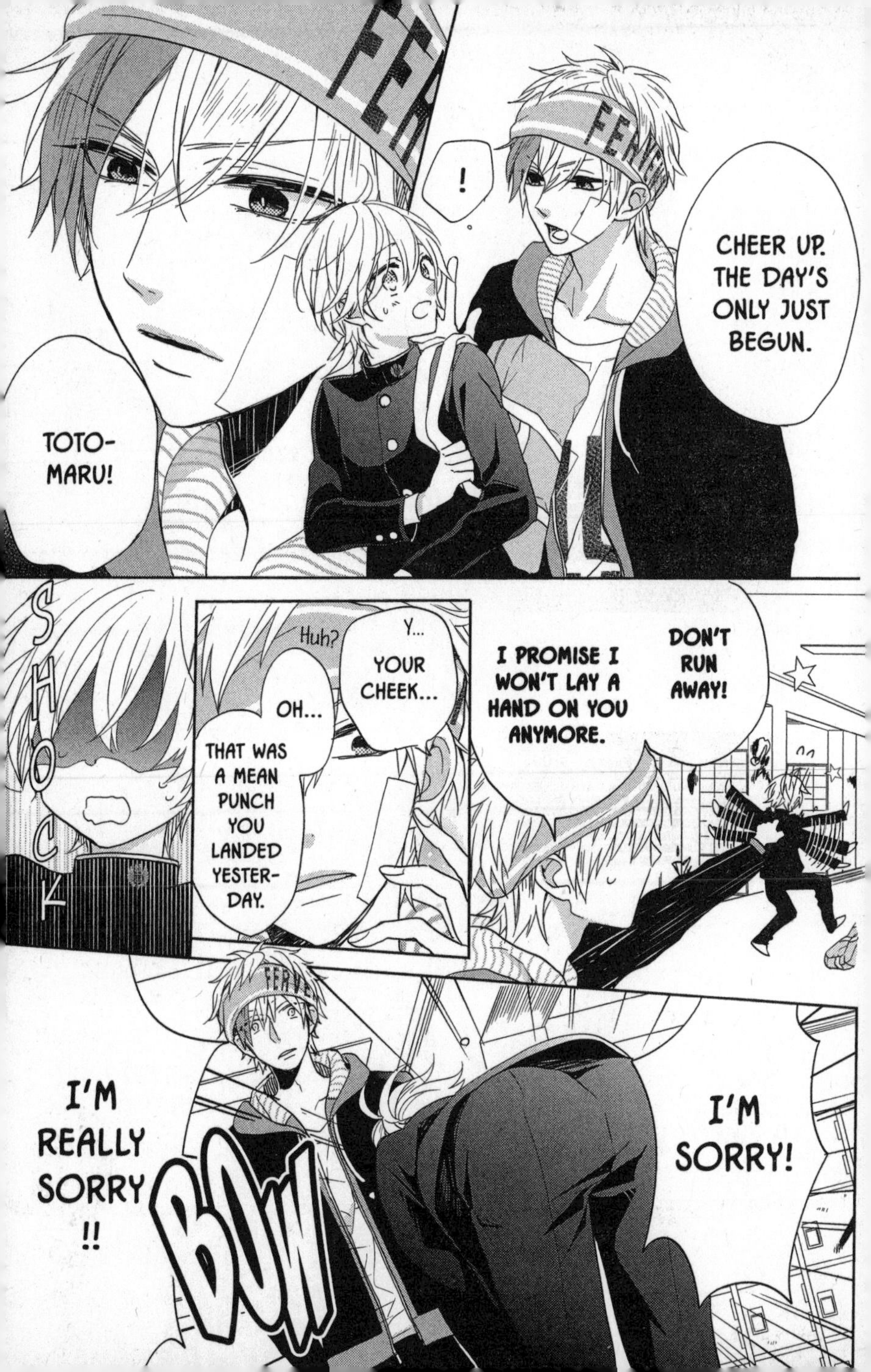
CHEER UP. THE DAY'S ONLY JUST BEGUN.
!
TOTO-MARU!
DON'T RUN AWAY!
I PROMISE I WON'T LAY A HAND ON YOU ANYMORE.
Y...
YOUR CHEEK...
Huh?
OH...
THAT WAS A MEAN PUNCH YOU LANDED YESTER-DAY.
SHOCK
I'M SORRY!
BOW
I'M REALLY SORRY!!

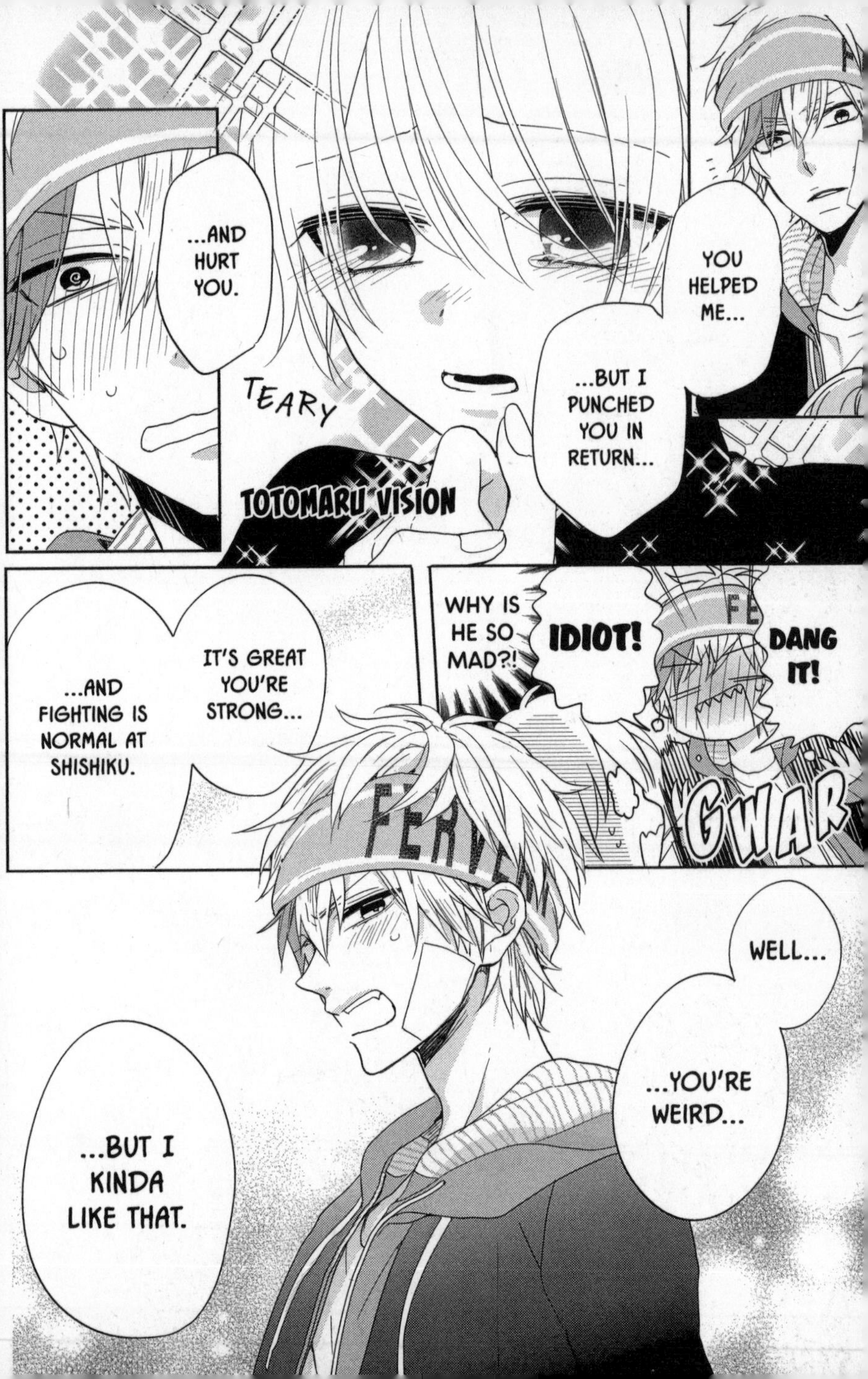
YOU HELPED ME...
...BUT I PUNCHED YOU IN RETURN...
...AND HURT YOU.
TEARY
TOTOMARU VISION
DANG IT!
IDIOT!
GWAR
WHY IS HE SO MAD?!
IT'S GREAT YOU'RE STRONG...
...AND FIGHTING IS NORMAL AT SHISHIKU.
WELL...
...YOU'RE WEIRD...
...BUT I KINDA LIKE THAT.

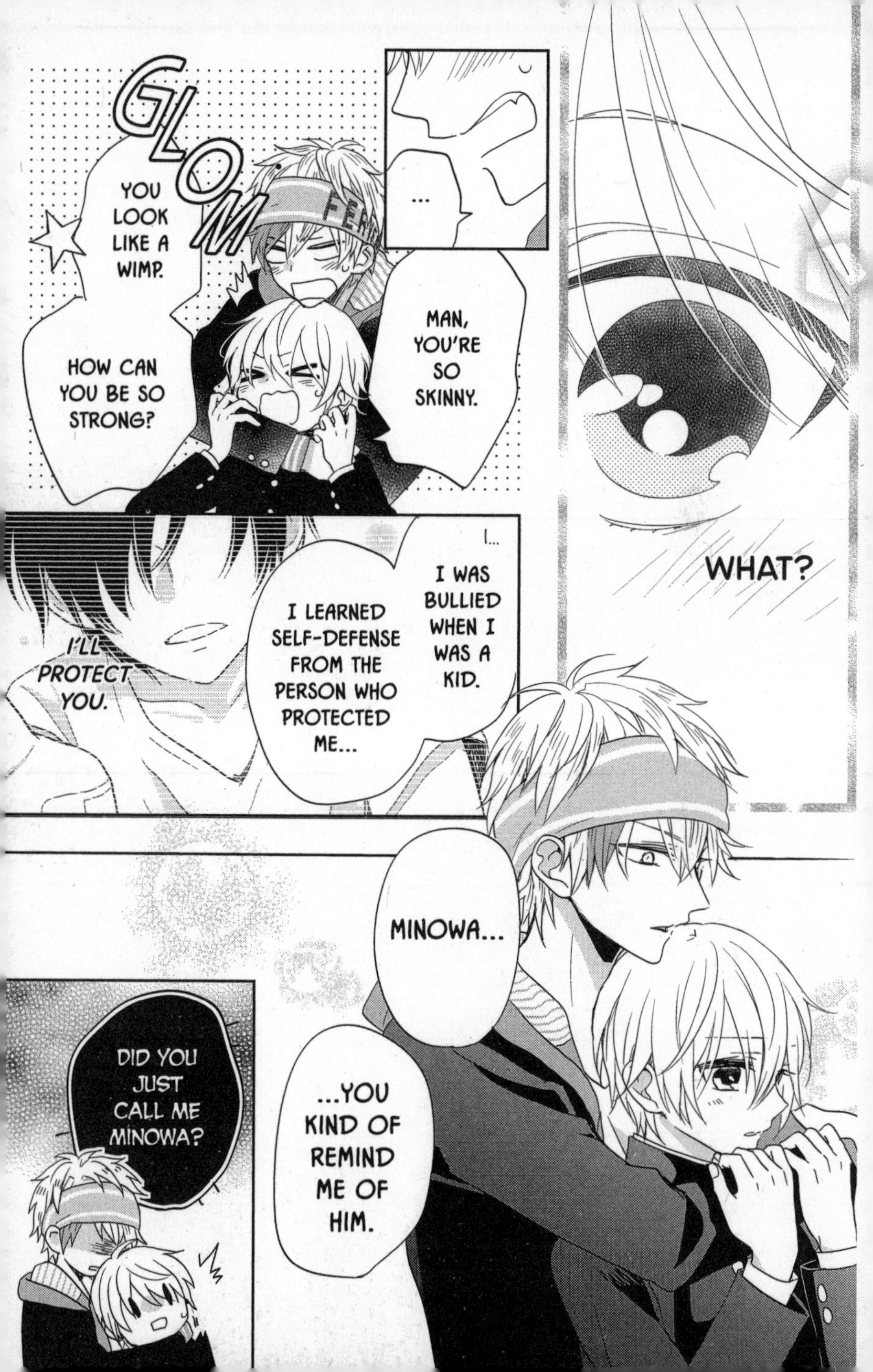
WHAT?
...
GLOM
MAN, YOU'RE SO SKINNY.
YOU LOOK LIKE A WIMP.
HOW CAN YOU BE SO STRONG?
I...
I WAS BULLIED WHEN I WAS A KID.
I LEARNED SELF-DEFENSE FROM THE PERSON WHO PROTECTED ME...
I'LL PROTECT YOU.
MINOWA...
...YOU KIND OF REMIND ME OF HIM.
DID YOU JUST CALL ME MINOWA?

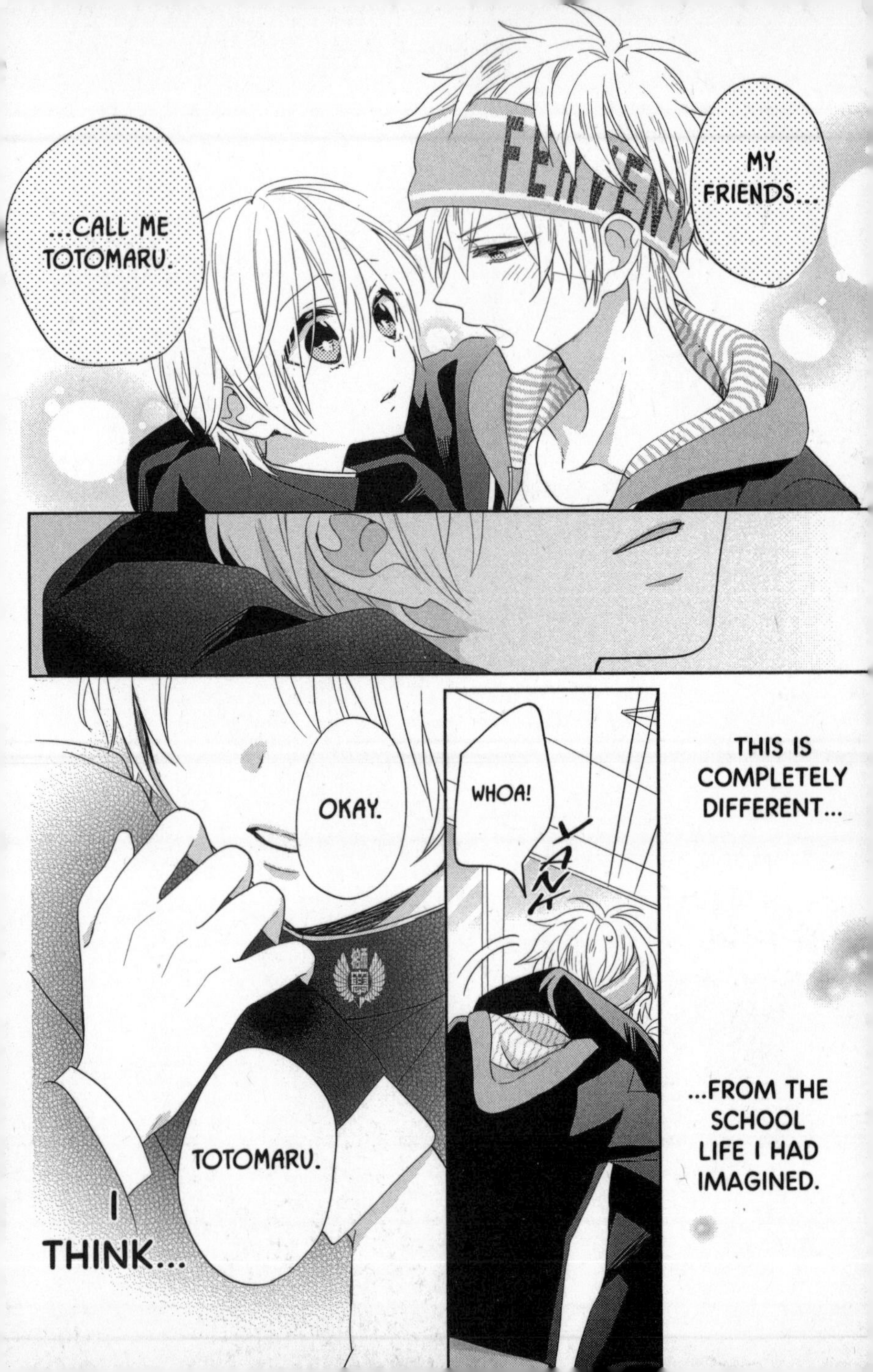
MY FRIENDS...
...CALL ME TOTOMARU.
THIS IS COMPLETELY DIFFERENT...
...FROM THE SCHOOL LIFE I HAD IMAGINED.
WHOA!
YANK
OKAY.
TOTOMARU.
I THINK...

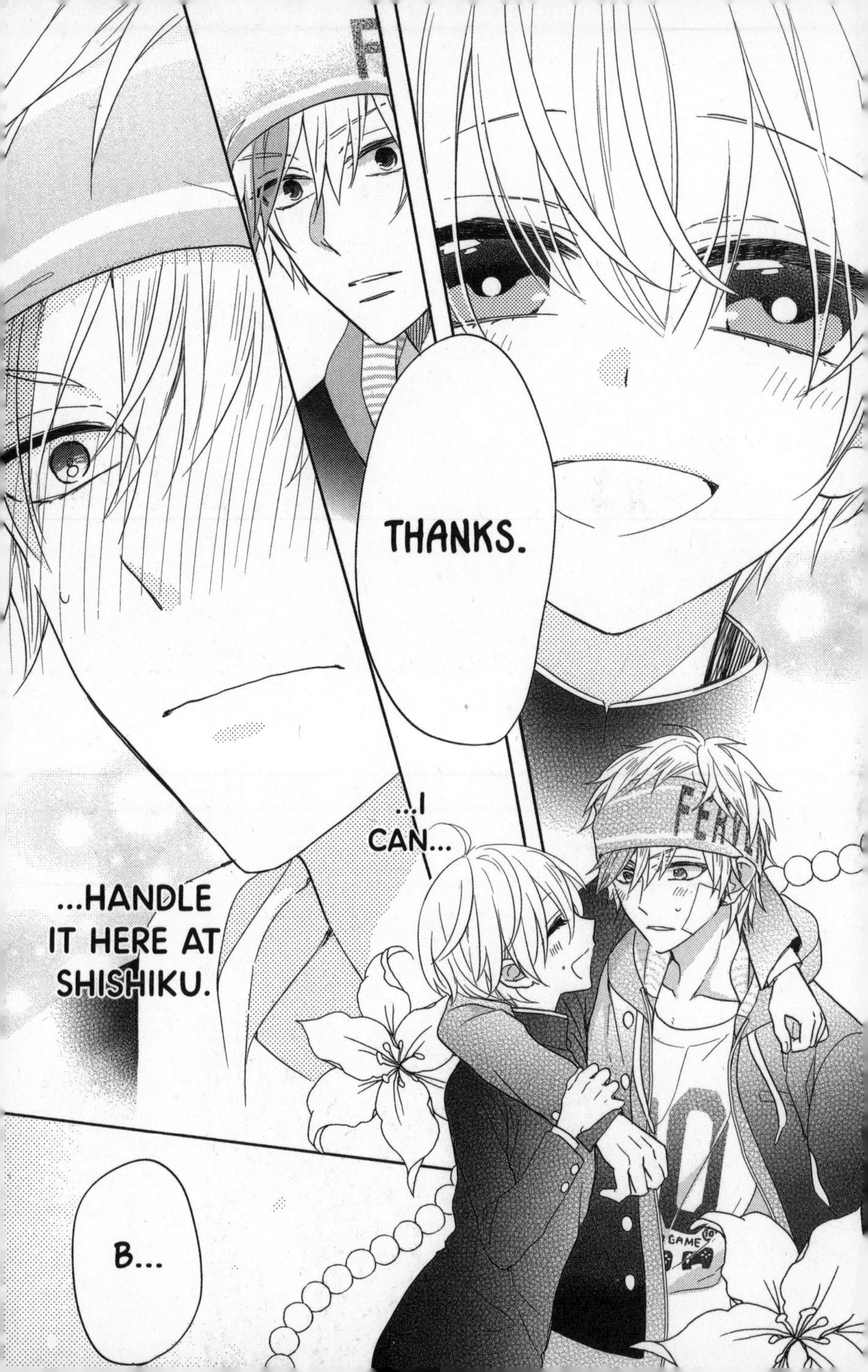
THANKS.
...I CAN...
...HANDLE IT HERE AT SHISHIKU.
B...

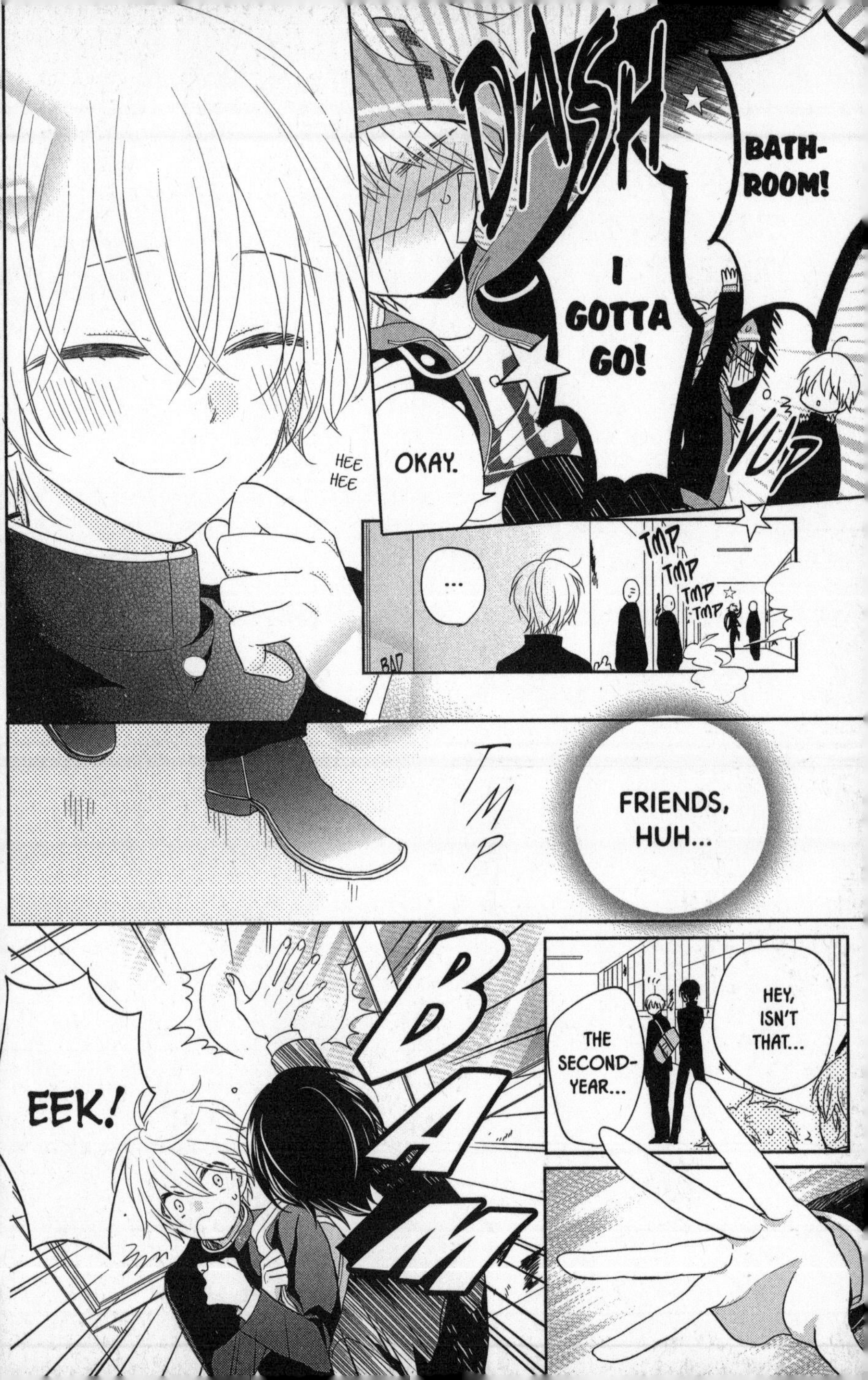
BATH-ROOM!
DASH
I GOTTA GO!
VUD
OKAY.
TMP TMP TMP TMP
...
BAD
HEE HEE
TMP
FRIENDS, HUH...
HEY, ISN'T THAT...
THE SECOND-YEAR...
BAM
EEK!

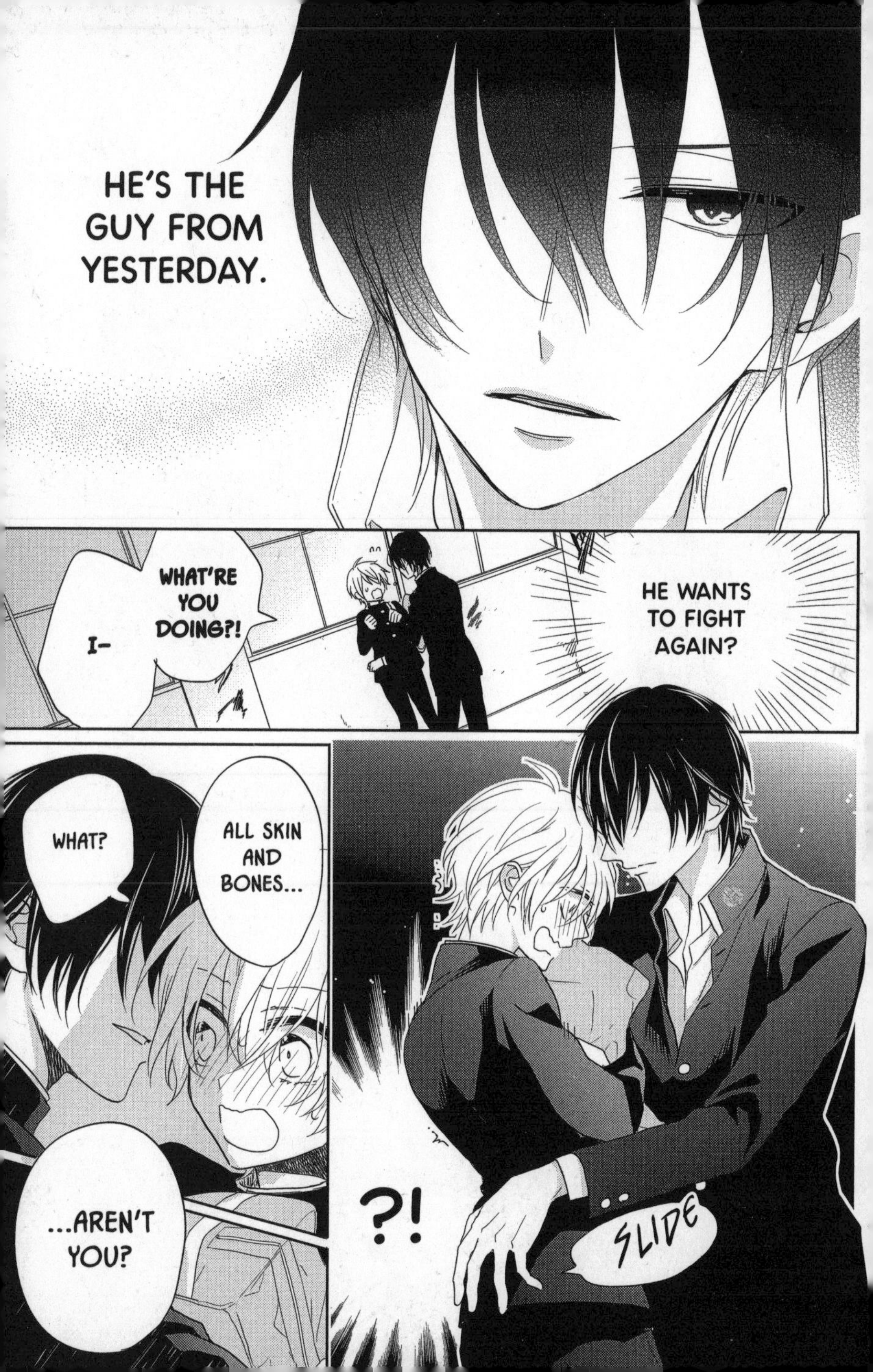
HE'S THE GUY FROM YESTERDAY.
HE WANTS TO FIGHT AGAIN?
WHAT'RE YOU DOING?!
I-
SLIDE
?!
ALL SKIN AND BONES...
WHAT?
...AREN'T YOU?

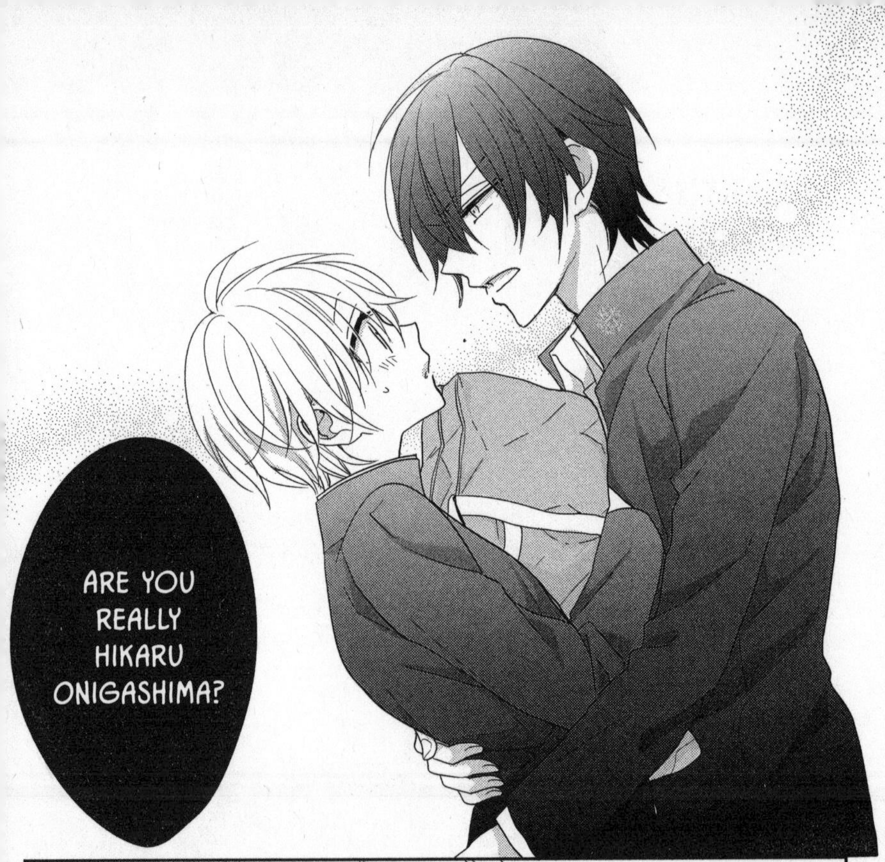
ARE YOU REALLY HIKARU ONIGASHIMA?

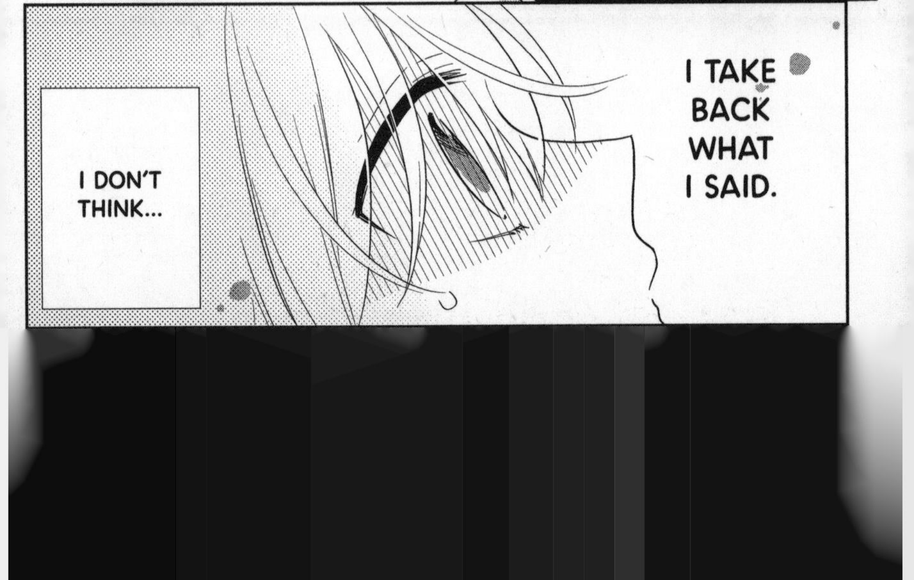
I TAKE BACK WHAT I SAID.
I DON'T THINK...

[redacted]

KENKA BANCHO Otome

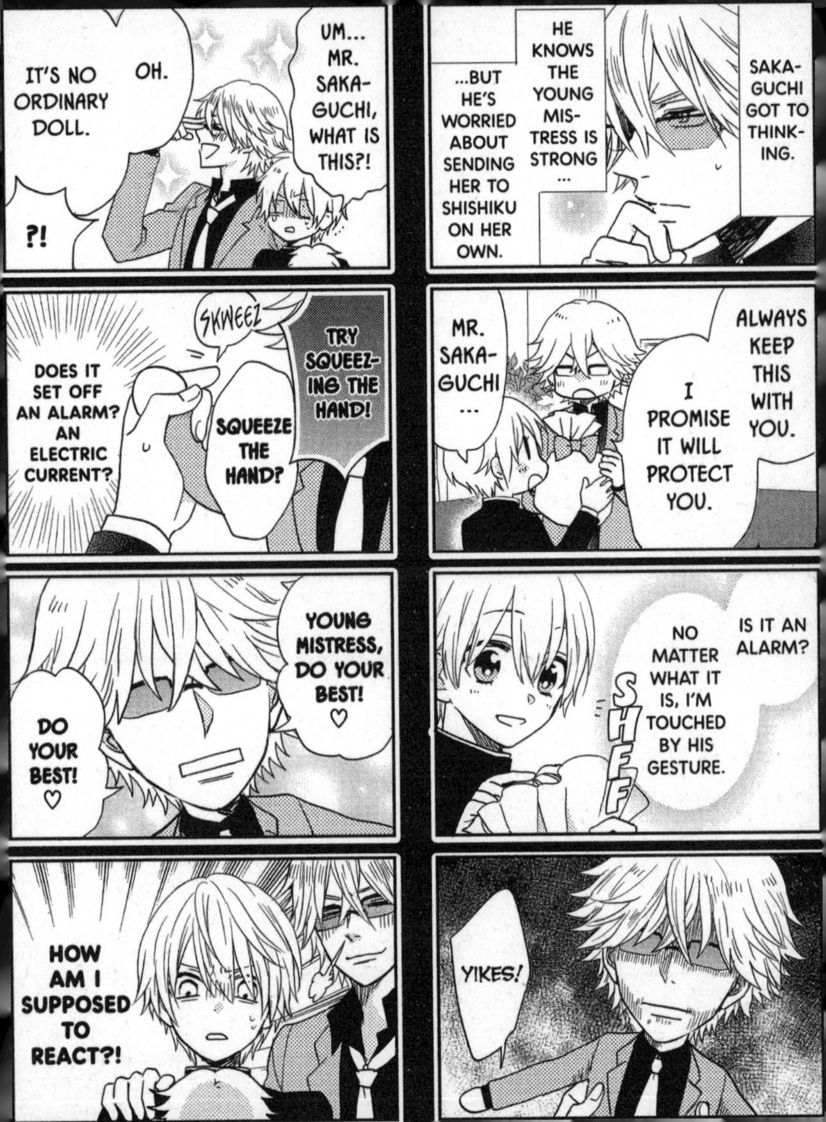
SAKAGUCHI GOT TO THINKING.
HE KNOWS THE YOUNG MISTRESS IS STRONG...
...BUT HE'S WORRIED ABOUT SENDING HER TO SHISHIKU ON HER OWN.
ALWAYS KEEP THIS WITH YOU.
I PROMISE IT WILL PROTECT YOU.
MR. SAKAGUCHI...
IS IT AN ALARM?
NO MATTER WHAT IT IS, I'M TOUCHED BY HIS GESTURE.
SHFF
YIKES!
UM... MR. SAKAGUCHI, WHAT IS THIS?!
OH.
IT'S NO ORDINARY DOLL.
?!
TRY SQUEEZING THE HAND!
SKWEEZ
SQUEEZE THE HAND?
DOES IT SET OFF AN ALARM? AN ELECTRIC CURRENT?
YOUNG MISTRESS, DO YOUR BEST! ♡
DO YOUR BEST! ♡
HOW AM I SUPPOSED TO REACT?!

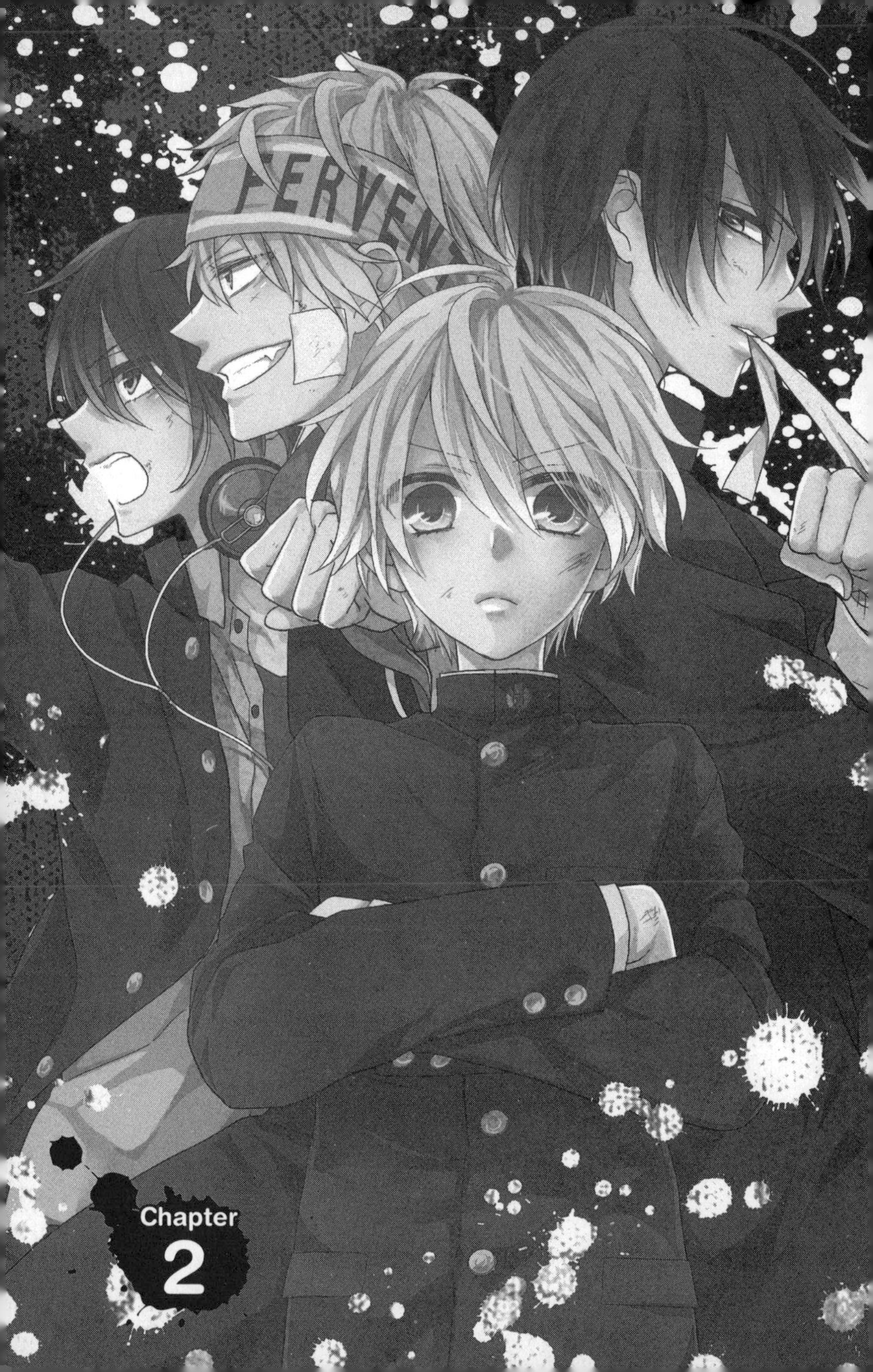
FERVEN
Chapter
2

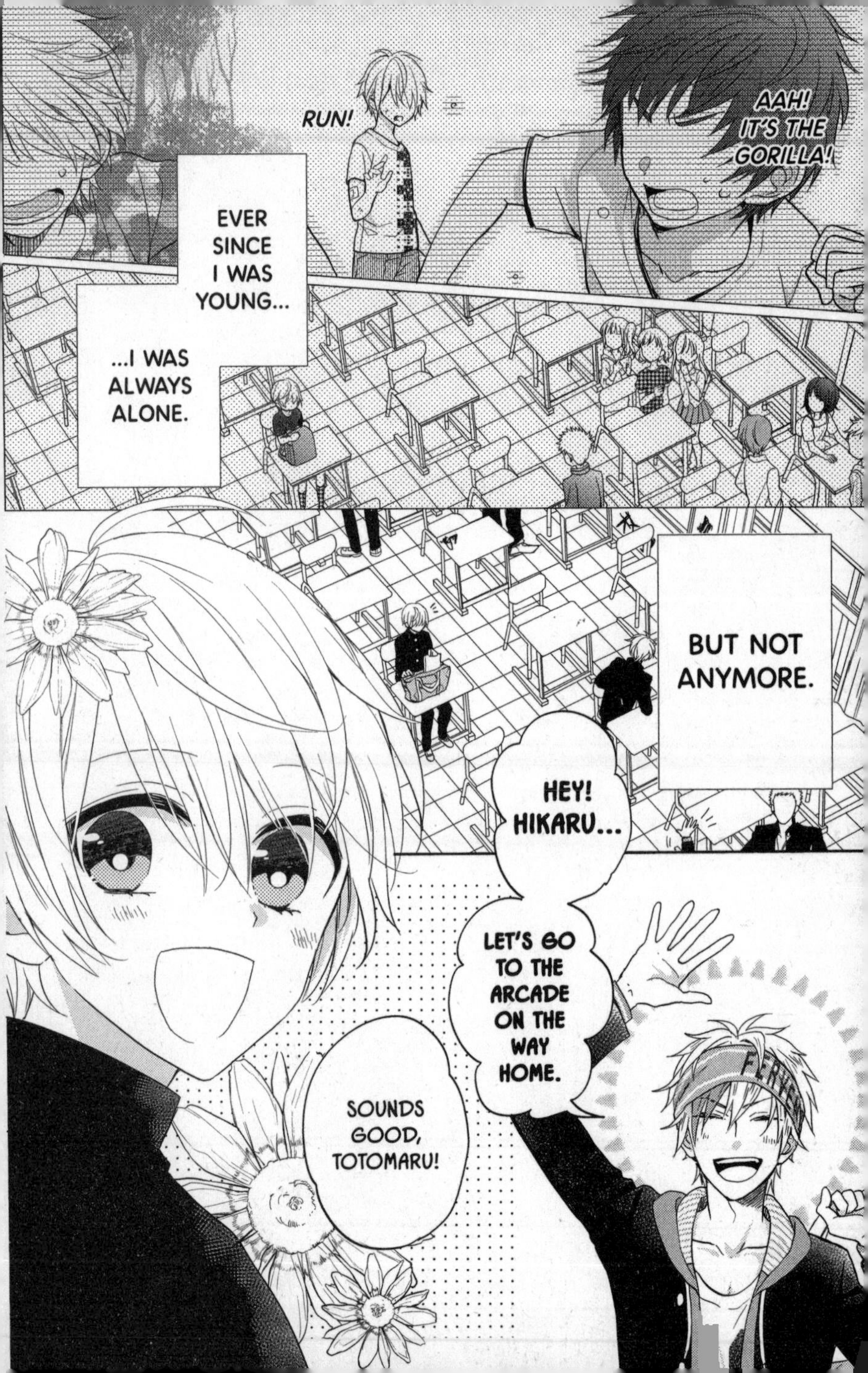
AAH! IT'S THE GORILLA!
RUN!
EVER SINCE I WAS YOUNG...
...I WAS ALWAYS ALONE.
BUT NOT ANYMORE.
HEY! HIKARU...
LET'S GO TO THE ARCADE ON THE WAY HOME.
SOUNDS GOOD, TOTOMARU!

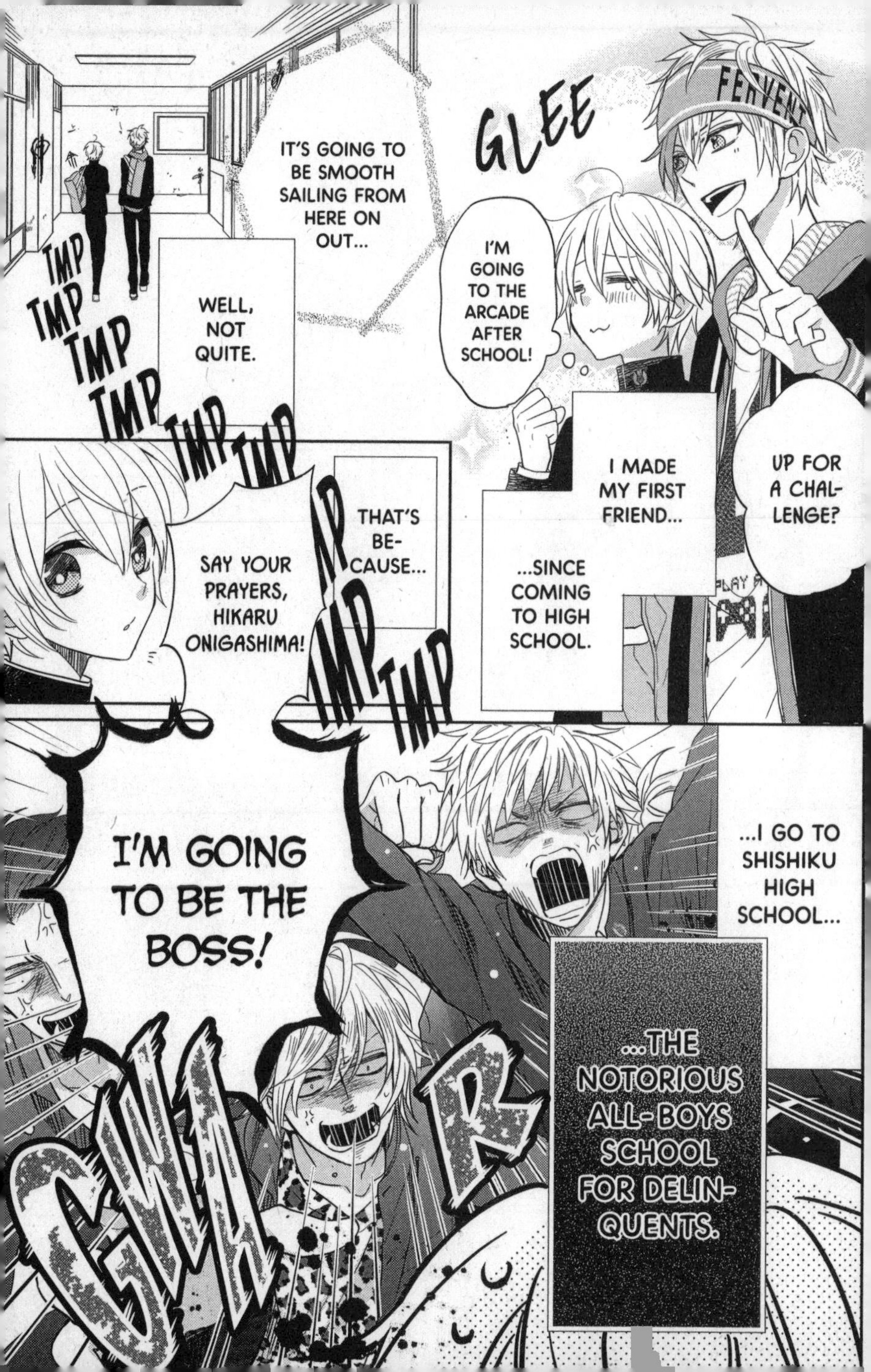
GLEE
UP FOR A CHAL-LENGE?
I'M GOING TO THE ARCADE AFTER SCHOOL!
I MADE MY FIRST FRIEND...
...SINCE COMING TO HIGH SCHOOL.
IT'S GOING TO BE SMOOTH SAILING FROM HERE ON OUT...
WELL, NOT QUITE.
TMP TMP TMP TMP TMP TMP
THAT'S BE-CAUSE...
SAY YOUR PRAYERS, HIKARU ONIGASHIMA!
TMP TMP
...I GO TO SHISHIKU HIGH SCHOOL...
...THE NOTORIOUS ALL-BOYS SCHOOL FOR DELIN-QUENTS.
I'M GOING TO BE THE BOSS!

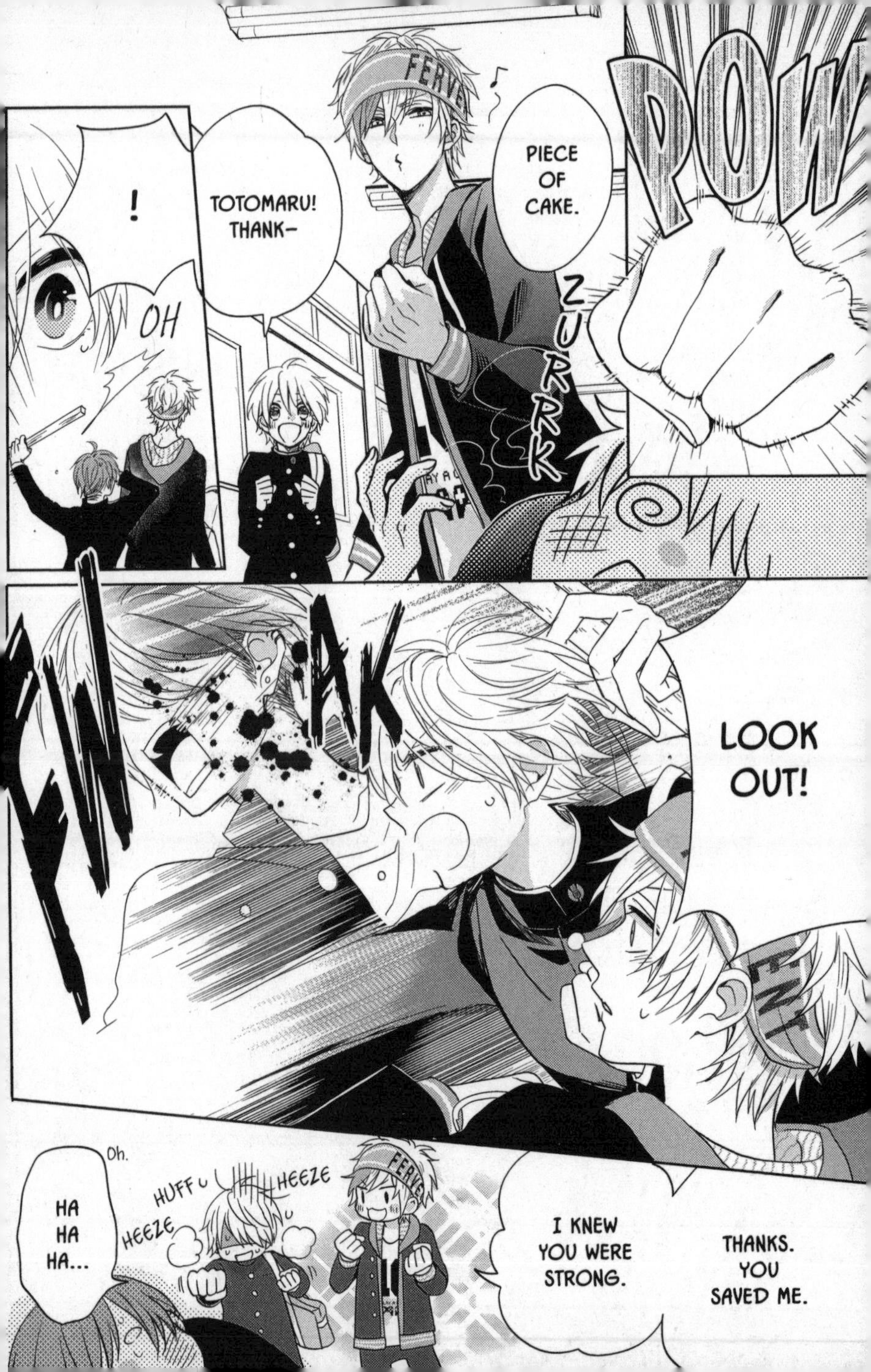
POW
PIECE OF CAKE.
TOTOMARU! THANK–
ZURRK
!
OH
LOOK OUT!
THANKS. YOU SAVED ME.
I KNEW YOU WERE STRONG.
HEEZE
HUFF
HEEZE
Oh.
HA HA HA...

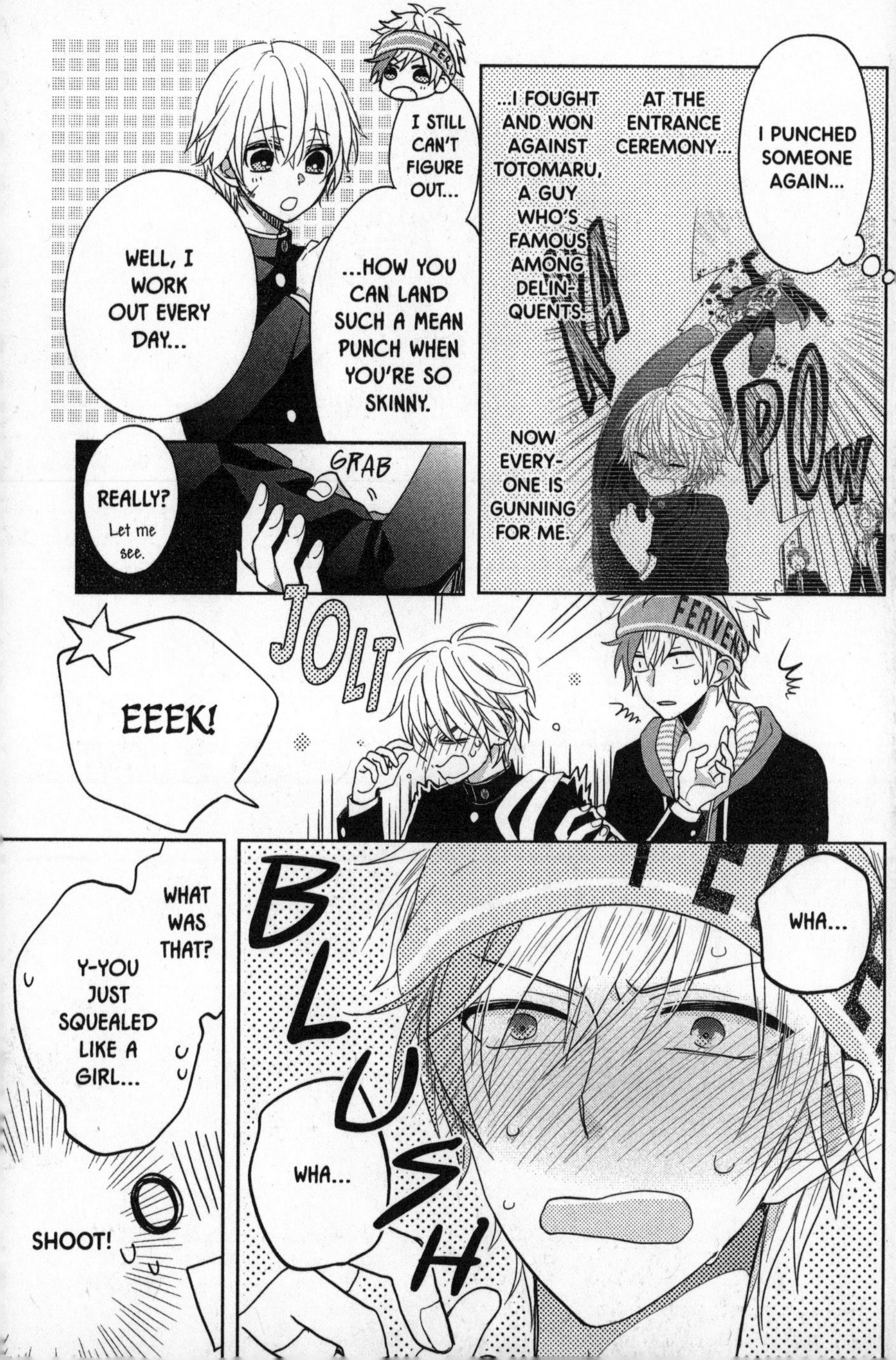
I PUNCHED SOMEONE AGAIN...
AT THE ENTRANCE CEREMONY...
...I FOUGHT AND WON AGAINST TOTOMARU, A GUY WHO'S FAMOUS AMONG DELINQUENTS.
POW
NOW EVERYONE IS GUNNING FOR ME.
I STILL CAN'T FIGURE OUT...
...HOW YOU CAN LAND SUCH A MEAN PUNCH WHEN YOU'RE SO SKINNY.
WELL, I WORK OUT EVERY DAY...
GRAB
REALLY? Let me see.
JOLT
EEEK!
WHA...
BLUSH
WHA...
WHAT WAS THAT?
Y-YOU JUST SQUEALED LIKE A GIRL...
SHOOT!

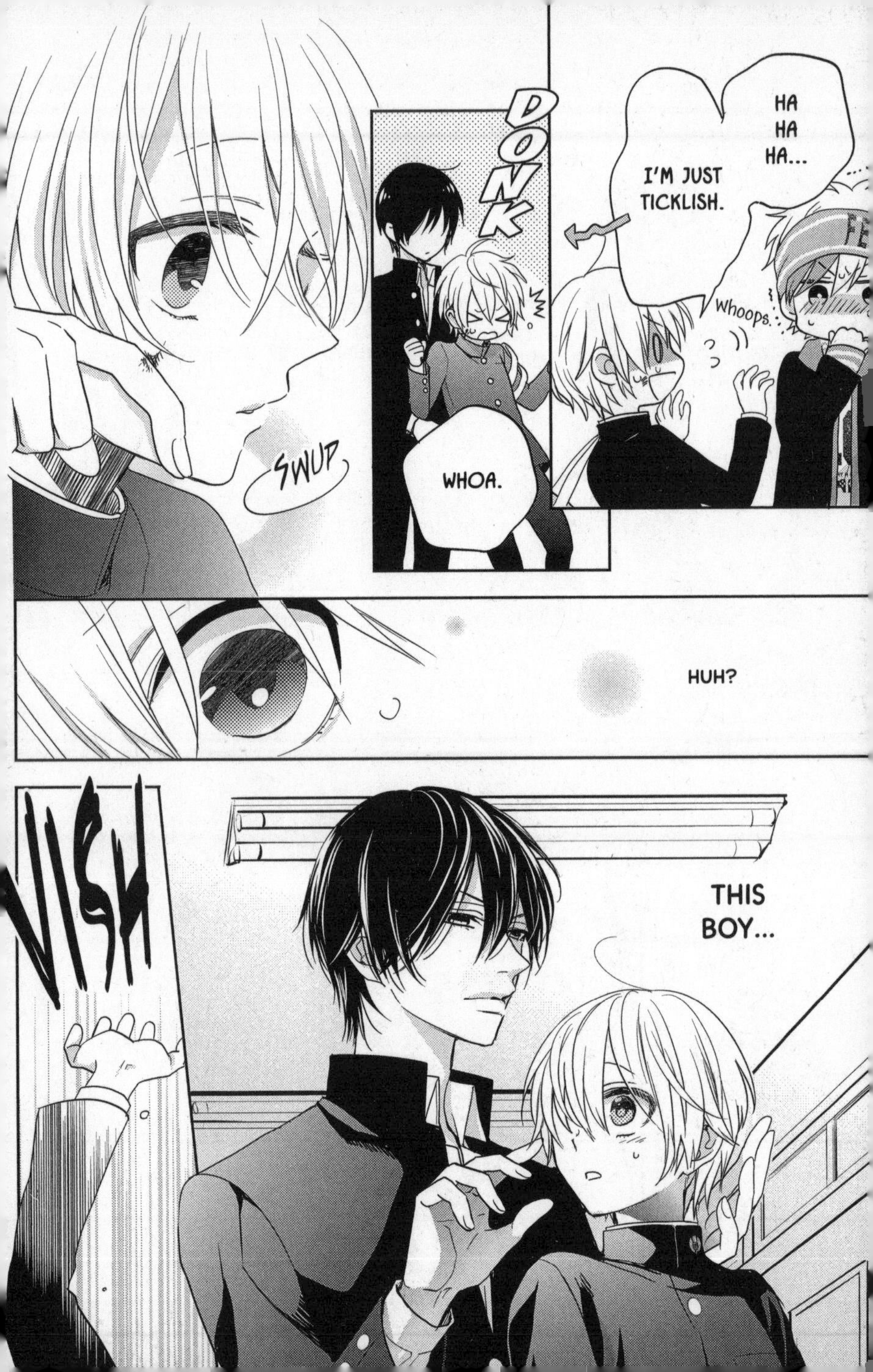
HA HA HA...
I'M JUST TICKLISH.
Whoops.
DONK
WHOA.
SWUP
HUH?
THIS BOY...
VISH

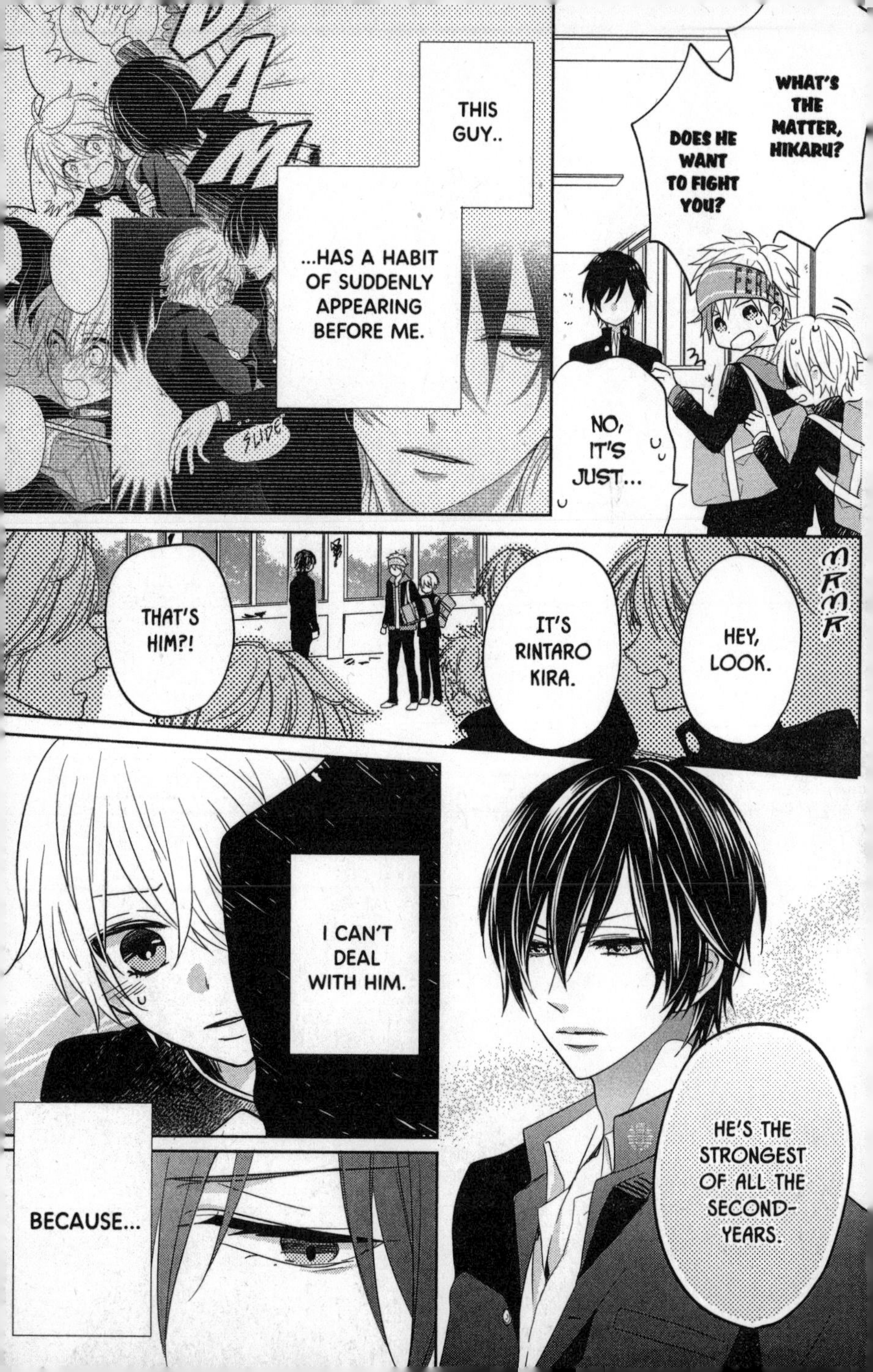
WHAT'S THE MATTER, HIKARU?
DOES HE WANT TO FIGHT YOU?
NO, IT'S JUST...
THIS GUY..
...HAS A HABIT OF SUDDENLY APPEARING BEFORE ME.
SLIDE
MRMR
HEY, LOOK.
IT'S RINTARO KIRA.
THAT'S HIM?!
HE'S THE STRONGEST OF ALL THE SECOND-YEARS.
I CAN'T DEAL WITH HIM.
BECAUSE...

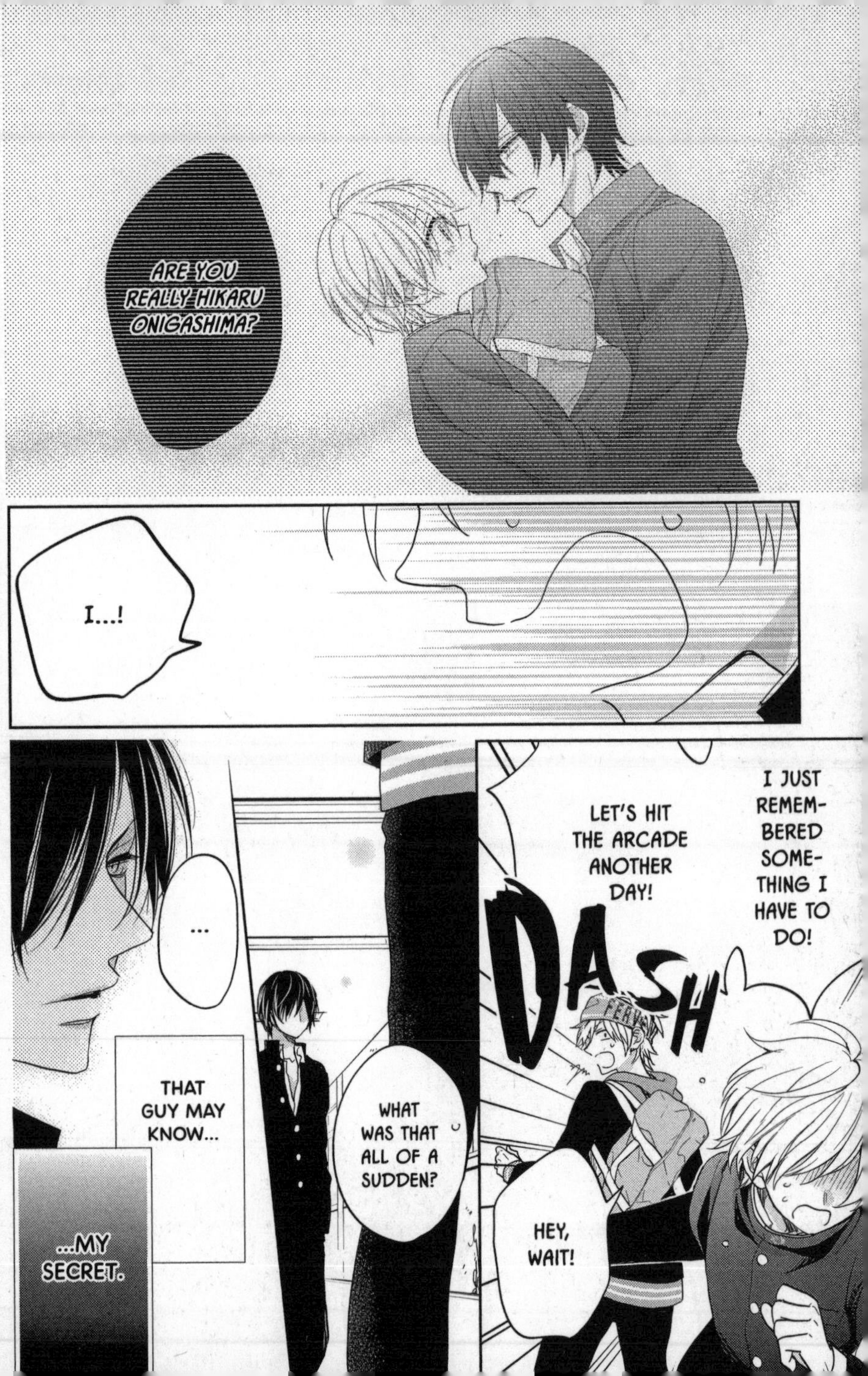
ARE YOU REALLY HIKARU ONIGASHIMA?
I...!
I JUST REMEMBERED SOMETHING I HAVE TO DO!
LET'S HIT THE ARCADE ANOTHER DAY!
DASH
HEY, WAIT!
WHAT WAS THAT ALL OF A SUDDEN?
...
THAT GUY MAY KNOW...
...MY SECRET.

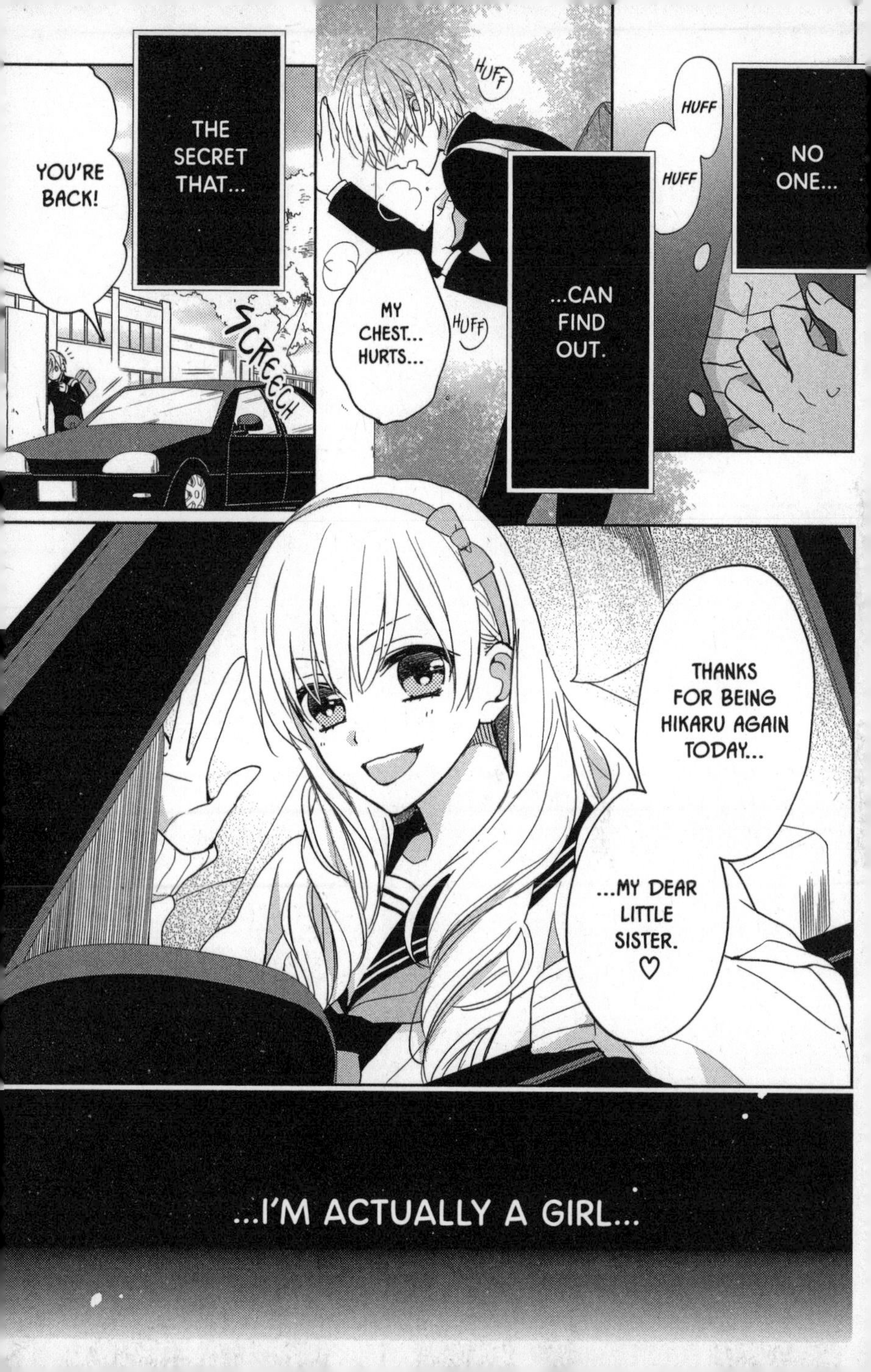
NO ONE...
HUFF
HUFF
...CAN FIND OUT.
HUFF
MY CHEST... HURTS...
HUFF
THE SECRET THAT...
YOU'RE BACK!
SCREECH
THANKS FOR BEING HIKARU AGAIN TODAY...
...MY DEAR LITTLE SISTER. ♡
...I'M ACTUALLY A GIRL...

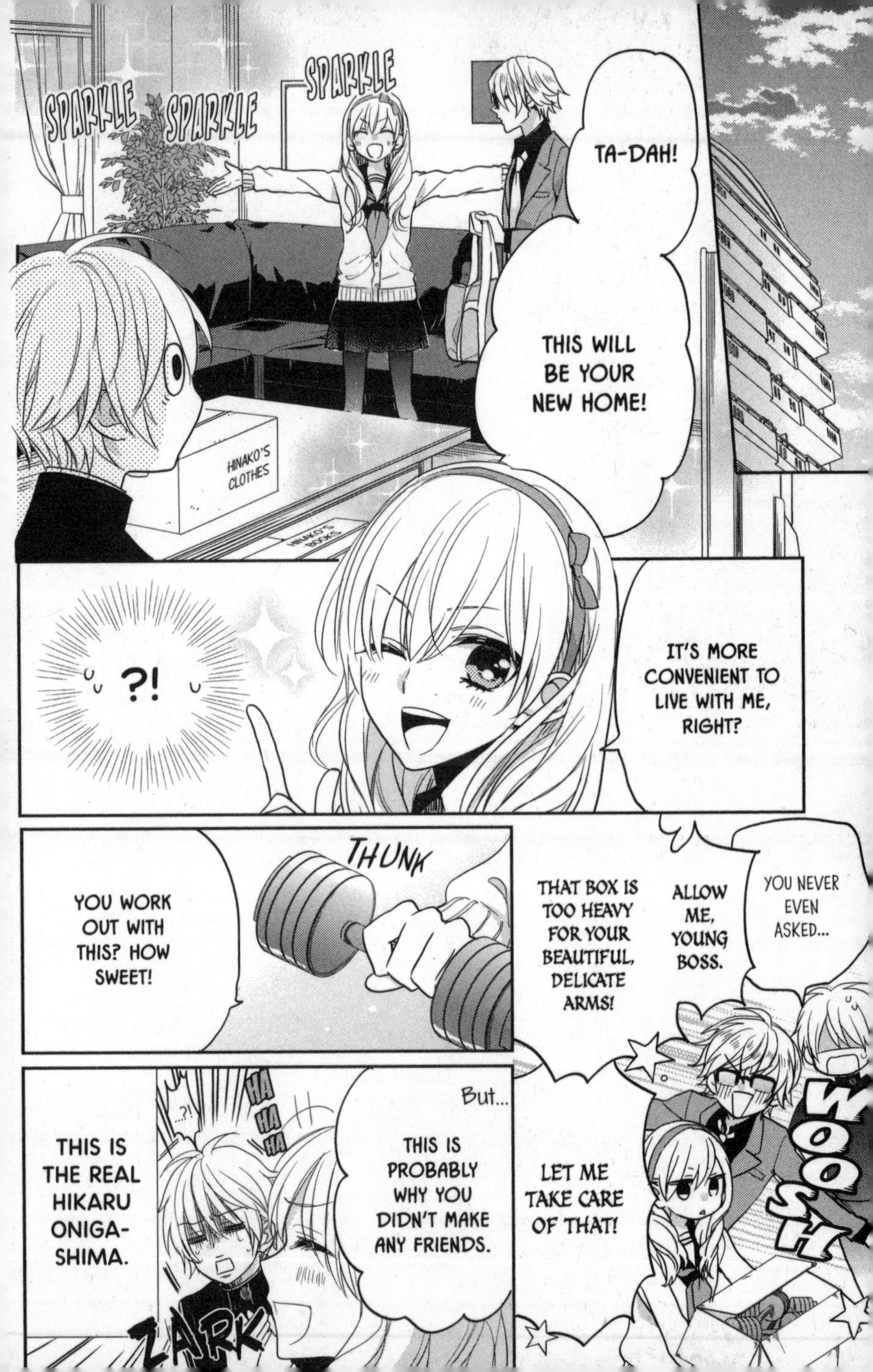
TA-DAH!
THIS WILL BE YOUR NEW HOME!
SPARKLE
SPARKLE
SPARKLE
HINAKO'S CLOTHES
HINAKO'S BOOKS
IT'S MORE CONVENIENT TO LIVE WITH ME, RIGHT?
?!
YOU NEVER EVEN ASKED...
ALLOW ME, YOUNG BOSS.
THAT BOX IS TOO HEAVY FOR YOUR BEAUTIFUL, DELICATE ARMS!
WOOSH
LET ME TAKE CARE OF THAT!
THUNK
YOU WORK OUT WITH THIS? HOW SWEET!
But...
THIS IS PROBABLY WHY YOU DIDN'T MAKE ANY FRIENDS.
HA HA HA
...?!
THIS IS THE REAL HIKARU ONIGA-SHIMA.
ZARK

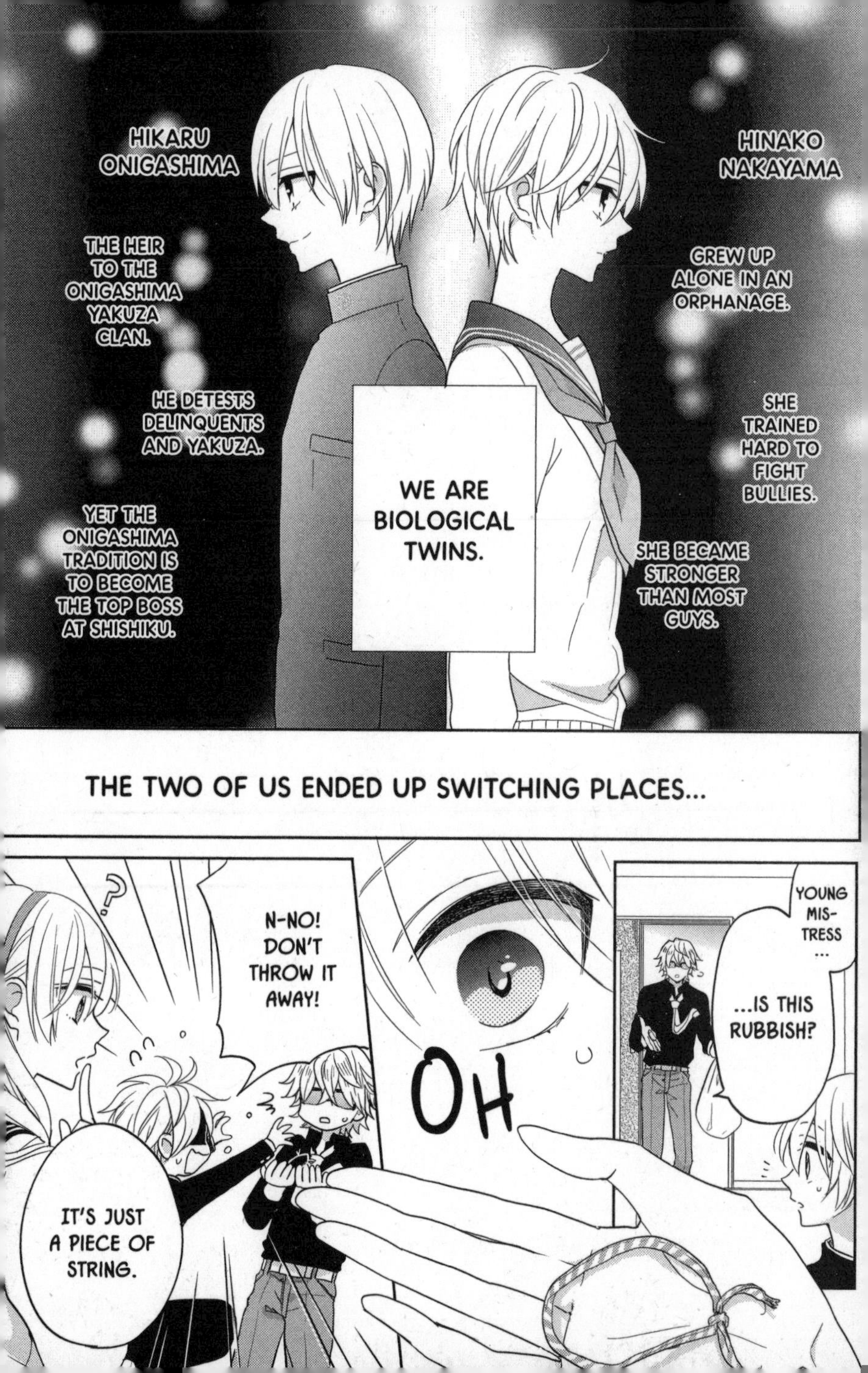
HINAKO NAKAYAMA
GREW UP ALONE IN AN ORPHANAGE.
SHE TRAINED HARD TO FIGHT BULLIES.
SHE BECAME STRONGER THAN MOST GUYS.
HIKARU ONIGASHIMA
THE HEIR TO THE ONIGASHIMA YAKUZA CLAN.
HE DETESTS DELINQUENTS AND YAKUZA.
YET THE ONIGASHIMA TRADITION IS TO BECOME THE TOP BOSS AT SHISHIKU.
WE ARE BIOLOGICAL TWINS.
THE TWO OF US ENDED UP SWITCHING PLACES...
YOUNG MISTRESS...
...IS THIS RUBBISH?
OH
N-NO! DON'T THROW IT AWAY!
IT'S JUST A PIECE OF STRING.

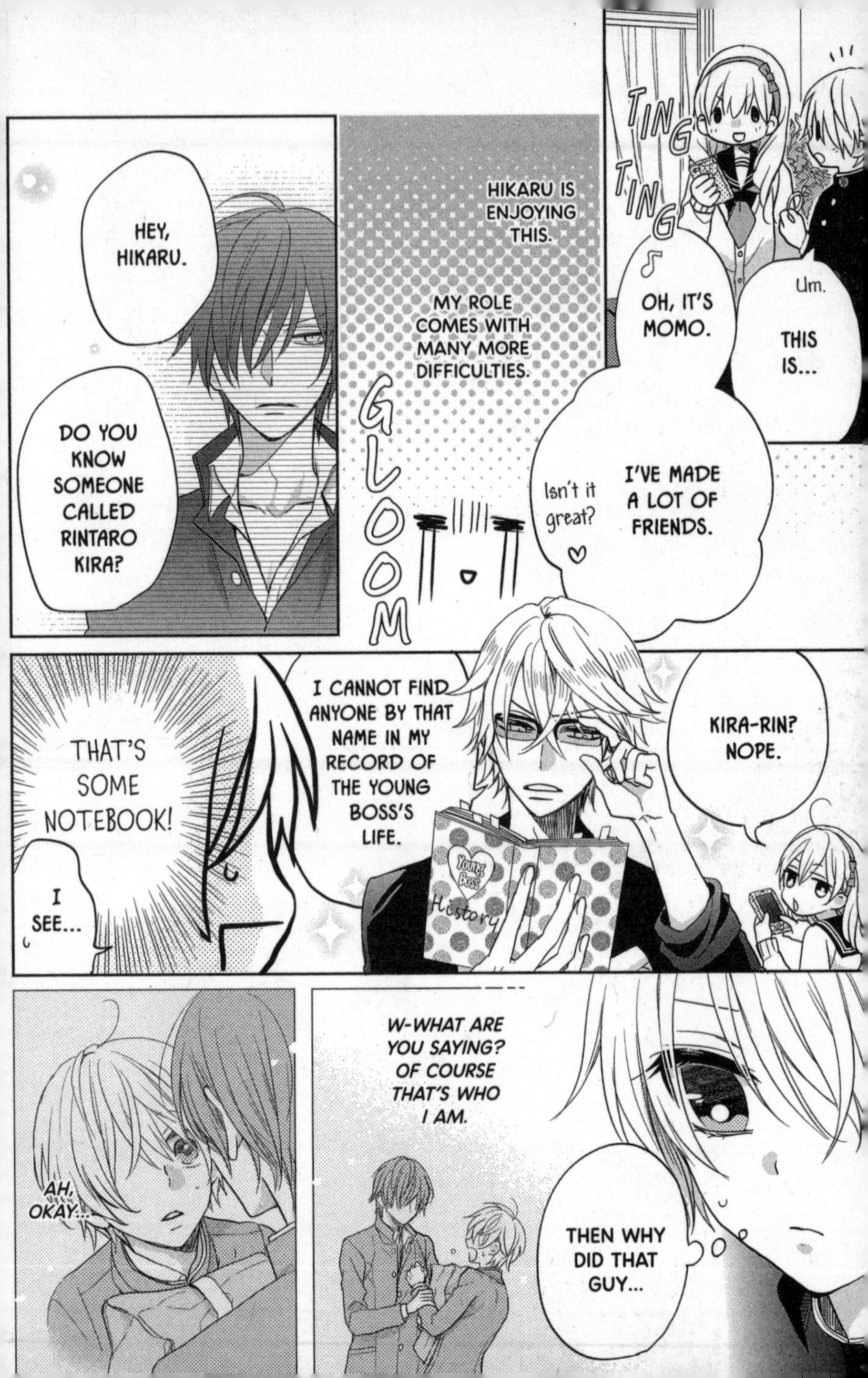
TING TING
Um.
THIS IS...
OH, IT'S MOMO.
I'VE MADE A LOT OF FRIENDS.
Isn't it great?
HIKARU IS ENJOYING THIS.
MY ROLE COMES WITH MANY MORE DIFFICULTIES.
GLOOM
HEY, HIKARU.
DO YOU KNOW SOMEONE CALLED RINTARO KIRA?
KIRA-RIN? NOPE.
I CANNOT FIND ANYONE BY THAT NAME IN MY RECORD OF THE YOUNG BOSS'S LIFE.
Young Boss History
THAT'S SOME NOTEBOOK!
I SEE...
W-WHAT ARE YOU SAYING? OF COURSE THAT'S WHO I AM.
THEN WHY DID THAT GUY...
AH, OKAY...

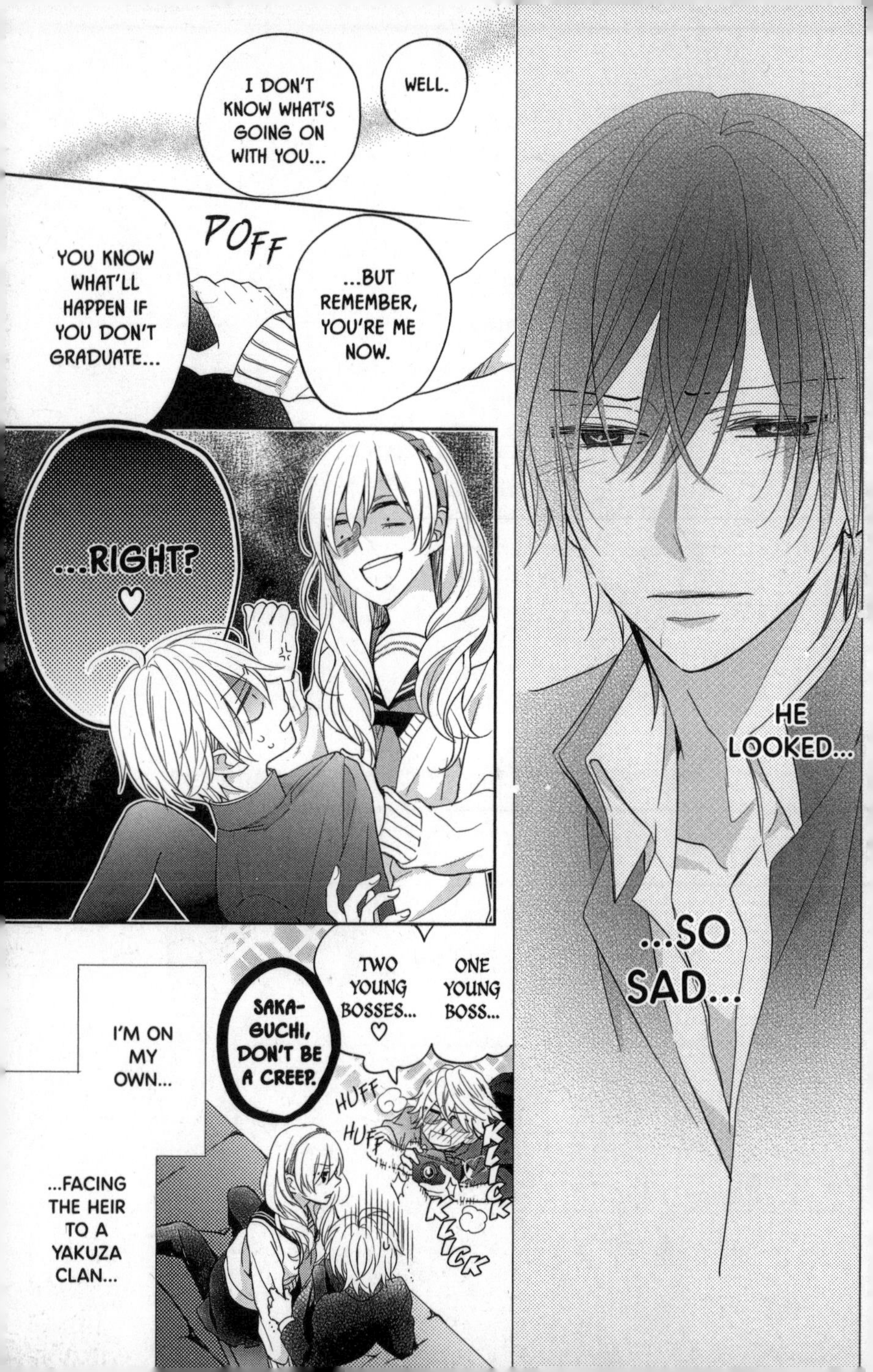
HE LOOKED...
...SO SAD...
WELL.
I DON'T KNOW WHAT'S GOING ON WITH YOU...
...BUT REMEMBER, YOU'RE ME NOW.
POFF
YOU KNOW WHAT'LL HAPPEN IF YOU DON'T GRADUATE...
...RIGHT? ♥
ONE YOUNG BOSS...
TWO YOUNG BOSSES... ♡
SAKA-GUCHI, DON'T BE A CREEP.
KLICK
KLICK
HUFF
HUFF
KLICK
I'M ON MY OWN...
...FACING THE HEIR TO A YAKUZA CLAN...

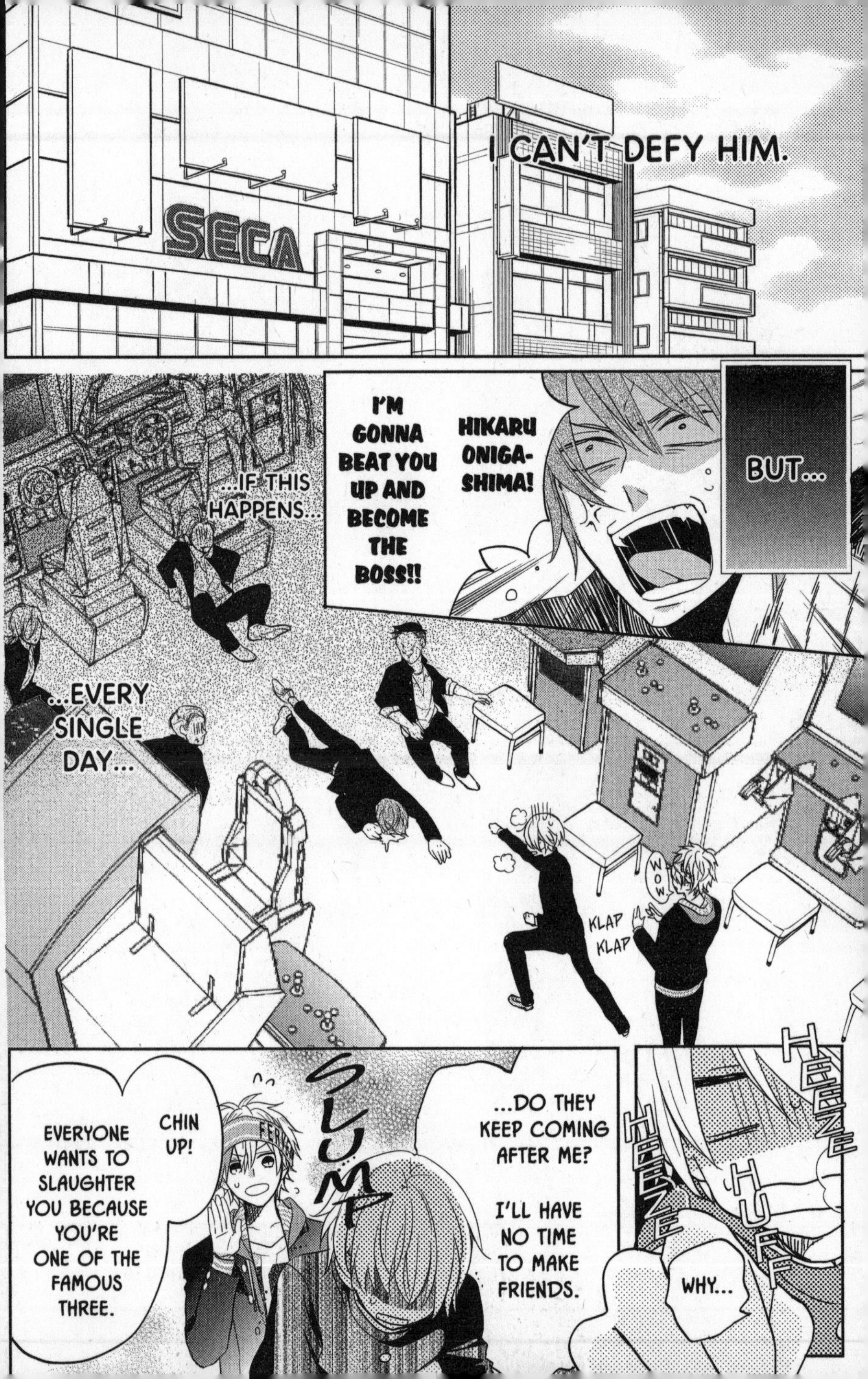
I CAN'T DEFY HIM.
SEGA
BUT...
HIKARU ONIGA-SHIMA!
I'M GONNA BEAT YOU UP AND BECOME THE BOSS!!
...IF THIS HAPPENS...
...EVERY SINGLE DAY...
WOW
KLAP KLAP
HEEEZE
HUFF
HEEEZE
WHY...
...DO THEY KEEP COMING AFTER ME?
I'LL HAVE NO TIME TO MAKE FRIENDS.
SLUMP
CHIN UP!
EVERYONE WANTS TO SLAUGHTER YOU BECAUSE YOU'RE ONE OF THE FAMOUS THREE.

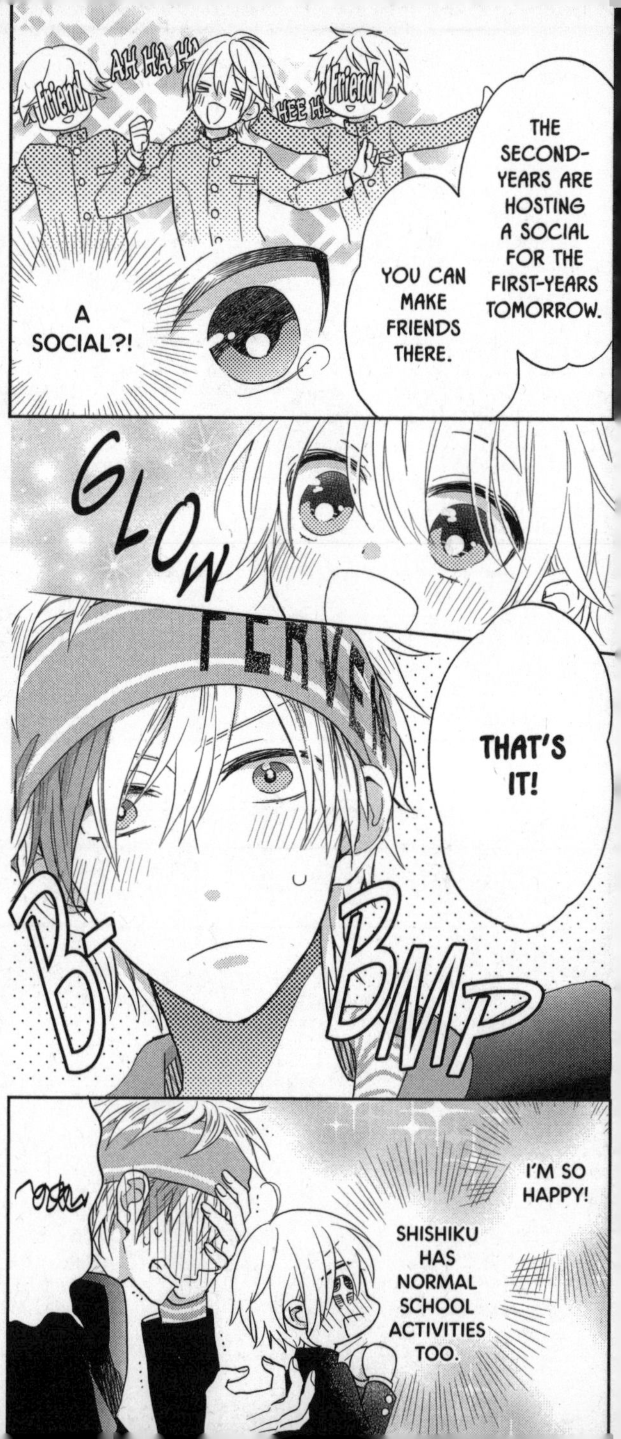
THE SECOND-YEARS ARE HOSTING A SOCIAL FOR THE FIRST-YEARS TOMORROW.
YOU CAN MAKE FRIENDS THERE.
A SOCIAL?!
GLOW
THAT'S IT!
B-BMP
I'M SO HAPPY!
SHISHIKU HAS NORMAL SCHOOL ACTIVITIES TOO.

FIRST-YEAR, VIOLET CLASS

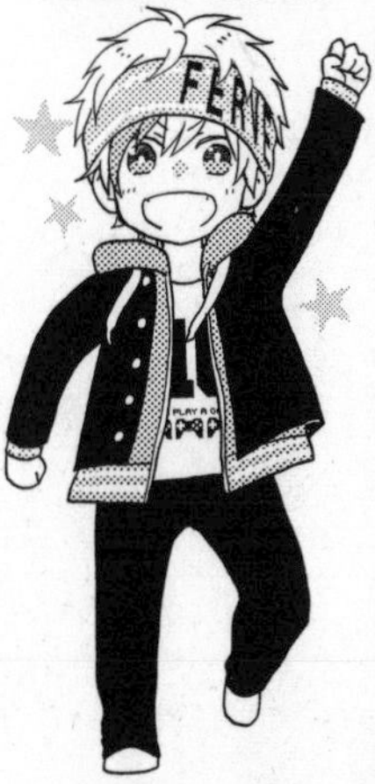

TOTOMARU MINOWA

Height: 5'7"
Weight: 140 lbs
Blood Type: B
Birthday: April 20
Skill: Karate

I wanted him to be a classmate Hinako could rely on. He's a good guy who is full of energy, and he's a great friend to others. I want to make him blush every single time.

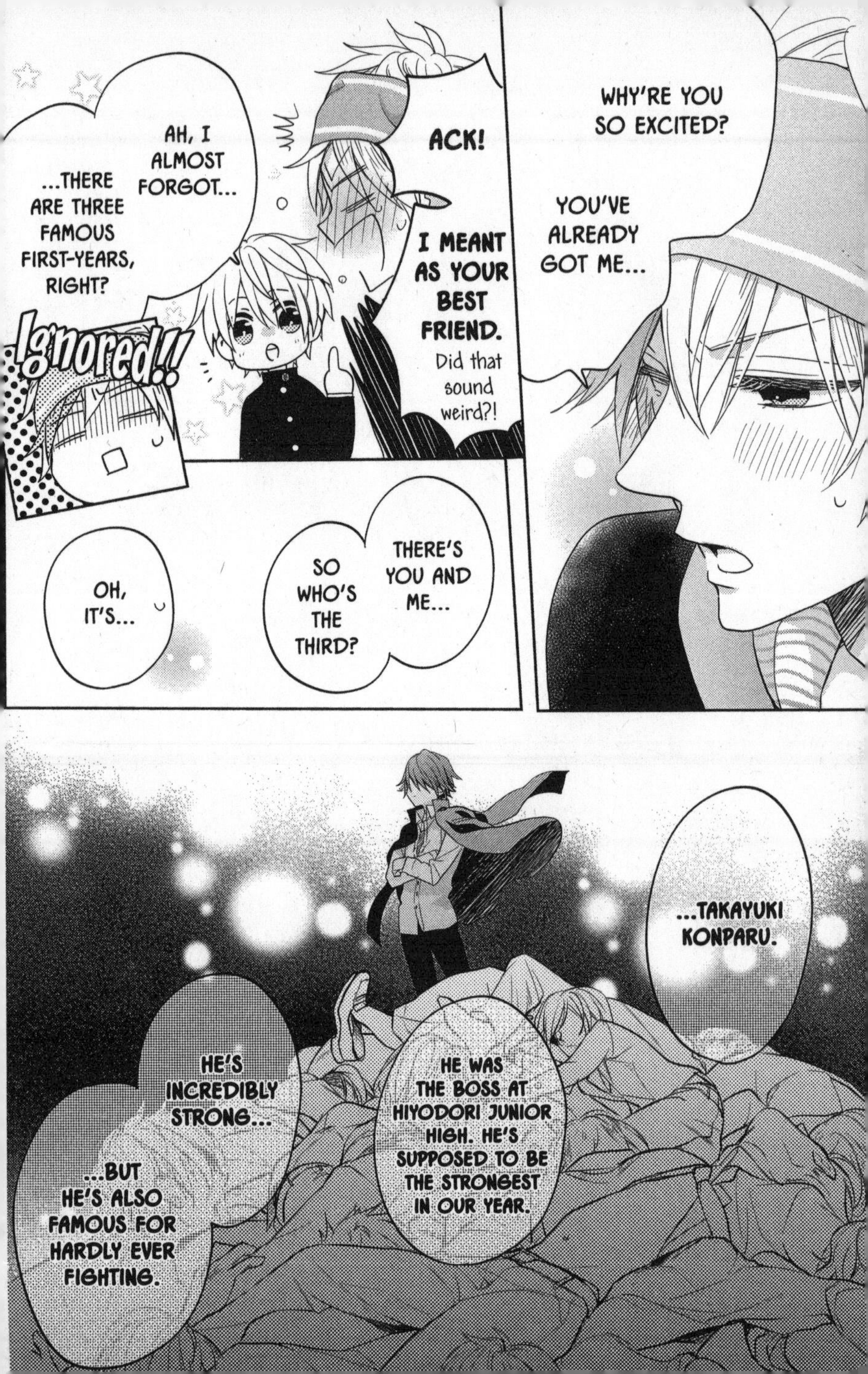
WHY'RE YOU SO EXCITED?
YOU'VE ALREADY GOT ME...
ACK!
I MEANT AS YOUR BEST FRIEND.
Did that sound weird?!
AH, I ALMOST FORGOT...
...THERE ARE THREE FAMOUS FIRST-YEARS, RIGHT?
Ignored!!
THERE'S YOU AND ME...
SO WHO'S THE THIRD?
OH, IT'S...
...TAKAYUKI KONPARU.
HE WAS THE BOSS AT HIYODORI JUNIOR HIGH. HE'S SUPPOSED TO BE THE STRONGEST IN OUR YEAR.
HE'S INCREDIBLY STRONG...
...BUT HE'S ALSO FAMOUS FOR HARDLY EVER FIGHTING.

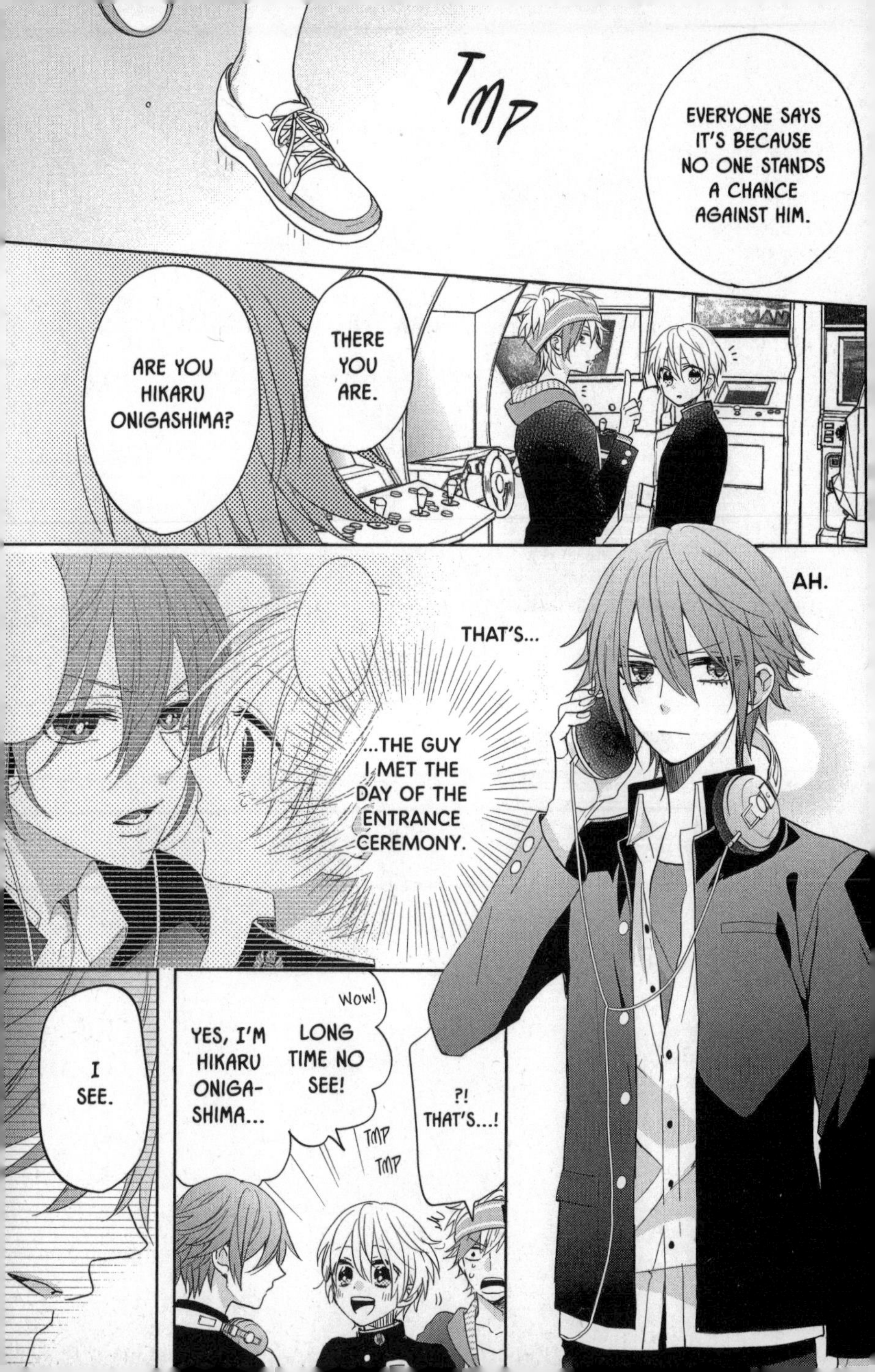
EVERYONE SAYS IT'S BECAUSE NO ONE STANDS A CHANCE AGAINST HIM.
TMP
THERE YOU ARE.
ARE YOU HIKARU ONIGASHIMA?
AH.
THAT'S...
...THE GUY I MET THE DAY OF THE ENTRANCE CEREMONY.
?! THAT'S...!
Wow!
LONG TIME NO SEE!
YES, I'M HIKARU ONIGA-SHIMA...
TMP
TMP
I SEE.

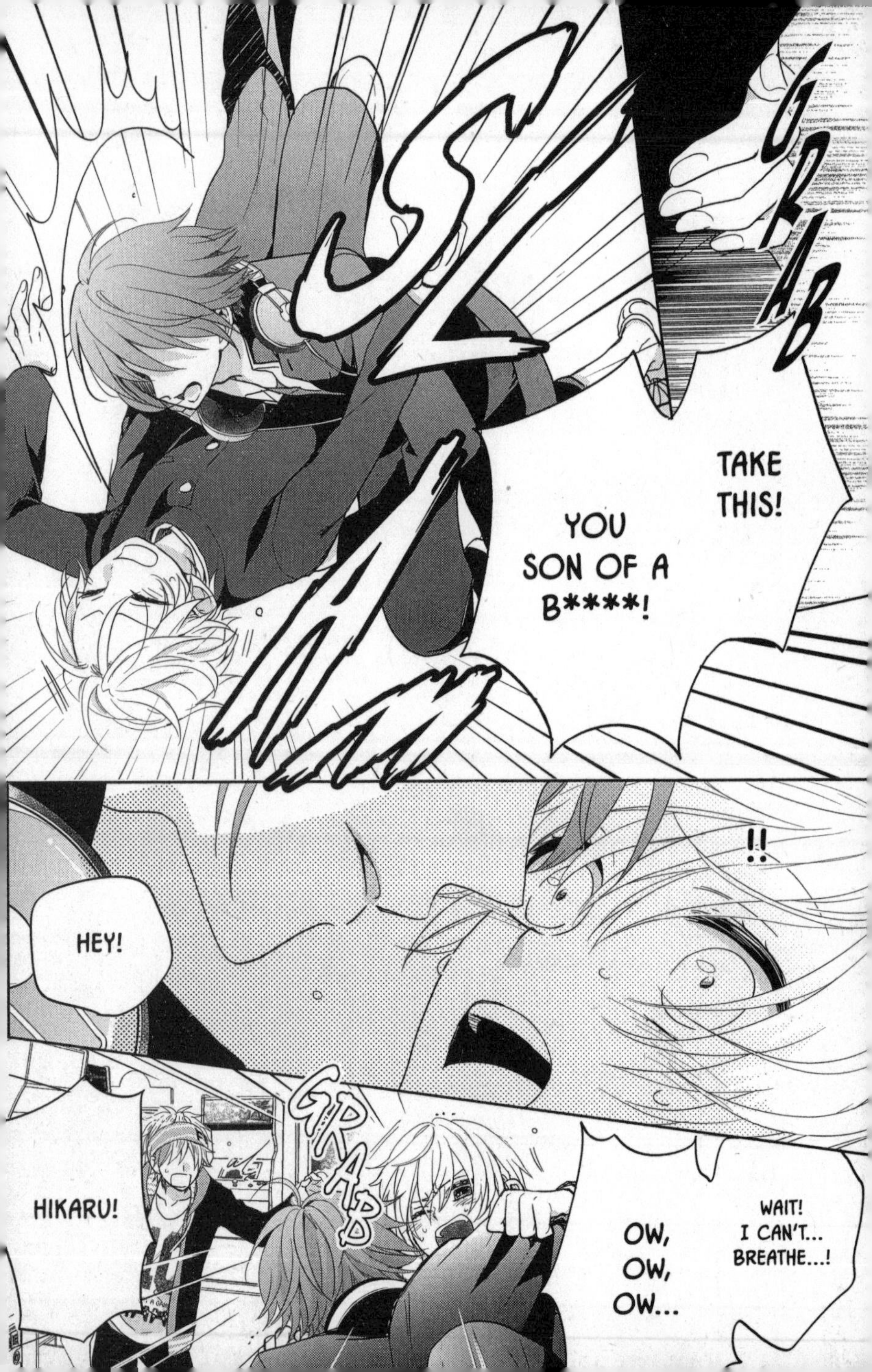
GRAB
TAKE THIS!
YOU SON OF A B****!
!!
HEY!
WAIT! I CAN'T... BREATHE...!
OW, OW, OW...
GRAB
HIKARU!

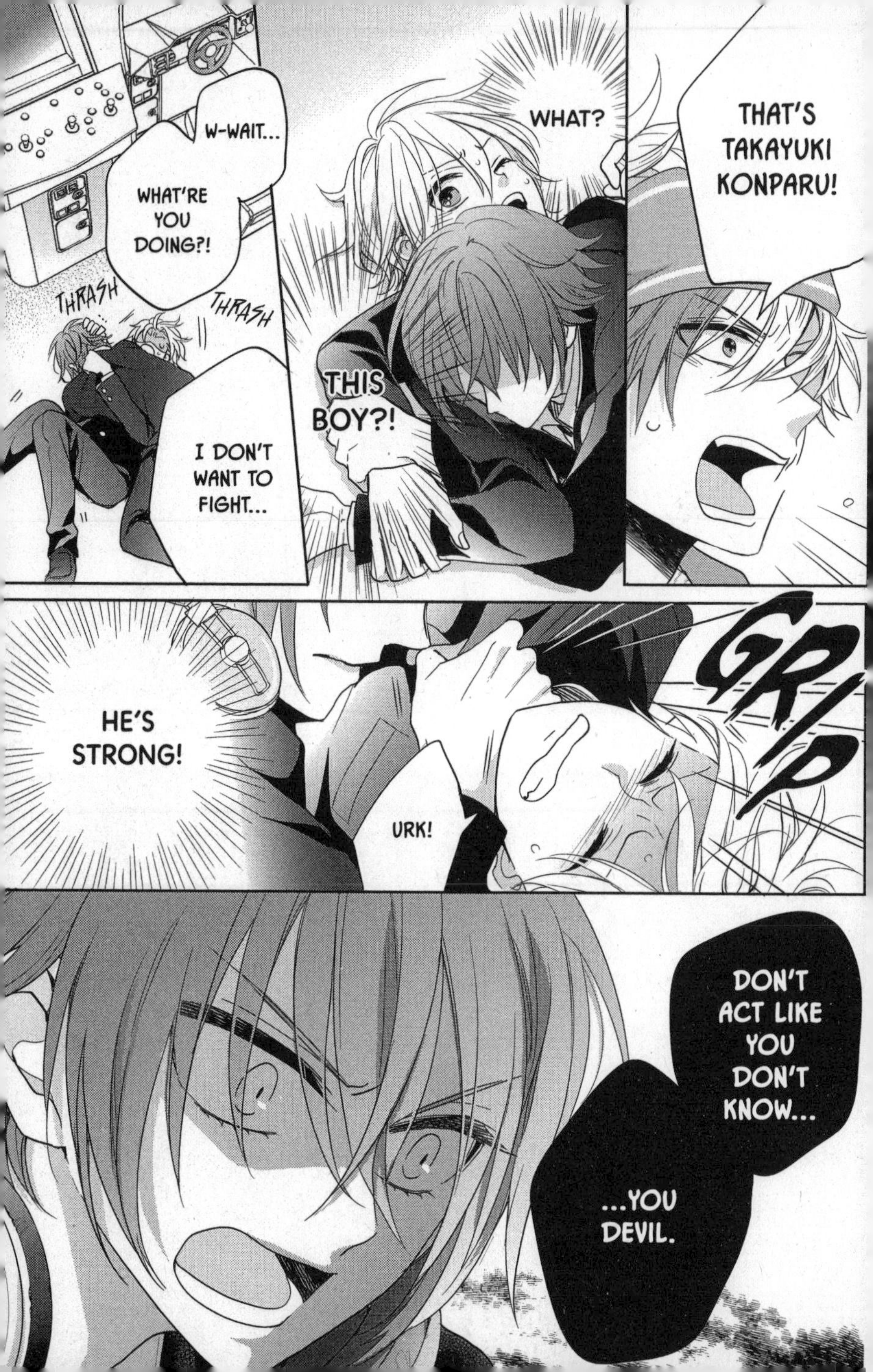
THAT'S TAKAYUKI KONPARU!
WHAT?
THIS BOY?!
W-WAIT...
WHAT'RE YOU DOING?!
THRASH
THRASH
I DON'T WANT TO FIGHT...
GRIP
URK!
HE'S STRONG!
DON'T ACT LIKE YOU DON'T KNOW...
...YOU DEVIL.

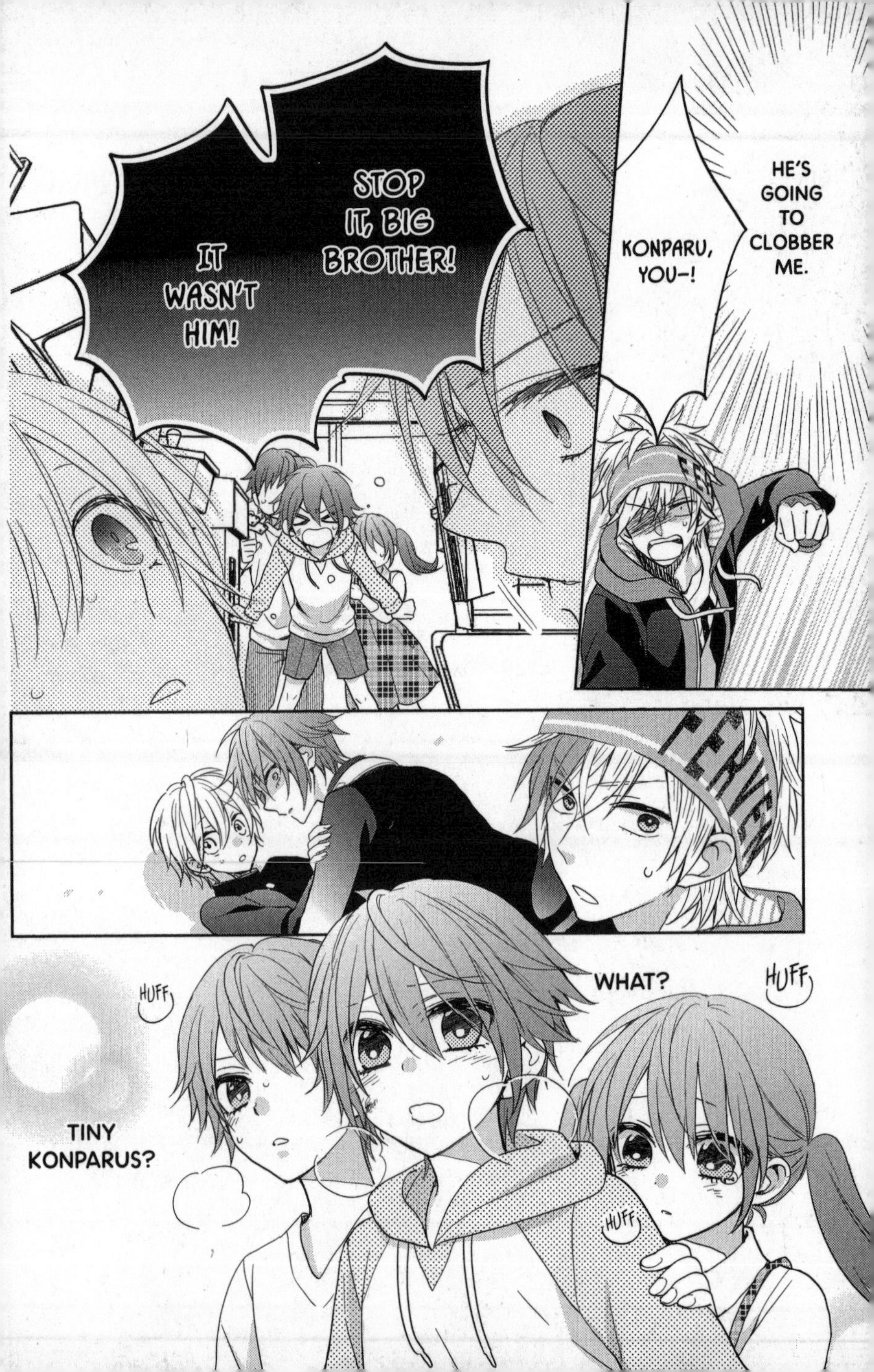
HE'S GOING TO CLOBBER ME.
KONPARU, YOU-!
STOP IT, BIG BROTHER!
IT WASN'T HIM!
HUFF
WHAT?
HUFF
TINY KONPARUS?
HUFF

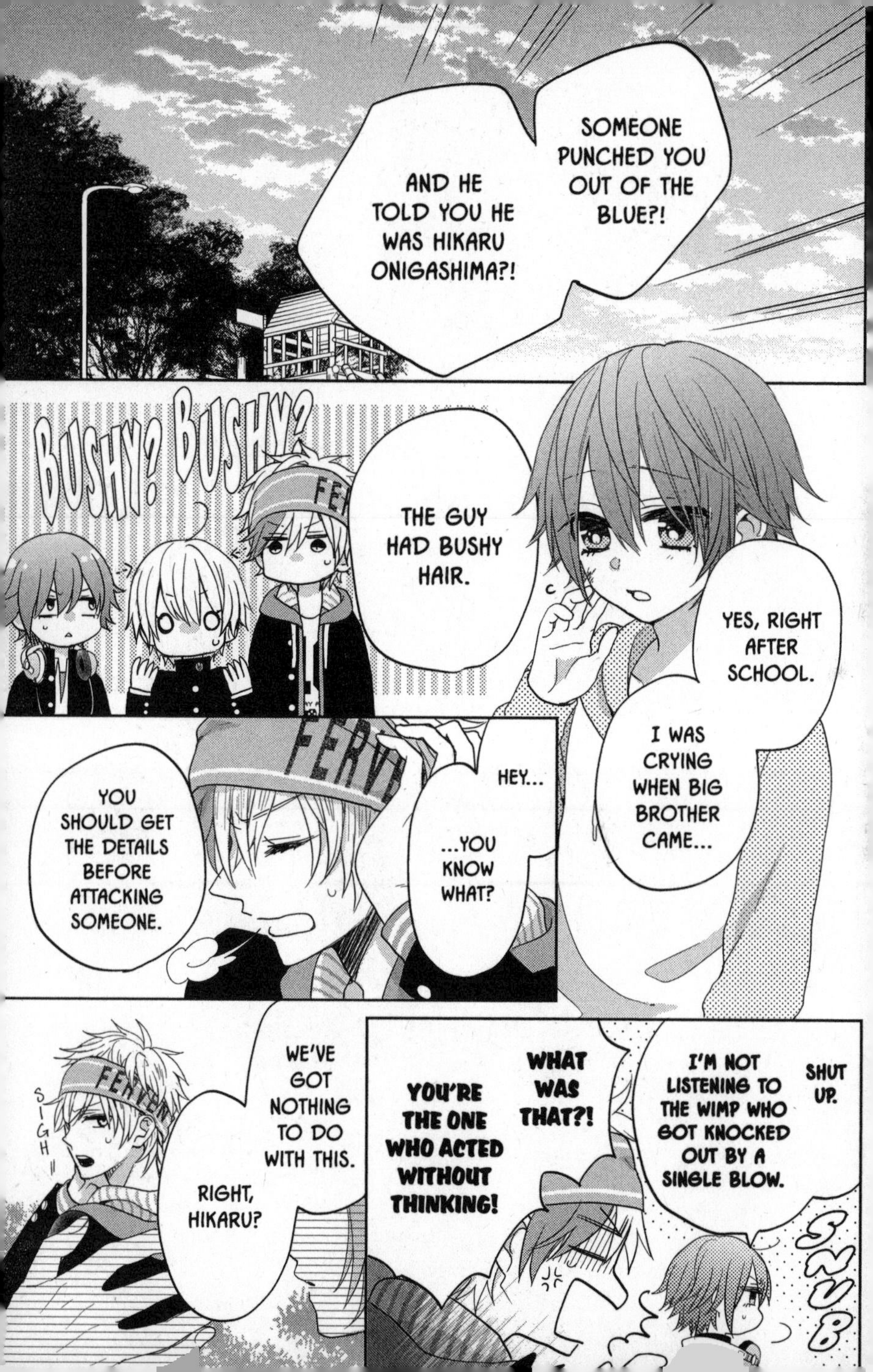
SOMEONE PUNCHED YOU OUT OF THE BLUE?!
AND HE TOLD YOU HE WAS HIKARU ONIGASHIMA?!
YES, RIGHT AFTER SCHOOL.
I WAS CRYING WHEN BIG BROTHER CAME...
THE GUY HAD BUSHY HAIR.
BUSHY? BUSHY?
FERV
HEY...
...YOU KNOW WHAT?
YOU SHOULD GET THE DETAILS BEFORE ATTACKING SOMEONE.
SHUT UP.
I'M NOT LISTENING TO THE WIMP WHO GOT KNOCKED OUT BY A SINGLE BLOW.
WHAT WAS THAT?!
YOU'RE THE ONE WHO ACTED WITHOUT THINKING!
SNUB
WE'VE GOT NOTHING TO DO WITH THIS.
RIGHT, HIKARU?
SIGH
FERVEN

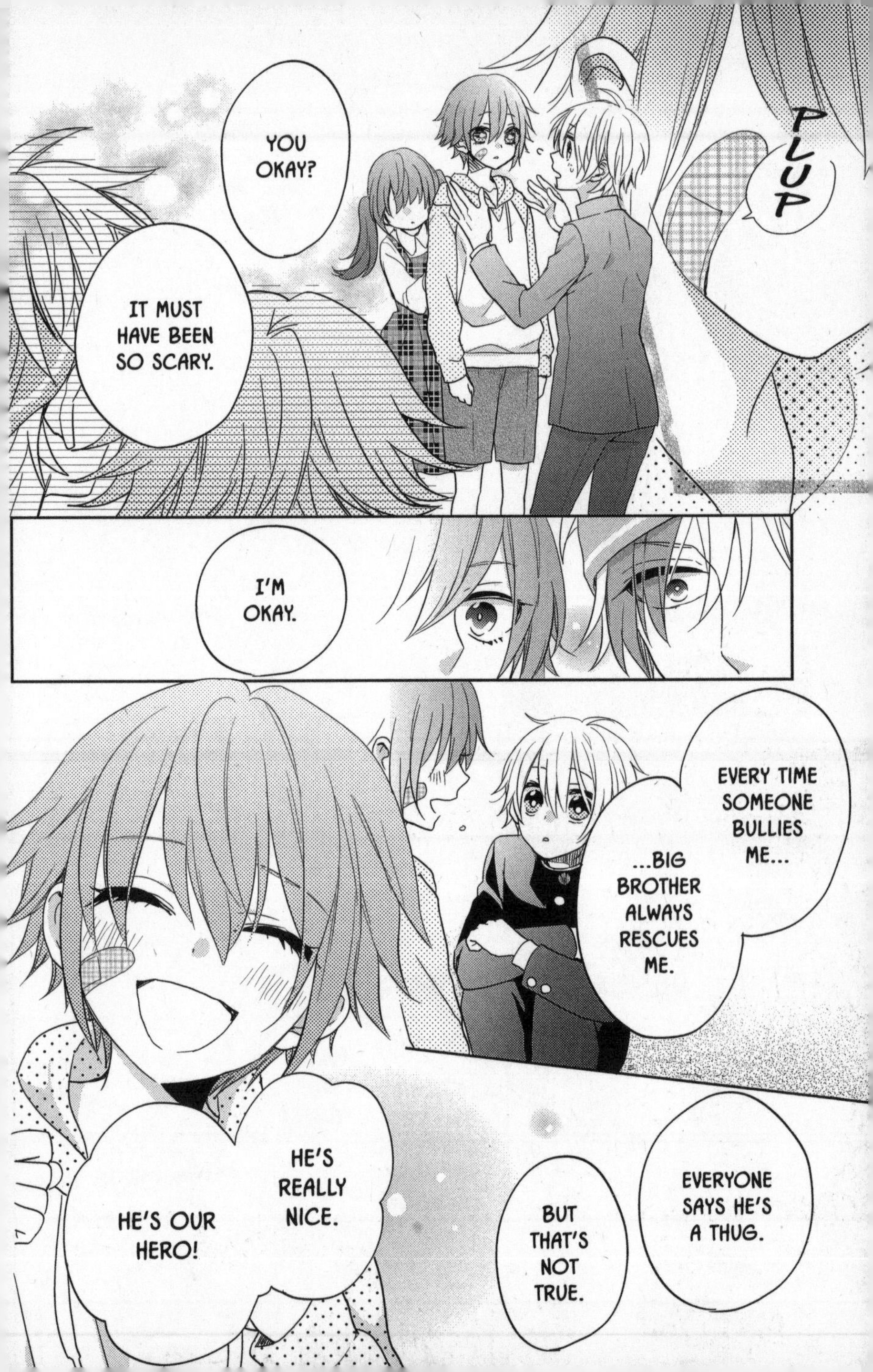
PLUP
YOU OKAY?
IT MUST HAVE BEEN SO SCARY.
I'M OKAY.
EVERY TIME SOMEONE BULLIES ME...
...BIG BROTHER ALWAYS RESCUES ME.
EVERYONE SAYS HE'S A THUG.
BUT THAT'S NOT TRUE.
HE'S REALLY NICE.
HE'S OUR HERO!

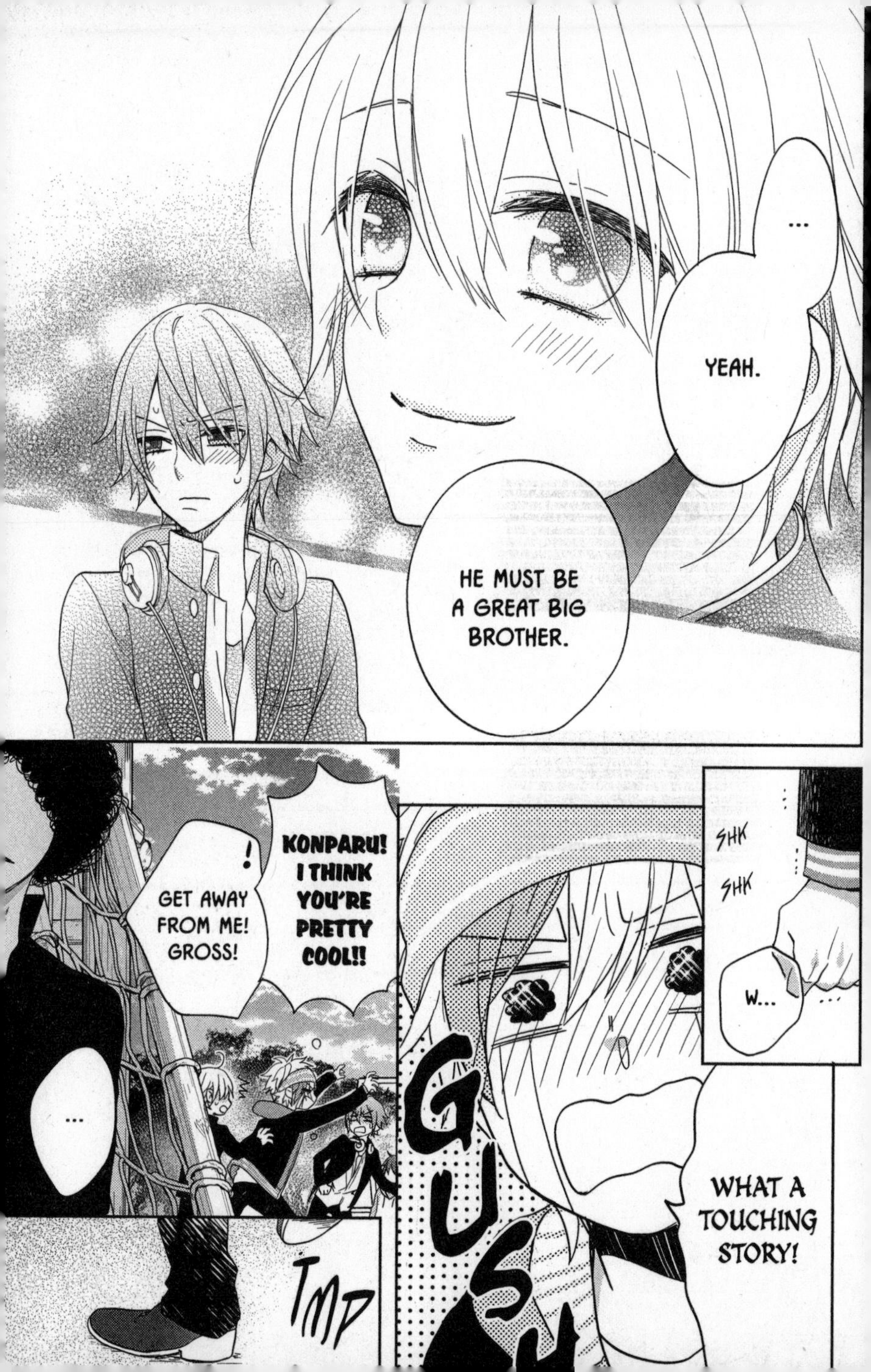
...
YEAH.
HE MUST BE A GREAT BIG BROTHER.
SHK
SHK
W...
WHAT A TOUCHING STORY!
GUSH
KONPARU! I THINK YOU'RE PRETTY COOL!!
! GET AWAY FROM ME! GROSS!
...
TMP

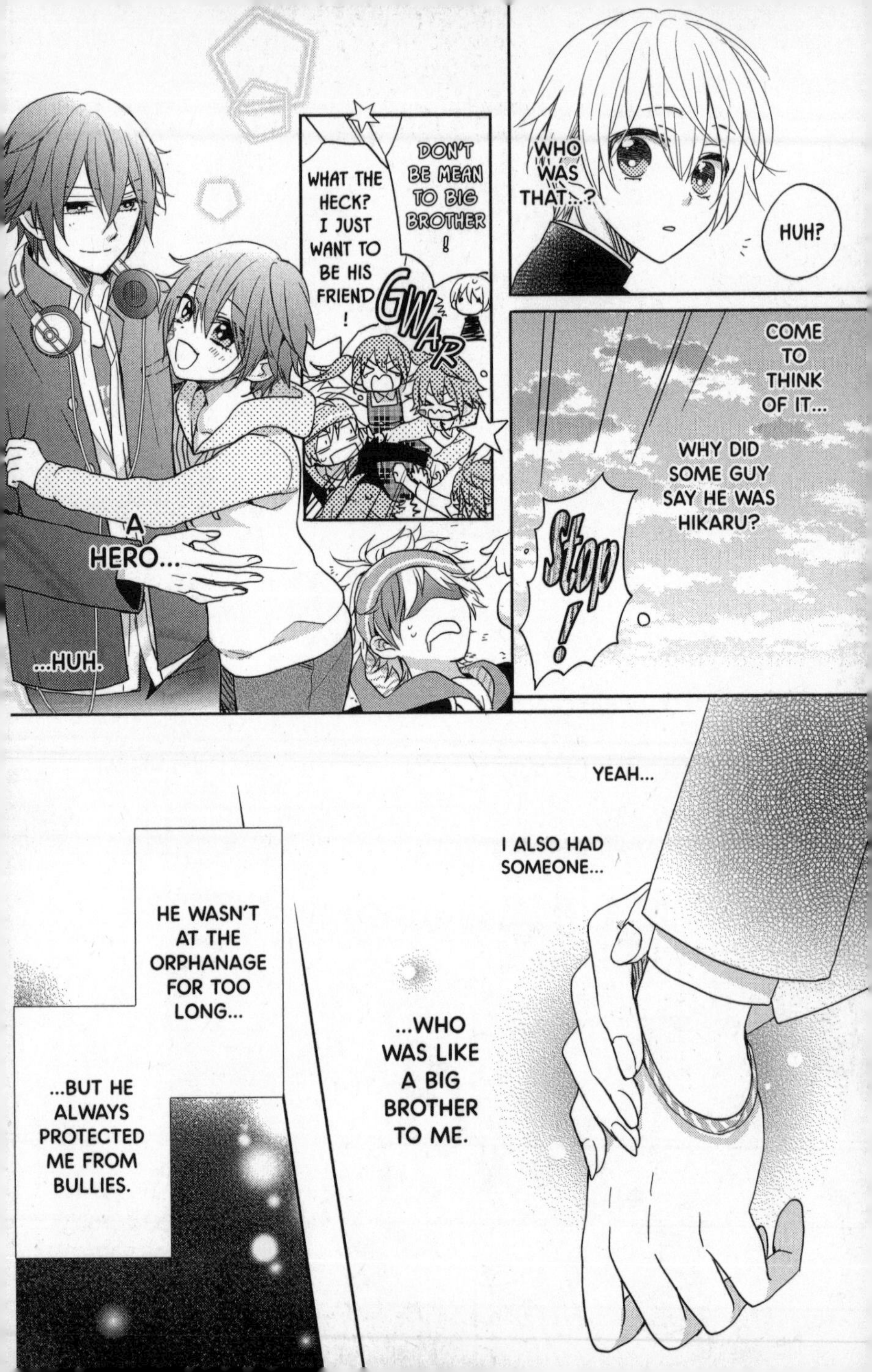
HUH?
WHO WAS THAT...?
COME TO THINK OF IT...
WHY DID SOME GUY SAY HE WAS HIKARU?
Stop!
DON'T BE MEAN TO BIG BROTHER!
WHAT THE HECK? I JUST WANT TO BE HIS FRIEND!
GWAR
A HERO...
...HUH.
YEAH...
I ALSO HAD SOMEONE...
...WHO WAS LIKE A BIG BROTHER TO ME.
HE WASN'T AT THE ORPHANAGE FOR TOO LONG...
...BUT HE ALWAYS PROTECTED ME FROM BULLIES.

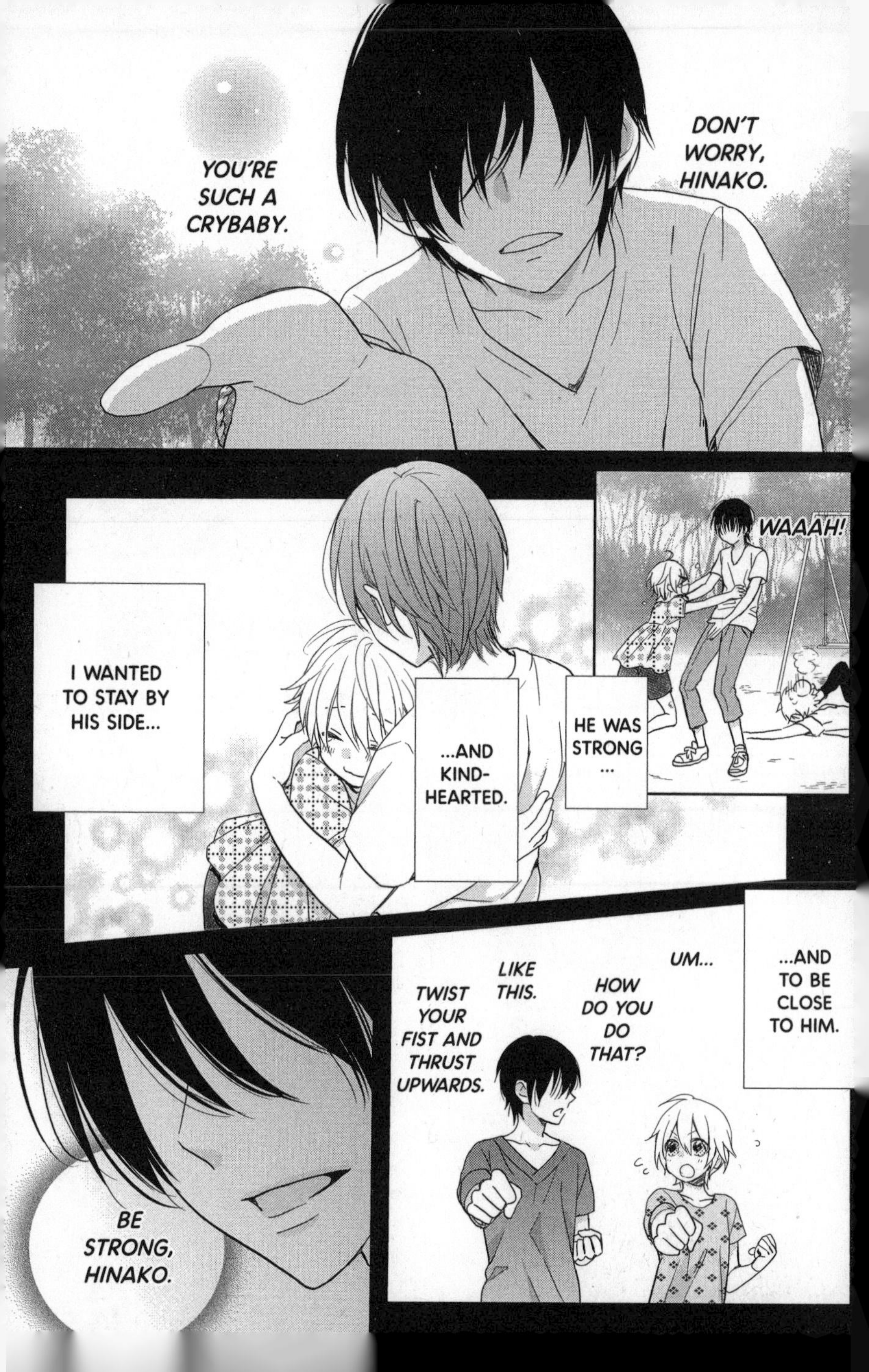
DON'T WORRY, HINAKO.
YOU'RE SUCH A CRYBABY.
WAAAH!
HE WAS STRONG...
...AND KIND-HEARTED.
I WANTED TO STAY BY HIS SIDE...
...AND TO BE CLOSE TO HIM.
UM...
HOW DO YOU DO THAT?
LIKE THIS.
TWIST YOUR FIST AND THRUST UPWARDS.
BE STRONG, HINAKO.

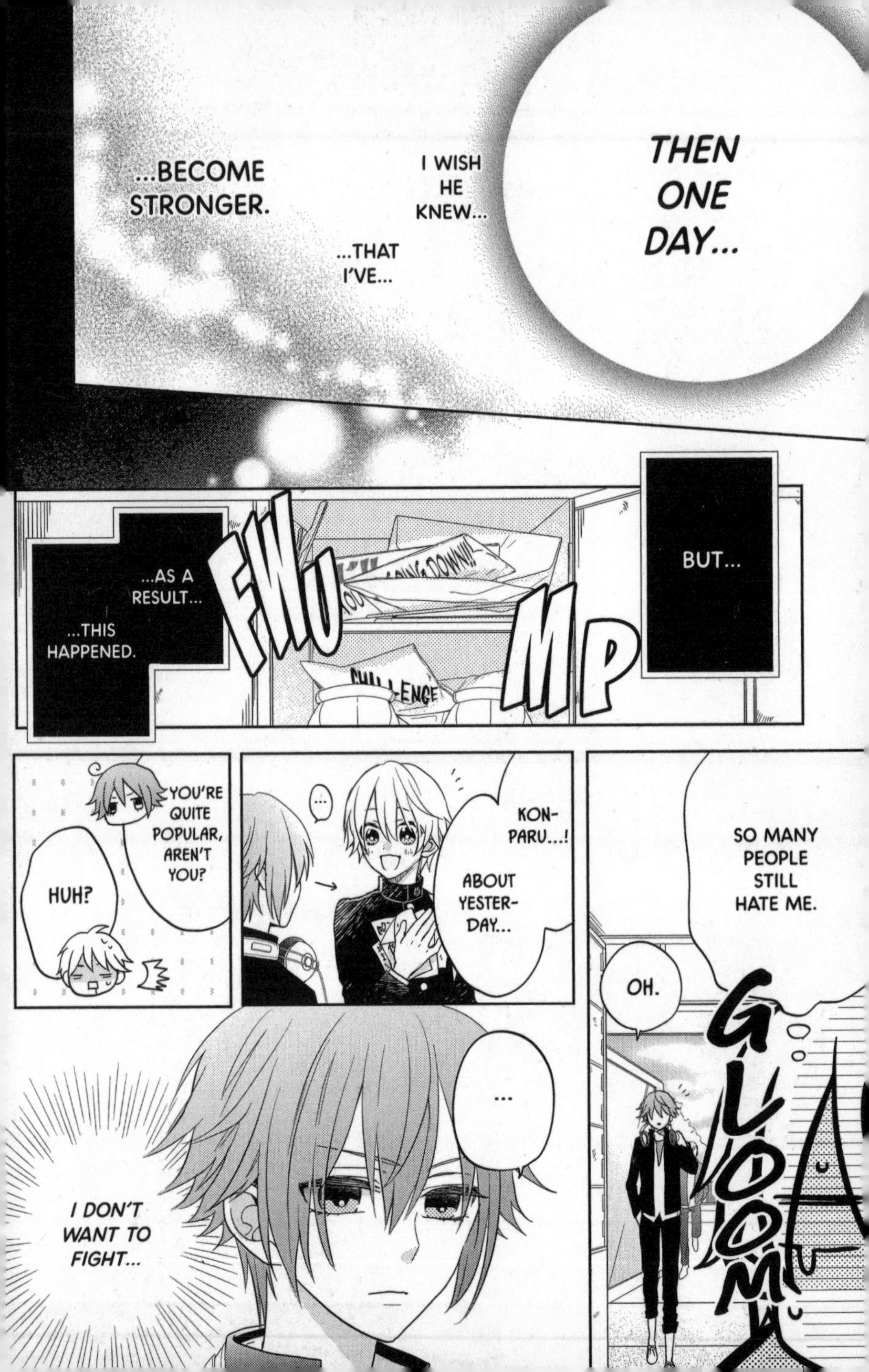
THEN ONE DAY...
I WISH HE KNEW...
...THAT I'VE...
...BECOME STRONGER.
BUT...
FWUMP
...AS A RESULT...
...THIS HAPPENED.
SO MANY PEOPLE STILL HATE ME.
OH.
GLOOM
KON-PARU...!
ABOUT YESTER-DAY...
...
YOU'RE QUITE POPULAR, AREN'T YOU?
HUH?
...
I DON'T WANT TO FIGHT...

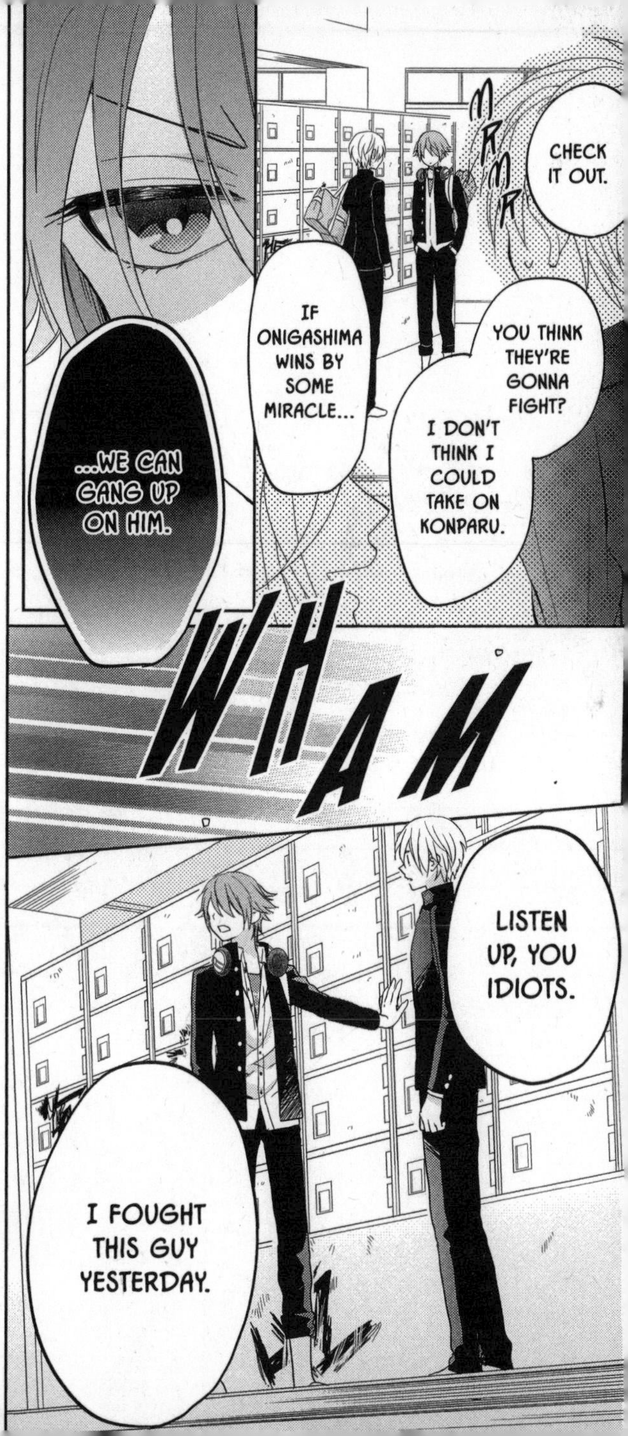
MRMR
CHECK IT OUT.
YOU THINK THEY'RE GONNA FIGHT?
I DON'T THINK I COULD TAKE ON KONPARU.
IF ONIGASHIMA WINS BY SOME MIRACLE...
...WE CAN GANG UP ON HIM.
WHAM
LISTEN UP, YOU IDIOTS.
I FOUGHT THIS GUY YESTERDAY.

FIRST-YEAR, WISTERIA CLASS

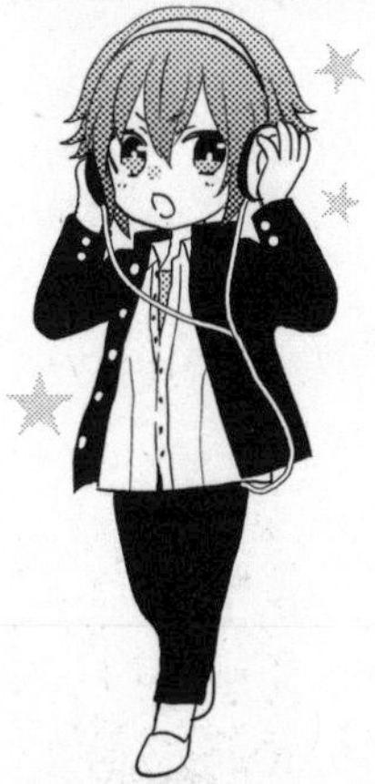

TAKAYUKI KONPARU

Height: 5'3"
Weight: 123 lbs
Blood Type: O
Birthday: January 19
Skill: Brazilian Jujitsu

Despite his pretty face, he's actually a tough guy. In the manga, he's reliable and plays the straight man to Totomaru. I want to show more of his big-brother side.

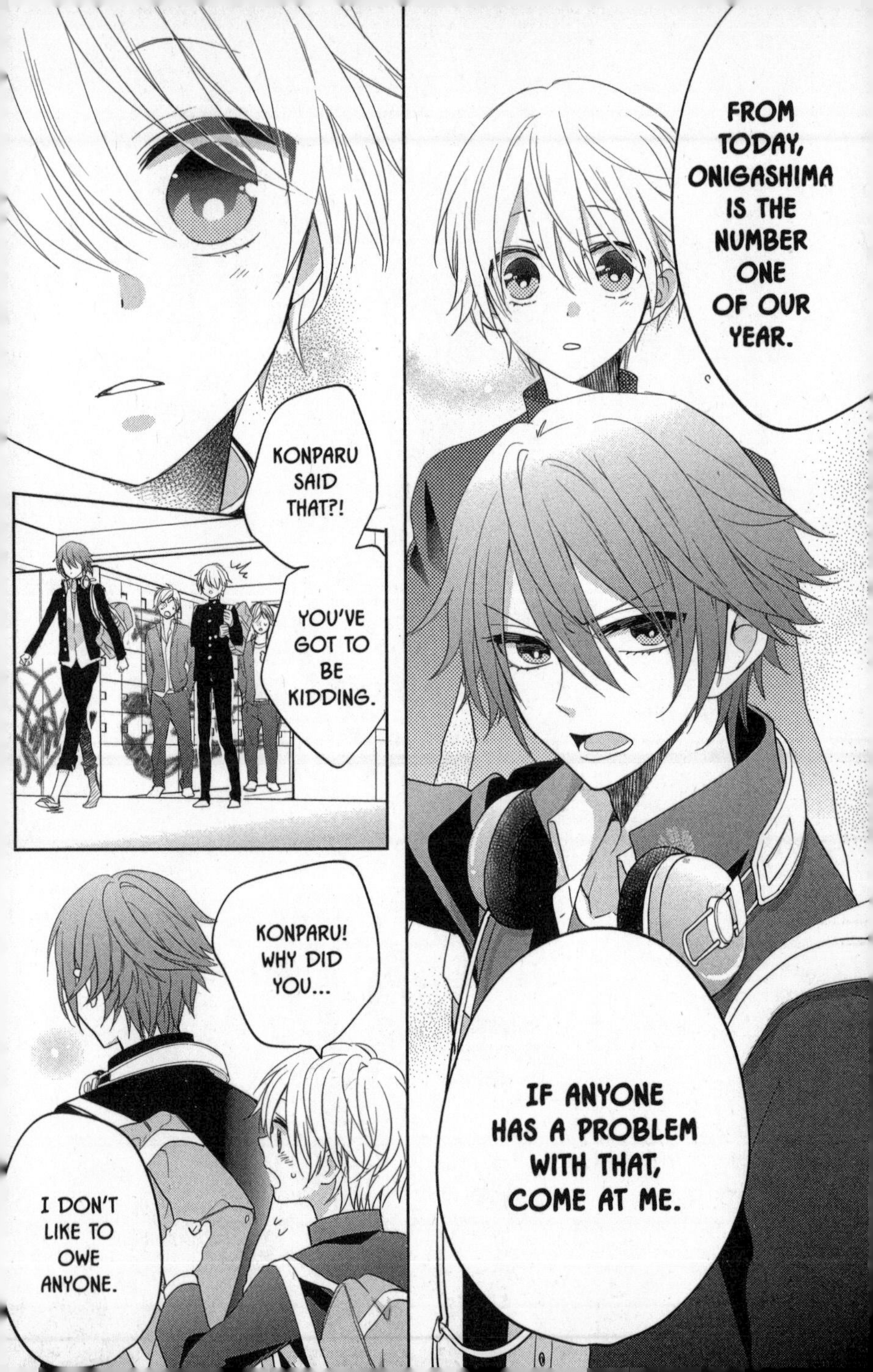
FROM TODAY, ONIGASHIMA IS THE NUMBER ONE OF OUR YEAR.
IF ANYONE HAS A PROBLEM WITH THAT, COME AT ME.
KONPARU SAID THAT?!
YOU'VE GOT TO BE KIDDING.
KONPARU! WHY DID YOU...
I DON'T LIKE TO OWE ANYONE.

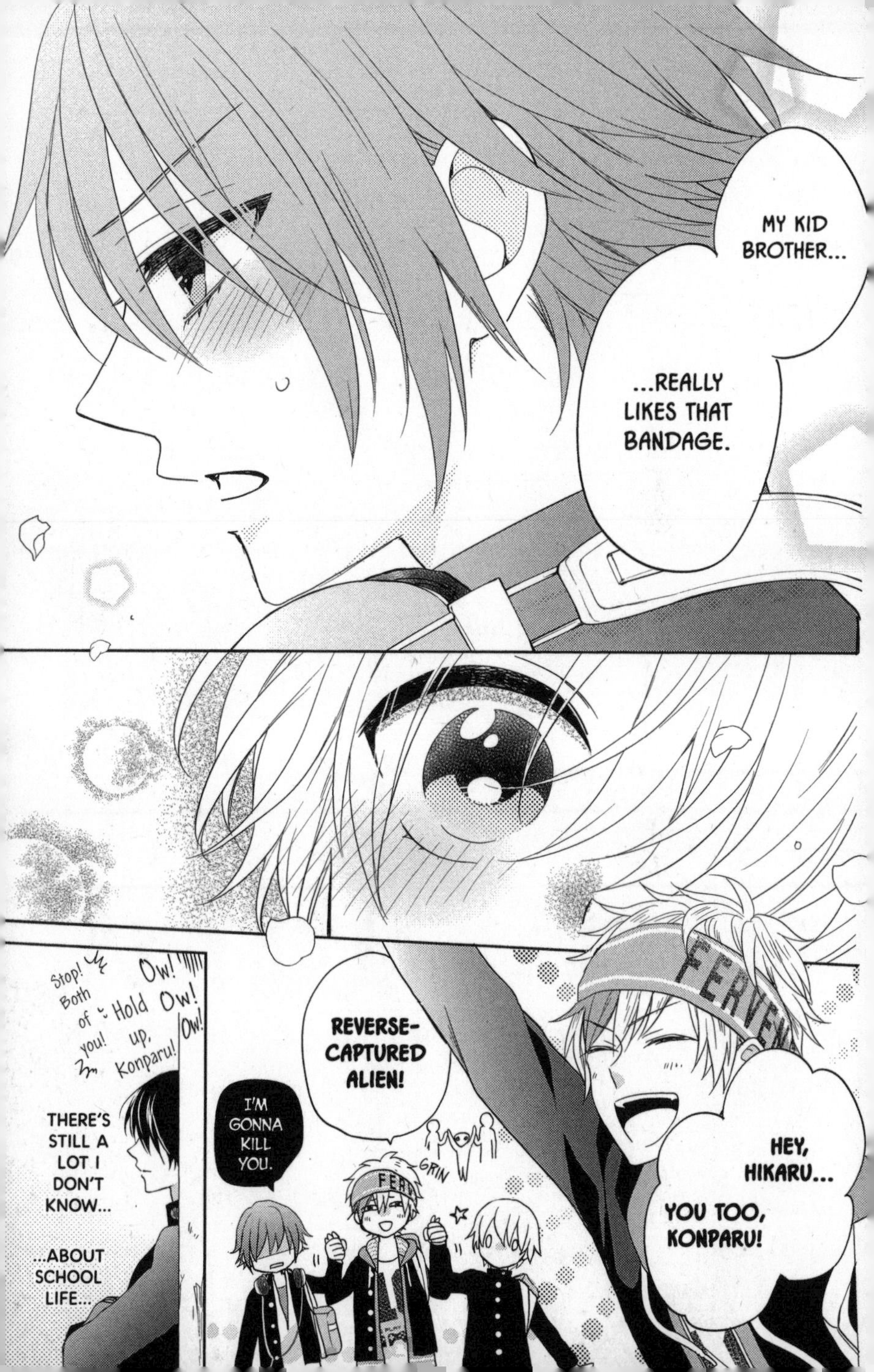
MY KID BROTHER...
...REALLY LIKES THAT BANDAGE.
HEY, HIKARU...
YOU TOO, KONPARU!
REVERSE-CAPTURED ALIEN!
I'M GONNA KILL YOU.
GRIN
Ow! Ow! Ow!
Hold up, Konparu!
Stop! Both of you!
THERE'S STILL A LOT I DON'T KNOW...
...ABOUT SCHOOL LIFE...

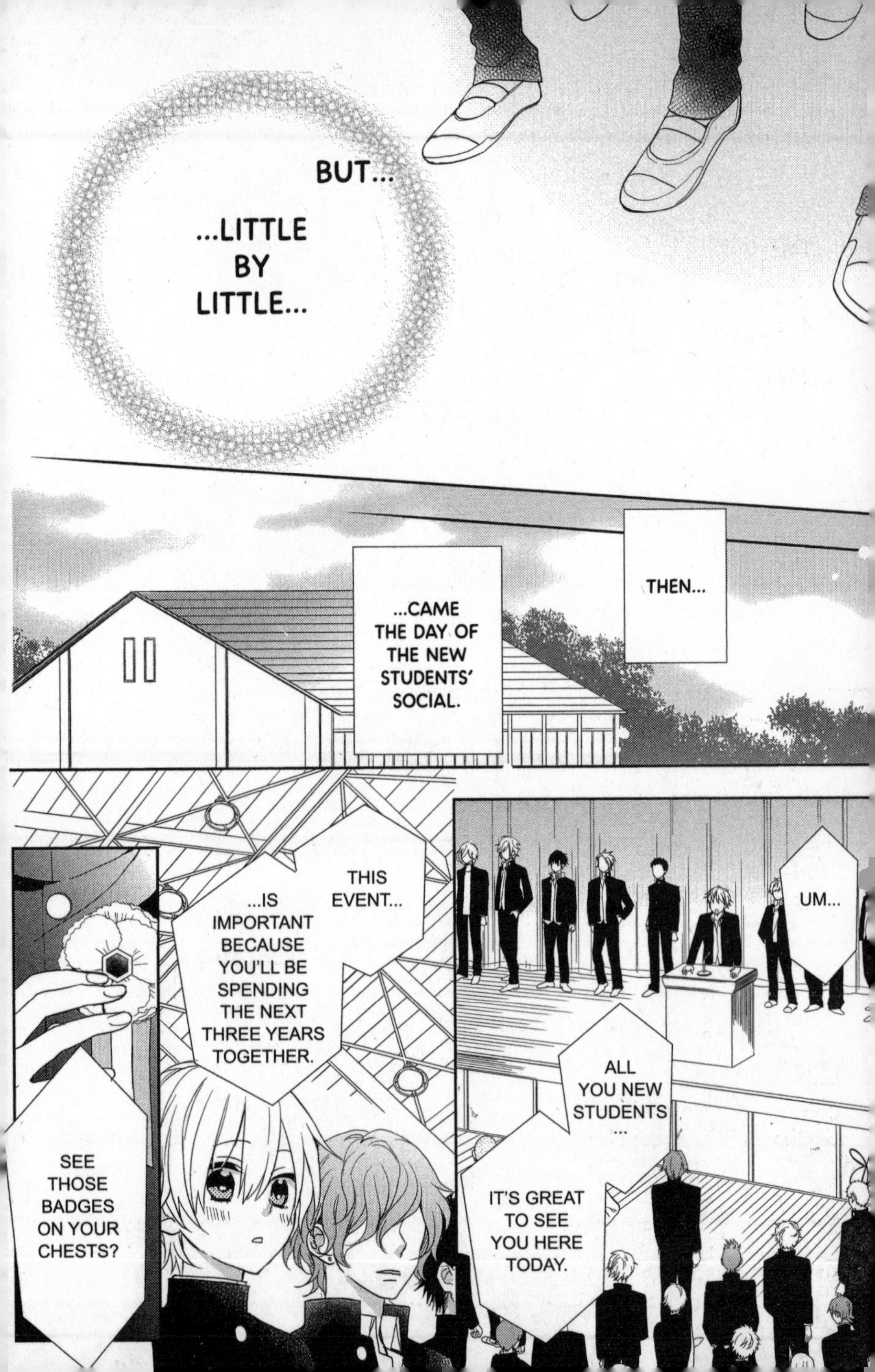
BUT...
...LITTLE BY LITTLE...
THEN...
...CAME THE DAY OF THE NEW STUDENTS' SOCIAL.
UM...
ALL YOU NEW STUDENTS ...
IT'S GREAT TO SEE YOU HERE TODAY.
THIS EVENT...
...IS IMPORTANT BECAUSE YOU'LL BE SPENDING THE NEXT THREE YEARS TOGETHER.
SEE THOSE BADGES ON YOUR CHESTS?

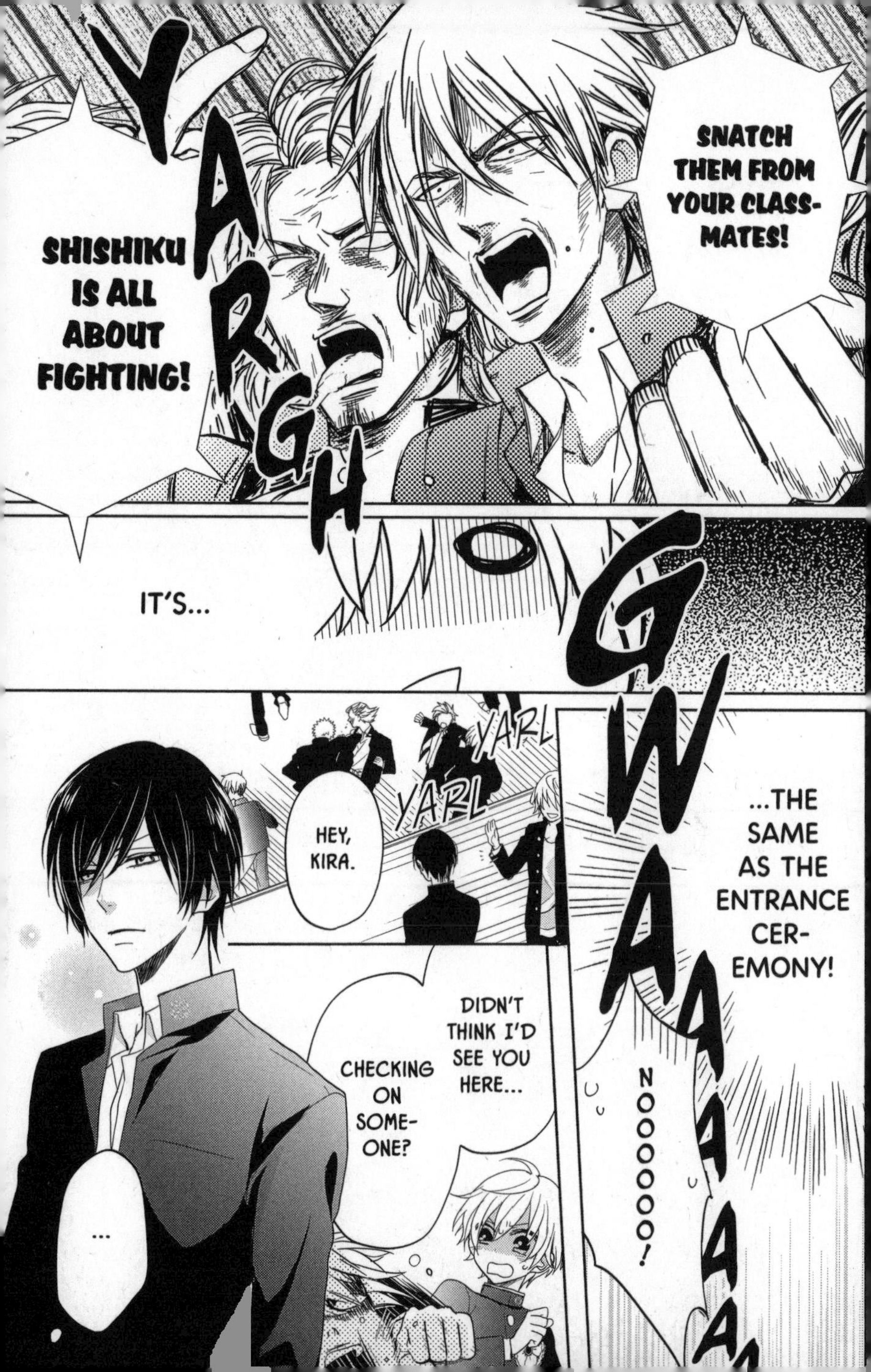

SNATCH THEM FROM YOUR CLASS-MATES!
SHISHIKU IS ALL ABOUT FIGHTING!
YARGH
IT'S...
GWAAAAA
...THE SAME AS THE ENTRANCE CER-EMONY!
NOOOOOO!
YARL
YARL
HEY, KIRA.
DIDN'T THINK I'D SEE YOU HERE...
CHECKING ON SOME-ONE?
...

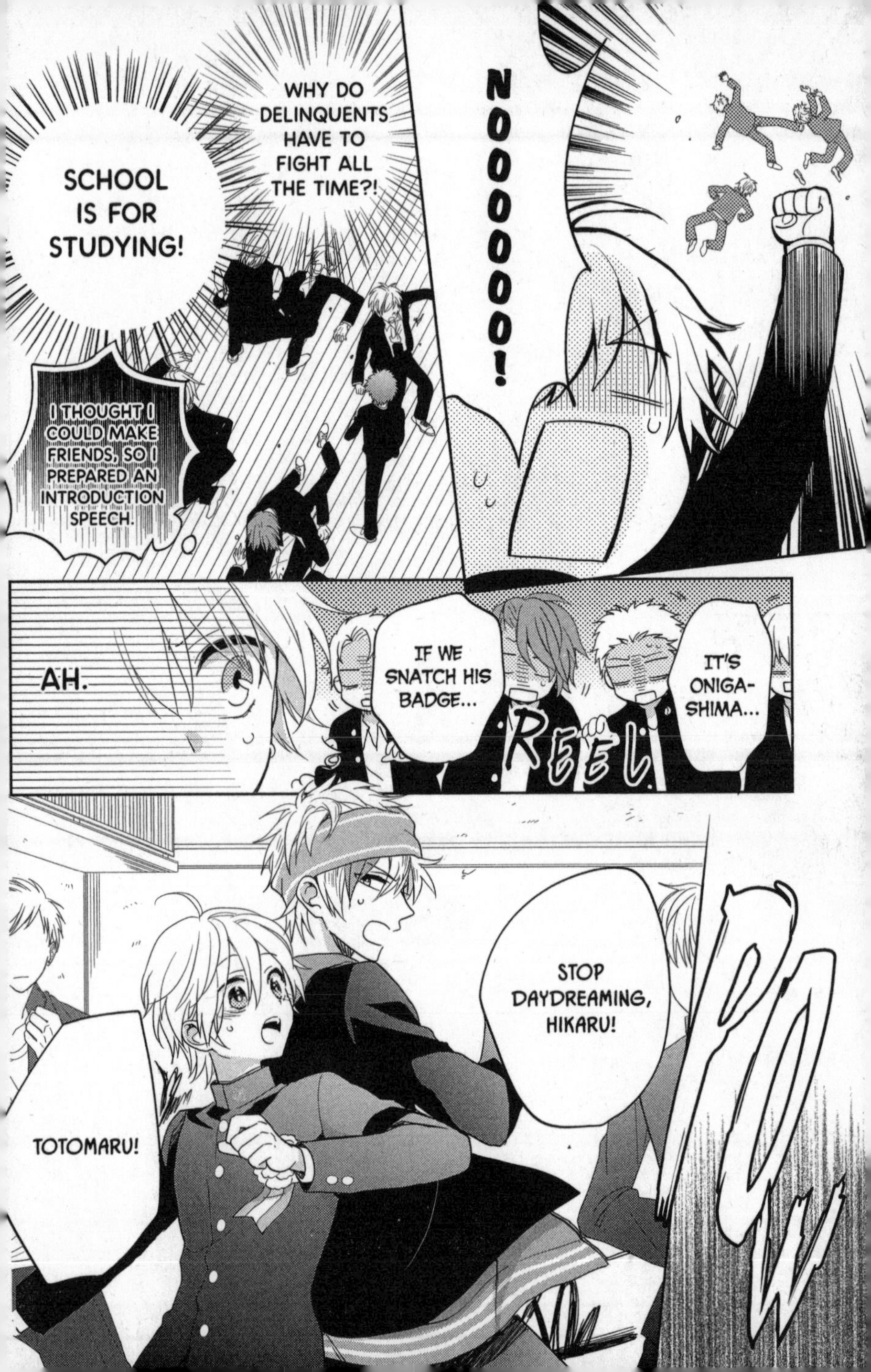
NOOOOOOOO!
WHY DO DELINQUENTS HAVE TO FIGHT ALL THE TIME?!
SCHOOL IS FOR STUDYING!
I THOUGHT I COULD MAKE FRIENDS, SO I PREPARED AN INTRODUCTION SPEECH.
IT'S ONIGA-SHIMA...
REEL
IF WE SNATCH HIS BADGE...
AH.
STOP DAYDREAMING, HIKARU!
TOTOMARU!

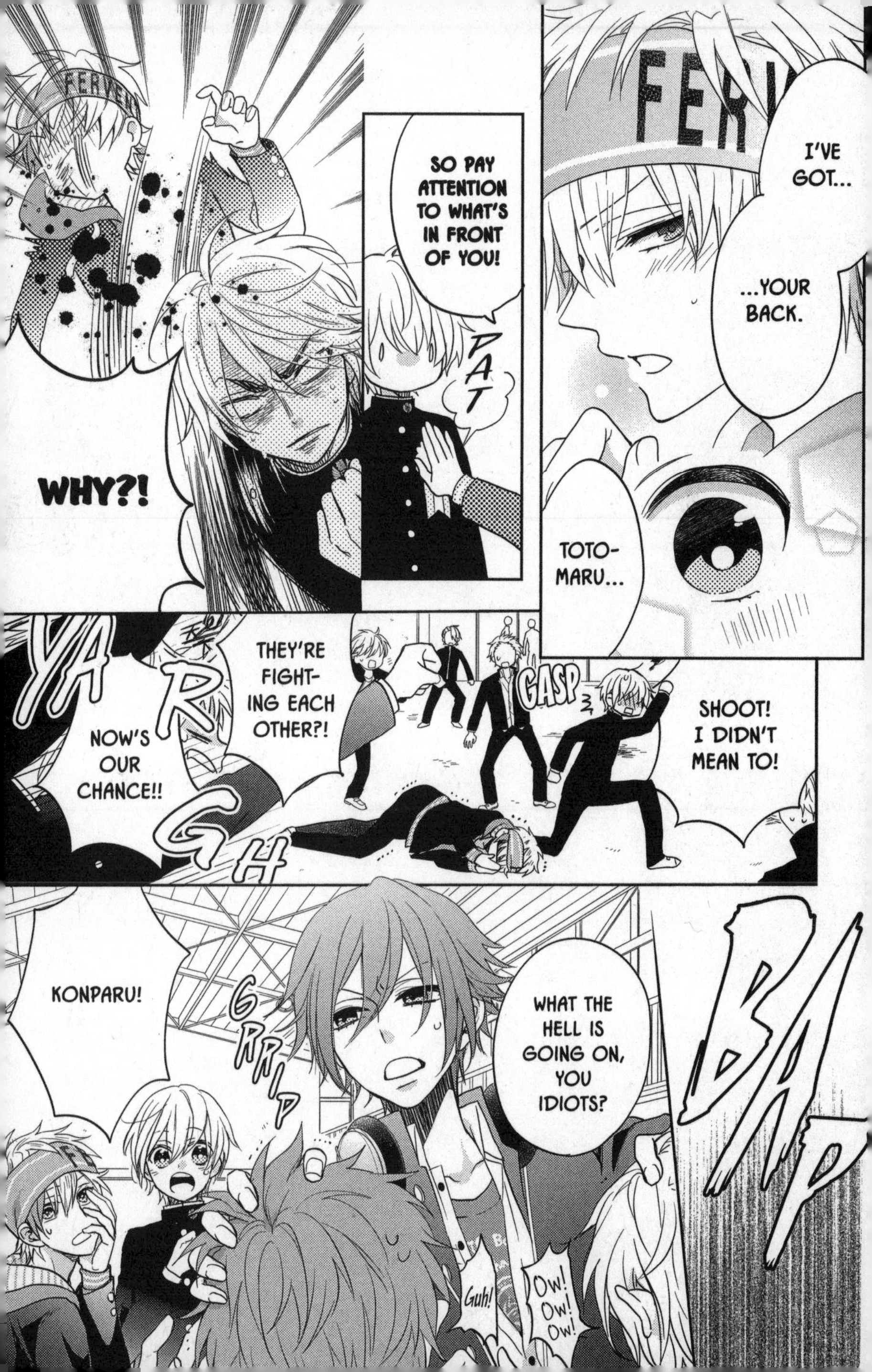
I'VE GOT...
...YOUR BACK.
TOTO-MARU...
SO PAY ATTENTION TO WHAT'S IN FRONT OF YOU!
PAT
WHY?!
SHOOT! I DIDN'T MEAN TO!
GASP
THEY'RE FIGHT-ING EACH OTHER?!
NOW'S OUR CHANCE!!
YARGH
BAP
WHAT THE HELL IS GOING ON, YOU IDIOTS?
GRRIP
KONPARU!
Ow! Ow! Ow!
Guh!

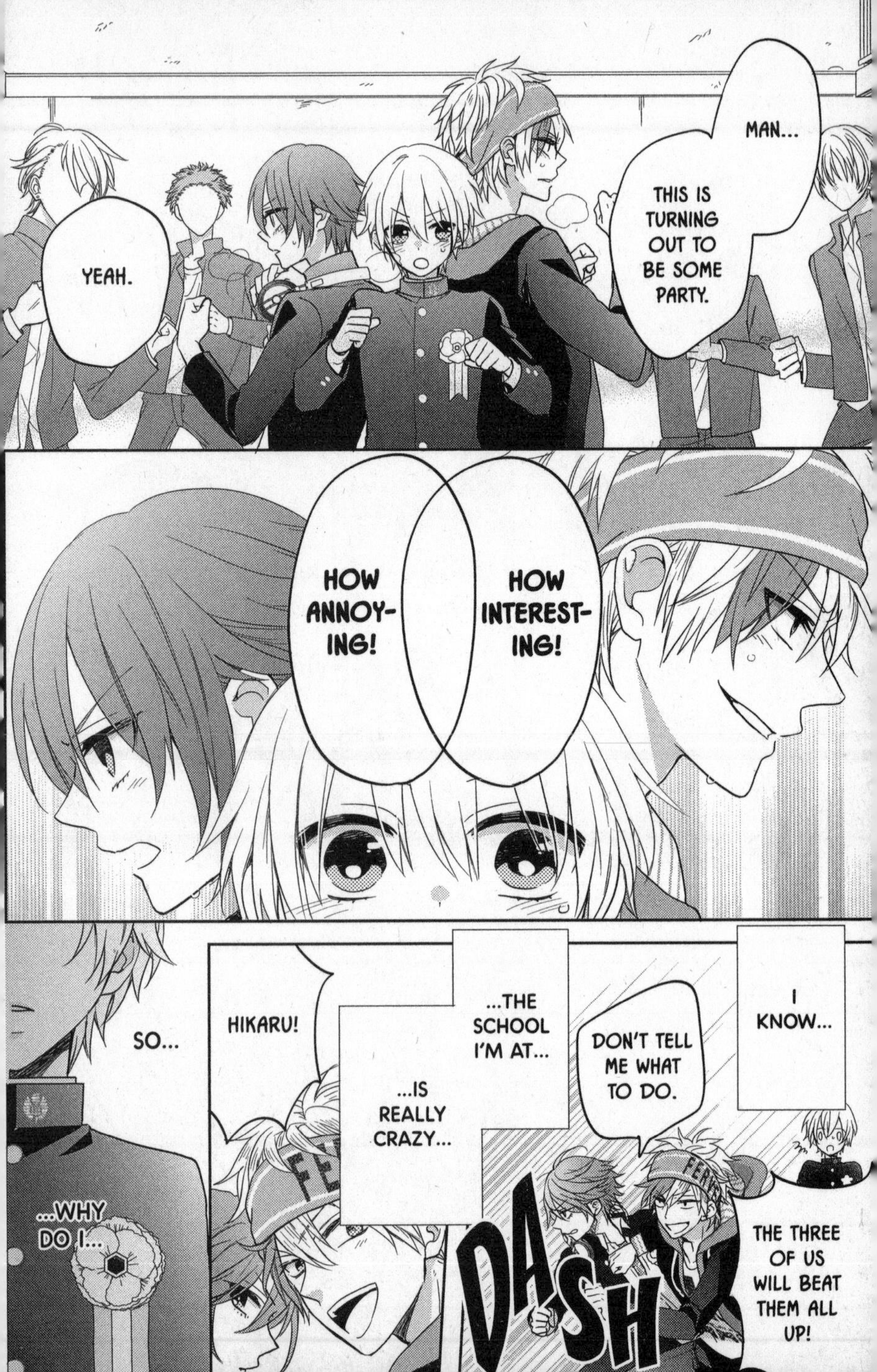
MAN...
THIS IS TURNING OUT TO BE SOME PARTY.
YEAH.
HOW INTERESTING!
HOW ANNOYING!
I KNOW...
...THE SCHOOL I'M AT...
...IS REALLY CRAZY...
THE THREE OF US WILL BEAT THEM ALL UP!
DON'T TELL ME WHAT TO DO.
DASH
HIKARU!
SO...
...WHY DO I...

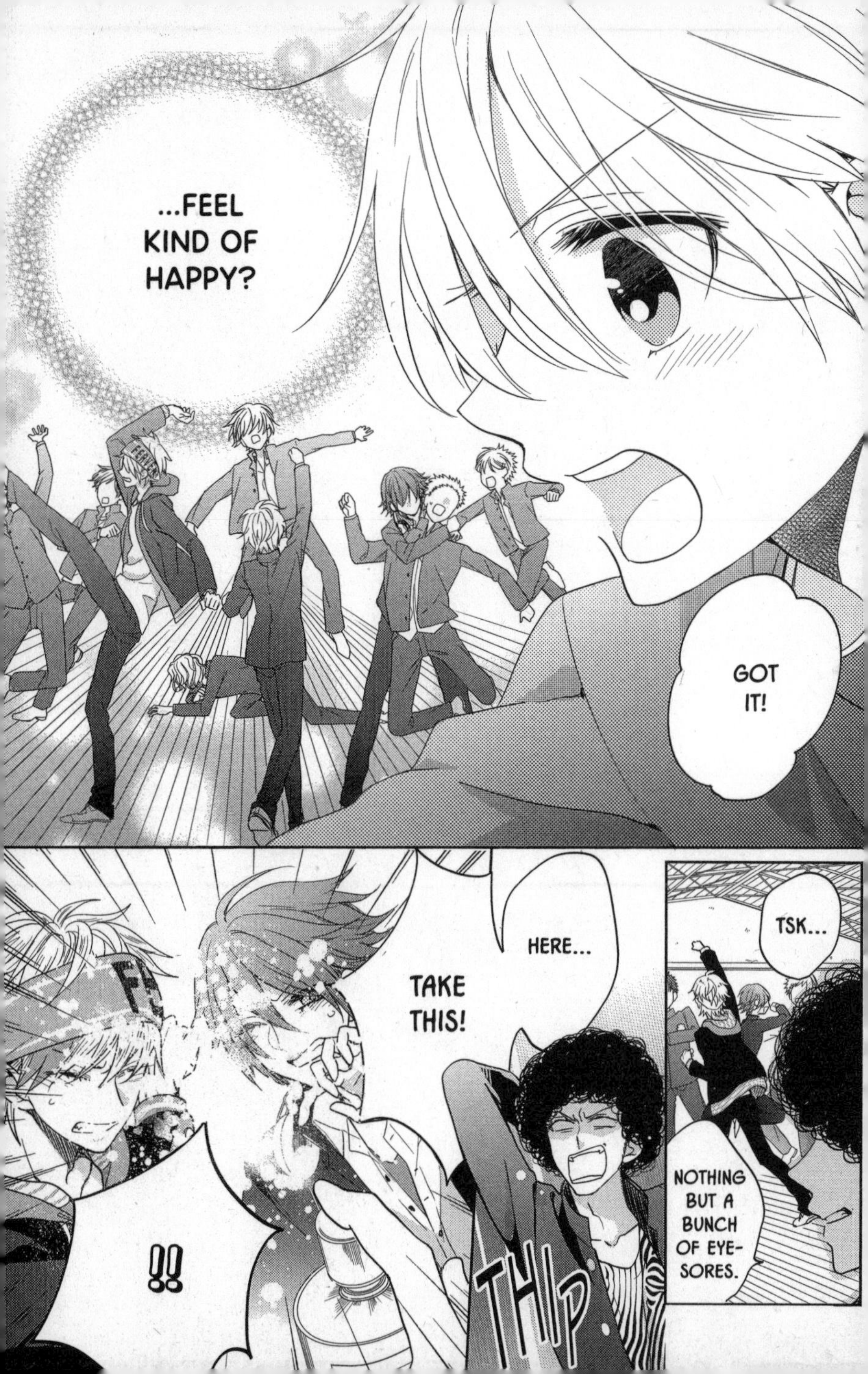
...FEEL KIND OF HAPPY?
GOT IT!
TSK...
NOTHING BUT A BUNCH OF EYE-SORES.
HERE...
TAKE THIS!
THIP
!!

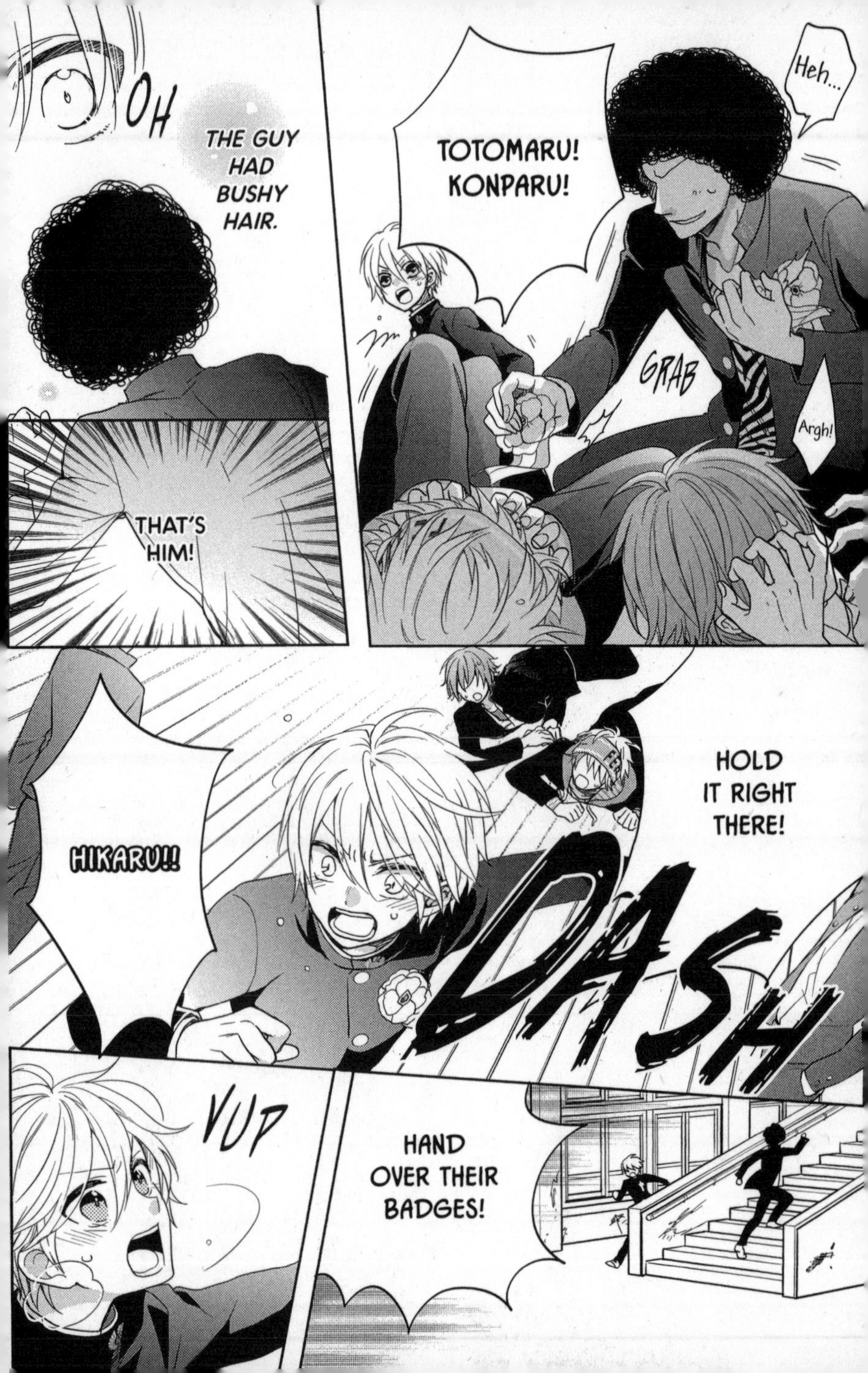
Heh...
TOTOMARU! KONPARU!
GRAB
Argh!
OH
THE GUY HAD BUSHY HAIR.
THAT'S HIM!
HOLD IT RIGHT THERE!
DASH
HIKARU!!
HAND OVER THEIR BADGES!
VUP

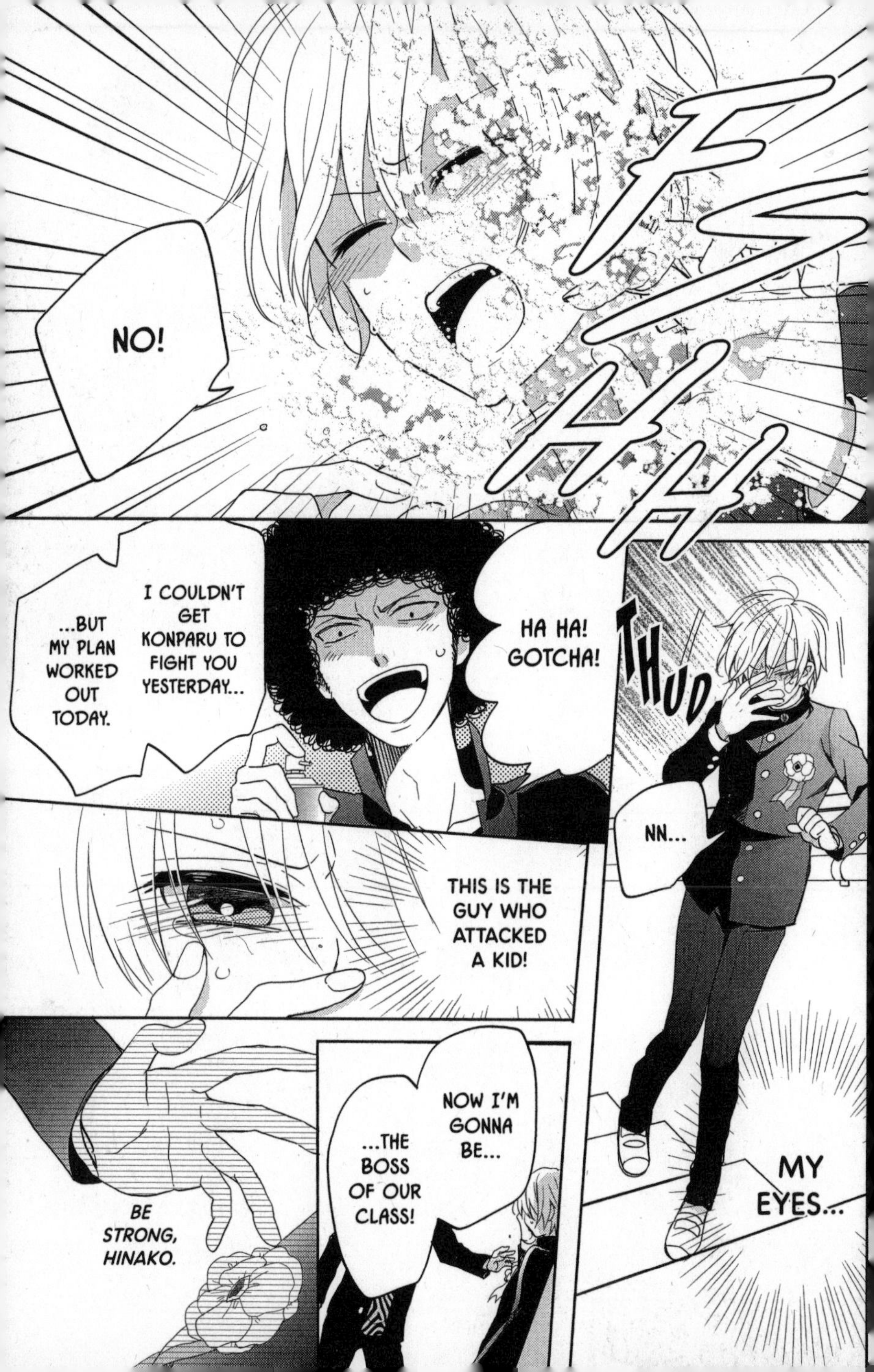
FSSHH
NO!
THUD
NN...
MY EYES...
HA HA! GOTCHA!
I COULDN'T GET KONPARU TO FIGHT YOU YESTERDAY...
...BUT MY PLAN WORKED OUT TODAY.
THIS IS THE GUY WHO ATTACKED A KID!
NOW I'M GONNA BE...
...THE BOSS OF OUR CLASS!
BE STRONG, HINAKO.

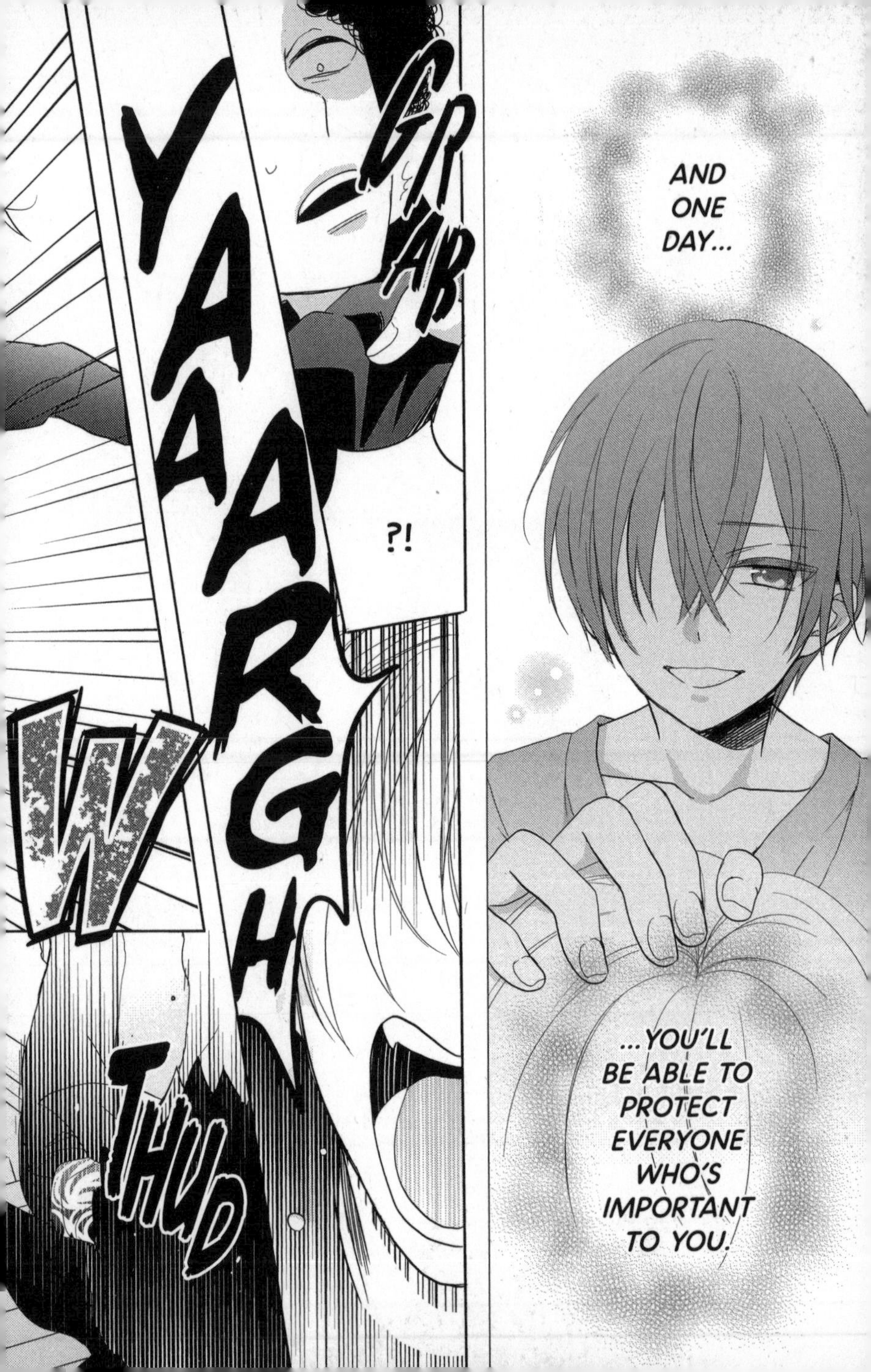
AND ONE DAY...
...YOU'LL BE ABLE TO PROTECT EVERYONE WHO'S IMPORTANT TO YOU.
GRAB
?!
YAAARGH
THUD

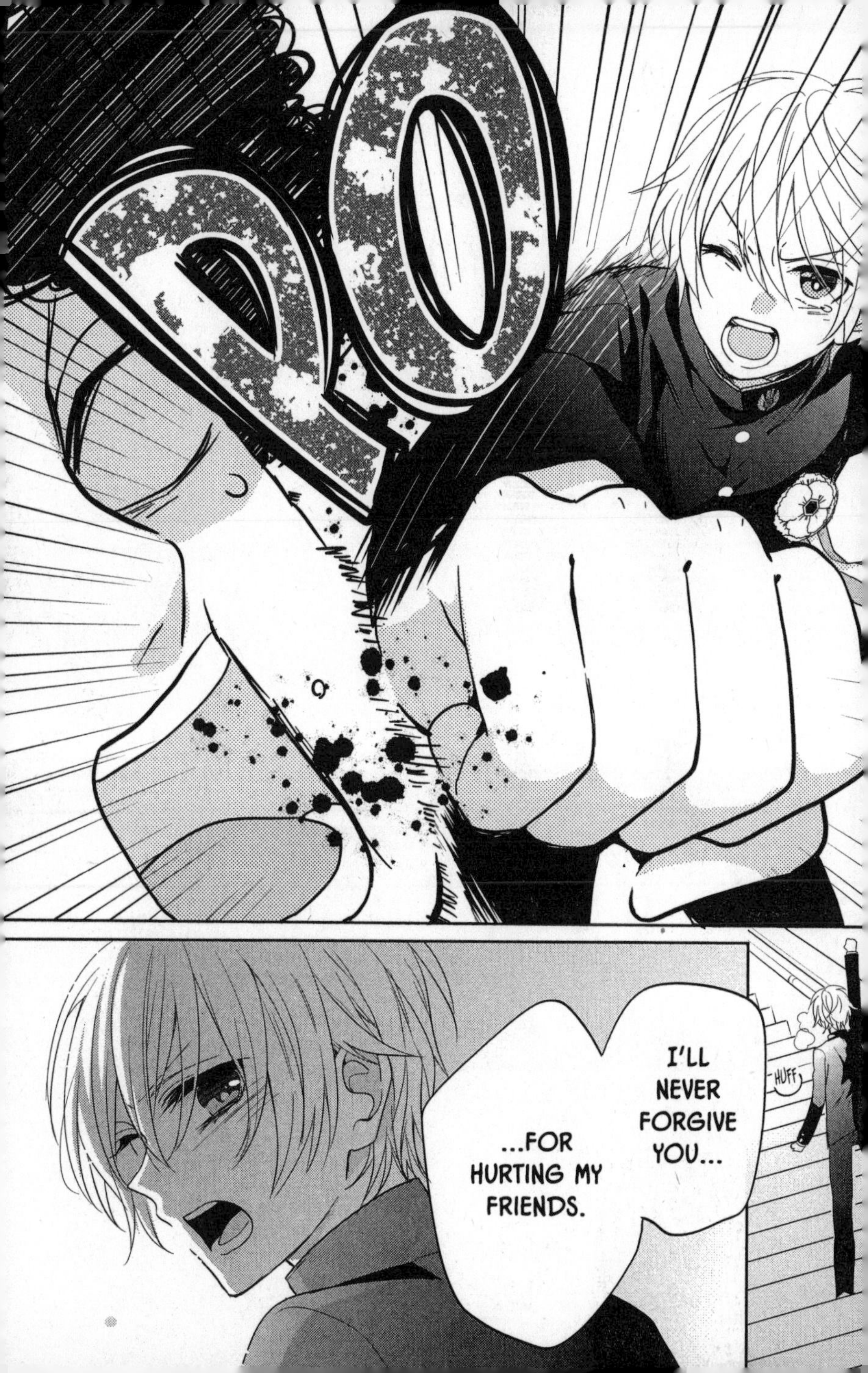
DO
HUFF
I'LL NEVER FORGIVE YOU...
...FOR HURTING MY FRIENDS.

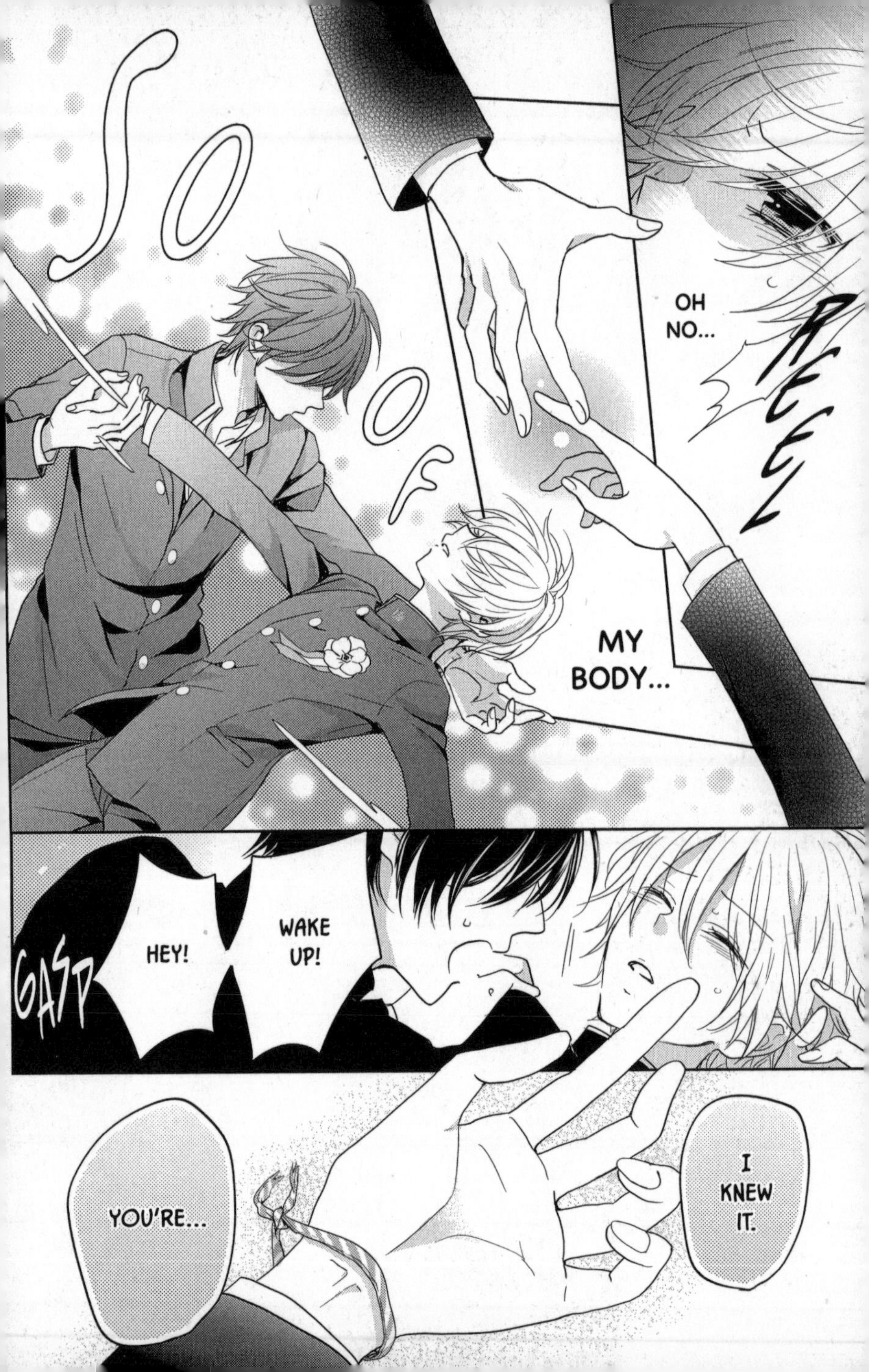

OH NO...
REEEL
MY BODY...
SOOOF
WAKE UP!
HEY!
GASP
I KNEW IT.
YOU'RE...

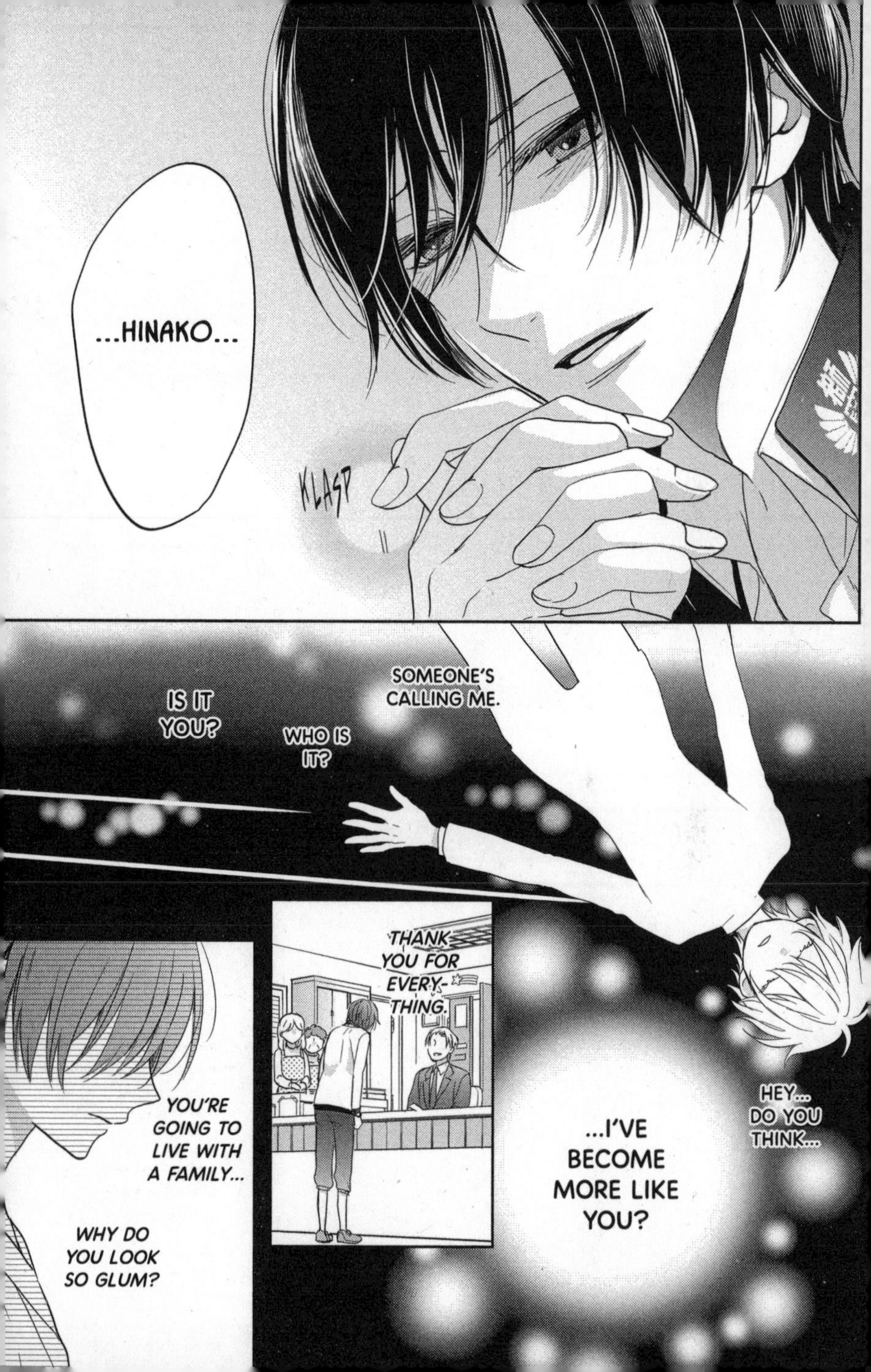
...HINAKO...
KLASP
SOMEONE'S CALLING ME.
WHO IS IT?
IS IT YOU?
HEY... DO YOU THINK...
...I'VE BECOME MORE LIKE YOU?
THANK YOU FOR EVERY-THING.
YOU'RE GOING TO LIVE WITH A FAMILY...
WHY DO YOU LOOK SO GLUM?

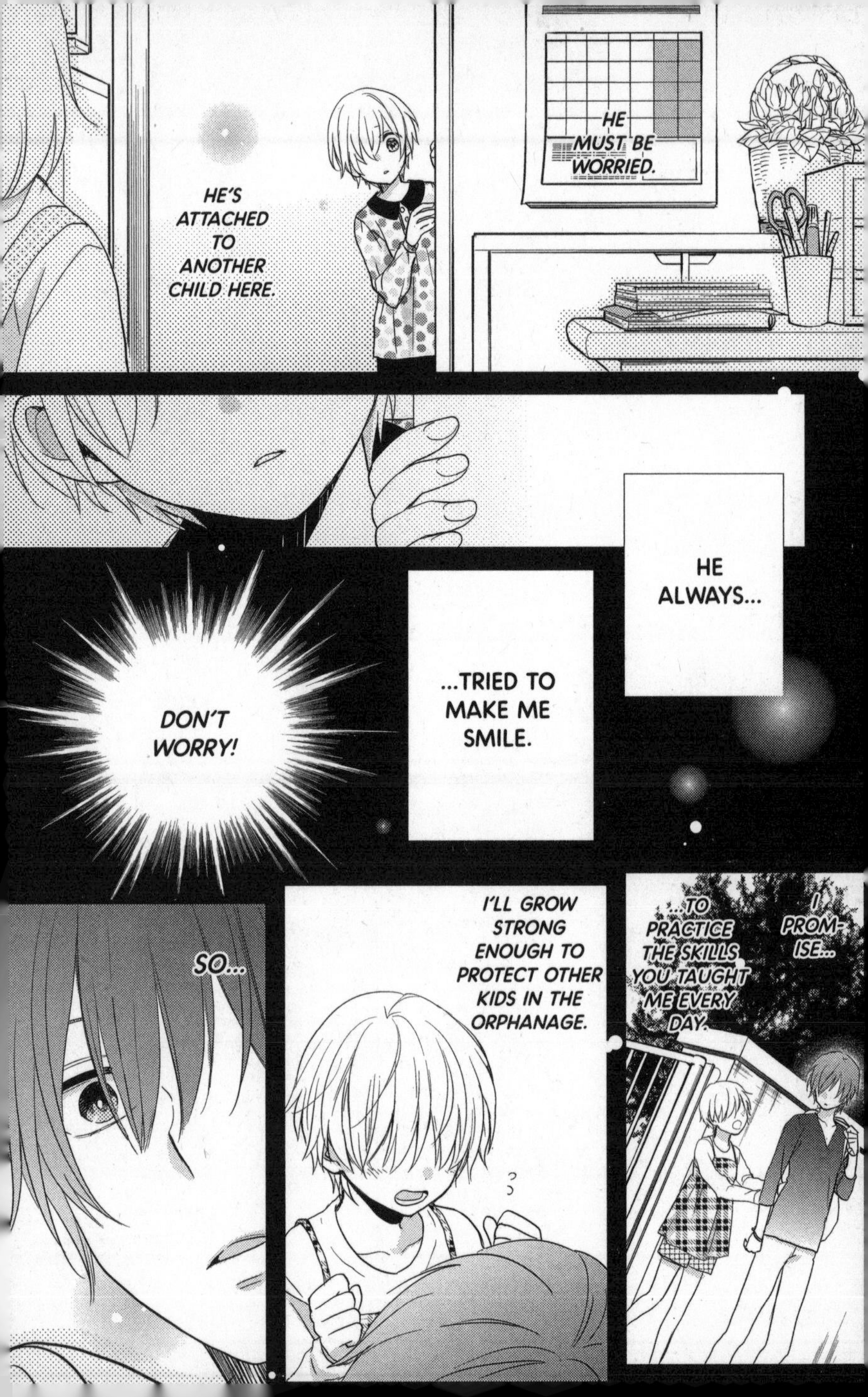
HE MUST BE WORRIED.
HE'S ATTACHED TO ANOTHER CHILD HERE.
HE ALWAYS...
...TRIED TO MAKE ME SMILE.
DON'T WORRY!
I PROMISE...
...TO PRACTICE THE SKILLS YOU TAUGHT ME EVERY DAY.
I'LL GROW STRONG ENOUGH TO PROTECT OTHER KIDS IN THE ORPHANAGE.
SO...

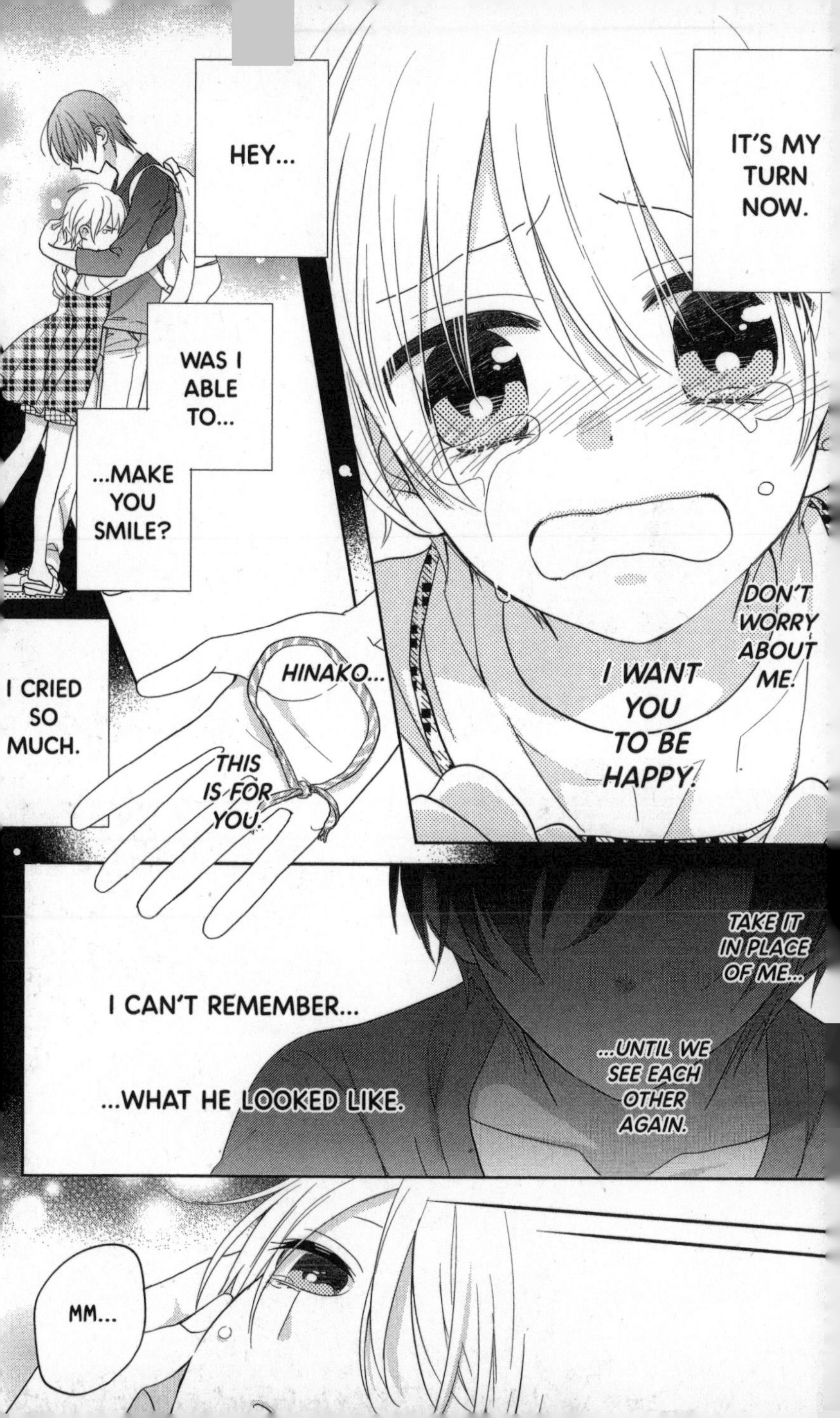
IT'S MY TURN NOW.
DON'T WORRY ABOUT ME.
I WANT YOU TO BE HAPPY.
HEY...
WAS I ABLE TO...
...MAKE YOU SMILE?
HINAKO...
I CRIED SO MUCH.
THIS IS FOR YOU.
TAKE IT IN PLACE OF ME...
...UNTIL WE SEE EACH OTHER AGAIN.
I CAN'T REMEMBER...
...WHAT HE LOOKED LIKE.
MM...

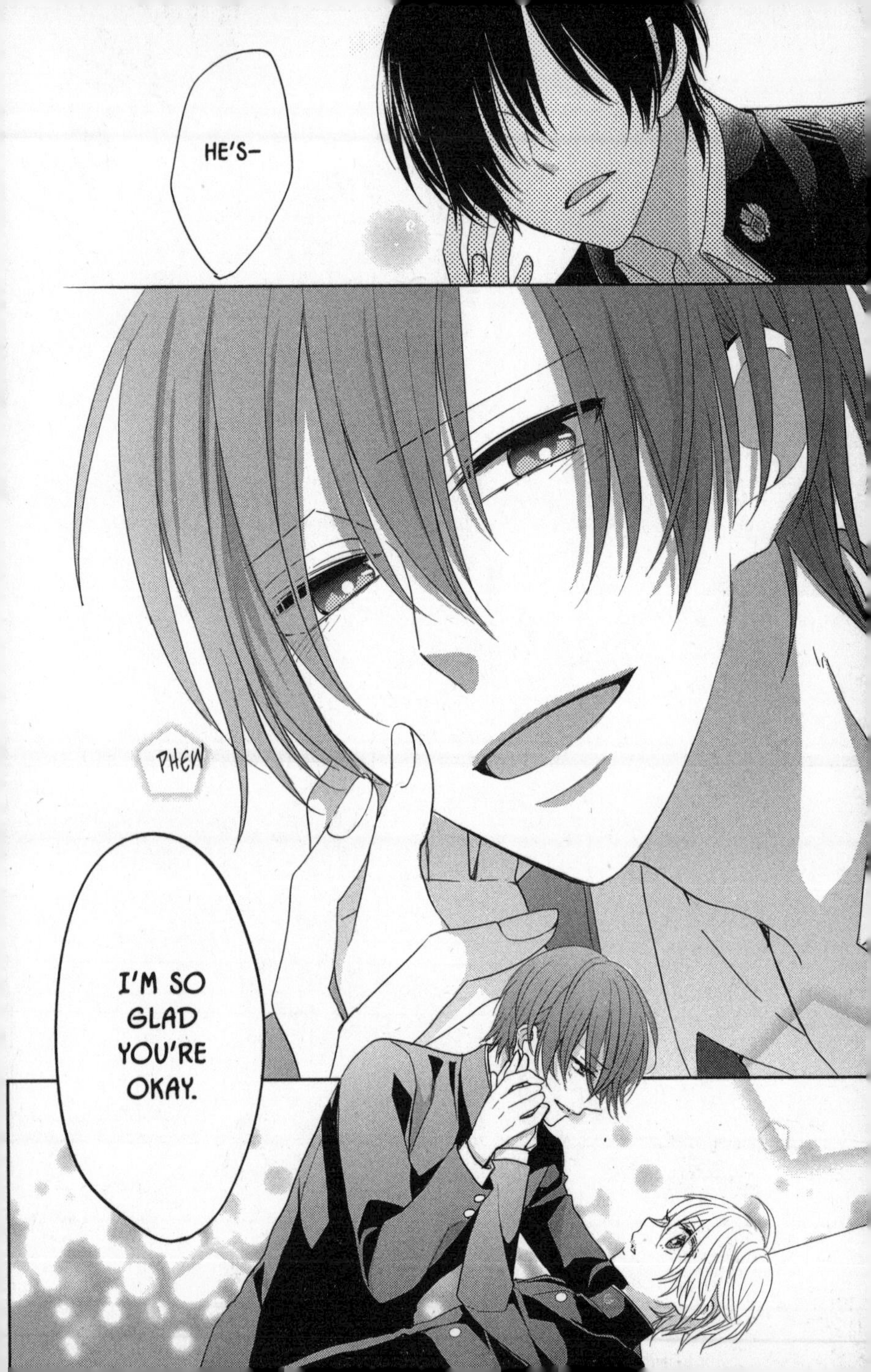
HE'S–
PHEW
I'M SO GLAD YOU'RE OKAY.

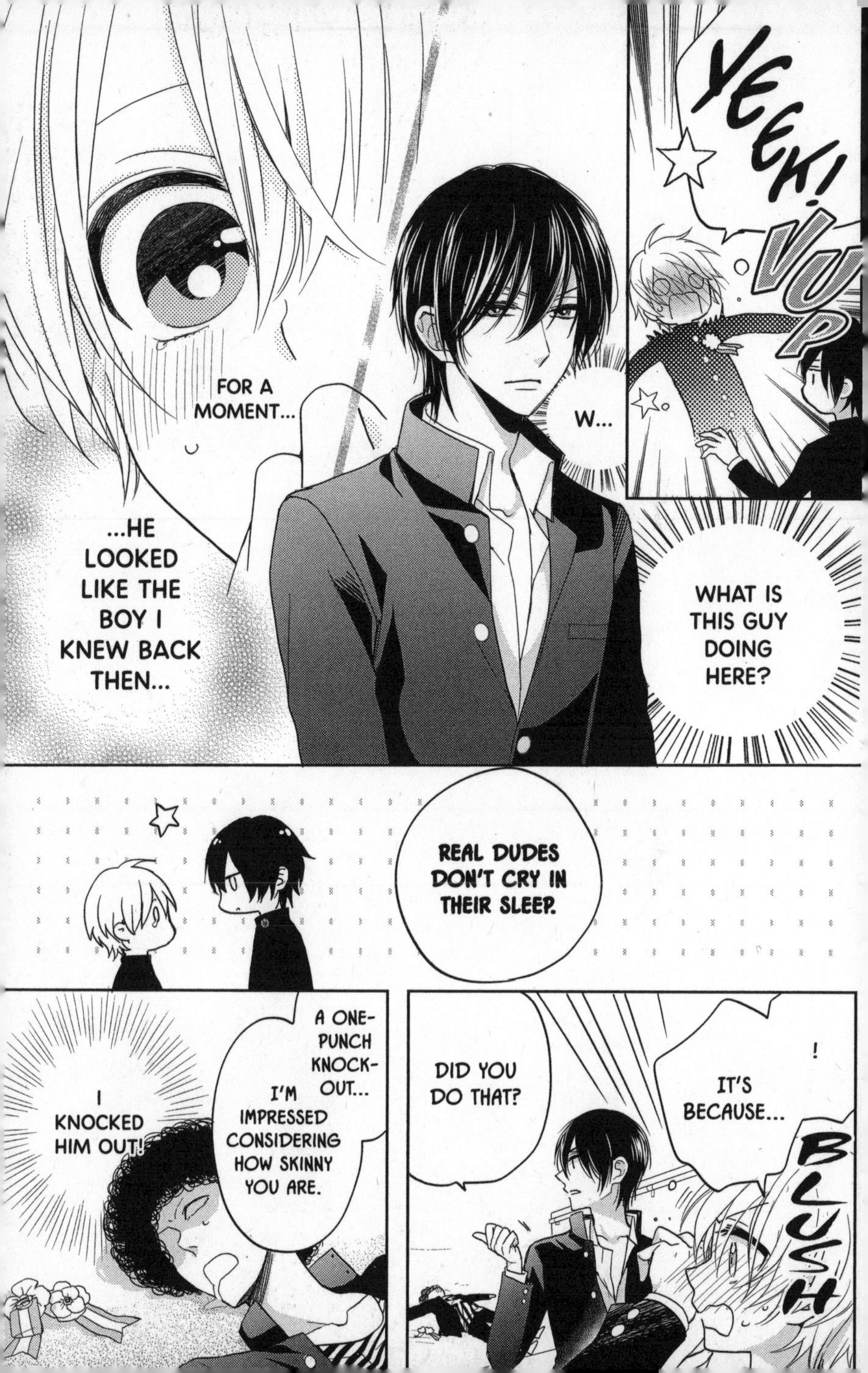
YEEK!
VUUP
W...
WHAT IS THIS GUY DOING HERE?
FOR A MOMENT...
...HE LOOKED LIKE THE BOY I KNEW BACK THEN...
REAL DUDES DON'T CRY IN THEIR SLEEP.
!
DID YOU DO THAT?
IT'S BECAUSE...
BLUSH
A ONE-PUNCH KNOCK-OUT...
I'M IMPRESSED CONSIDERING HOW SKINNY YOU ARE.
I KNOCKED HIM OUT!

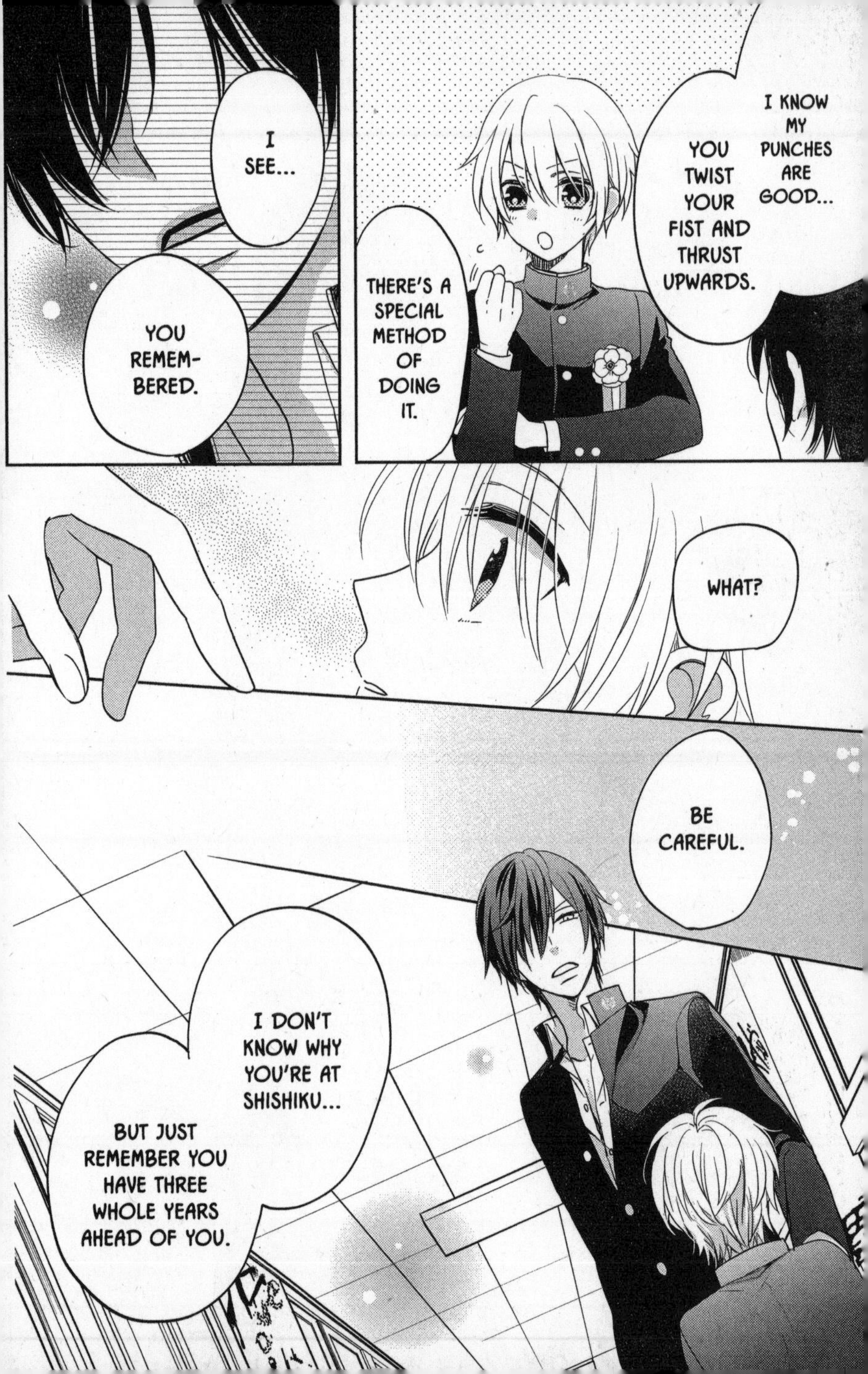
I KNOW MY PUNCHES ARE GOOD...
YOU TWIST YOUR FIST AND THRUST UPWARDS.
THERE'S A SPECIAL METHOD OF DOING IT.
I SEE...
YOU REMEM-BERED.
WHAT?
BE CAREFUL.
I DON'T KNOW WHY YOU'RE AT SHISHIKU...
BUT JUST REMEMBER YOU HAVE THREE WHOLE YEARS AHEAD OF YOU.

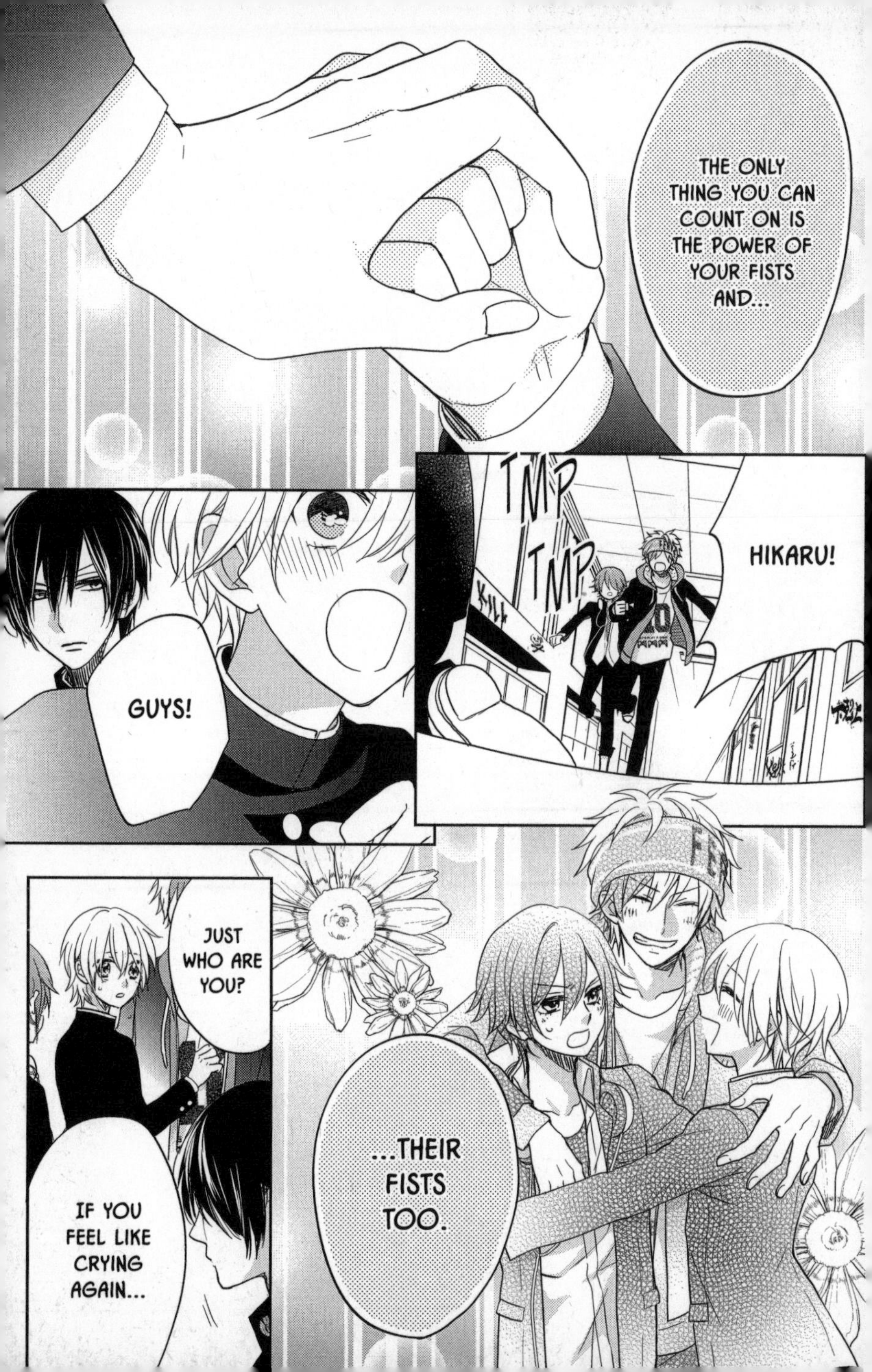
THE ONLY THING YOU CAN COUNT ON IS THE POWER OF YOUR FISTS AND...
TMP TMP
HIKARU!
GUYS!
...THEIR FISTS TOO.
JUST WHO ARE YOU?
IF YOU FEEL LIKE CRYING AGAIN...

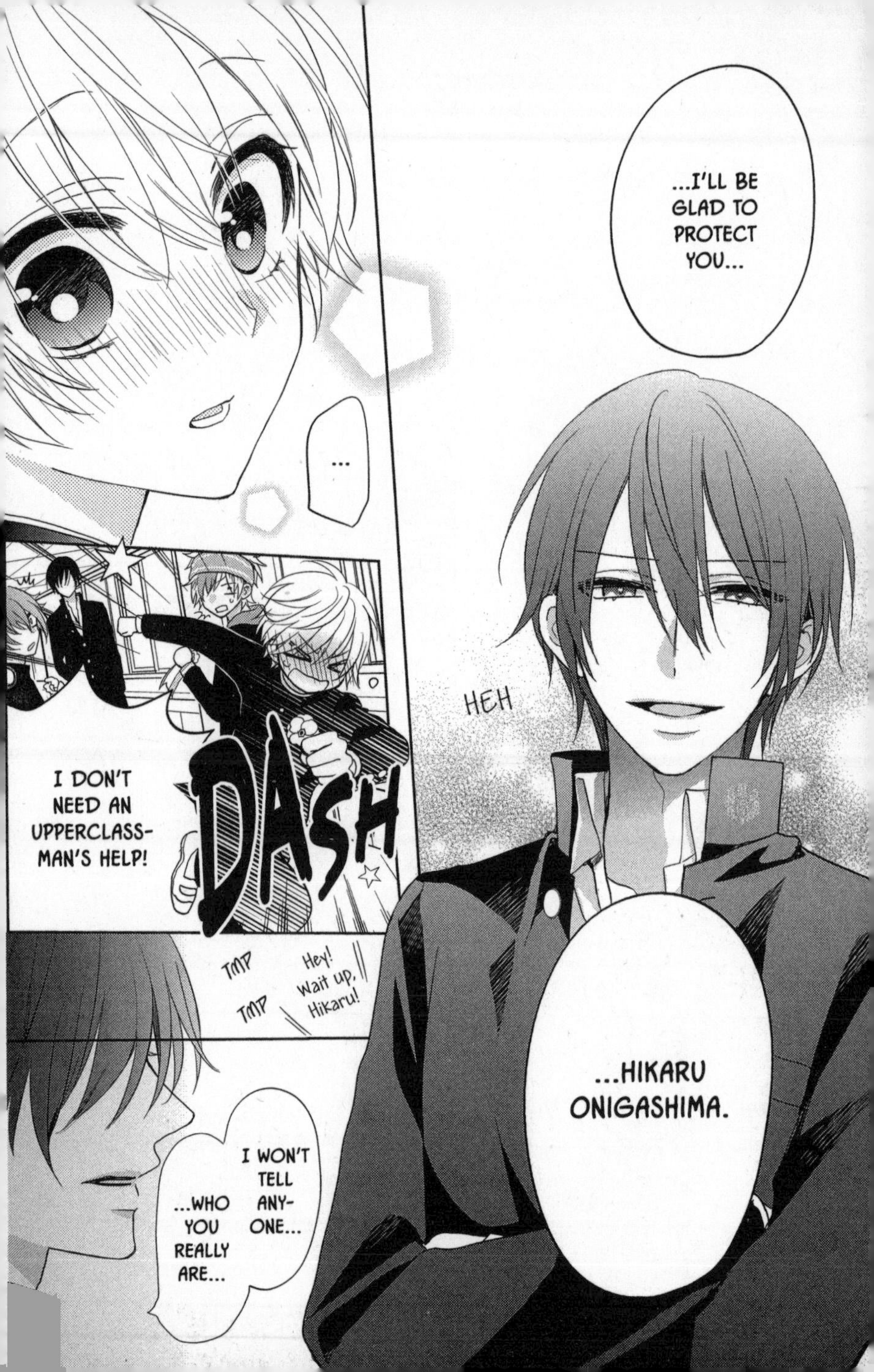

...I'LL BE GLAD TO PROTECT YOU...
HEH
...HIKARU ONIGASHIMA.
...
I DON'T NEED AN UPPERCLASSMAN'S HELP!
DASH
Hey! Wait up, Hikaru!
TMP
TMP
I WON'T TELL ANYONE...
...WHO YOU REALLY ARE...

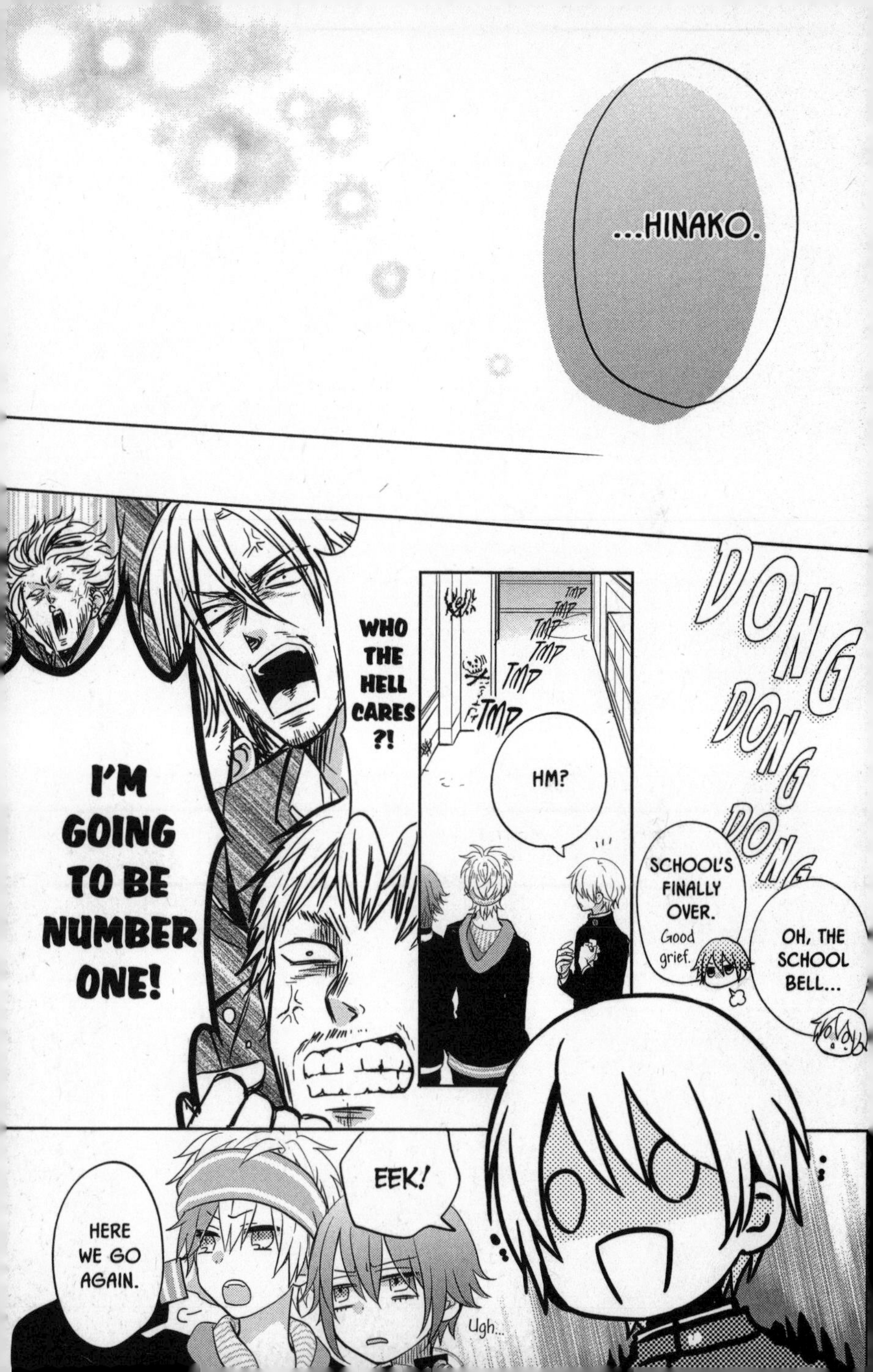
...HINAKO.
DONG DONG DONG
SCHOOL'S FINALLY OVER.
Good grief.
OH, THE SCHOOL BELL...
TMP TMP TMP TMP TMP TMP
HM?
WHO THE HELL CARES?!
I'M GOING TO BE NUMBER ONE!
EEK!
HERE WE GO AGAIN.
Ugh...

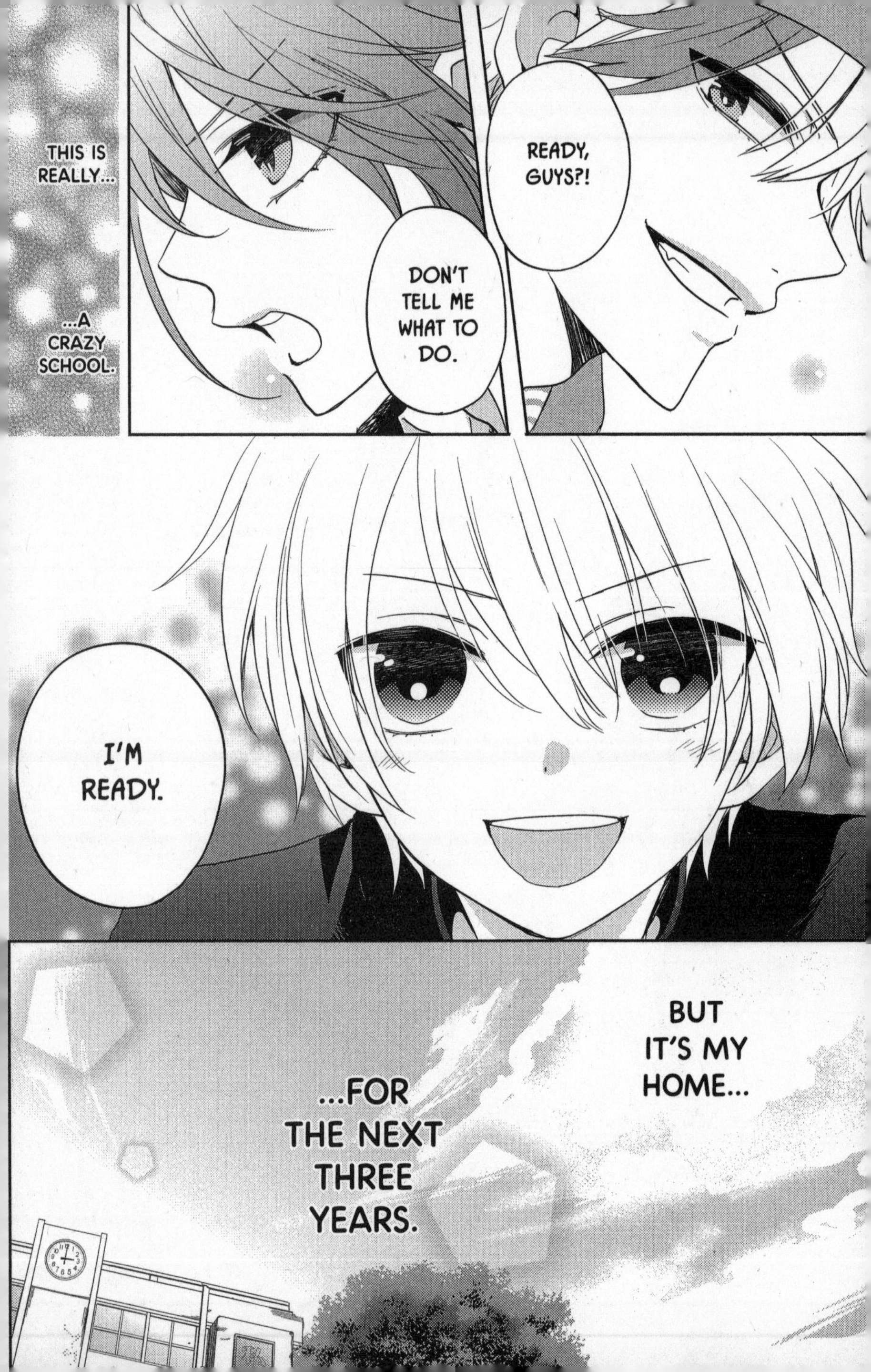
READY, GUYS?!
DON'T TELL ME WHAT TO DO.
THIS IS REALLY...
...A CRAZY SCHOOL.
I'M READY.
BUT IT'S MY HOME...
...FOR THE NEXT THREE YEARS.

KENKA BANCHO
Otome

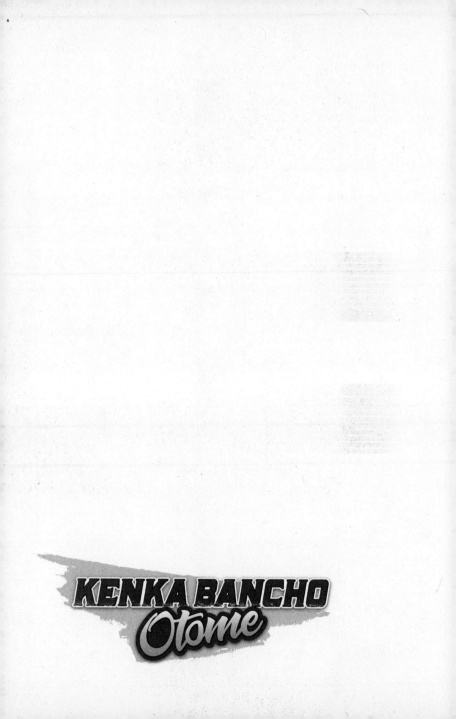

LOOK BACK AND OUR EYES MEET AGAIN

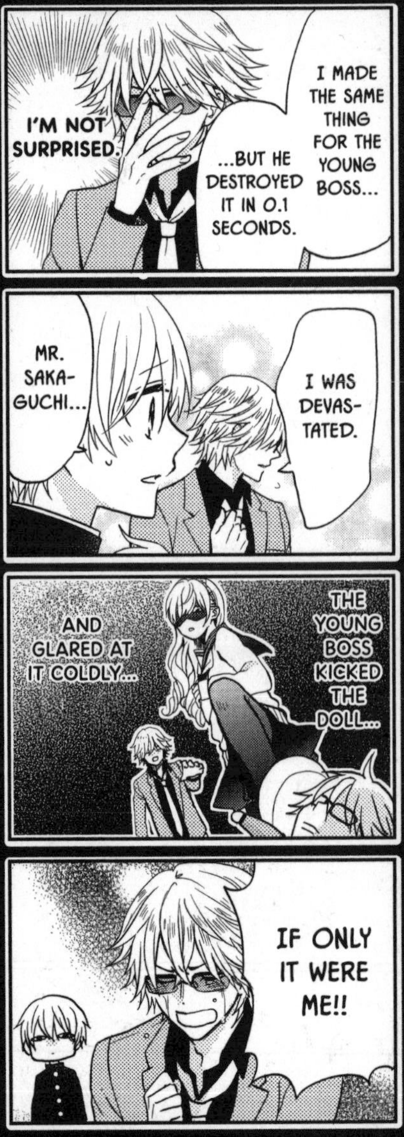
I MADE THE SAME THING FOR THE YOUNG BOSS...
...BUT HE DESTROYED IT IN 0.1 SECONDS.
I'M NOT SURPRISED.
I WAS DEVAS-TATED.
MR. SAKA-GUCHI...
THE YOUNG BOSS KICKED THE DOLL...
AND GLARED AT IT COLDLY...
IF ONLY IT WERE ME!!

BECAUSE IT'S LOVE

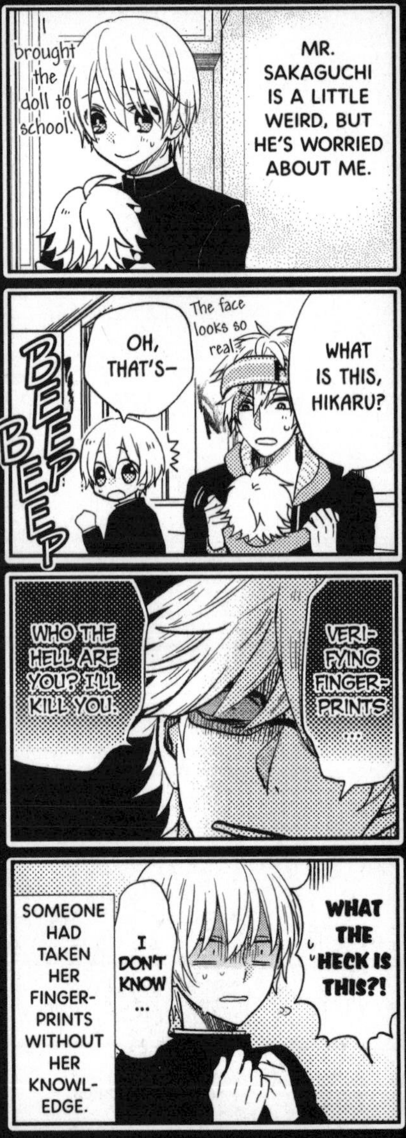
MR. SAKAGUCHI IS A LITTLE WEIRD, BUT HE'S WORRIED ABOUT ME.
I brought the doll to school.
WHAT IS THIS, HIKARU?
The face looks so real.
OH, THAT'S—
BEEP BEEP
VERI-FYING FINGER-PRINTS...
WHO THE HELL ARE YOU? I'LL KILL YOU.
WHAT THE HECK IS THIS?!
I DON'T KNOW...
SOMEONE HAD TAKEN HER FINGER-PRINTS WITHOUT HER KNOWL-EDGE.

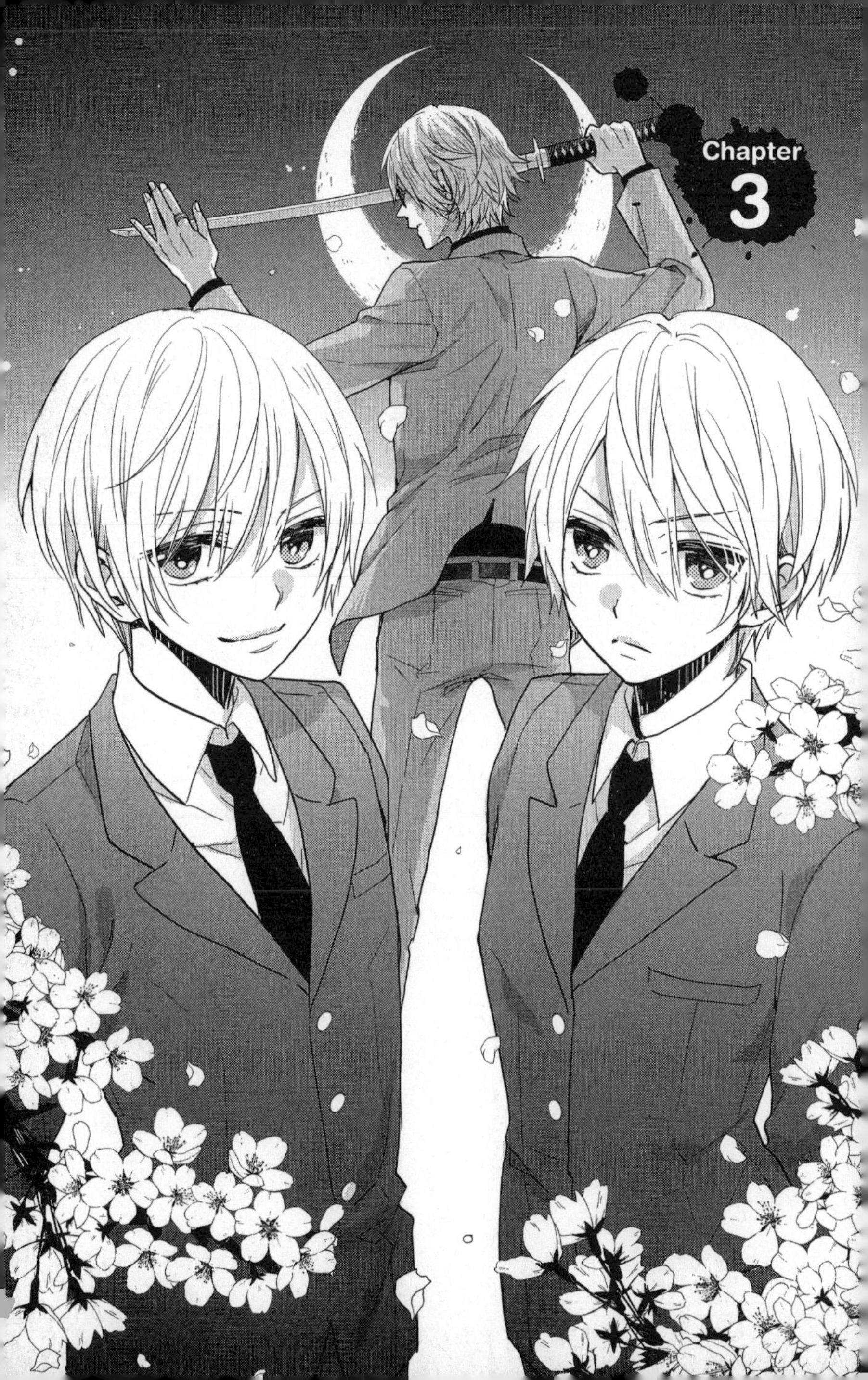
Chapter
3

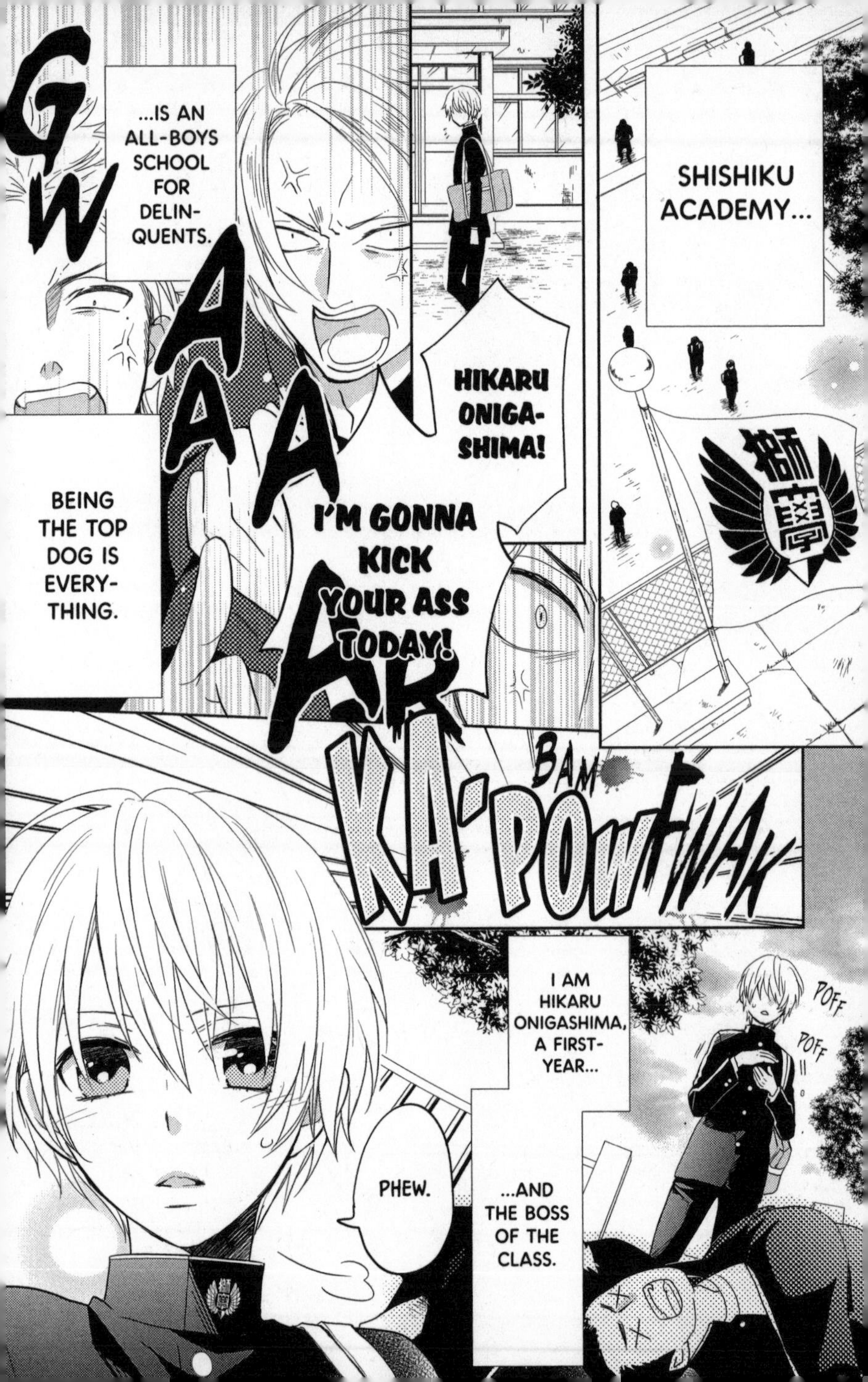
SHISHIKU ACADEMY...
HIKARU ONIGA-SHIMA!
I'M GONNA KICK YOUR ASS TODAY!
...IS AN ALL-BOYS SCHOOL FOR DELIN-QUENTS.
GWAAAR
BEING THE TOP DOG IS EVERY-THING.
BAM
KA-POW
FWAK
I AM HIKARU ONIGASHIMA, A FIRST-YEAR...
POFF
POFF
...AND THE BOSS OF THE CLASS.
PHEW.

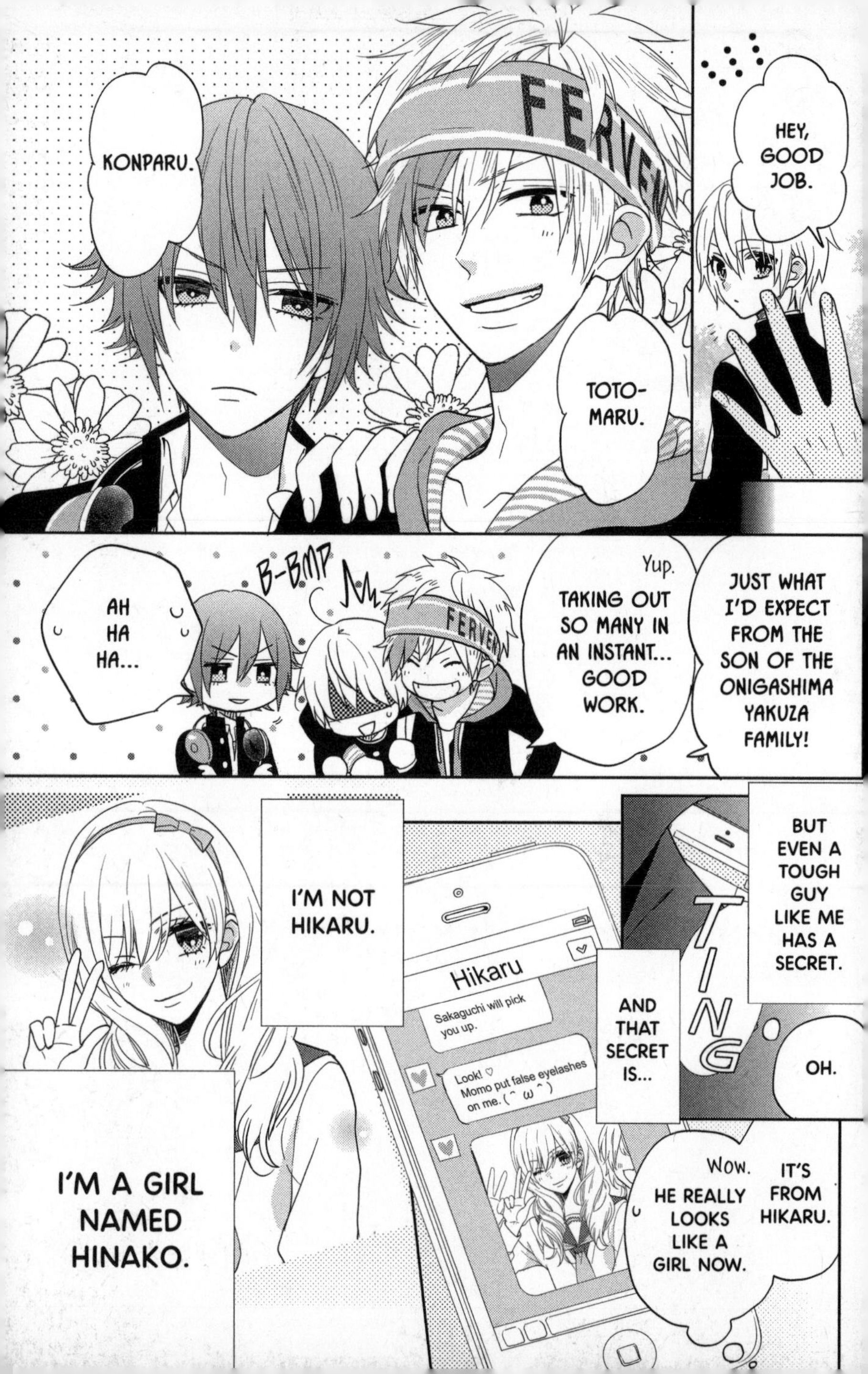
HEY, GOOD JOB.
TOTO-MARU.
KONPARU.
JUST WHAT I'D EXPECT FROM THE SON OF THE ONIGASHIMA YAKUZA FAMILY!
Yup.
TAKING OUT SO MANY IN AN INSTANT... GOOD WORK.
B-BMP
AH HA HA...
BUT EVEN A TOUGH GUY LIKE ME HAS A SECRET.
TING
OH.
AND THAT SECRET IS...
IT'S FROM HIKARU.
Wow.
HE REALLY LOOKS LIKE A GIRL NOW.
Hikaru
Sakaguchi will pick you up.
Look! ♡ Momo put false eyelashes on me. (^ ω ^)
I'M NOT HIKARU.
I'M A GIRL NAMED HINAKO.

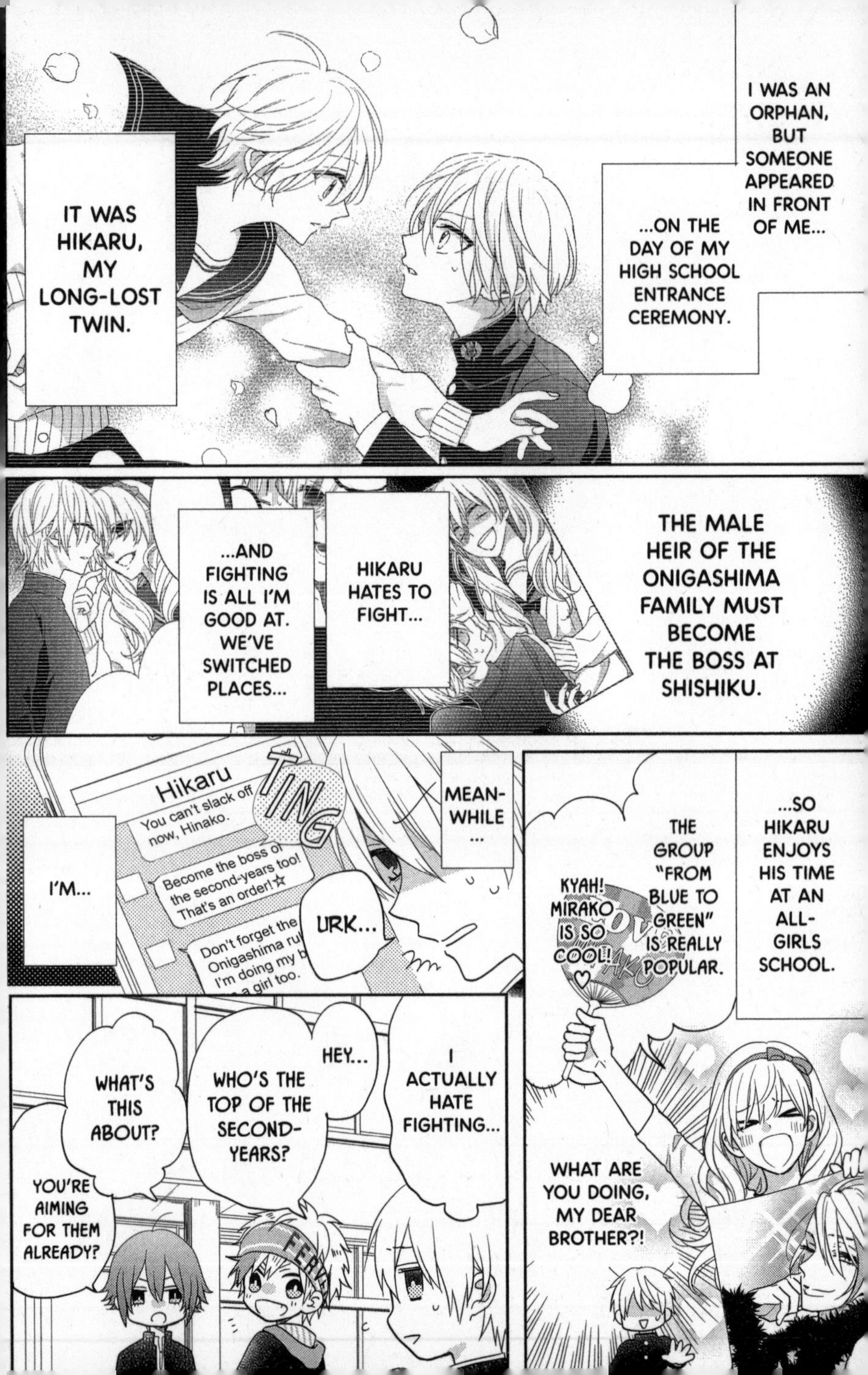
I WAS AN ORPHAN, BUT SOMEONE APPEARED IN FRONT OF ME...
...ON THE DAY OF MY HIGH SCHOOL ENTRANCE CEREMONY.
IT WAS HIKARU, MY LONG-LOST TWIN.
THE MALE HEIR OF THE ONIGASHIMA FAMILY MUST BECOME THE BOSS AT SHISHIKU.
HIKARU HATES TO FIGHT...
...AND FIGHTING IS ALL I'M GOOD AT. WE'VE SWITCHED PLACES...
...SO HIKARU ENJOYS HIS TIME AT AN ALL-GIRLS SCHOOL.
THE GROUP "FROM BLUE TO GREEN" IS REALLY POPULAR.
KYAH! MIRAKO IS SO COOL! ♥
WHAT ARE YOU DOING, MY DEAR BROTHER?!
MEAN-WHILE...
TING
Hikaru
You can't slack off now, Hinako.
Become the boss of the second-years too! That's an order!☆
Don't forget the
URK...
I'M...
I ACTUALLY HATE FIGHTING...
HEY...
WHO'S THE TOP OF THE SECOND-YEARS?
WHAT'S THIS ABOUT?
YOU'RE AIMING FOR THEM ALREADY?

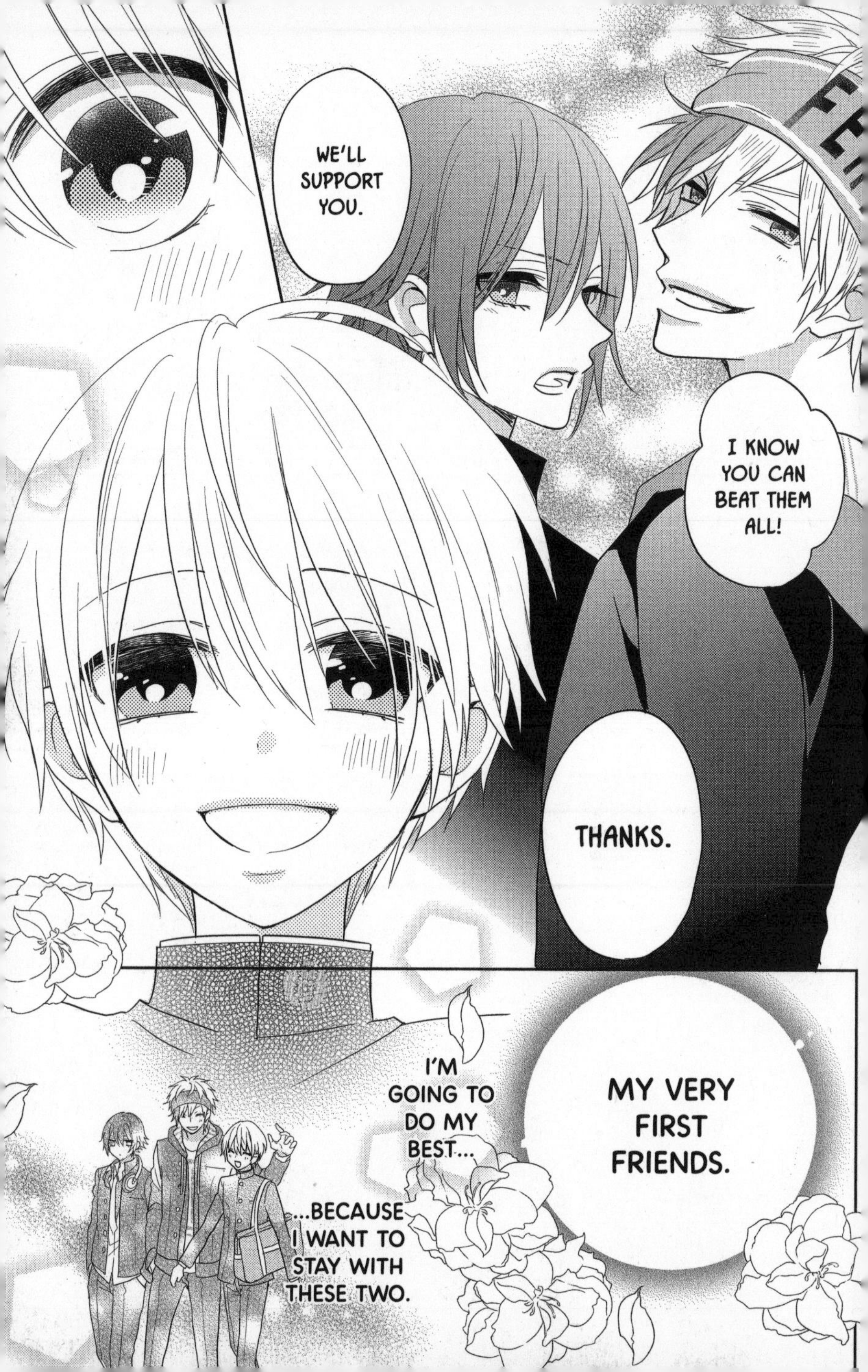
WE'LL SUPPORT YOU.
I KNOW YOU CAN BEAT THEM ALL!
THANKS.
MY VERY FIRST FRIENDS.
I'M GOING TO DO MY BEST...
...BECAUSE I WANT TO STAY WITH THESE TWO.

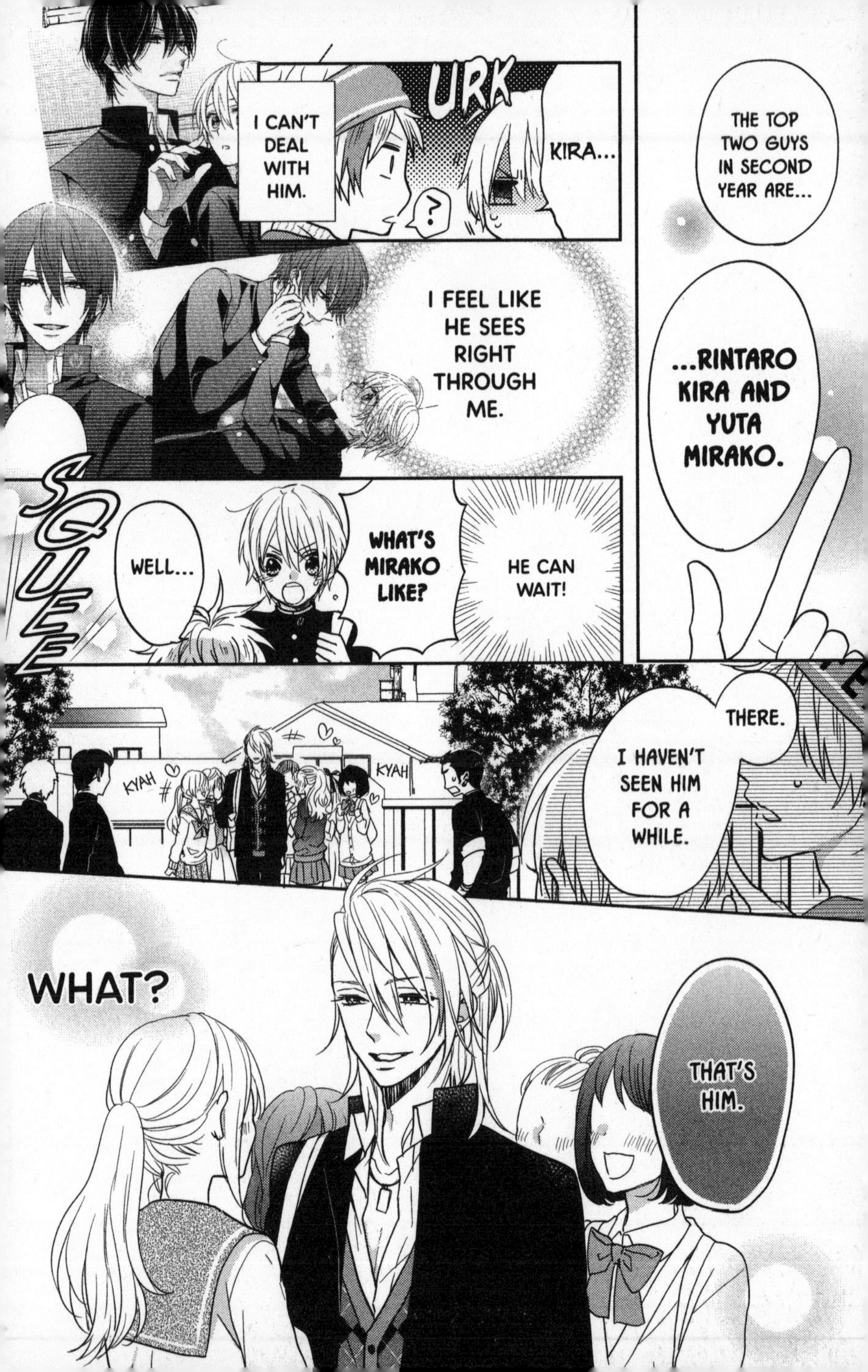
THE TOP TWO GUYS IN SECOND YEAR ARE...
...RINTARO KIRA AND YUTA MIRAKO.
KIRA...
?
URK
I CAN'T DEAL WITH HIM.
I FEEL LIKE HE SEES RIGHT THROUGH ME.
HE CAN WAIT!
WHAT'S MIRAKO LIKE?
WELL...
SQUEEE
THERE.
I HAVEN'T SEEN HIM FOR A WHILE.
KYAH
KYAH
THAT'S HIM.
WHAT?

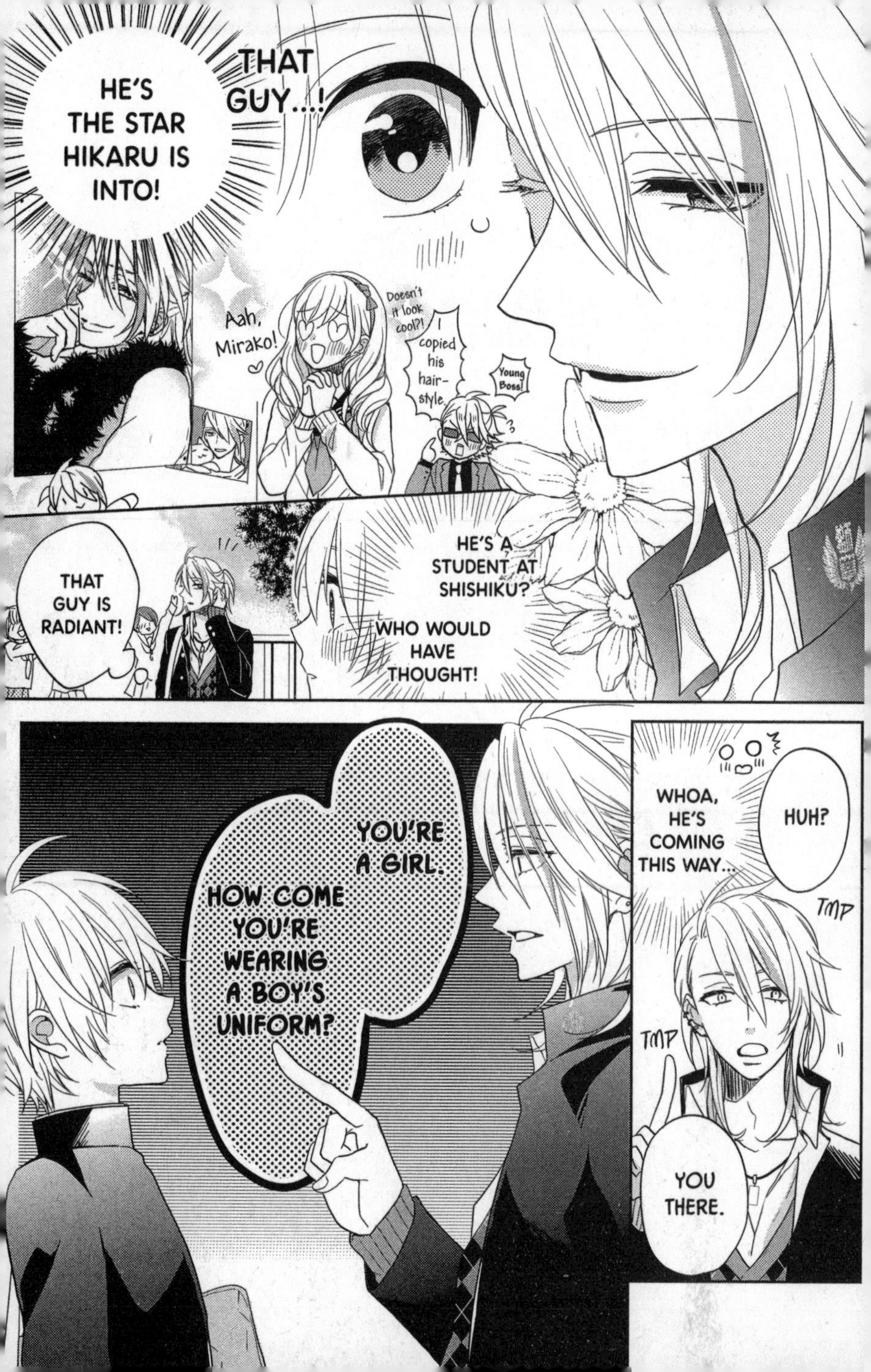
THAT GUY...!
HE'S THE STAR HIKARU IS INTO!
Young Boss!
Doesn't it look cool?! I copied his hairstyle.
Aah, Mirako!
HE'S A STUDENT AT SHISHIKU?
WHO WOULD HAVE THOUGHT!
THAT GUY IS RADIANT!
HUH?
WHOA, HE'S COMING THIS WAY...
TMP
TMP
YOU THERE.
YOU'RE A GIRL.
HOW COME YOU'RE WEARING A BOY'S UNIFORM?

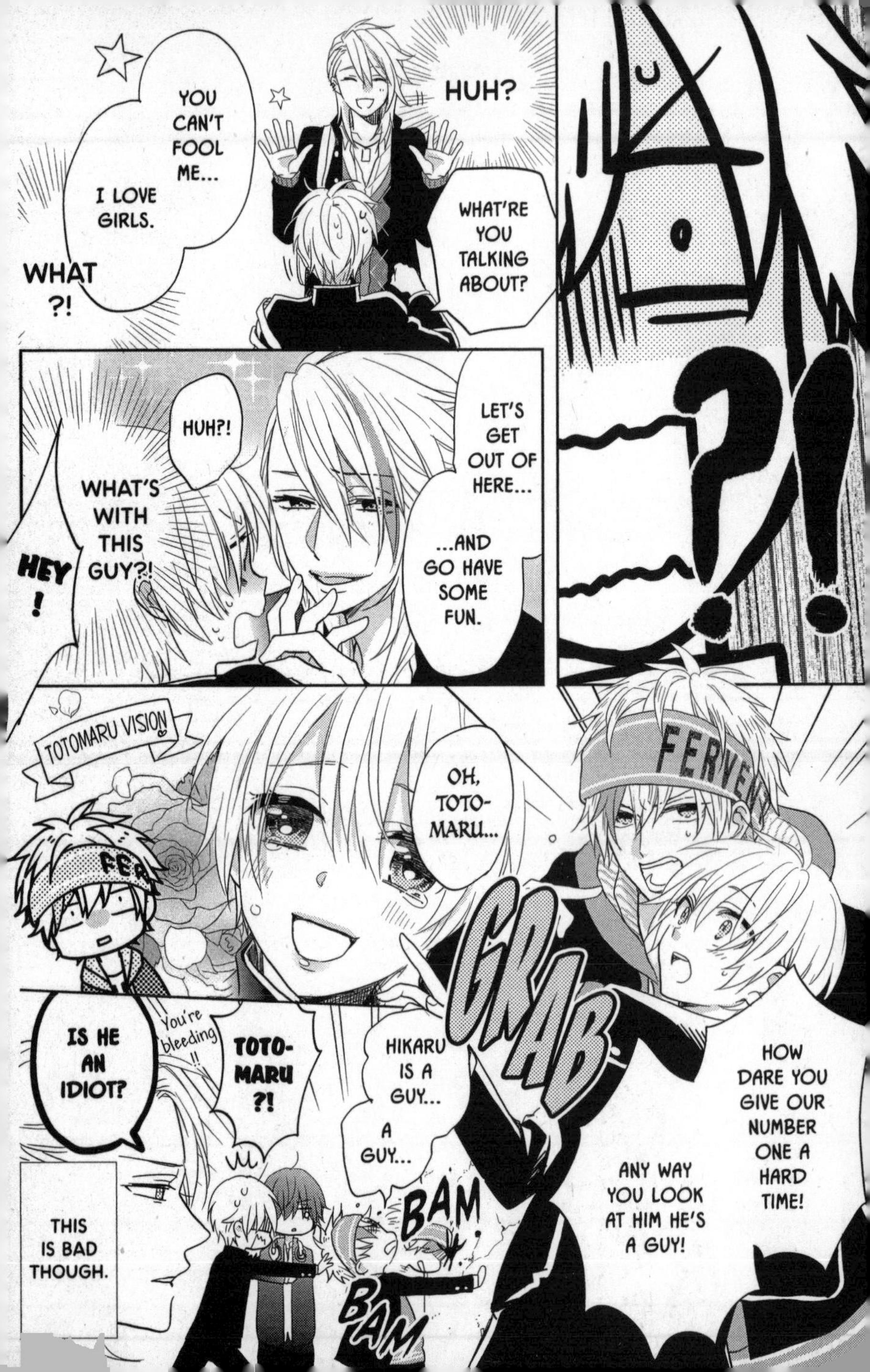
?!
HUH?
WHAT'RE YOU TALKING ABOUT?
YOU CAN'T FOOL ME... I LOVE GIRLS.
WHAT ?!
LET'S GET OUT OF HERE...
...AND GO HAVE SOME FUN.
HUH?!
WHAT'S WITH THIS GUY?!
HEY !
FERVENT
HOW DARE YOU GIVE OUR NUMBER ONE A HARD TIME!
GRAB
OH, TOTO-MARU...
TOTOMARU VISION
FER
ANY WAY YOU LOOK AT HIM HE'S A GUY!
HIKARU IS A GUY...
A GUY...
TOTO-MARU ?!
You're bleeding !!
IS HE AN IDIOT?
BAM
BAM
THIS IS BAD THOUGH.

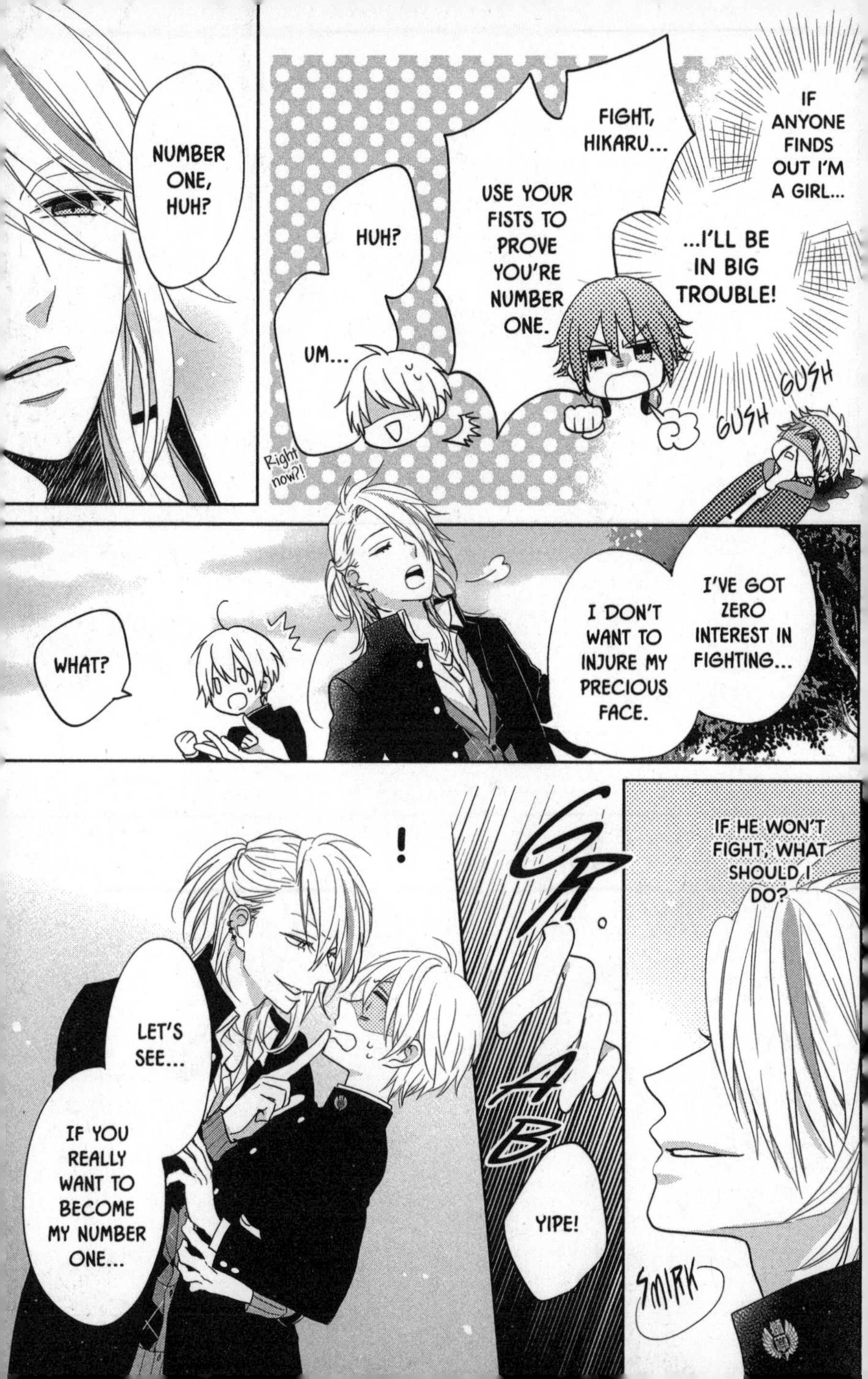

IF ANYONE FINDS OUT I'M A GIRL...
...I'LL BE IN BIG TROUBLE!
FIGHT, HIKARU...
USE YOUR FISTS TO PROVE YOU'RE NUMBER ONE.
GUSH
GUSH
HUH?
UM...
Right now?!
NUMBER ONE, HUH?
I'VE GOT ZERO INTEREST IN FIGHTING...
I DON'T WANT TO INJURE MY PRECIOUS FACE.
WHAT?
IF HE WON'T FIGHT, WHAT SHOULD I DO?
SMIRK
GRAB
YIPE!
!
LET'S SEE...
IF YOU REALLY WANT TO BECOME MY NUMBER ONE...

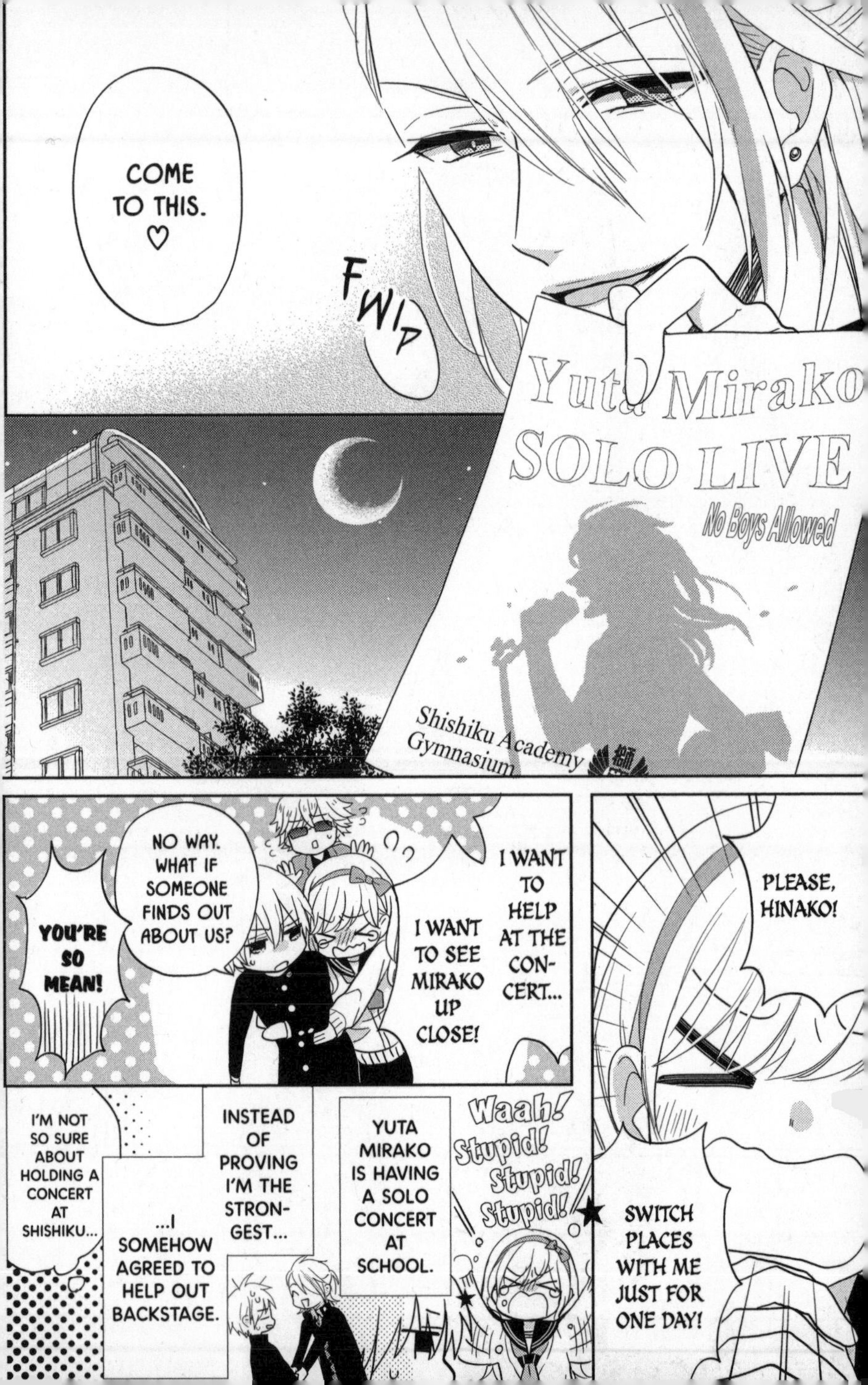
COME TO THIS. ♡
FWIP
Yuta Mirako SOLO LIVE
No Boys Allowed
Shishiku Academy Gymnasium
PLEASE, HINAKO!
SWITCH PLACES WITH ME JUST FOR ONE DAY!
I WANT TO HELP AT THE CONCERT...
I WANT TO SEE MIRAKO UP CLOSE!
NO WAY. WHAT IF SOMEONE FINDS OUT ABOUT US?
YOU'RE SO MEAN!
Waah! Stupid! Stupid! Stupid!
YUTA MIRAKO IS HAVING A SOLO CONCERT AT SCHOOL.
INSTEAD OF PROVING I'M THE STRONGEST...
...I SOMEHOW AGREED TO HELP OUT BACKSTAGE.
I'M NOT SO SURE ABOUT HOLDING A CONCERT AT SHISHIKU...

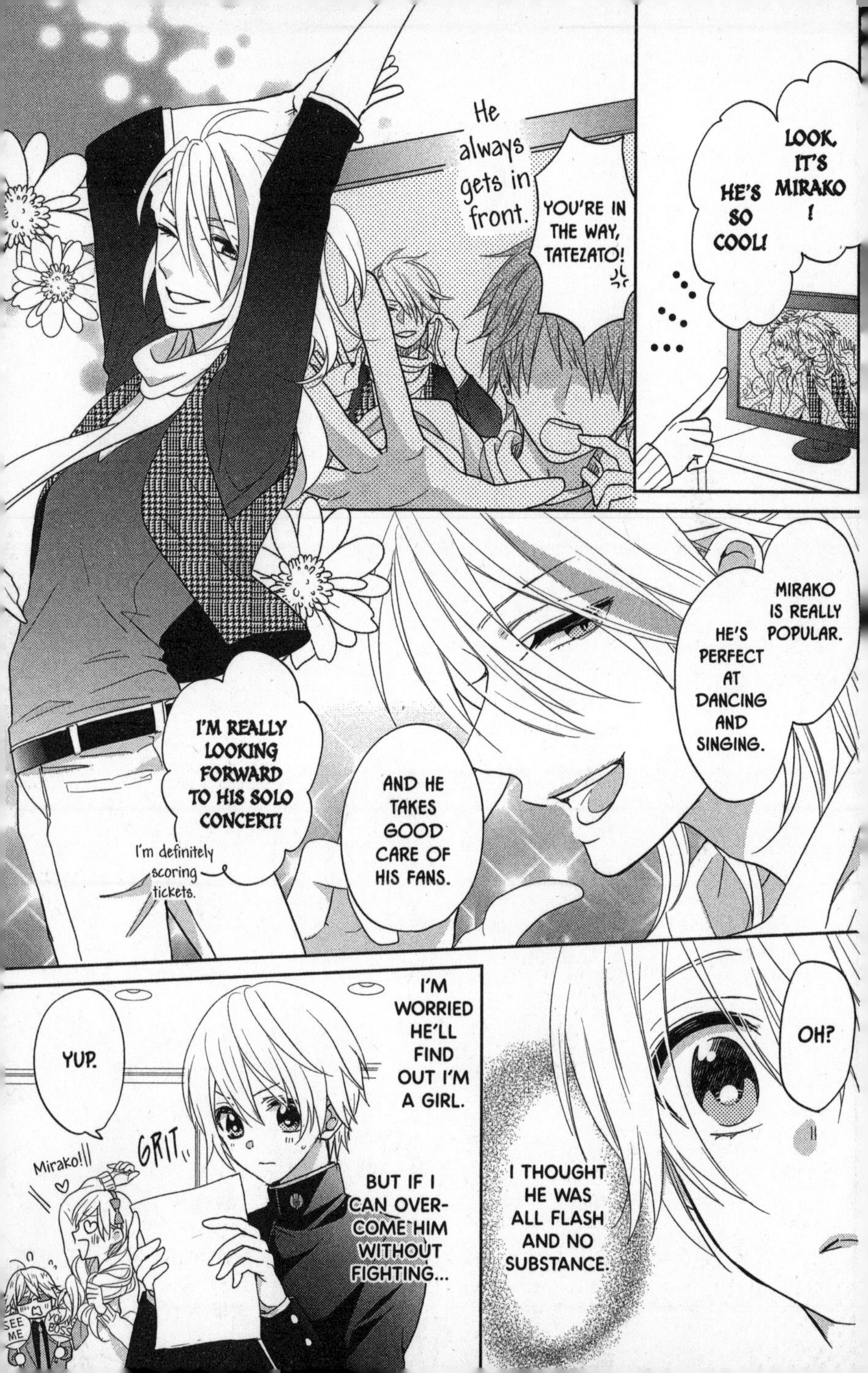
LOOK, IT'S MIRAKO!
HE'S SO COOL!
...
...
...
YOU'RE IN THE WAY, TATEZATO!
He always gets in front.
MIRAKO IS REALLY POPULAR.
HE'S PERFECT AT DANCING AND SINGING.
AND HE TAKES GOOD CARE OF HIS FANS.
I'M REALLY LOOKING FORWARD TO HIS SOLO CONCERT!
I'm definitely scoring tickets.
OH?
I THOUGHT HE WAS ALL FLASH AND NO SUBSTANCE.
I'M WORRIED HE'LL FIND OUT I'M A GIRL.
BUT IF I CAN OVER-COME HIM WITHOUT FIGHTING...
YUP.
GRIT
Mirako!!
SEE ME
YOUNG BOSS

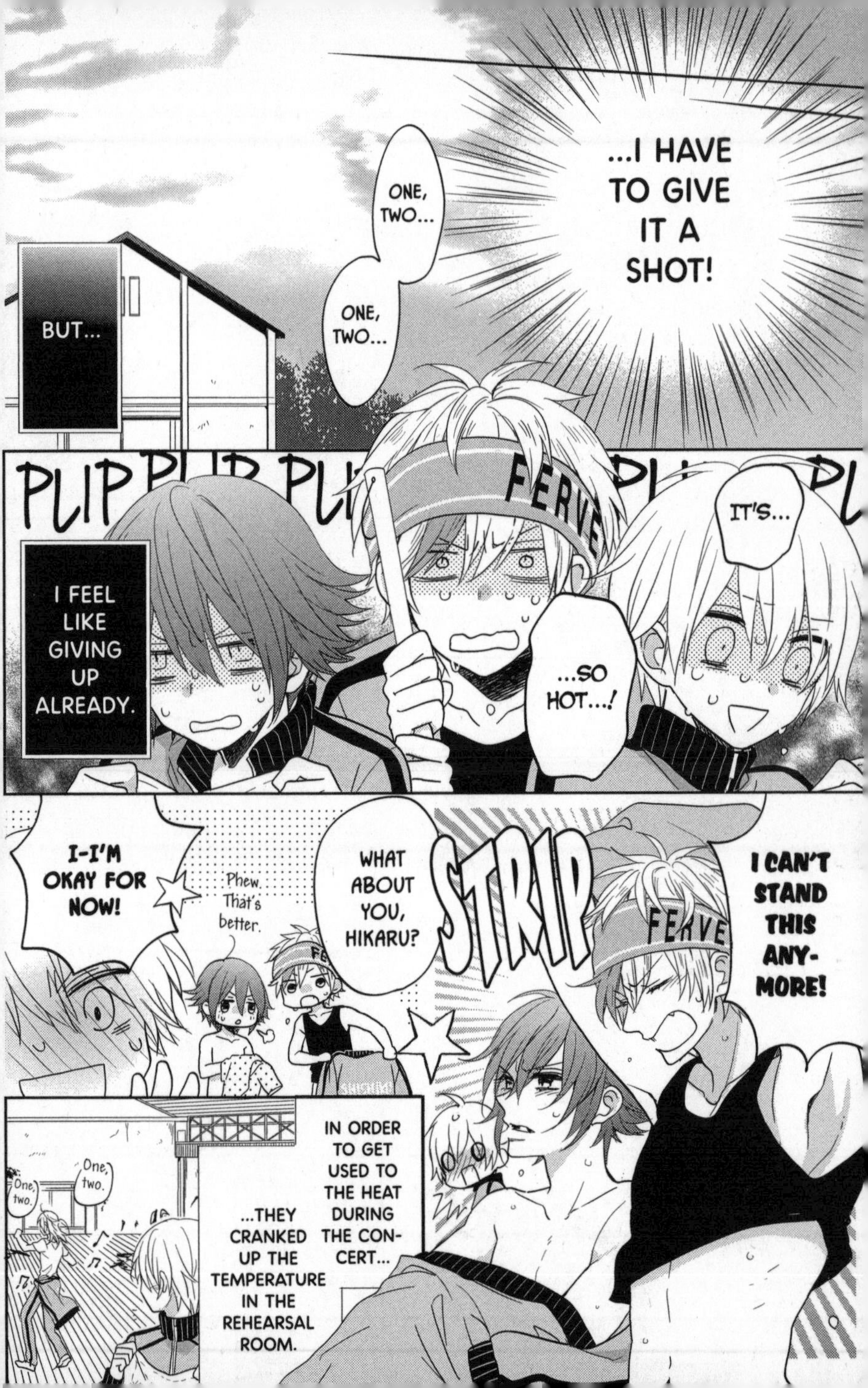
...I HAVE TO GIVE IT A SHOT!
ONE, TWO...
ONE, TWO...
BUT...
PLIP
FERVE
IT'S...
...SO HOT...!
I FEEL LIKE GIVING UP ALREADY.
I CAN'T STAND THIS ANYMORE!
FERVE
STRIP
WHAT ABOUT YOU, HIKARU?
Phew. That's better.
I-I'M OKAY FOR NOW!
IN ORDER TO GET USED TO THE HEAT DURING THE CON-CERT...
...THEY CRANKED UP THE TEMPERATURE IN THE REHEARSAL ROOM.
One, two.
One, two.

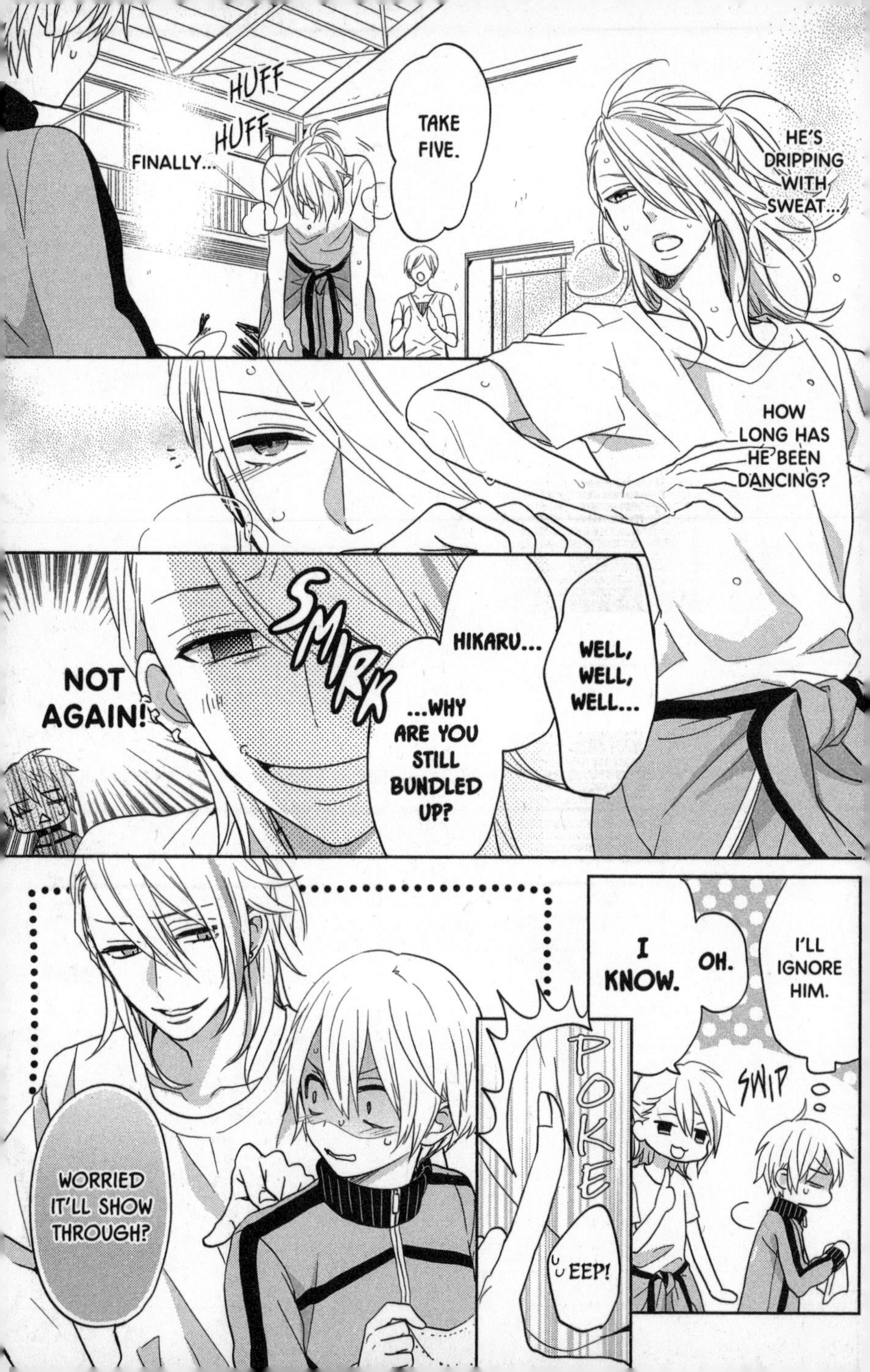
HE'S DRIPPING WITH SWEAT...
TAKE FIVE.
HUFF
HUFF
FINALLY...
HOW LONG HAS HE BEEN DANCING?
WELL, WELL, WELL...
HIKARU...
...WHY ARE YOU STILL BUNDLED UP?
SMIRK
NOT AGAIN!
I'LL IGNORE HIM.
OH.
I KNOW.
SWIP
POKE
EEP!
WORRIED IT'LL SHOW THROUGH?

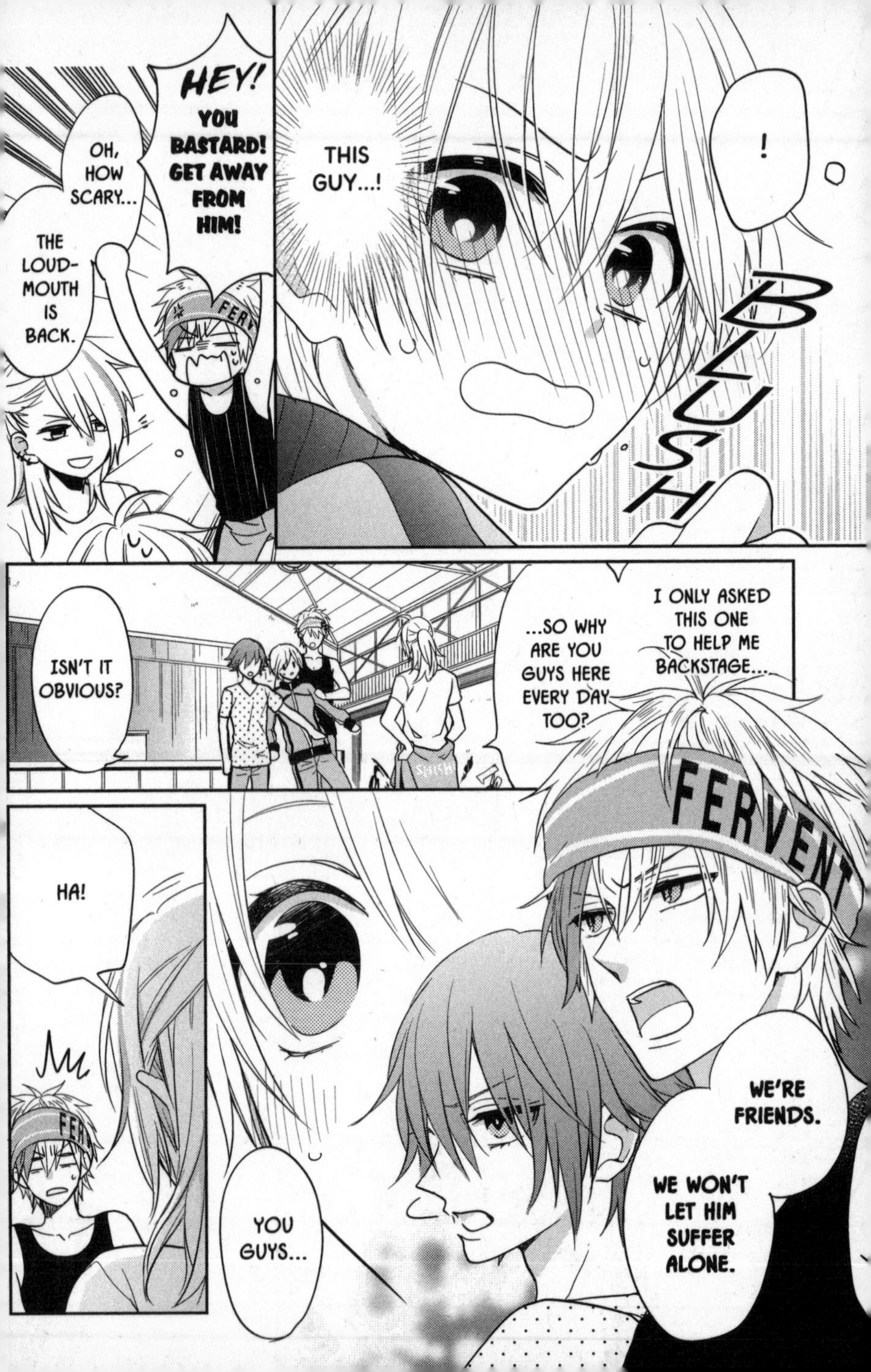
!
BLUSH
THIS GUY...!
HEY!
YOU BASTARD! GET AWAY FROM HIM!
OH, HOW SCARY...
THE LOUD-MOUTH IS BACK.
I ONLY ASKED THIS ONE TO HELP ME BACKSTAGE...
...SO WHY ARE YOU GUYS HERE EVERY DAY TOO?
ISN'T IT OBVIOUS?
FERVENT
WE'RE FRIENDS.
WE WON'T LET HIM SUFFER ALONE.
YOU GUYS...
HA!

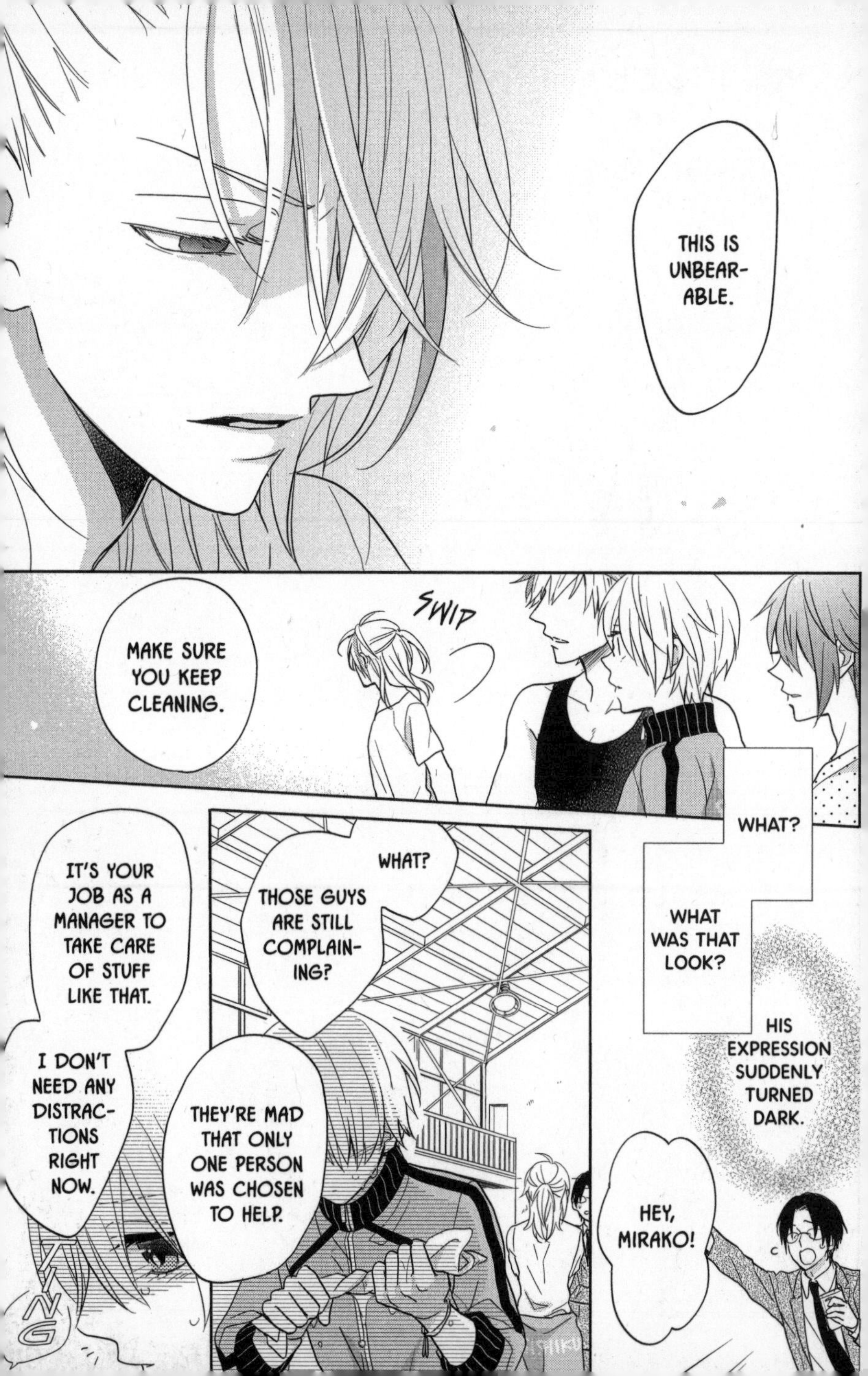
THIS IS UNBEARABLE.
SWIP
MAKE SURE YOU KEEP CLEANING.
WHAT?
WHAT WAS THAT LOOK?
HIS EXPRESSION SUDDENLY TURNED DARK.
HEY, MIRAKO!
WHAT?
THOSE GUYS ARE STILL COMPLAIN-ING?
THEY'RE MAD THAT ONLY ONE PERSON WAS CHOSEN TO HELP.
IT'S YOUR JOB AS A MANAGER TO TAKE CARE OF STUFF LIKE THAT.
I DON'T NEED ANY DISTRAC-TIONS RIGHT NOW.
KING

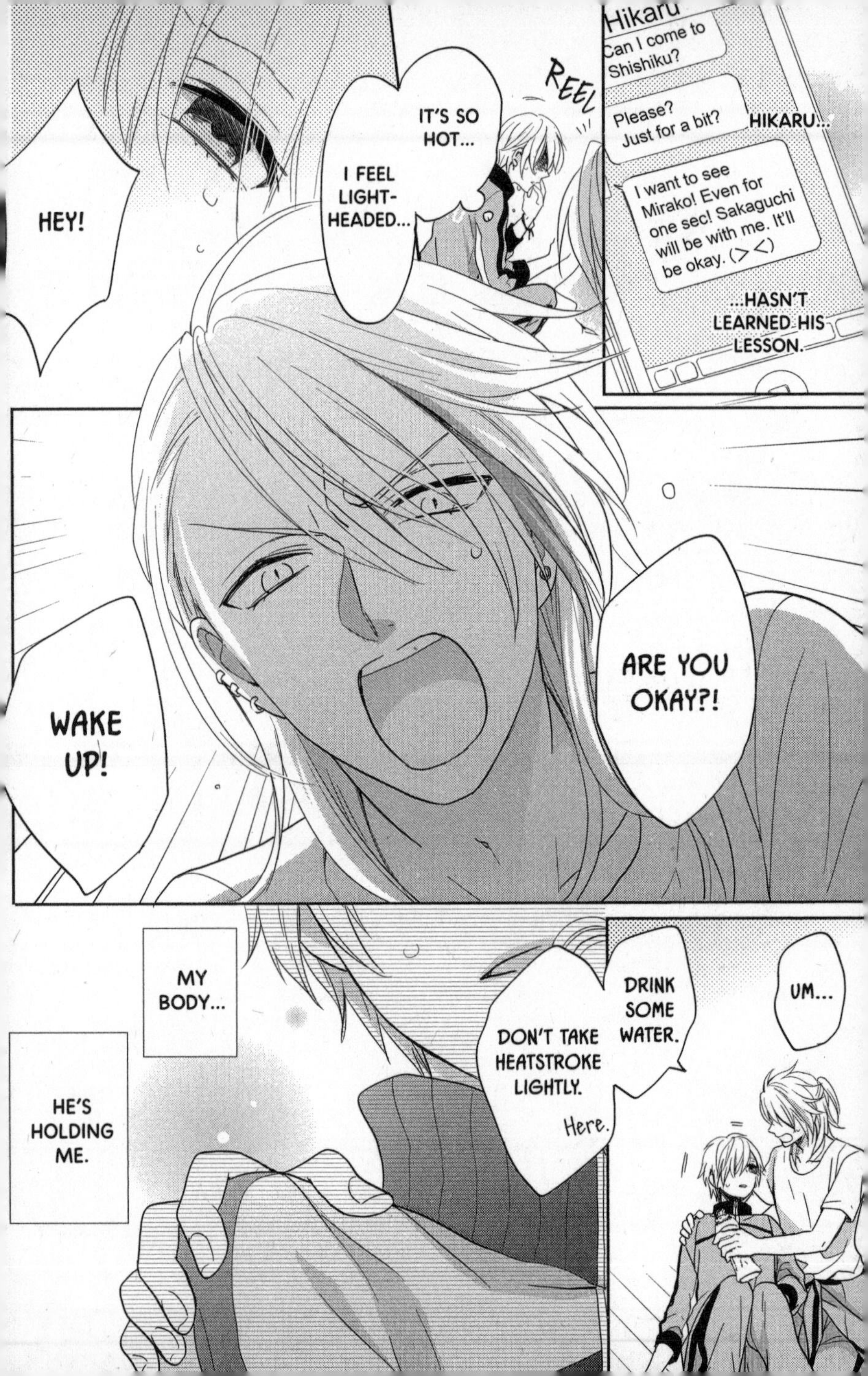
Hikaru
Can I come to Shishiku?
Please? Just for a bit?
I want to see Mirako! Even for one sec! Sakaguchi will be with me. It'll be okay. (><)
HIKARU...
...HASN'T LEARNED HIS LESSON.
REEL
IT'S SO HOT...
I FEEL LIGHT-HEADED...
HEY!
ARE YOU OKAY?!
WAKE UP!
UM...
DRINK SOME WATER.
DON'T TAKE HEATSTROKE LIGHTLY.
Here.
MY BODY...
HE'S HOLDING ME.

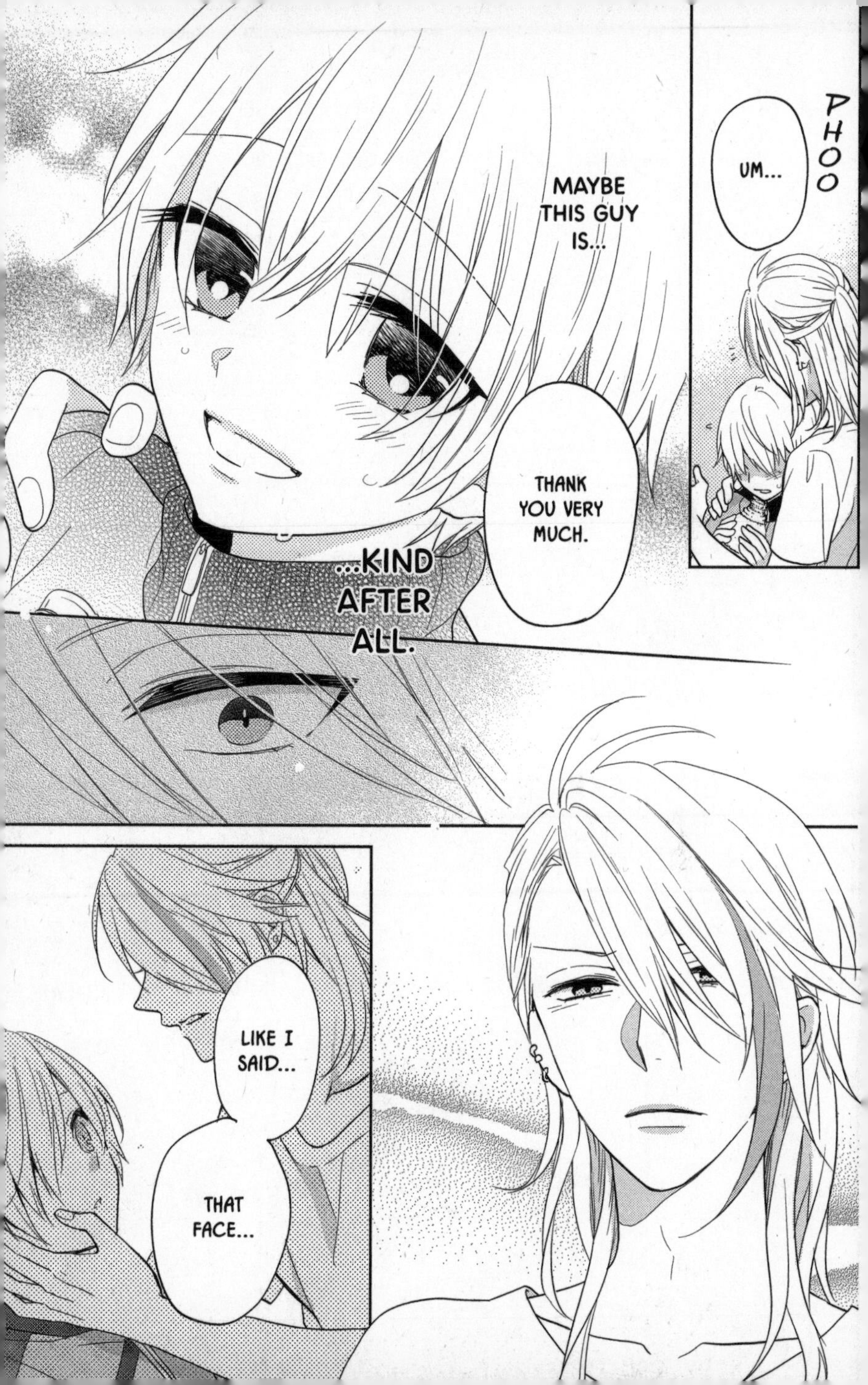
PHOO
UM...
MAYBE THIS GUY IS...
THANK YOU VERY MUCH.
...KIND AFTER ALL.
LIKE I SAID...
THAT FACE...

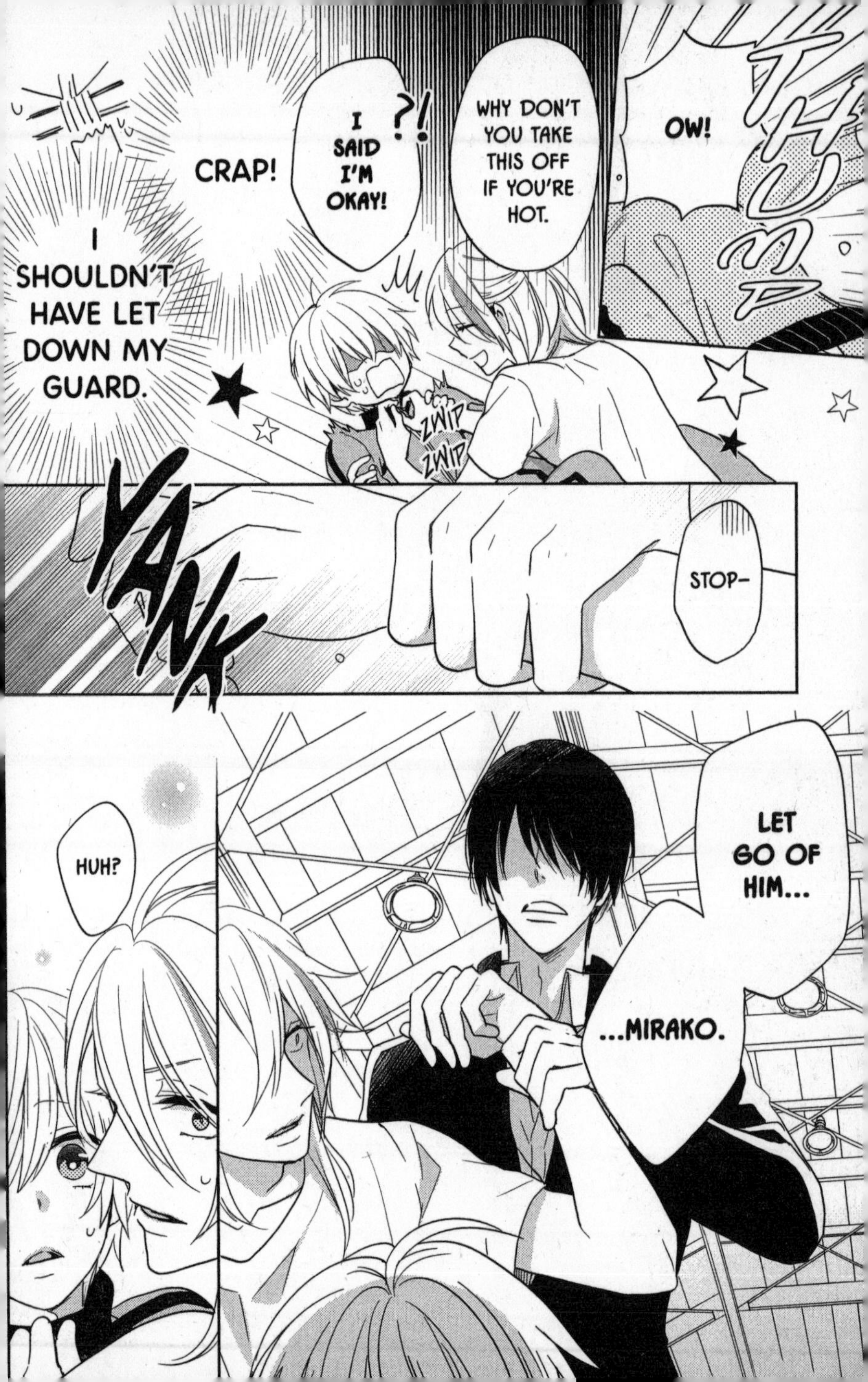
THUMP
OW!
WHY DON'T YOU TAKE THIS OFF IF YOU'RE HOT.
?!
I SAID I'M OKAY!
CRAP!
I SHOULDN'T HAVE LET DOWN MY GUARD.
ZWIP ZWIP
STOP-
YANK
LET GO OF HIM...
...MIRAKO.
HUH?

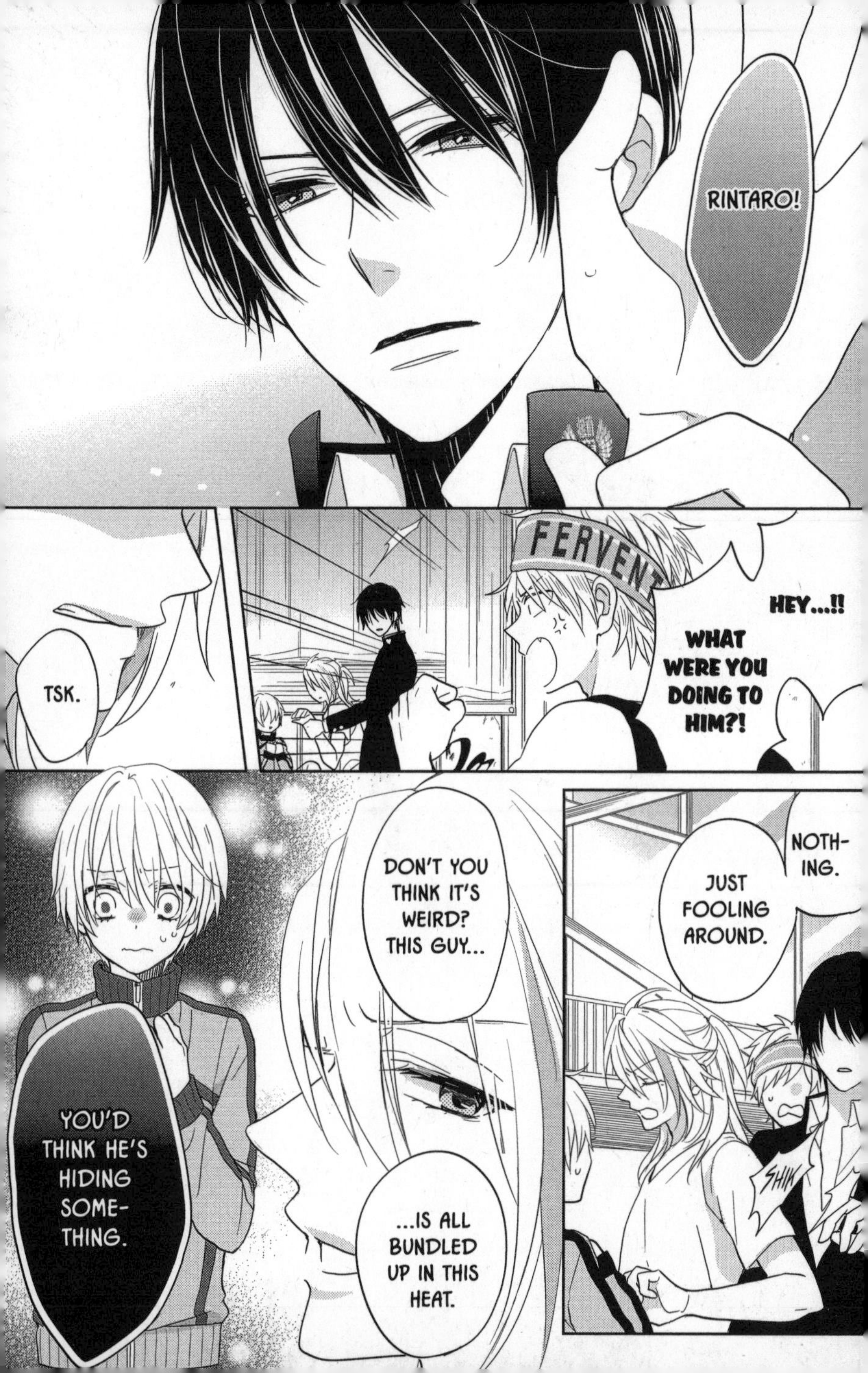
RINTARO!
FERVENT
HEY...!!
WHAT WERE YOU DOING TO HIM?!
TSK.
NOTH-ING.
JUST FOOLING AROUND.
SHIK
DON'T YOU THINK IT'S WEIRD? THIS GUY...
...IS ALL BUNDLED UP IN THIS HEAT.
YOU'D THINK HE'S HIDING SOME-THING.

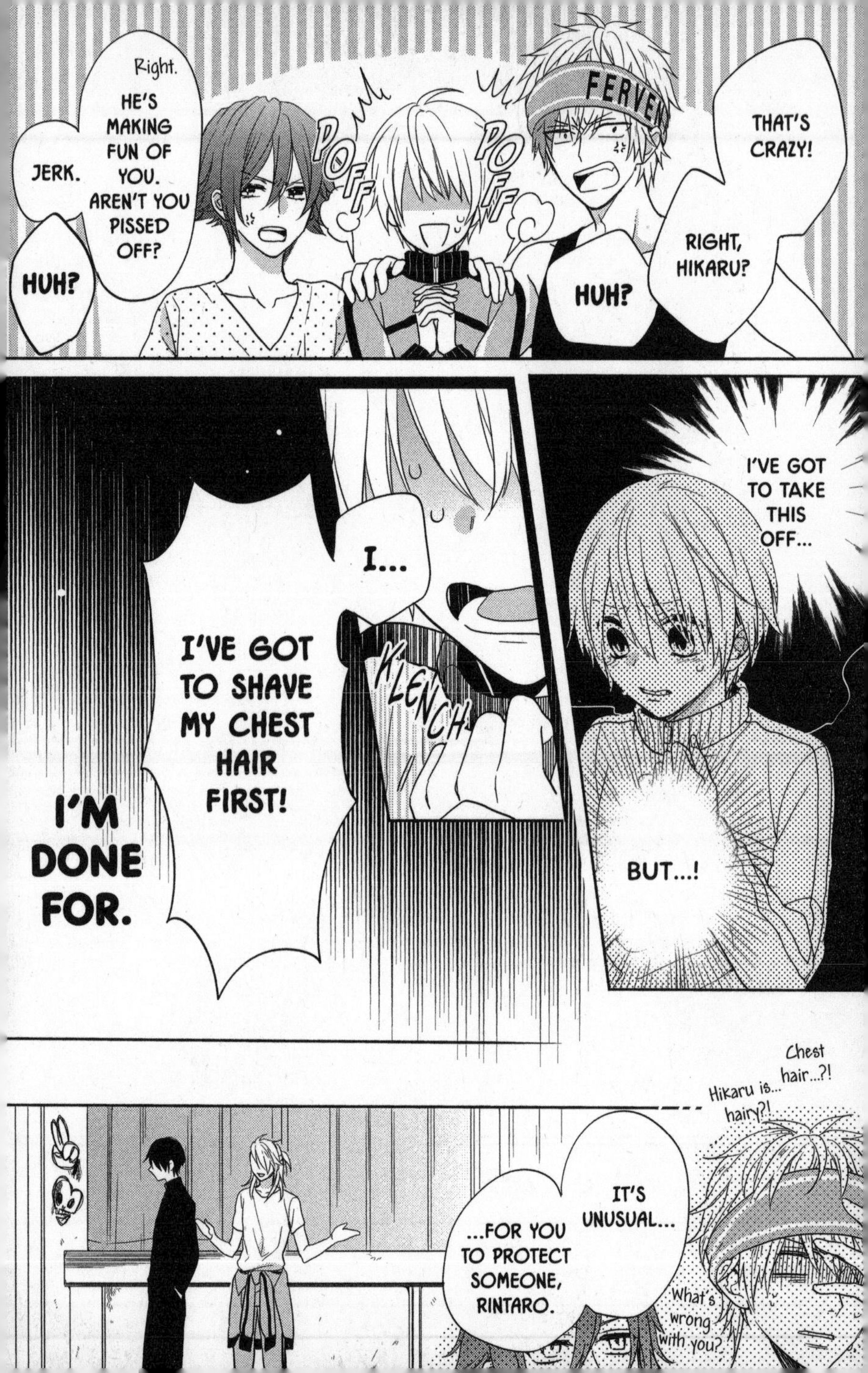
FERVEN
THAT'S CRAZY!
RIGHT, HIKARU?
HUH?
POFF
POFF
Right.
HE'S MAKING FUN OF YOU. AREN'T YOU PISSED OFF?
JERK.
HUH?
I'VE GOT TO TAKE THIS OFF...
BUT...!
I...
KLENCH
I'VE GOT TO SHAVE MY CHEST HAIR FIRST!
I'M DONE FOR.
Chest hair...?!
Hikaru is... hairy?!
What's wrong with you?
IT'S UNUSUAL...
...FOR YOU TO PROTECT SOMEONE, RINTARO.

SECOND-YEAR, LILY CLASS

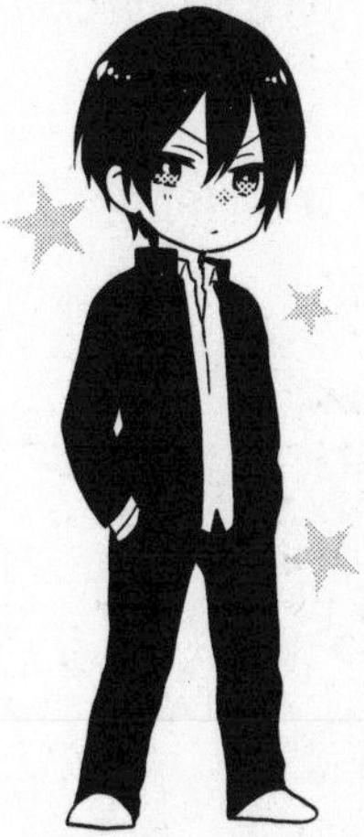

RINTARO KIRA

Height: 5'8"
Weight: 145 lbs
Blood Type: A
Birthday: October 24
Skill: Boxing

✿

He's a cool guy who looks out for Hinako. But if you notice, he's always right behind her. Maybe he has a built-in sensor to detect her. I secretly call him Kira-rin.

He's a cutie.

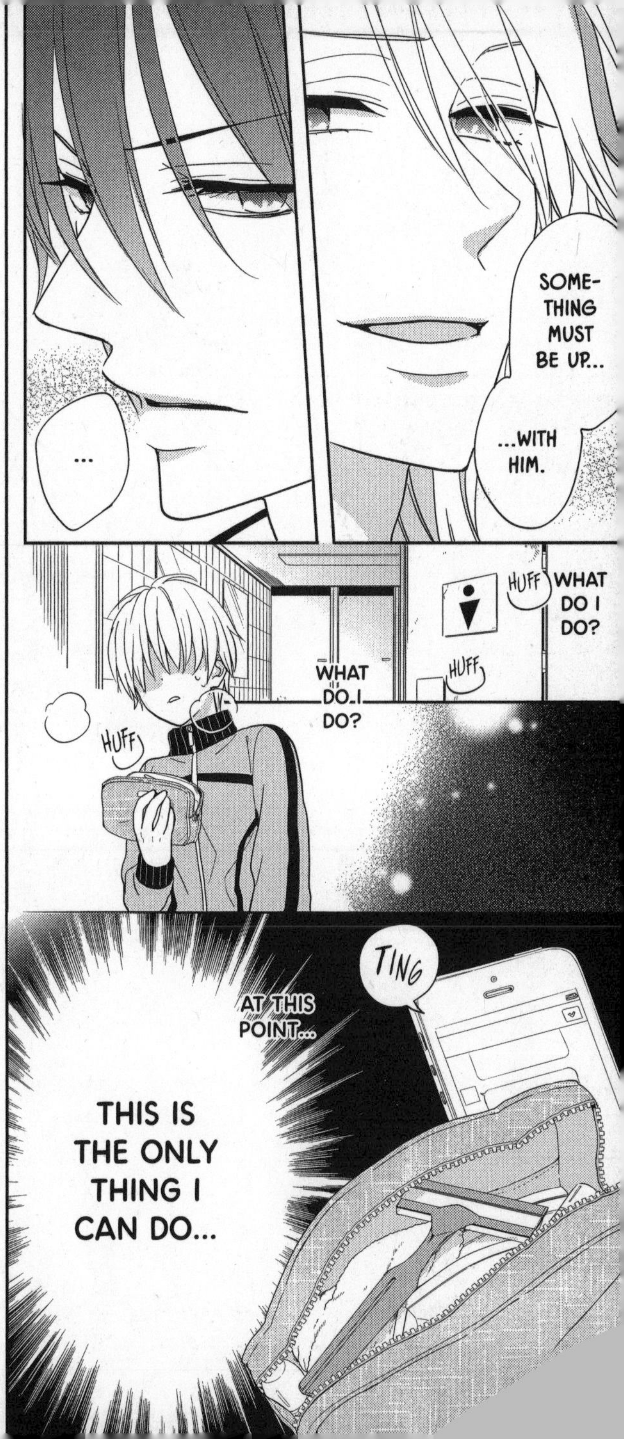
SOME-THING MUST BE UP...
...WITH HIM.
...
WHAT DO I DO?
HUFF
HUFF
WHAT DO I DO?
HUFF
TING
AT THIS POINT...
THIS IS THE ONLY THING I CAN DO...

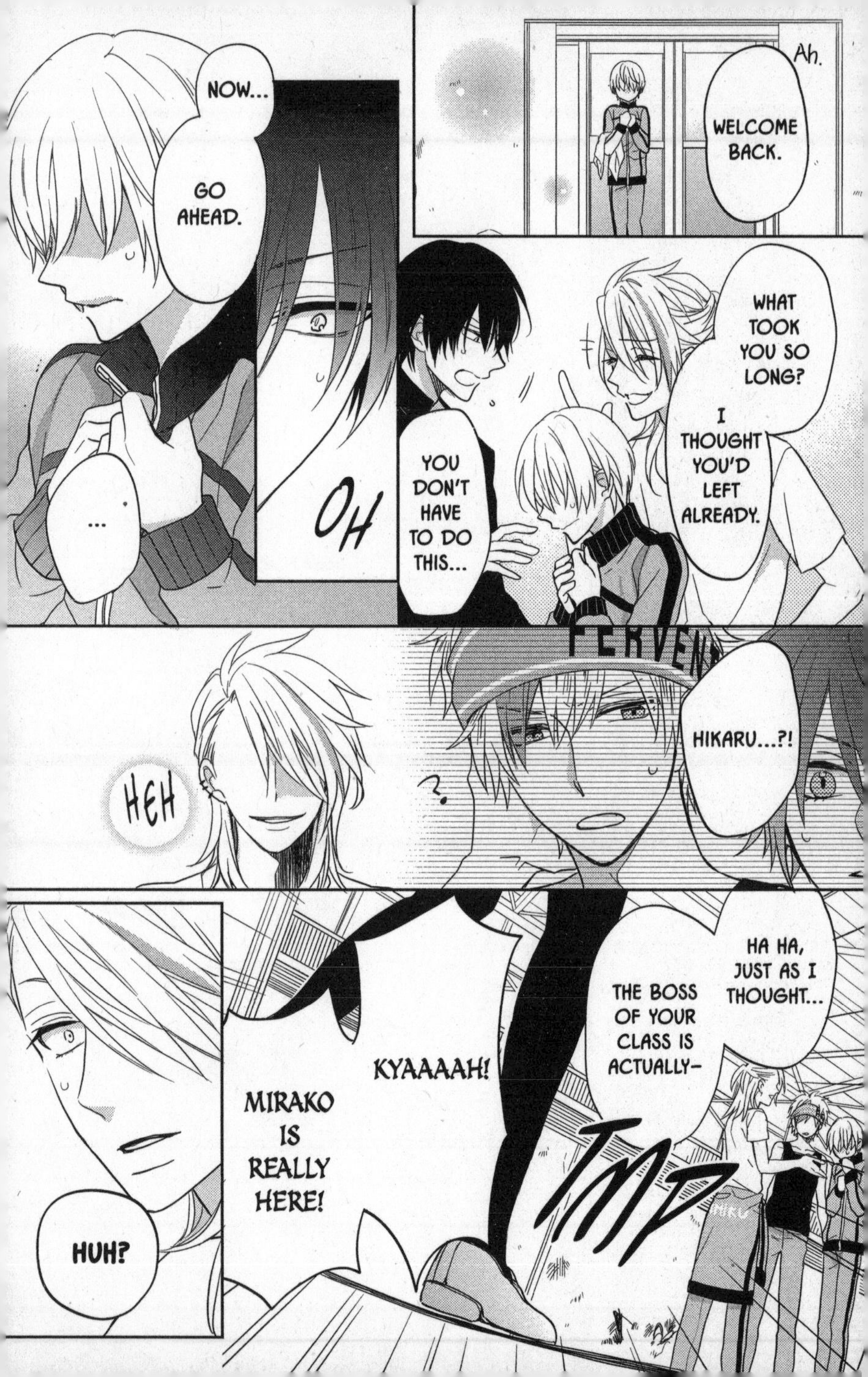
Ah.
WELCOME BACK.
WHAT TOOK YOU SO LONG? I THOUGHT YOU'D LEFT ALREADY.
YOU DON'T HAVE TO DO THIS...
OH
NOW... GO AHEAD.
...
HIKARU...?!
?
HEH
HA HA, JUST AS I THOUGHT...
THE BOSS OF YOUR CLASS IS ACTUALLY–
KYAAAAH!
MIRAKO IS REALLY HERE!
HUH?

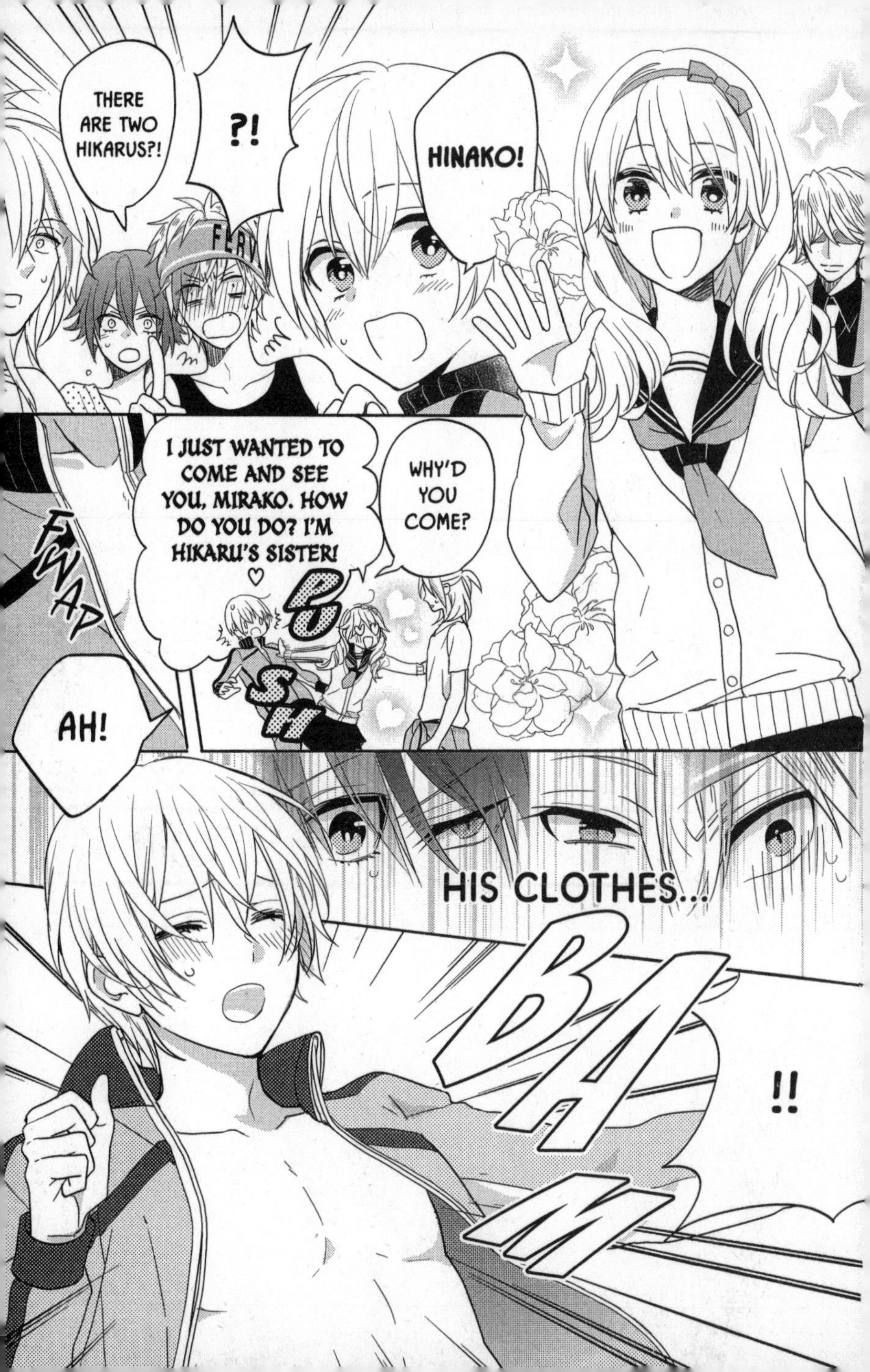
HINAKO!
?!
THERE ARE TWO HIKARUS?!
WHY'D YOU COME?
I JUST WANTED TO COME AND SEE YOU, MIRAKO. HOW DO YOU DO? I'M HIKARU'S SISTER! ♡
BOSH
FWAP
AH!
HIS CLOTHES...
BAM
!!

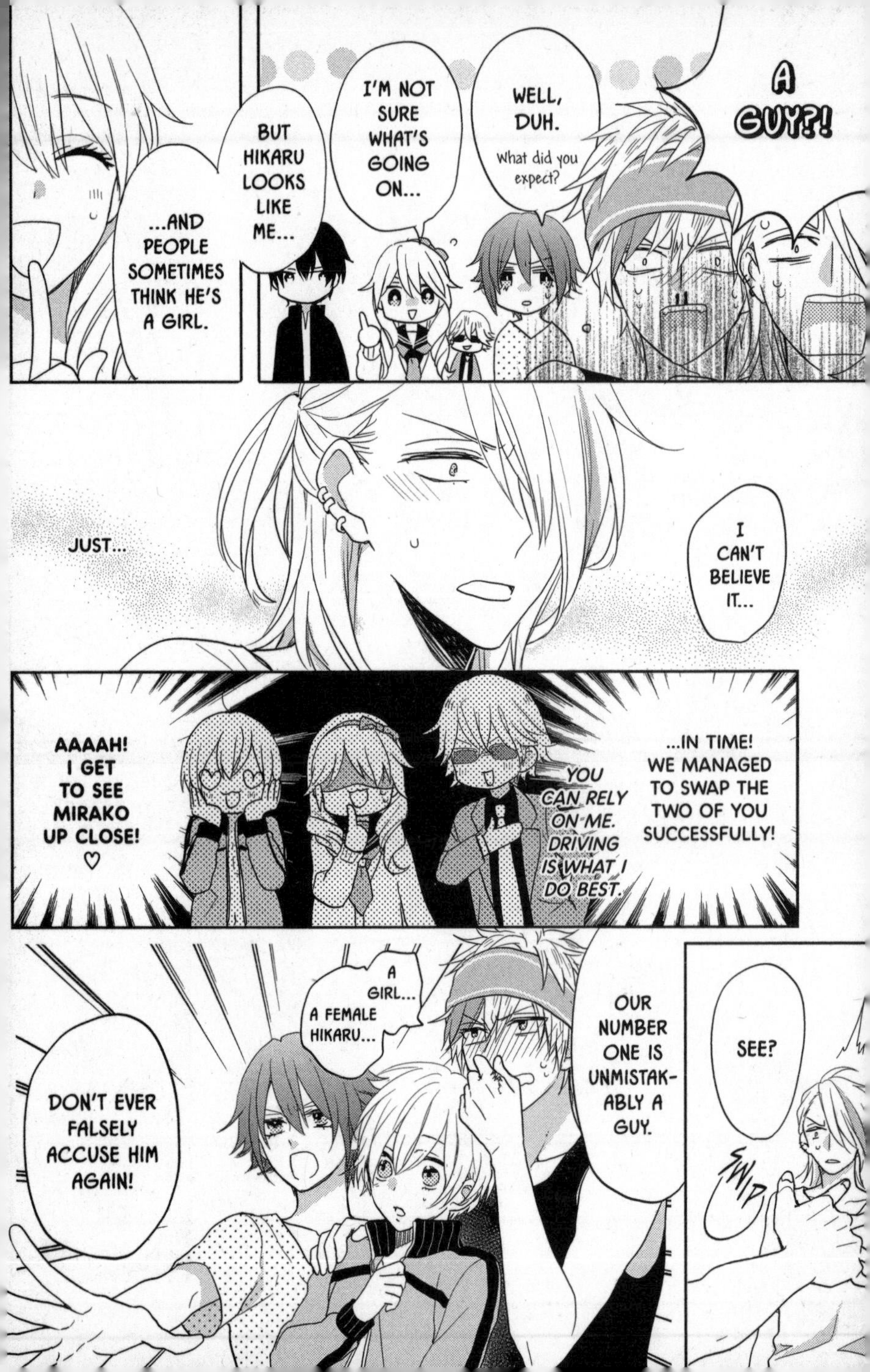
A GUY?!
WELL, DUH. What did you expect?
I'M NOT SURE WHAT'S GOING ON...
BUT HIKARU LOOKS LIKE ME...
...AND PEOPLE SOMETIMES THINK HE'S A GIRL.
I CAN'T BELIEVE IT...
JUST...
...IN TIME! WE MANAGED TO SWAP THE TWO OF YOU SUCCESSFULLY!
YOU CAN RELY ON ME. DRIVING IS WHAT I DO BEST.
AAAAH! I GET TO SEE MIRAKO UP CLOSE! ♡
SEE?
SWIP
OUR NUMBER ONE IS UNMISTAK-ABLY A GUY.
A GIRL... A FEMALE HIKARU...
DON'T EVER FALSELY ACCUSE HIM AGAIN!

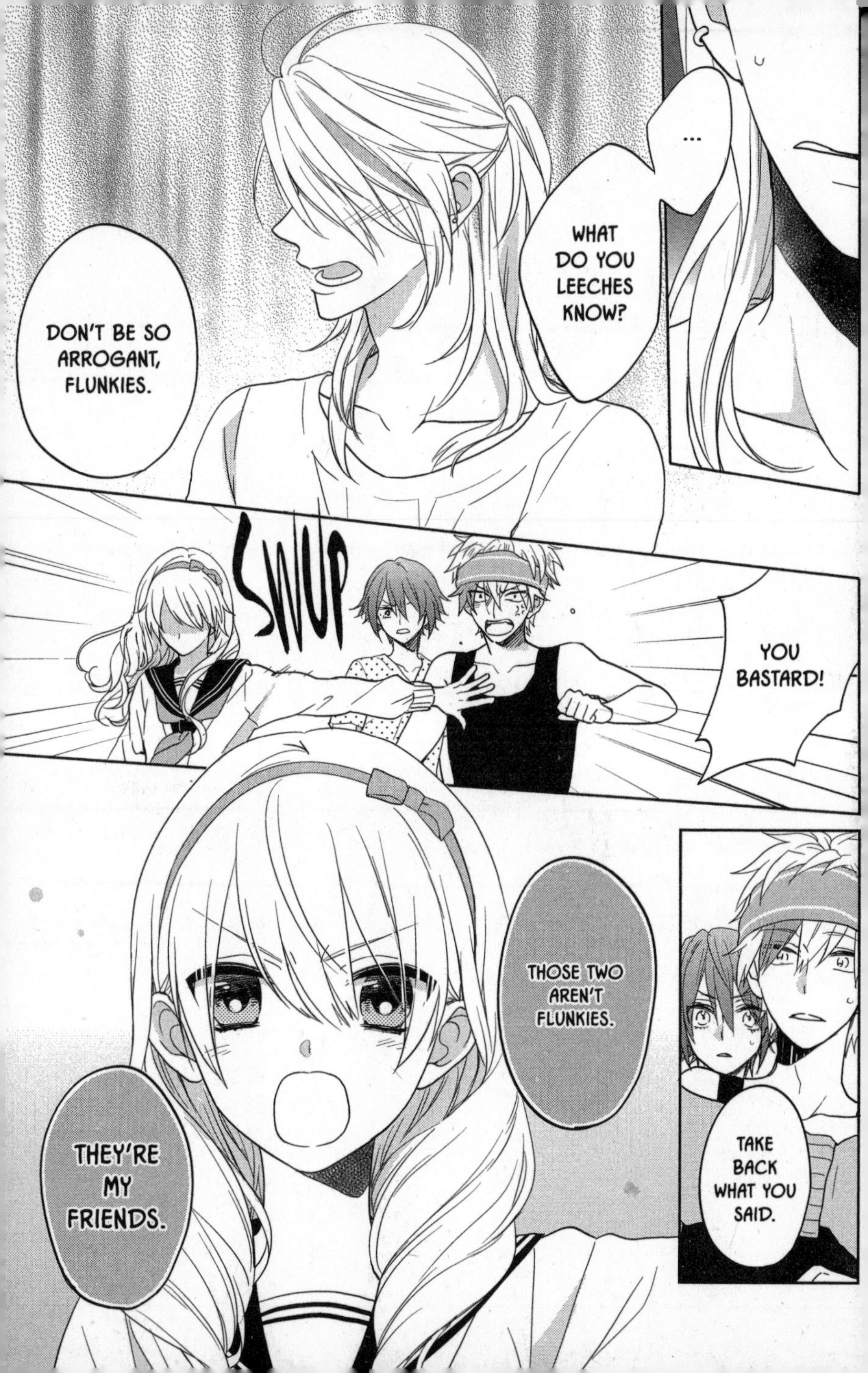
...
WHAT DO YOU LEECHES KNOW?
DON'T BE SO ARROGANT, FLUNKIES.
YOU BASTARD!
SWUP
TAKE BACK WHAT YOU SAID.
THOSE TWO AREN'T FLUNKIES.
THEY'RE MY FRIENDS.

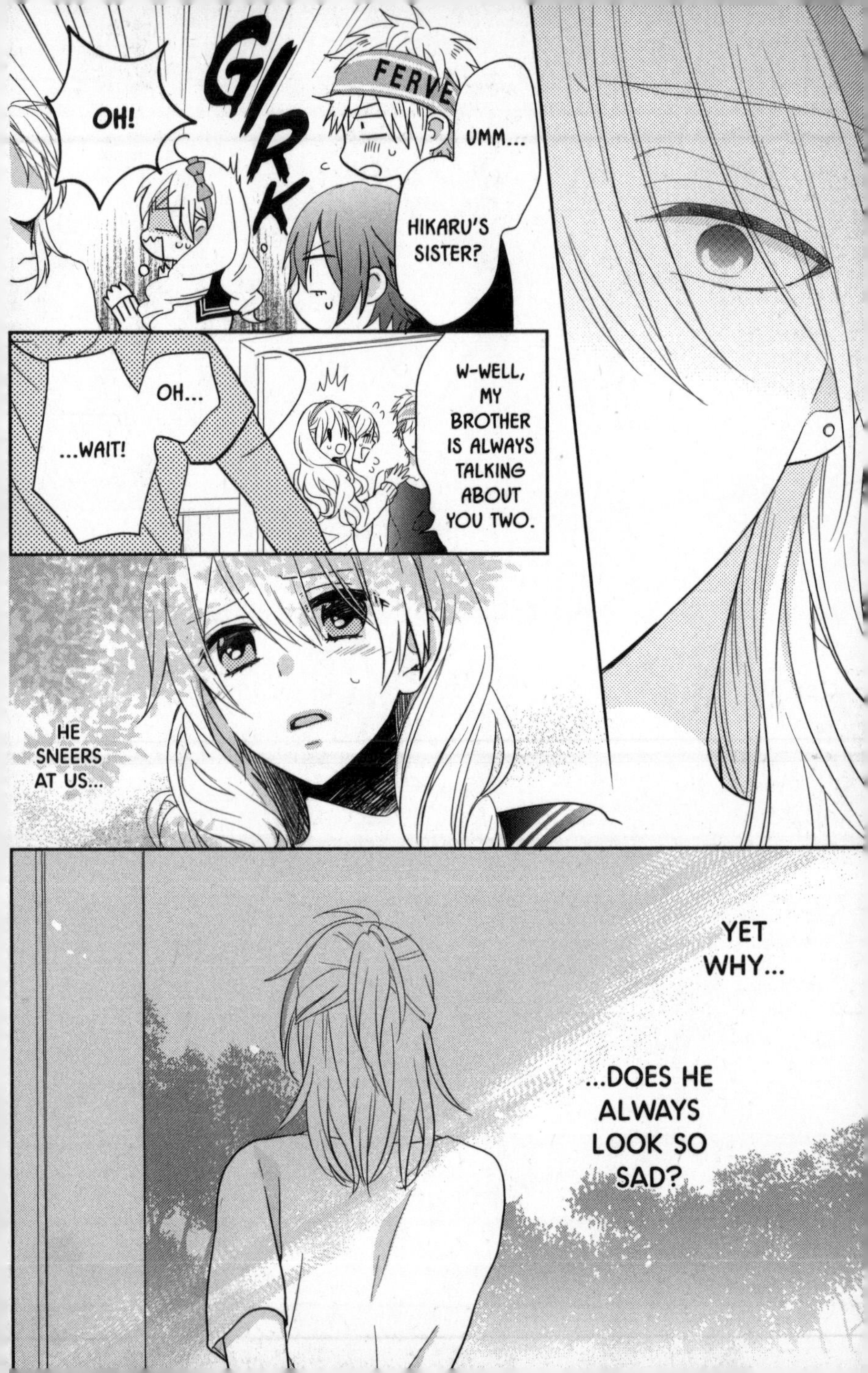
FERVE
UMM...
HIKARU'S SISTER?
GIRK
OH!
W-WELL, MY BROTHER IS ALWAYS TALKING ABOUT YOU TWO.
OH...
...WAIT!
HE SNEERS AT US...
YET WHY...
...DOES HE ALWAYS LOOK SO SAD?

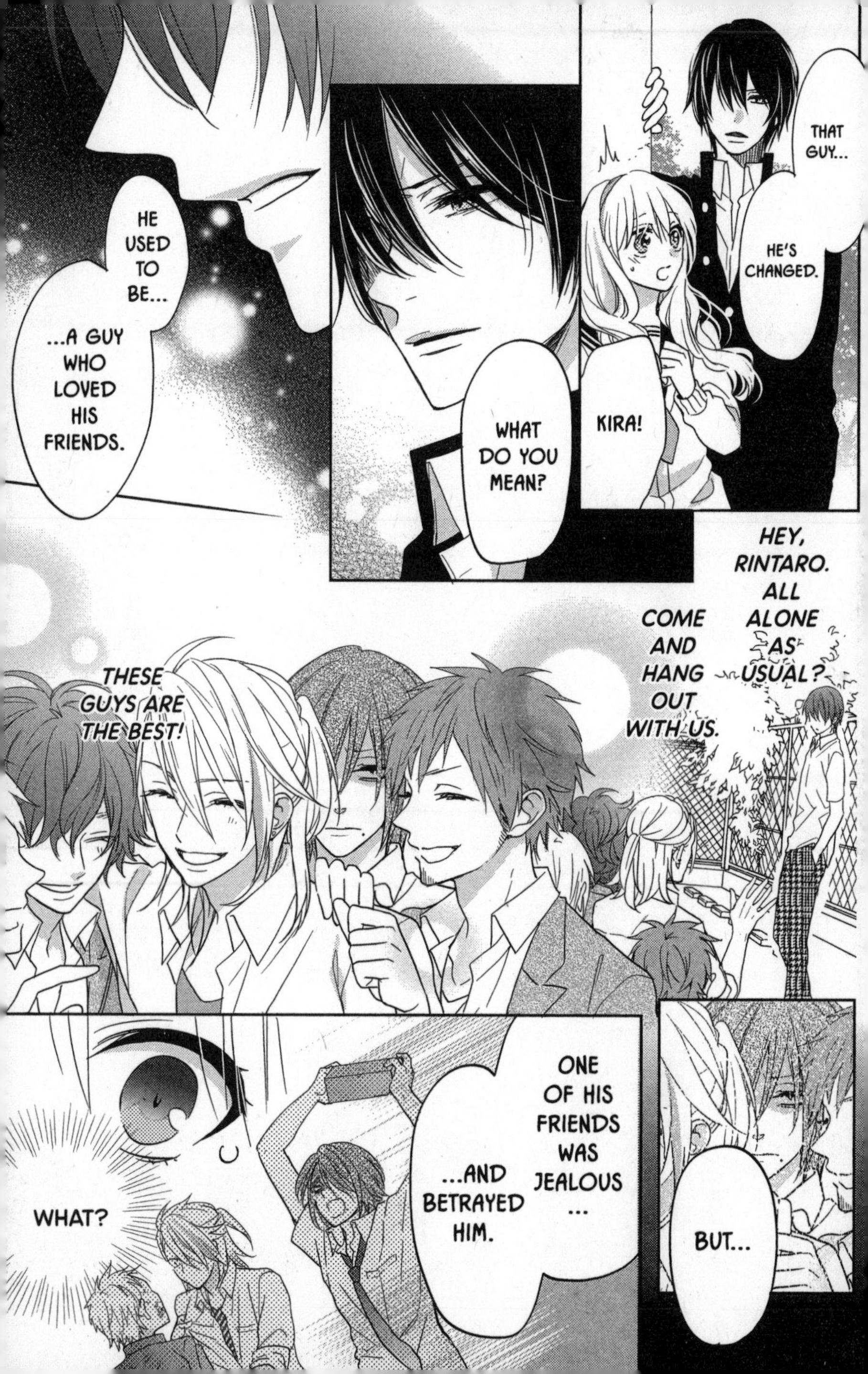
THAT GUY...
HE'S CHANGED.
KIRA!
WHAT DO YOU MEAN?
HE USED TO BE...
...A GUY WHO LOVED HIS FRIENDS.
HEY, RINTARO. ALL ALONE AS USUAL?
COME AND HANG OUT WITH US.
THESE GUYS ARE THE BEST!
BUT...
ONE OF HIS FRIENDS WAS JEALOUS...
...AND BETRAYED HIM.
WHAT?

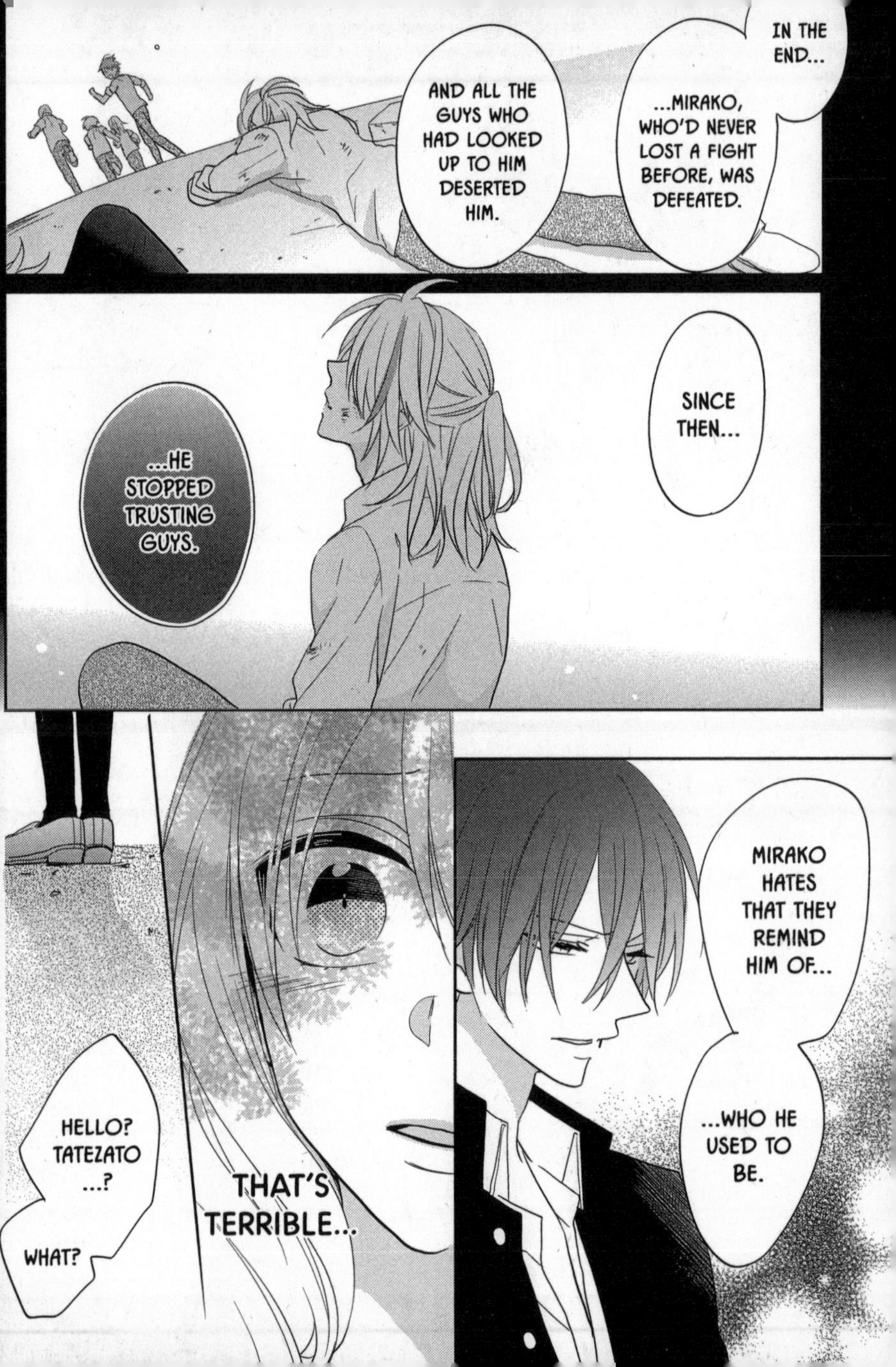
IN THE END...
...MIRAKO, WHO'D NEVER LOST A FIGHT BEFORE, WAS DEFEATED.
AND ALL THE GUYS WHO HAD LOOKED UP TO HIM DESERTED HIM.
SINCE THEN...
...HE STOPPED TRUSTING GUYS.
MIRAKO HATES THAT THEY REMIND HIM OF...
...WHO HE USED TO BE.
THAT'S TERRIBLE...
HELLO? TATEZATO ...?
WHAT?

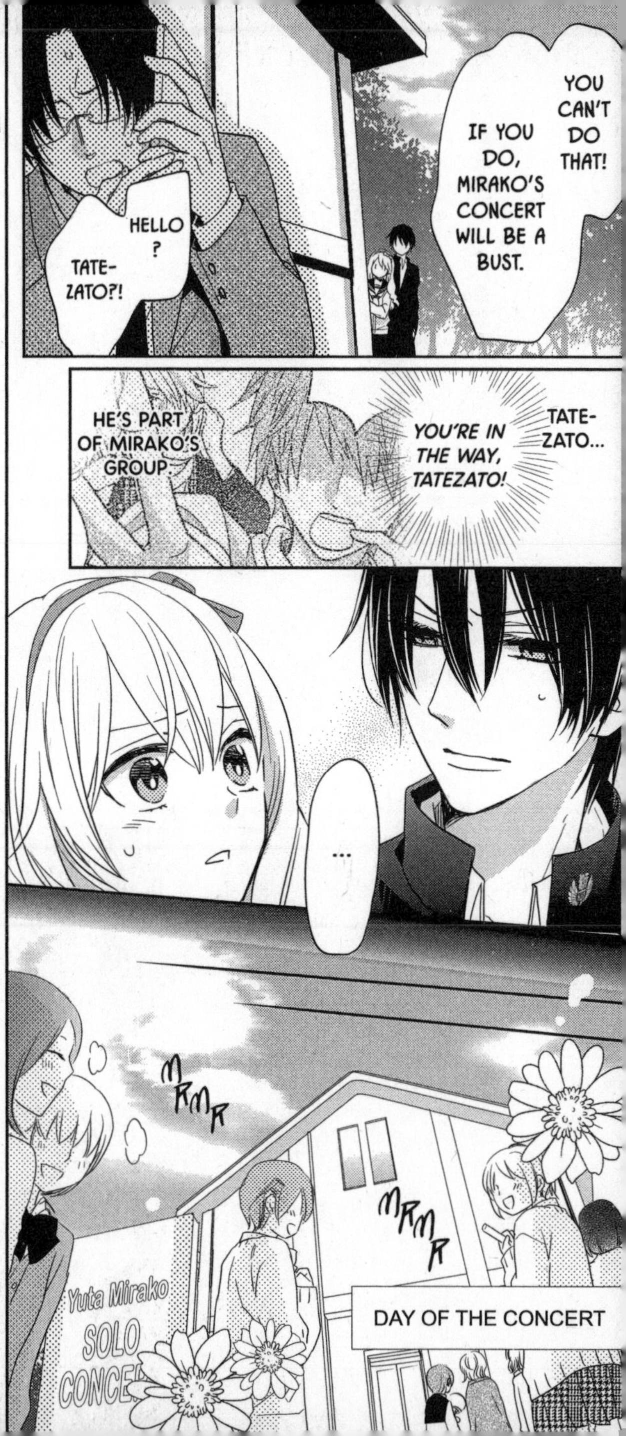
YOU CAN'T DO THAT!
IF YOU DO, MIRAKO'S CONCERT WILL BE A BUST.
HELLO?
TATE-ZATO?!
TATE-ZATO...
YOU'RE IN THE WAY, TATEZATO!
HE'S PART OF MIRAKO'S GROUP.
...
MRMR
MRMR
DAY OF THE CONCERT
Yuta Mirako
SOLO
CONCE

SECOND-YEAR, CHERRY BLOSSOM CLASS

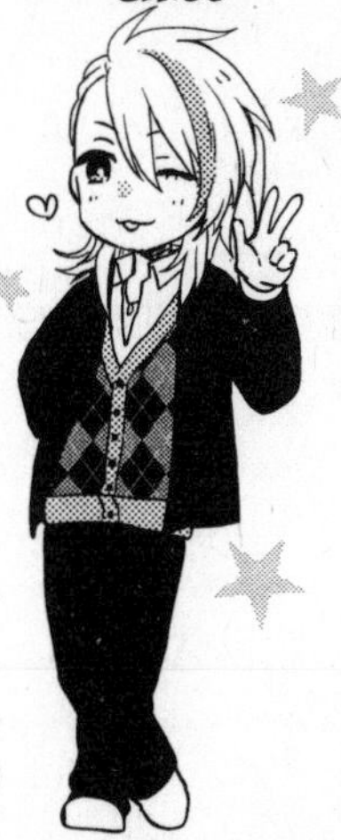

YUTA MIRAKO

Height: 5'7"
Weight: 128 lbs
Blood Type: AB
Birthday: July 26
Skill: Kickboxing

Many say that's he's got a great personality. I like the way he's quirky. You don't see many idols who are also delinquents, do you? I wish he'd be better friends with Rintaro, though.

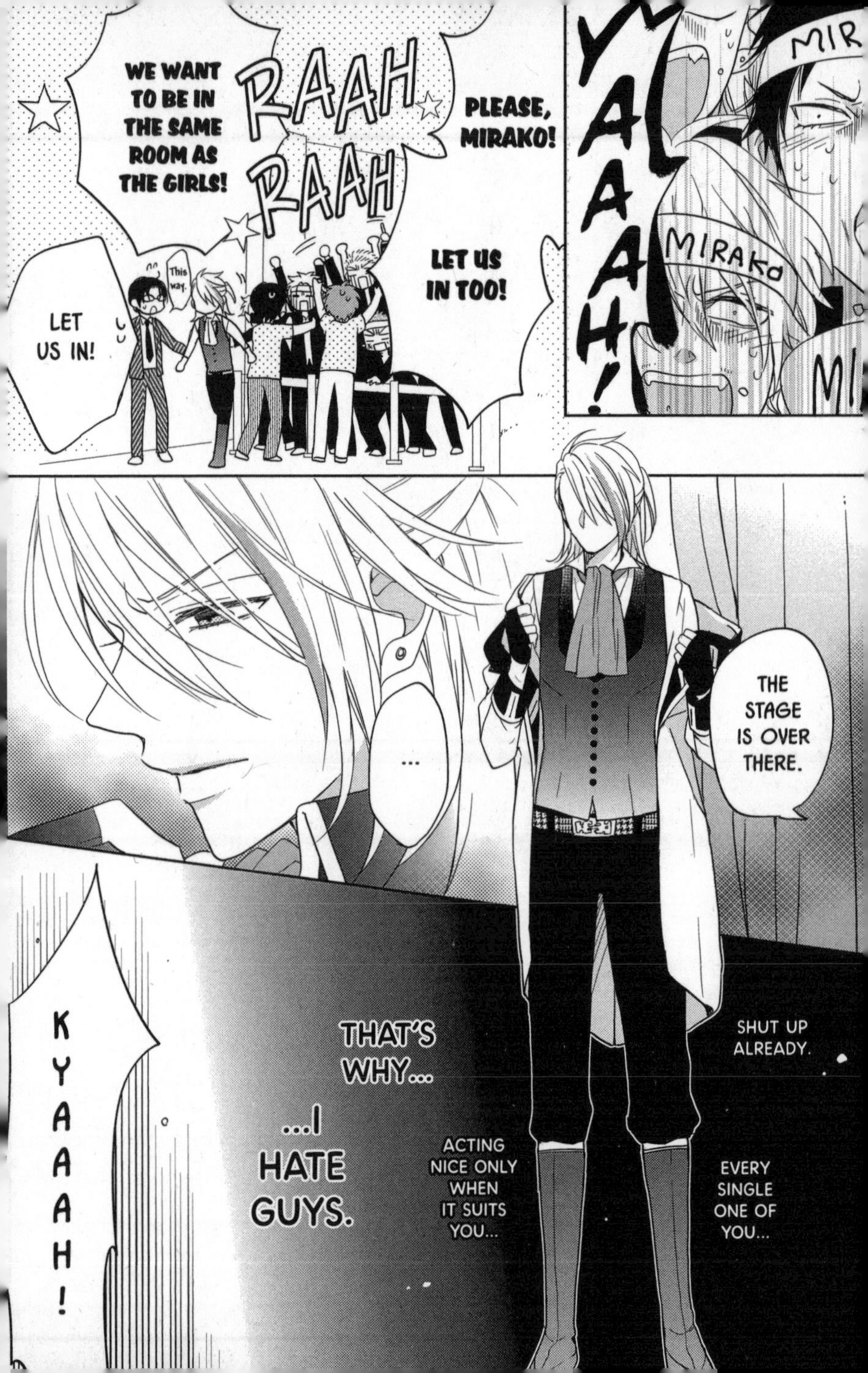
YAAAAH!
MIR
MIRAKO
MI
PLEASE, MIRAKO!
RAAH RAAH
WE WANT TO BE IN THE SAME ROOM AS THE GIRLS!
LET US IN TOO!
This way.
LET US IN!
THE STAGE IS OVER THERE.
SHUT UP ALREADY.
EVERY SINGLE ONE OF YOU...
ACTING NICE ONLY WHEN IT SUITS YOU...
THAT'S WHY...
...I HATE GUYS.
...
KYAAAAH!

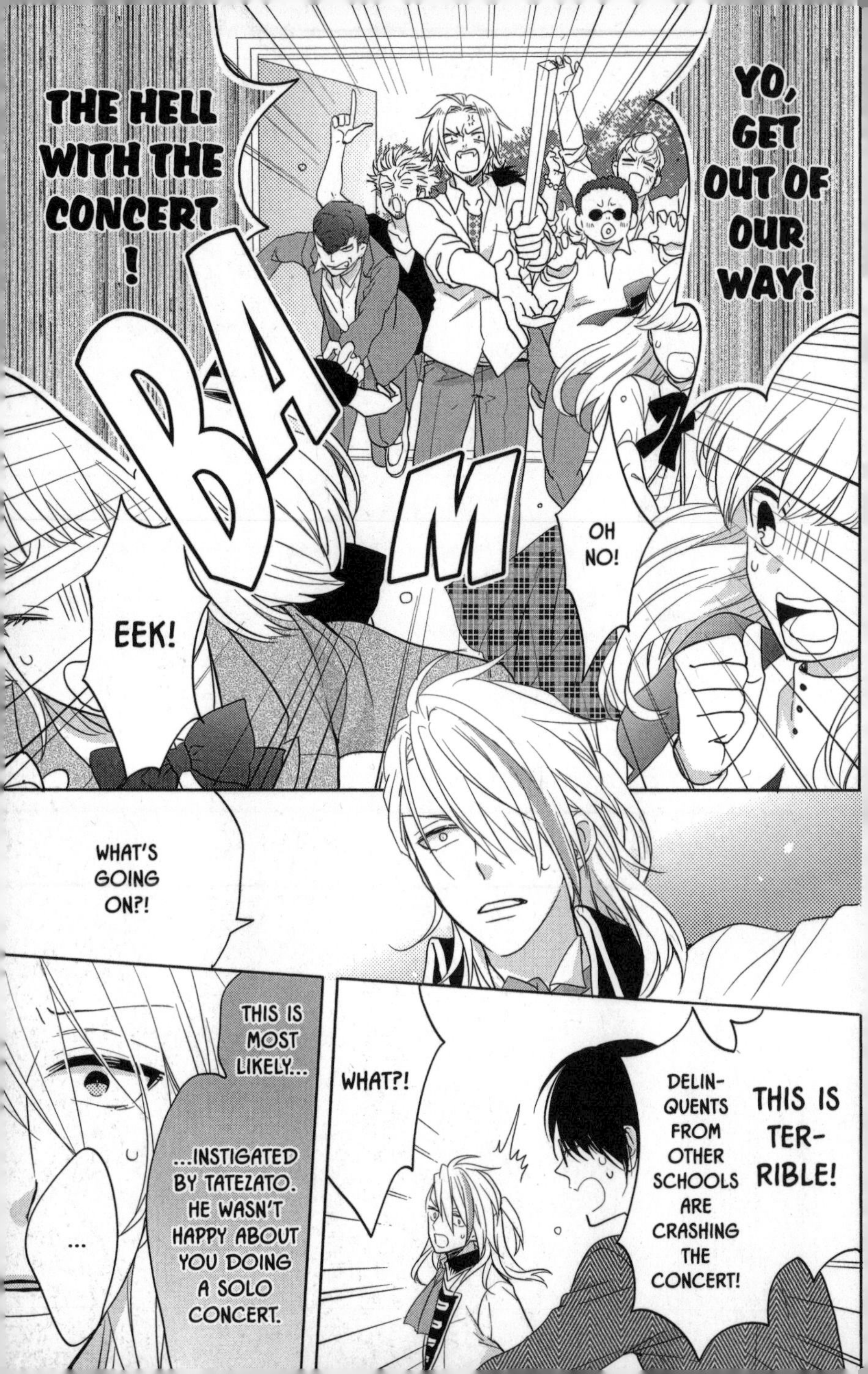
YO, GET OUT OF OUR WAY!
THE HELL WITH THE CONCERT!
BAM
OH NO!
EEK!
WHAT'S GOING ON?!
THIS IS TERRIBLE!
DELIN-QUENTS FROM OTHER SCHOOLS ARE CRASHING THE CONCERT!
WHAT?!
THIS IS MOST LIKELY...
...INSTIGATED BY TATEZATO. HE WASN'T HAPPY ABOUT YOU DOING A SOLO CONCERT.
...

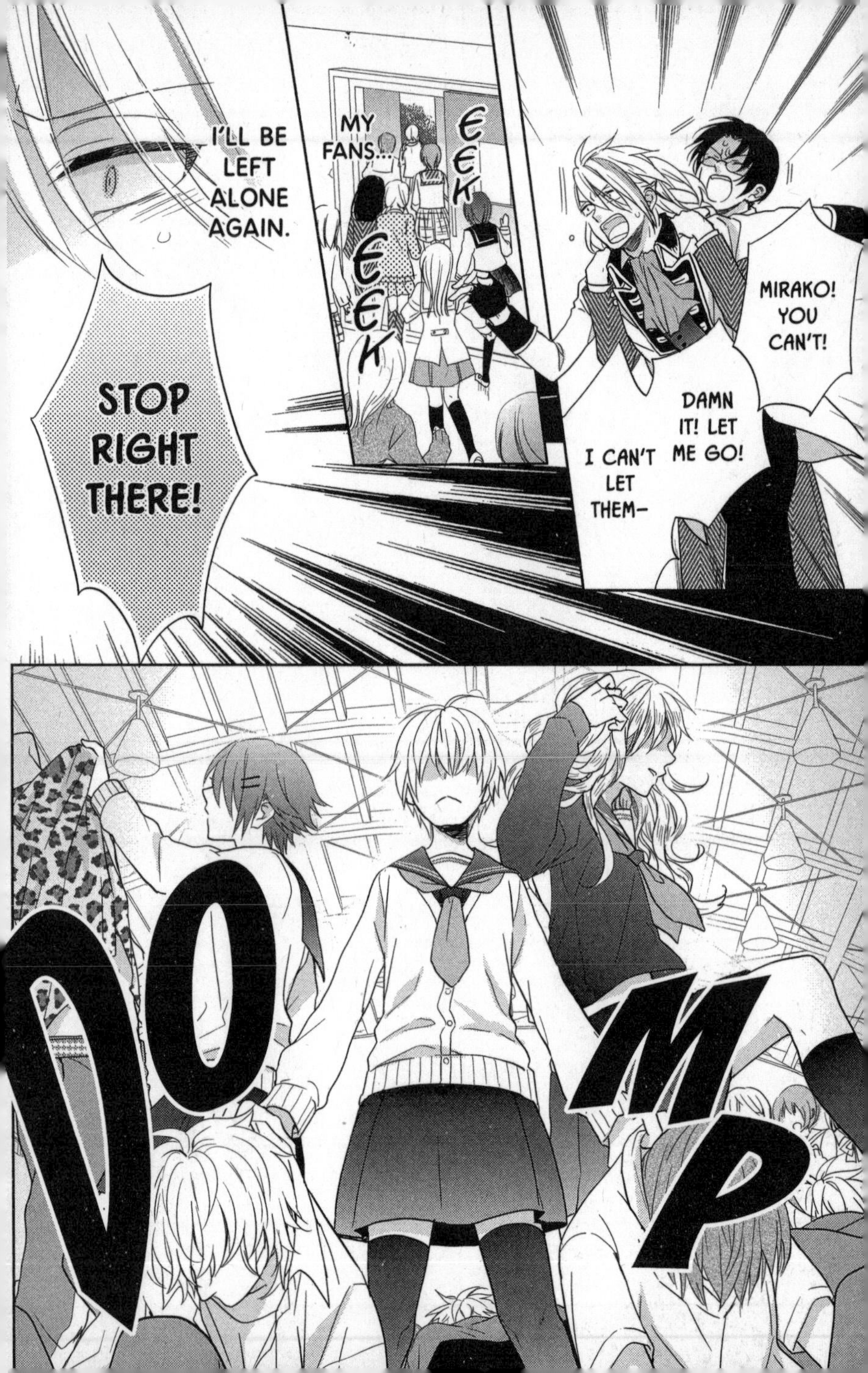
MIRAKO! YOU CAN'T!
DAMN IT! LET ME GO!
I CAN'T LET THEM—
EEK
MY FANS...
EEK
I'LL BE LEFT ALONE AGAIN.
STOP RIGHT THERE!
DOMP

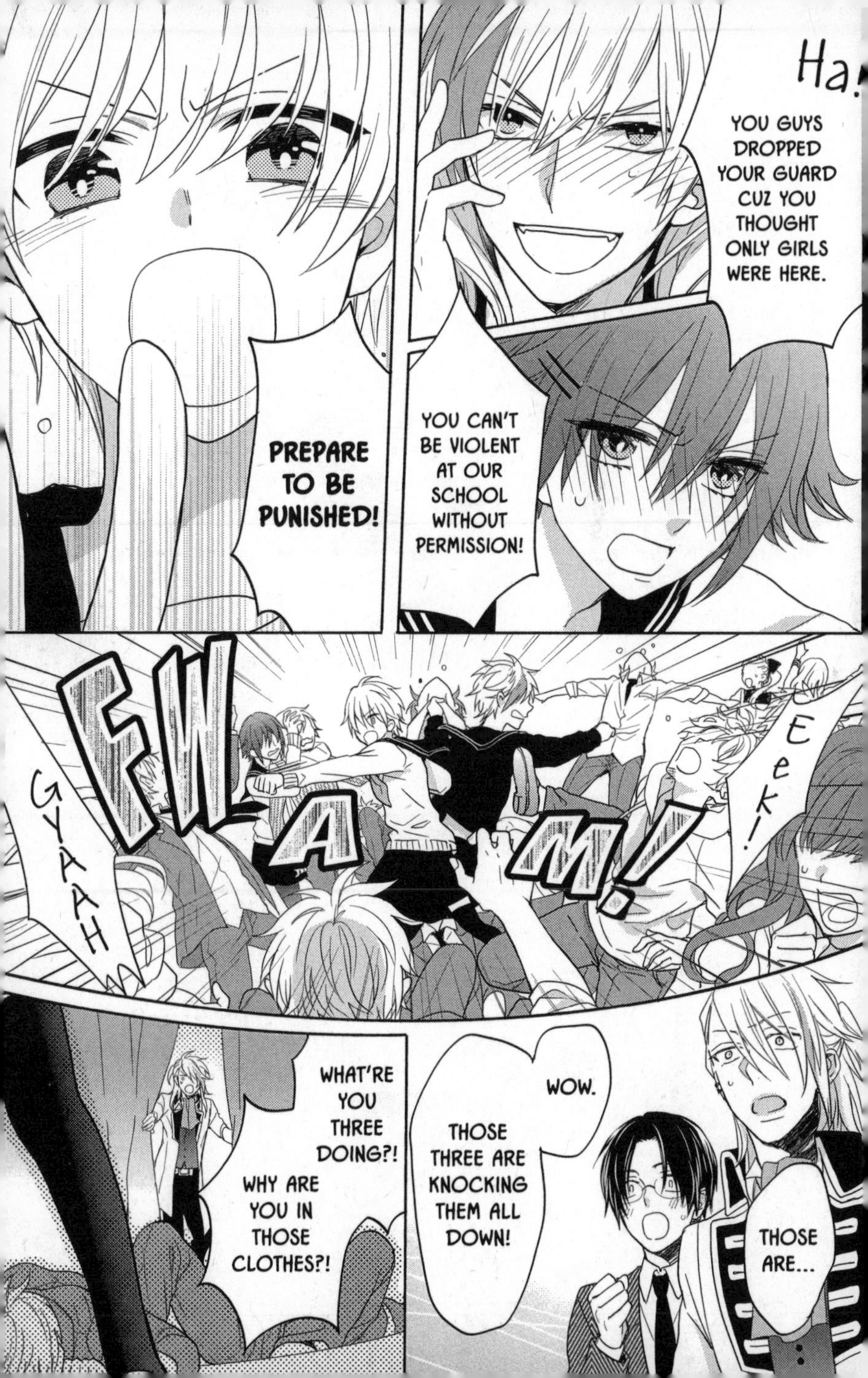
Ha!
YOU GUYS DROPPED YOUR GUARD CUZ YOU THOUGHT ONLY GIRLS WERE HERE.
YOU CAN'T BE VIOLENT AT OUR SCHOOL WITHOUT PERMISSION!
PREPARE TO BE PUNISHED!
Eek!
FWAM!
GYAAAH
THOSE ARE...
WOW.
THOSE THREE ARE KNOCKING THEM ALL DOWN!
WHAT'RE YOU THREE DOING?!
WHY ARE YOU IN THOSE CLOTHES?!

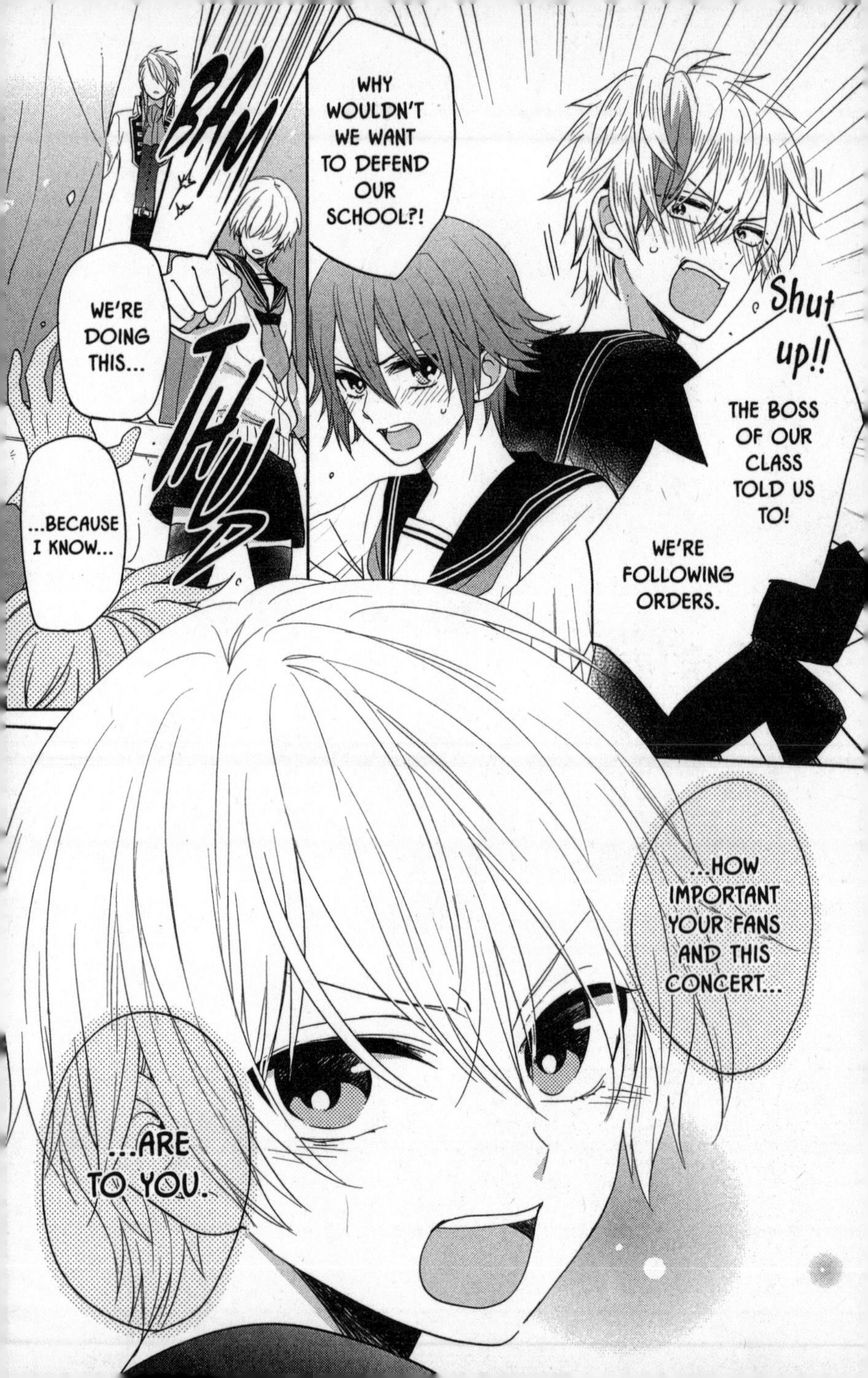
WHY WOULDN'T WE WANT TO DEFEND OUR SCHOOL?!
Shut up!!
THE BOSS OF OUR CLASS TOLD US TO!
WE'RE FOLLOWING ORDERS.
BAM
WE'RE DOING THIS...
THUD
...BECAUSE I KNOW...
...HOW IMPORTANT YOUR FANS AND THIS CONCERT...
...ARE TO YOU.

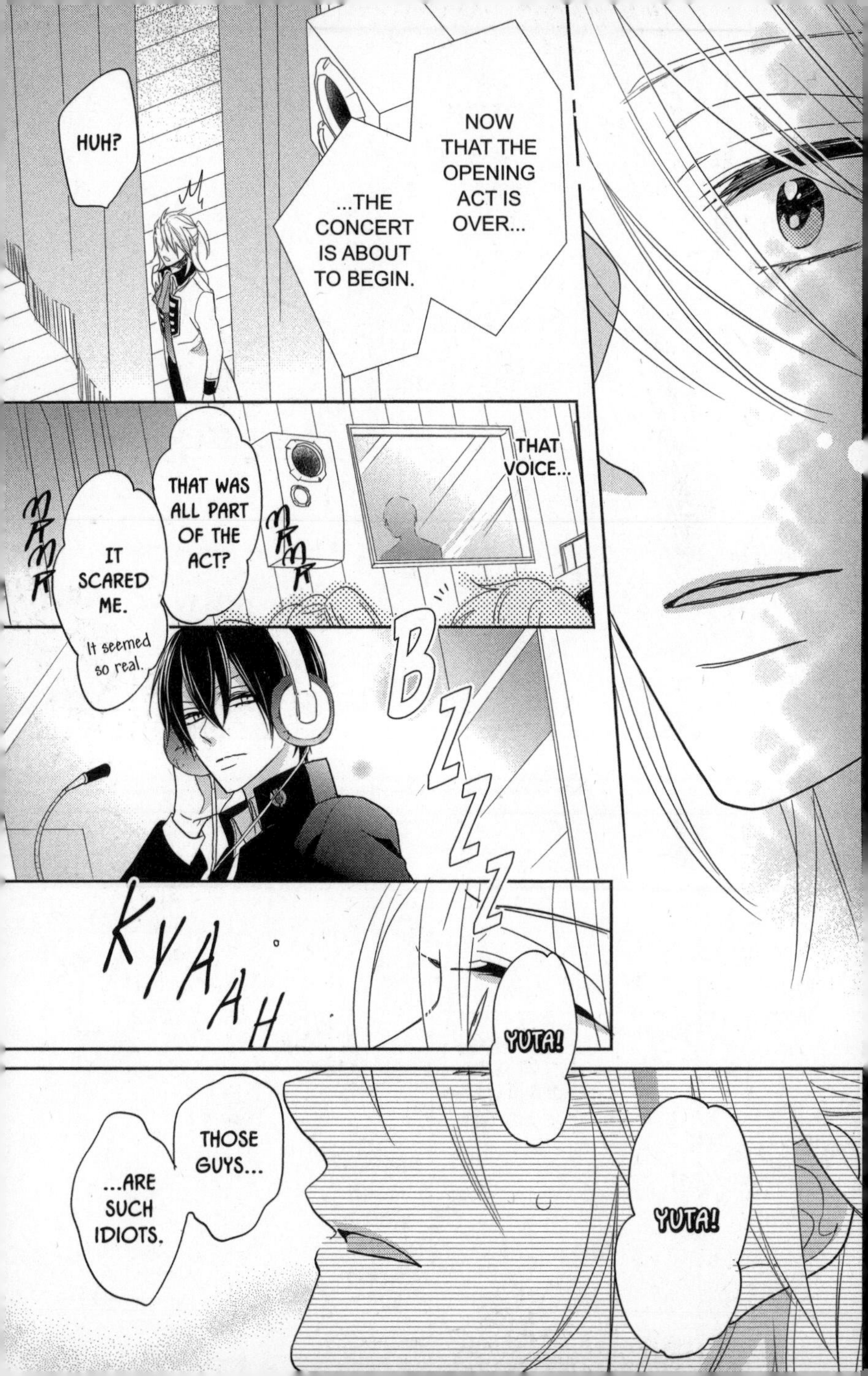
NOW THAT THE OPENING ACT IS OVER...
...THE CONCERT IS ABOUT TO BEGIN.
HUH?
THAT WAS ALL PART OF THE ACT?
IT SCARED ME.
It seemed so real.
MMMM
MMMM
THAT VOICE...
BZZZZ
KYAAH
YUTA!
YUTA!
THOSE GUYS...
...ARE SUCH IDIOTS.

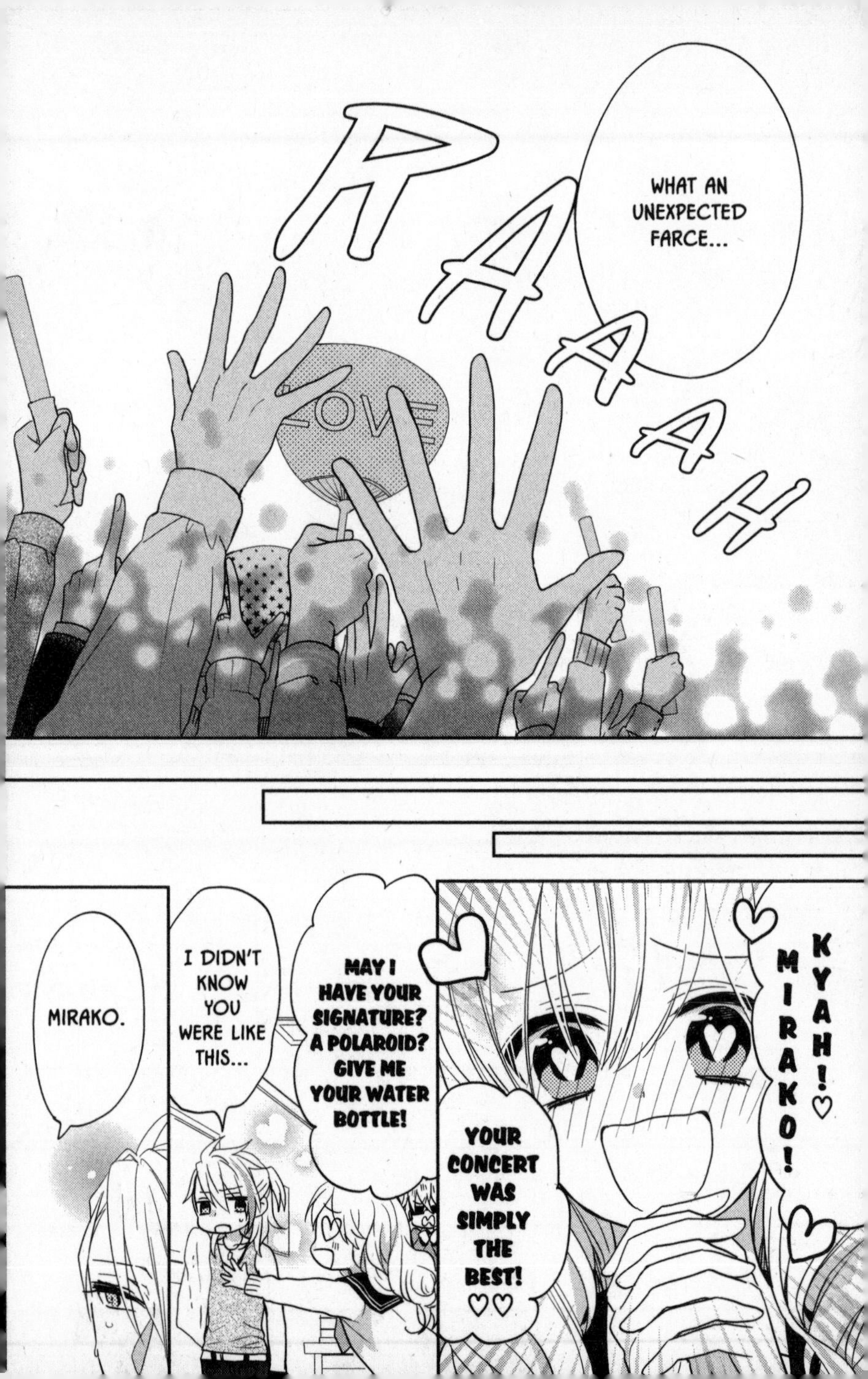
WHAT AN UNEXPECTED FARCE...
RAAAAH
KYAH! MIRAKO! ♡
YOUR CONCERT WAS SIMPLY THE BEST! ♡♡
MAY I HAVE YOUR SIGNATURE? A POLAROID? GIVE ME YOUR WATER BOTTLE!
I DIDN'T KNOW YOU WERE LIKE THIS...
MIRAKO.

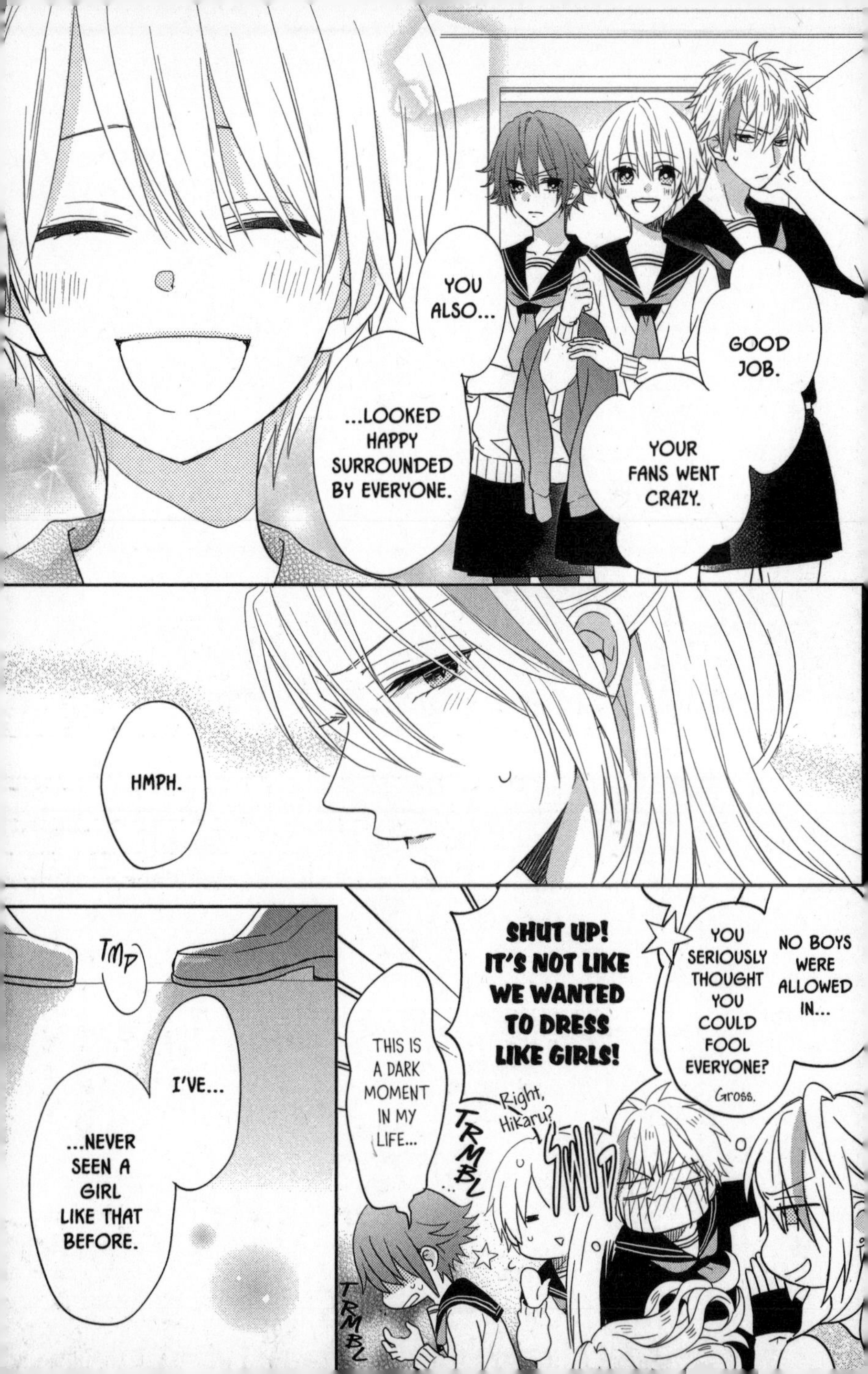
GOOD JOB.
YOUR FANS WENT CRAZY.
YOU ALSO...
...LOOKED HAPPY SURROUNDED BY EVERYONE.
HMPH.
NO BOYS WERE ALLOWED IN...
YOU SERIOUSLY THOUGHT YOU COULD FOOL EVERYONE?
Gross.
SHUT UP! IT'S NOT LIKE WE WANTED TO DRESS LIKE GIRLS!
Right, Hikaru?
SWIP
THIS IS A DARK MOMENT IN MY LIFE...
TRMBL
TRMBL
TMP
I'VE...
...NEVER SEEN A GIRL LIKE THAT BEFORE.

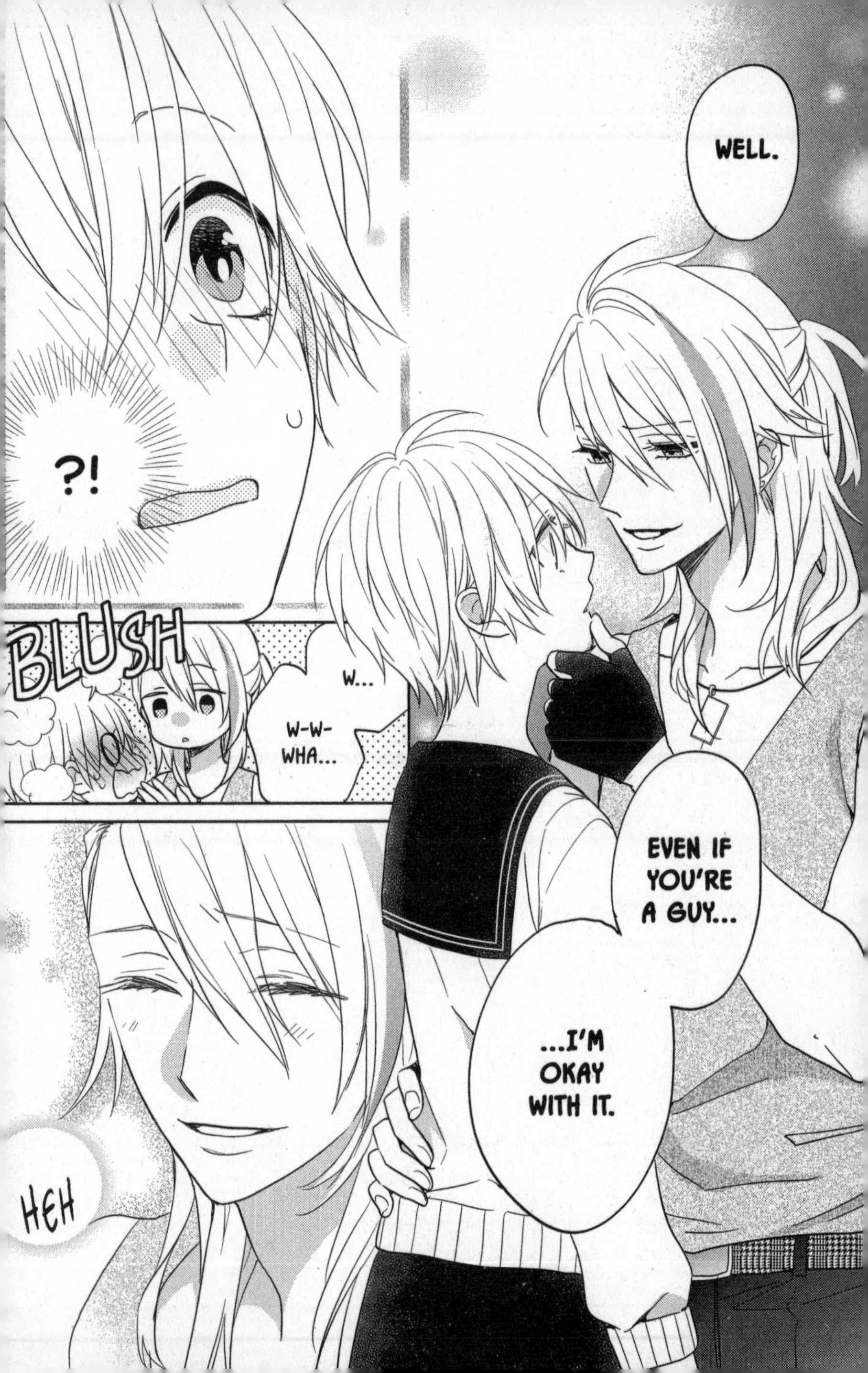
WELL.
EVEN IF YOU'RE A GUY...
...I'M OKAY WITH IT.
?!
BLUSH
W...
W-W-WHA...
HEH

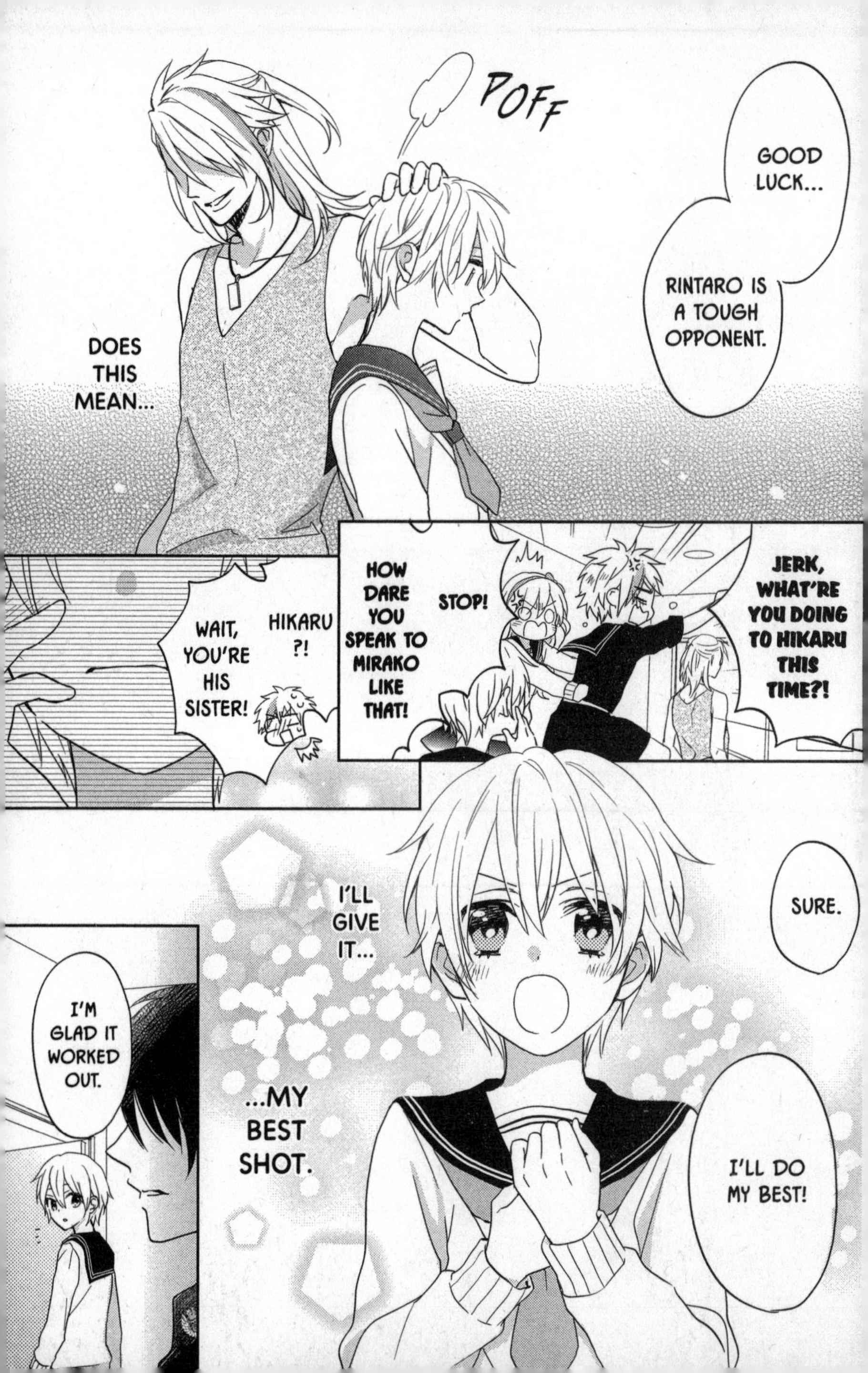
POFF
GOOD LUCK...
RINTARO IS A TOUGH OPPONENT.
DOES THIS MEAN...
JERK, WHAT'RE YOU DOING TO HIKARU THIS TIME?!
STOP!
HOW DARE YOU SPEAK TO MIRAKO LIKE THAT!
HIKARU ?!
WAIT, YOU'RE HIS SISTER!
SURE.
I'LL DO MY BEST!
I'LL GIVE IT...
...MY BEST SHOT.
I'M GLAD IT WORKED OUT.

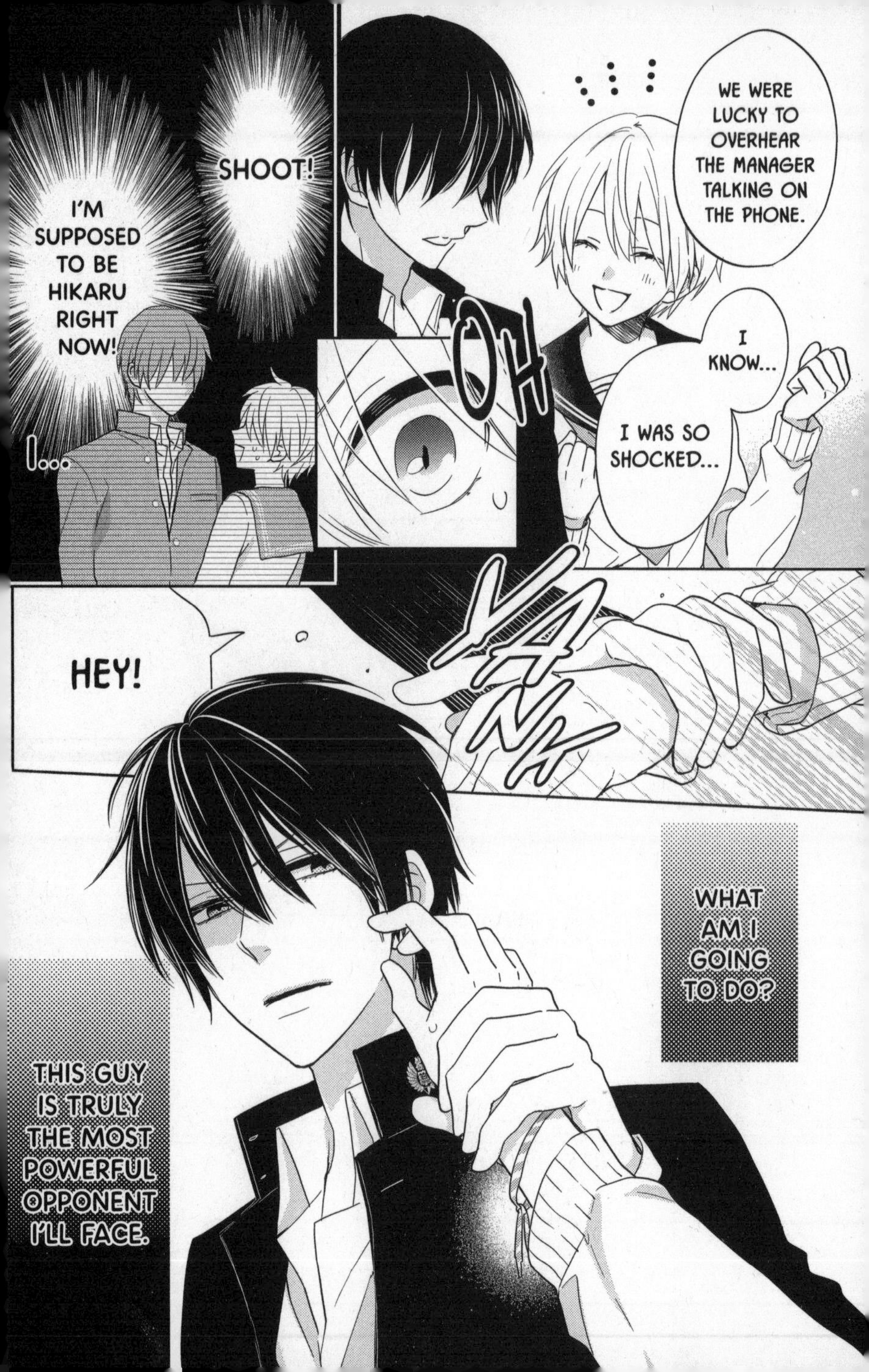
...
WE WERE LUCKY TO OVERHEAR THE MANAGER TALKING ON THE PHONE.
I KNOW...
I WAS SO SHOCKED...
OH
SHOOT!
I'M SUPPOSED TO BE HIKARU RIGHT NOW!
I...
YANK
HEY!
WHAT AM I GOING TO DO?
THIS GUY IS TRULY THE MOST POWERFUL OPPONENT I'LL FACE.

KENKA BANCHO
Otome

IT'S TABOO TO STAND OUT

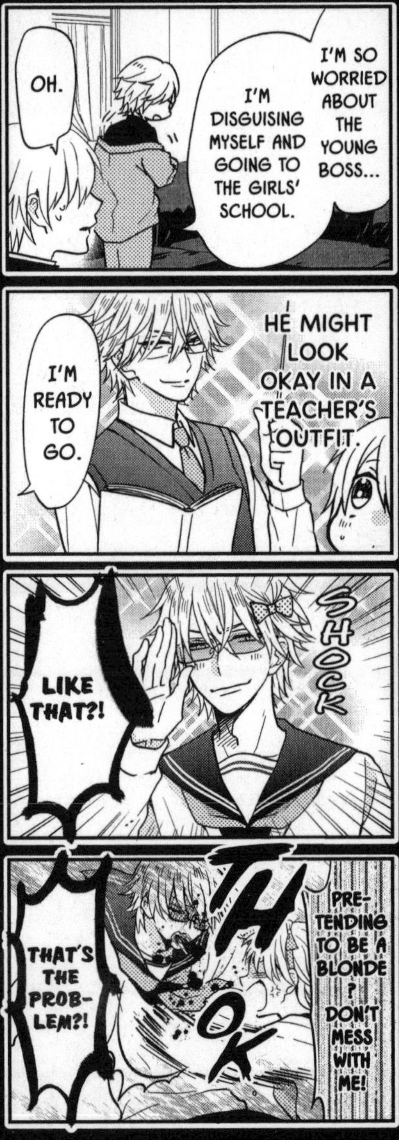
I'M SO WORRIED ABOUT THE YOUNG BOSS...
I'M DISGUISING MYSELF AND GOING TO THE GIRLS' SCHOOL.
OH.
HE MIGHT LOOK OKAY IN A TEACHER'S OUTFIT.
I'M READY TO GO.
SHOCK
LIKE THAT?!
PRE-TENDING TO BE A BLONDE? DON'T MESS WITH ME!
THAT'S THE PROB-LEM?!

CARROT & STICK, HOT & COLD

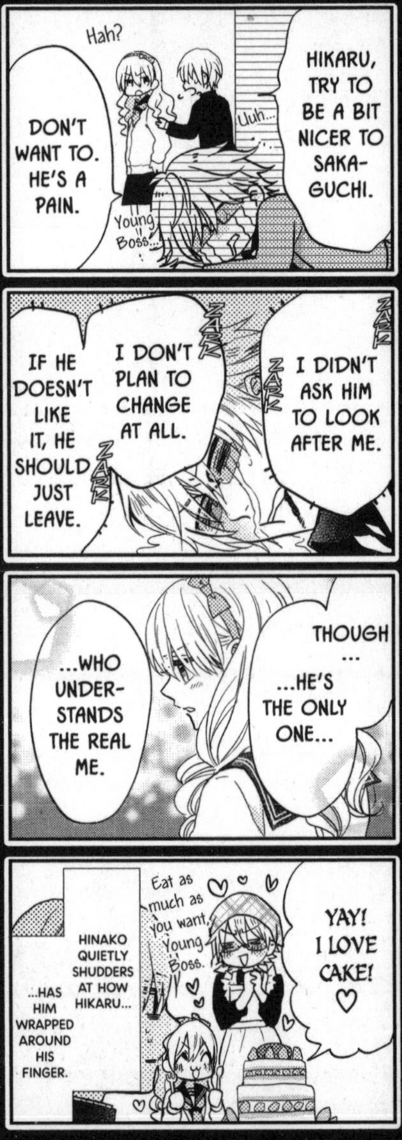
HIKARU, TRY TO BE A BIT NICER TO SAKA-GUCHI.
Uuh...
Hah?
DON'T WANT TO. HE'S A PAIN.
Young Boss...
ZARK
I DIDN'T ASK HIM TO LOOK AFTER ME.
I DON'T PLAN TO CHANGE AT ALL.
IF HE DOESN'T LIKE IT, HE SHOULD JUST LEAVE.
THOUGH...
...HE'S THE ONLY ONE...
...WHO UNDER-STANDS THE REAL ME.
YAY! I LOVE CAKE! ♡
Eat as much as you want, Young Boss.
HINAKO QUIETLY SHUDDERS AT HOW HIKARU...
...HAS HIM WRAPPED AROUND HIS FINGER.

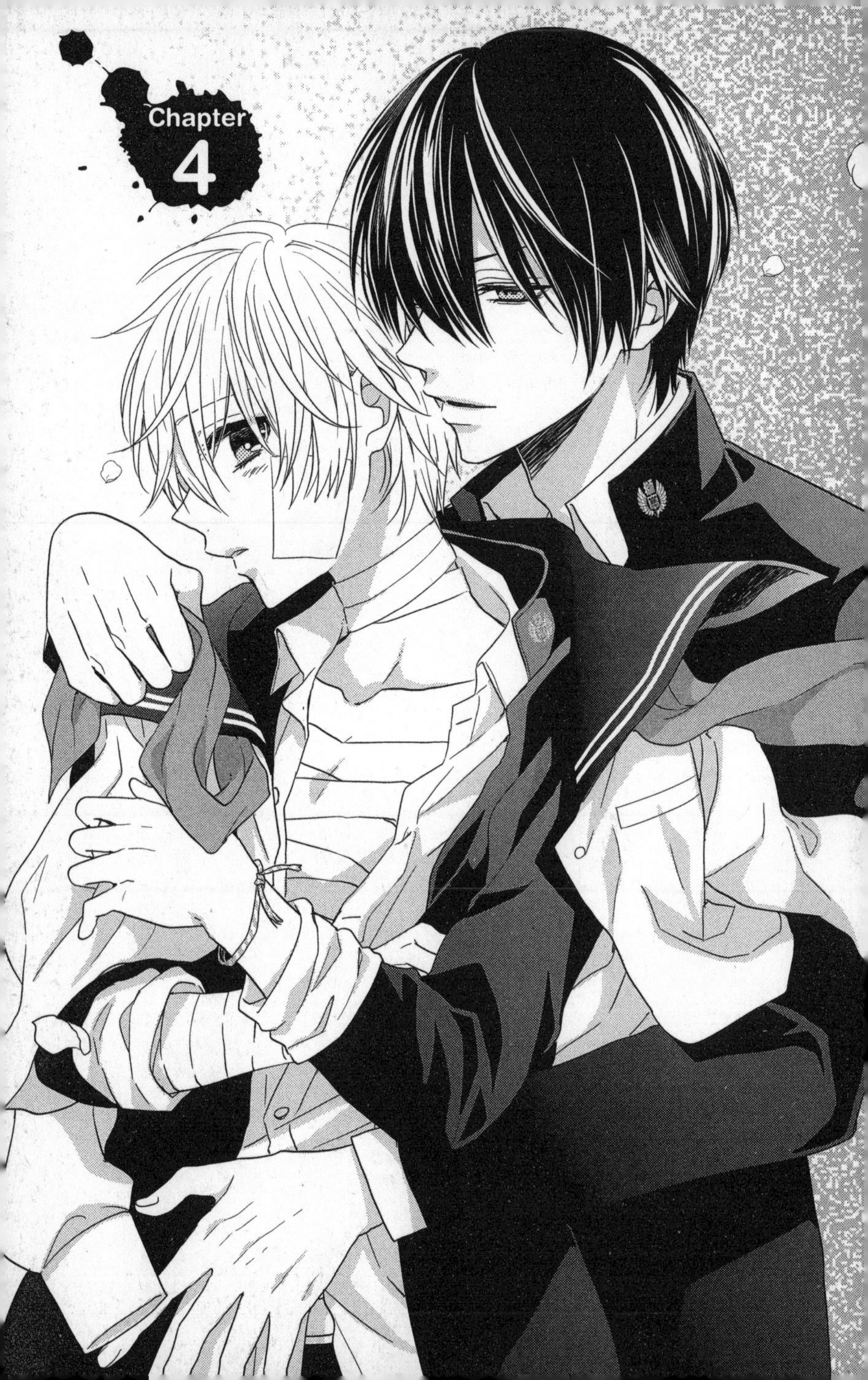
Chapter
4

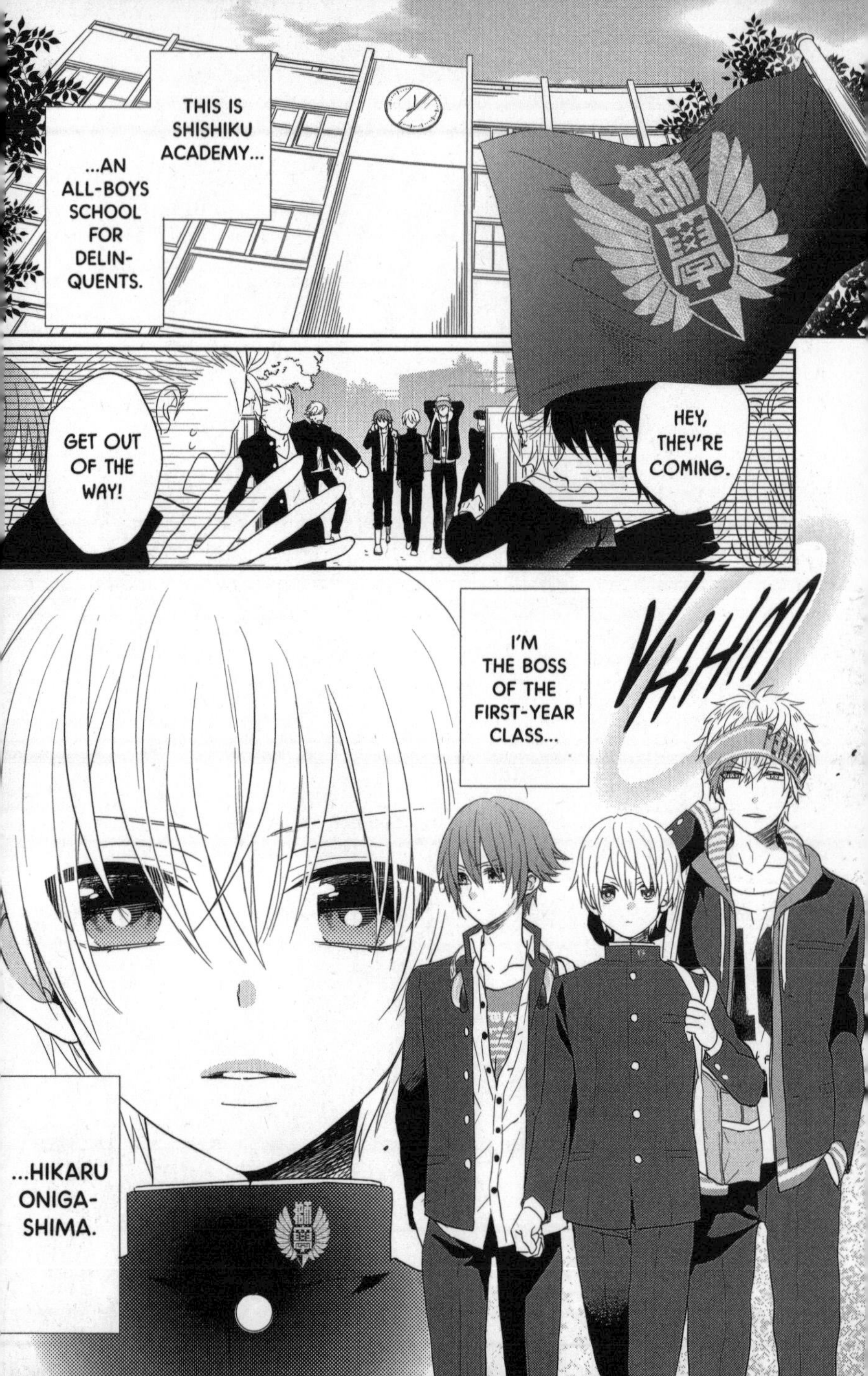
THIS IS SHISHIKU ACADEMY...
...AN ALL-BOYS SCHOOL FOR DELIN- QUENTS.
HEY, THEY'RE COMING.
GET OUT OF THE WAY!
I'M THE BOSS OF THE FIRST-YEAR CLASS...
...HIKARU ONIGA- SHIMA.

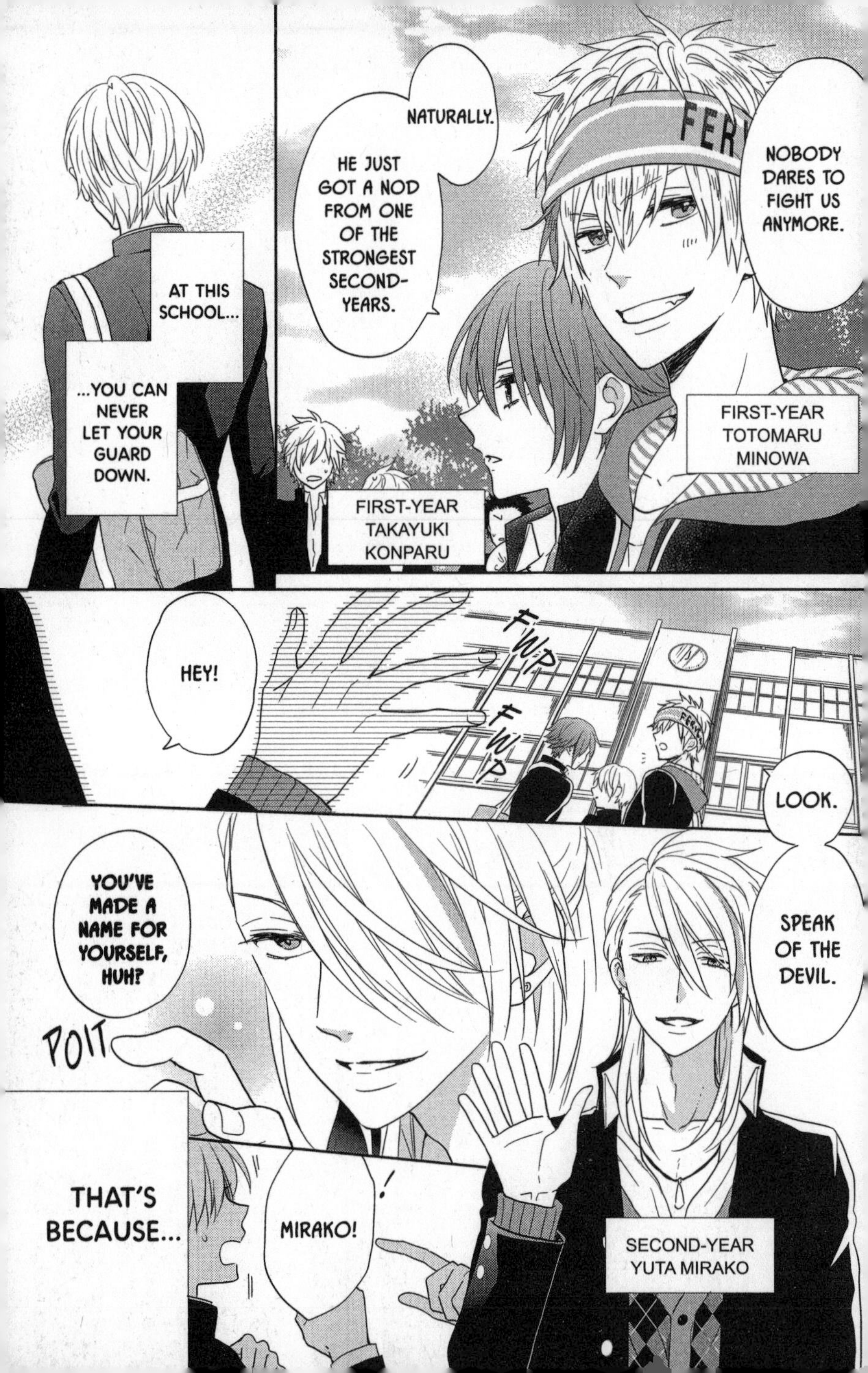
NOBODY DARES TO FIGHT US ANYMORE.
NATURALLY.
HE JUST GOT A NOD FROM ONE OF THE STRONGEST SECOND-YEARS.
FIRST-YEAR TOTOMARU MINOWA
FIRST-YEAR TAKAYUKI KONPARU
AT THIS SCHOOL...
...YOU CAN NEVER LET YOUR GUARD DOWN.
LOOK.
HEY!
FWP
FWP
SPEAK OF THE DEVIL.
SECOND-YEAR YUTA MIRAKO
YOU'VE MADE A NAME FOR YOURSELF, HUH?
POIT
MIRAKO!
THAT'S BECAUSE...

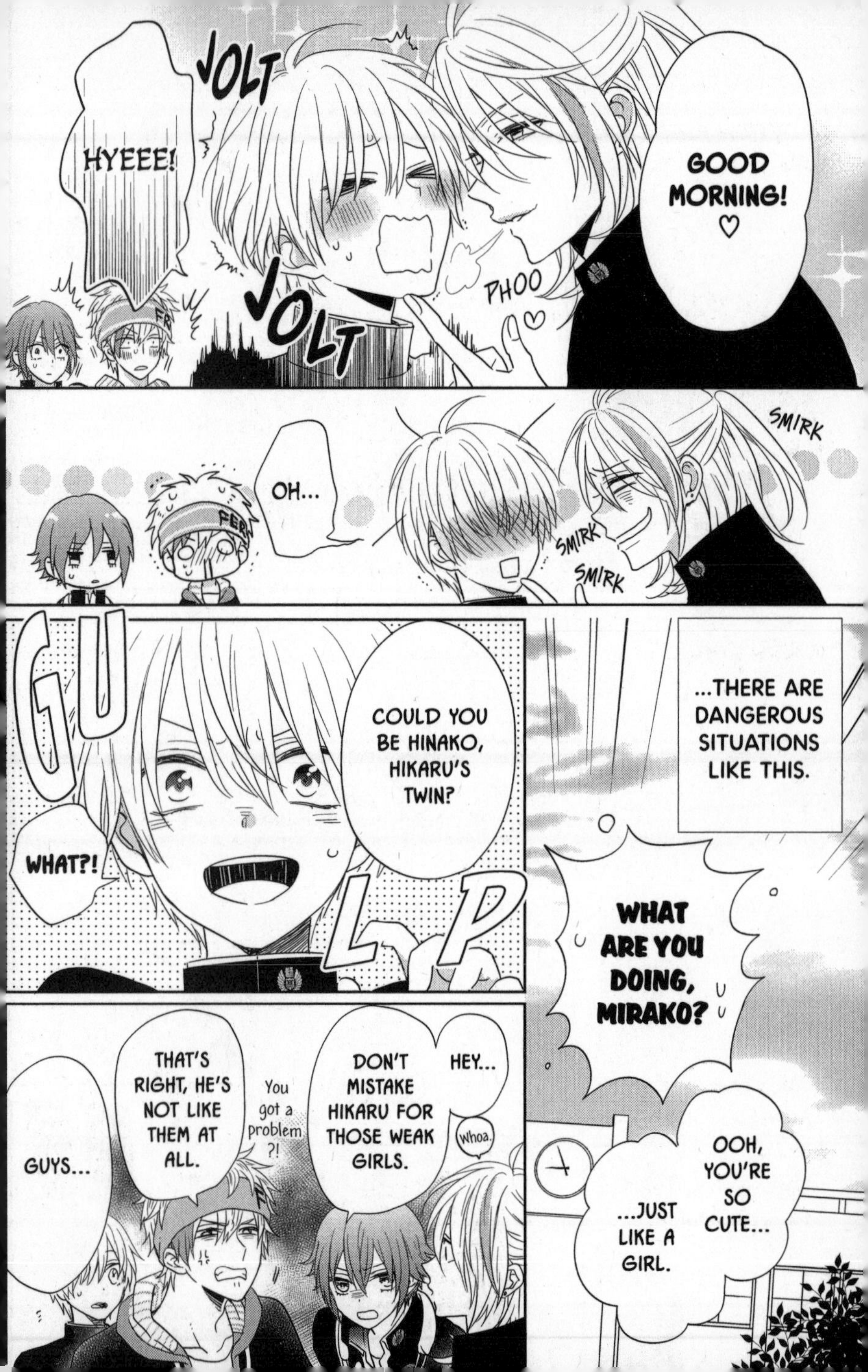
GOOD MORNING! ♡
PHOO ♡
JOLT
JOLT
HYEEE!
SMIRK
SMIRK
SMIRK
OH...
...THERE ARE DANGEROUS SITUATIONS LIKE THIS.
WHAT ARE YOU DOING, MIRAKO?
OOH, YOU'RE SO CUTE...
...JUST LIKE A GIRL.
COULD YOU BE HINAKO, HIKARU'S TWIN?
GU
LP
WHAT?!
HEY...
Whoa.
DON'T MISTAKE HIKARU FOR THOSE WEAK GIRLS.
You got a problem?!
THAT'S RIGHT, HE'S NOT LIKE THEM AT ALL.
GUYS...

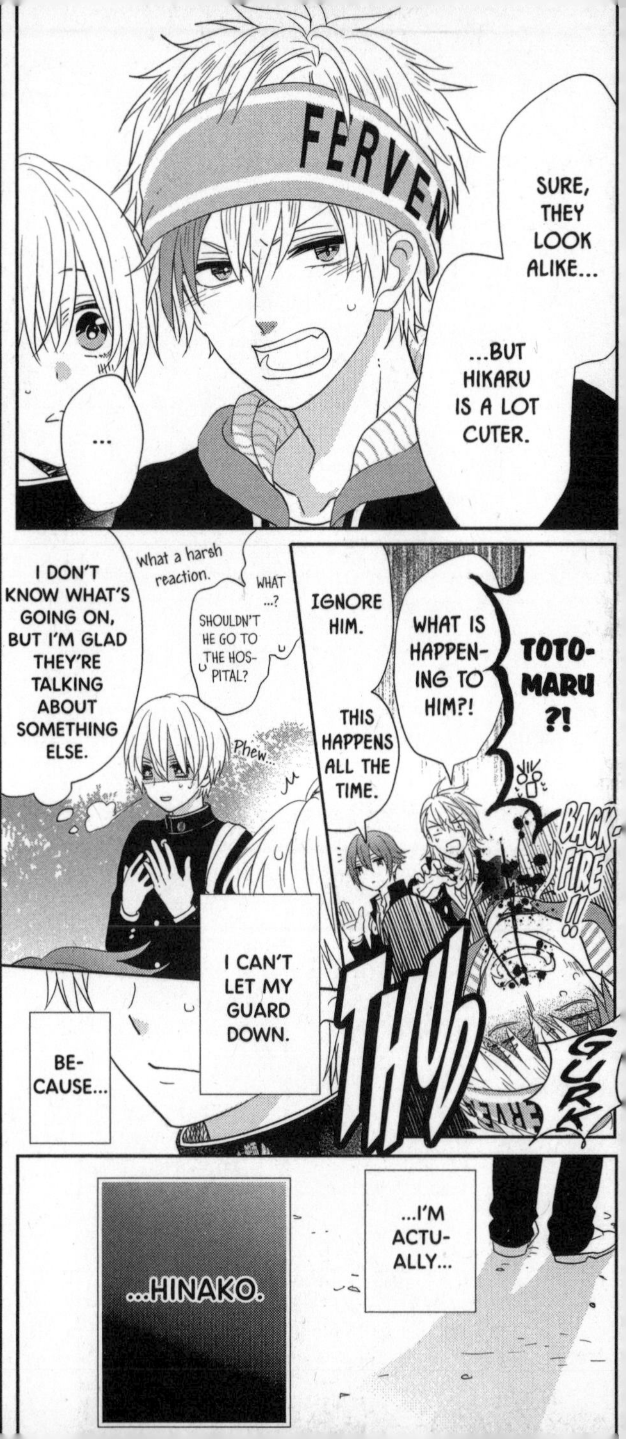
FERVEN
SURE, THEY LOOK ALIKE...
...BUT HIKARU IS A LOT CUTER.
...
TOTO-MARU?!
WHAT IS HAPPEN-ING TO HIM?!
IGNORE HIM.
THIS HAPPENS ALL THE TIME.
BACK-FIRE!!
GURK
THUD
WHAT ...?
SHOULDN'T HE GO TO THE HOS-PITAL?
What a harsh reaction.
I DON'T KNOW WHAT'S GOING ON, BUT I'M GLAD THEY'RE TALKING ABOUT SOMETHING ELSE.
Phew...
I CAN'T LET MY GUARD DOWN.
BE-CAUSE...
...I'M ACTU-ALLY...
...HINAKO.

THIRD-YEAR, PAULOWNIA CLASS

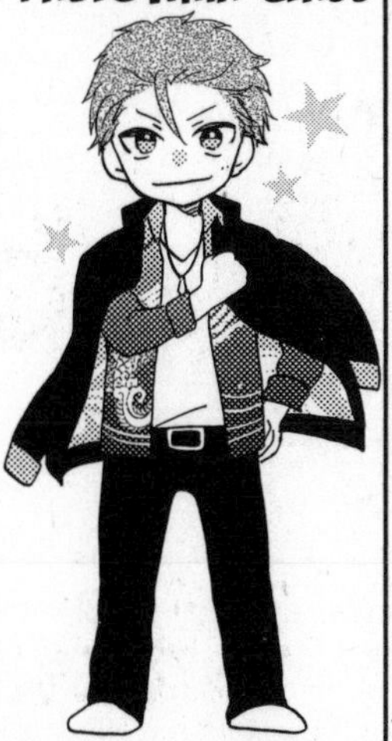

HOUOU ONIGASHIMA

Height: 5'9"
Weight: 165 lbs
Blood Type: O
Birthday: December 16

He's still a secret character. Check out the game to find out who he really is. When I see him, I suddenly have this strange desire for him to carry me on his shoulders.

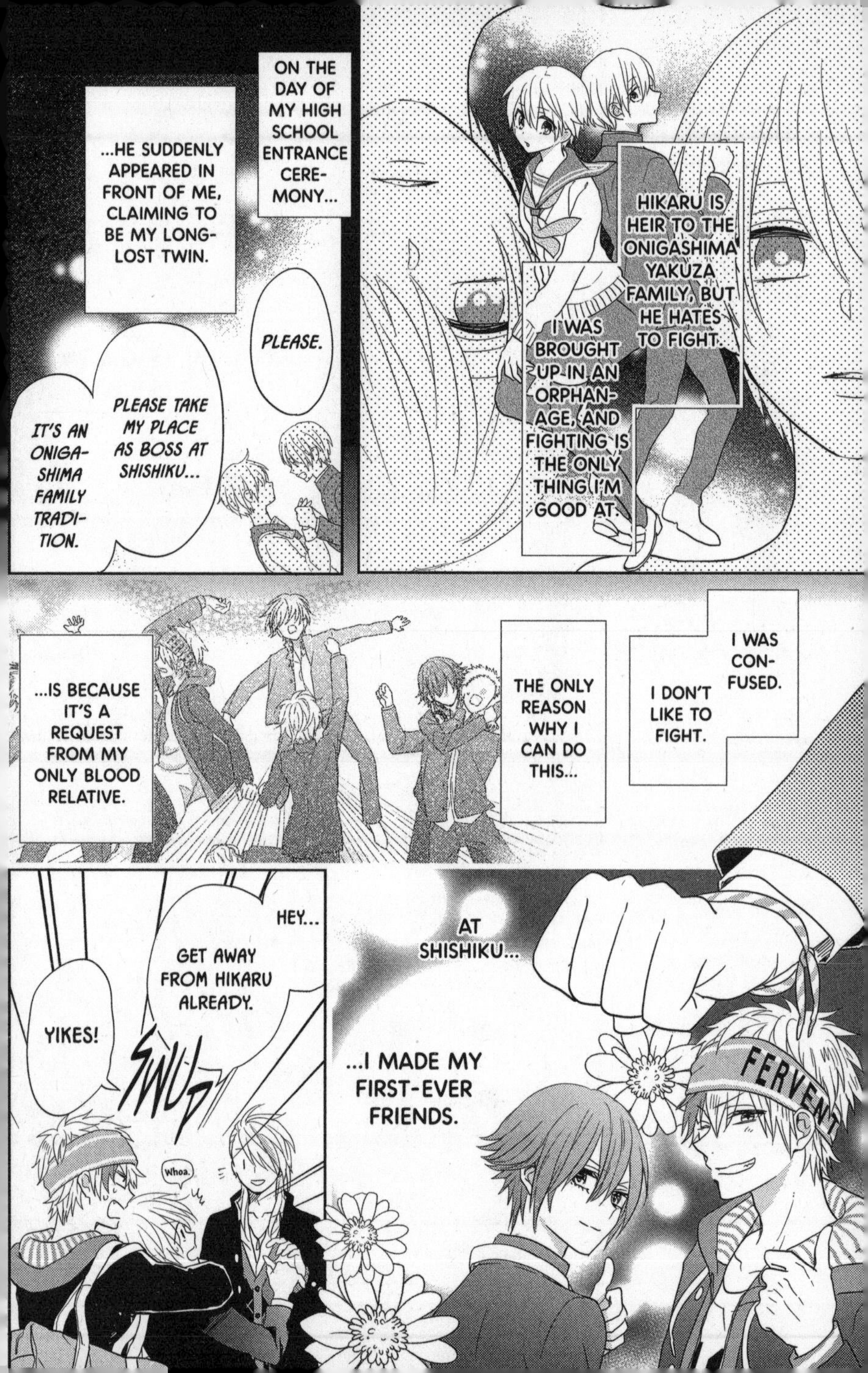
HIKARU IS HEIR TO THE ONIGASHIMA YAKUZA FAMILY, BUT HE HATES TO FIGHT.
I WAS BROUGHT UP IN AN ORPHANAGE, AND FIGHTING IS THE ONLY THING I'M GOOD AT.
ON THE DAY OF MY HIGH SCHOOL ENTRANCE CEREMONY...
...HE SUDDENLY APPEARED IN FRONT OF ME, CLAIMING TO BE MY LONG-LOST TWIN.
PLEASE.
PLEASE TAKE MY PLACE AS BOSS AT SHISHIKU...
IT'S AN ONIGASHIMA FAMILY TRADITION.
I WAS CONFUSED.
I DON'T LIKE TO FIGHT.
THE ONLY REASON WHY I CAN DO THIS...
...IS BECAUSE IT'S A REQUEST FROM MY ONLY BLOOD RELATIVE.
AT SHISHIKU...
...I MADE MY FIRST-EVER FRIENDS.
FERVENT
HEY...
GET AWAY FROM HIKARU ALREADY.
YIKES!
SWUP
Whoa.

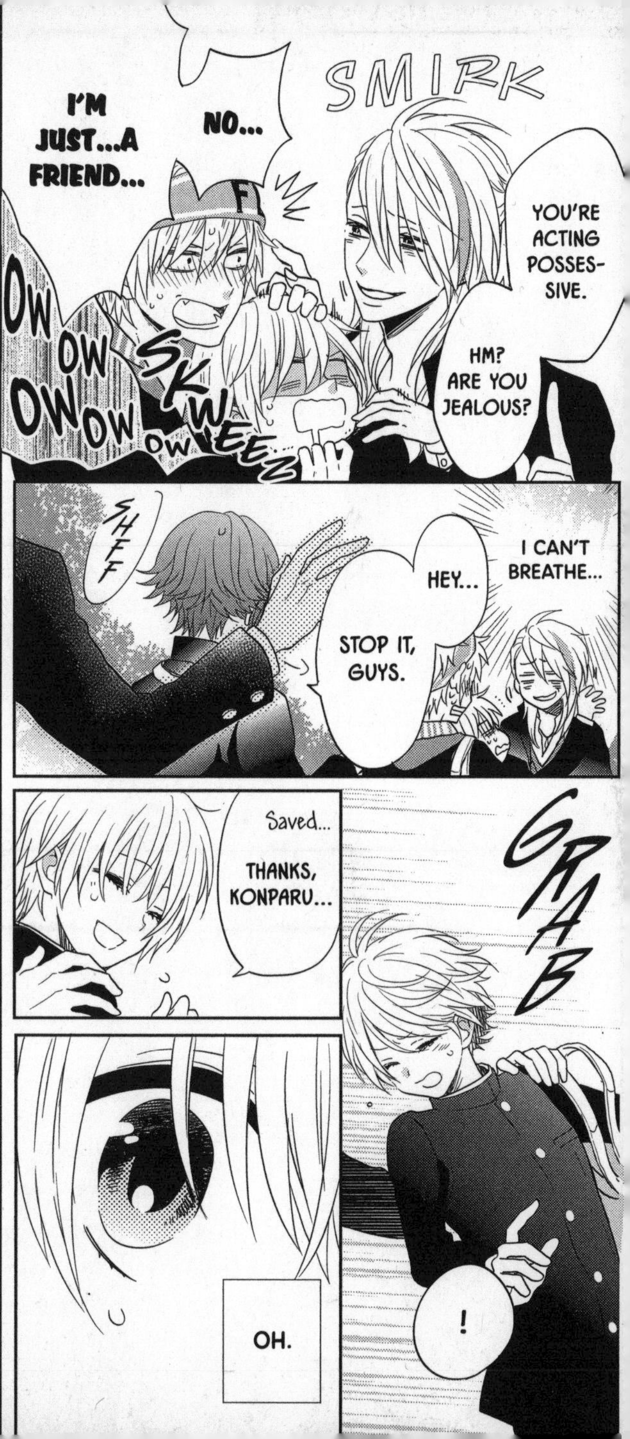
SMIRK
YOU'RE ACTING POSSES-SIVE.
HM? ARE YOU JEALOUS?
NO...
I'M JUST...A FRIEND...
SKWEEZ
OW OW OW OW OW OW
I CAN'T BREATHE...
HEY...
STOP IT, GUYS.
SHEFF
GRAB
!
Saved...
THANKS, KONPARU...
OH.

THE INVINCIBLE ONIGASHIMA GROUP

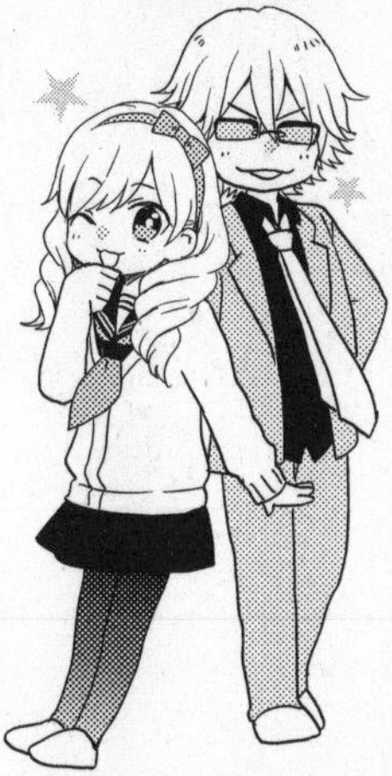

HIKARU ONIGASHIMA (MALE)

Height: 5'3"
Weight: 115 lbs
Blood Type: ?
Birthday: ?
Skill: Nail art

HARUO SAKAGUCHI

Height: 6'
Weight: 163 lbs
Blood Type: A
Birthday: March 30
Skill: Cooking

❀

I love these two. I want to keep following them.

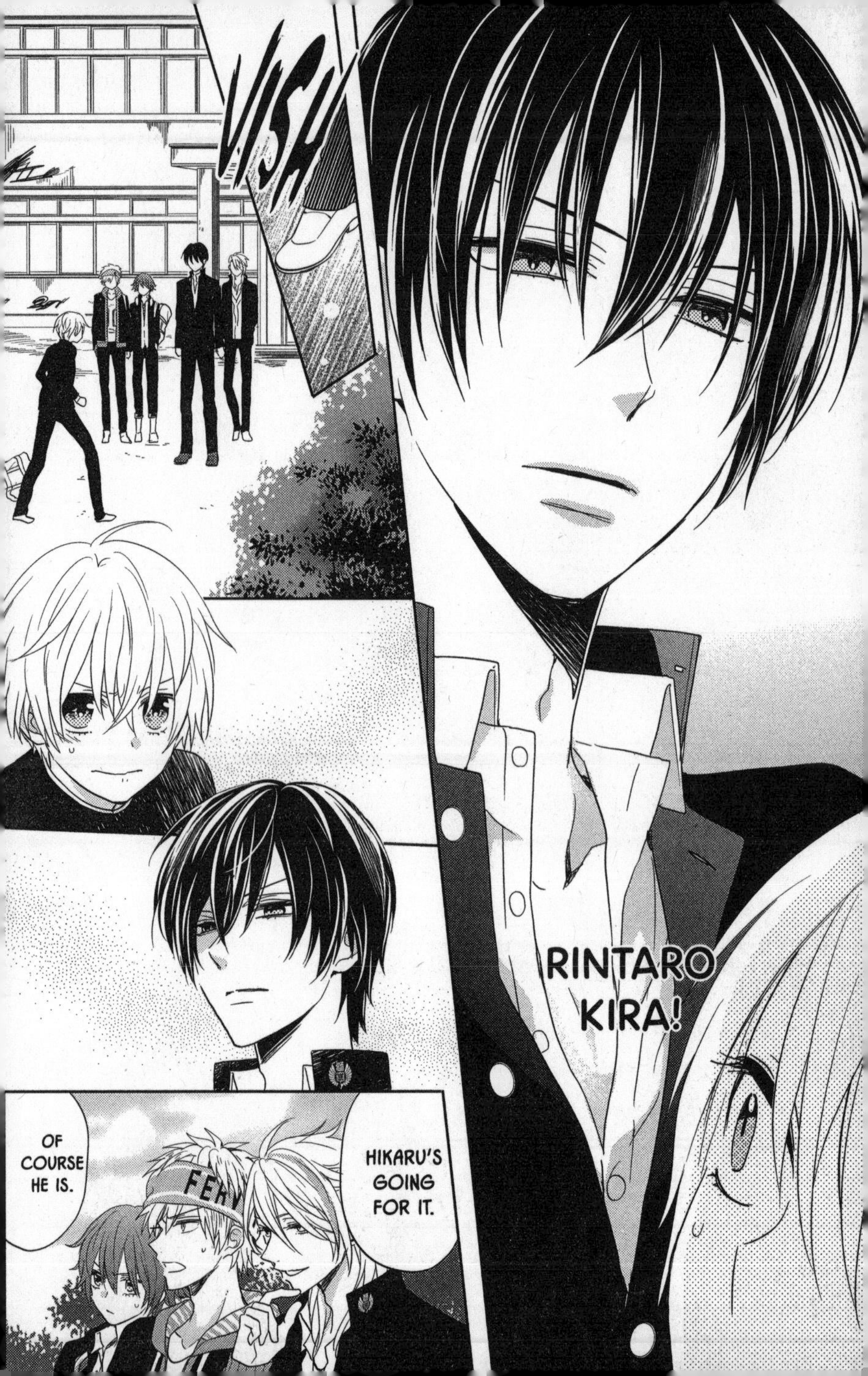
VISH
RINTARO KIRA!
HIKARU'S GOING FOR IT.
OF COURSE HE IS.

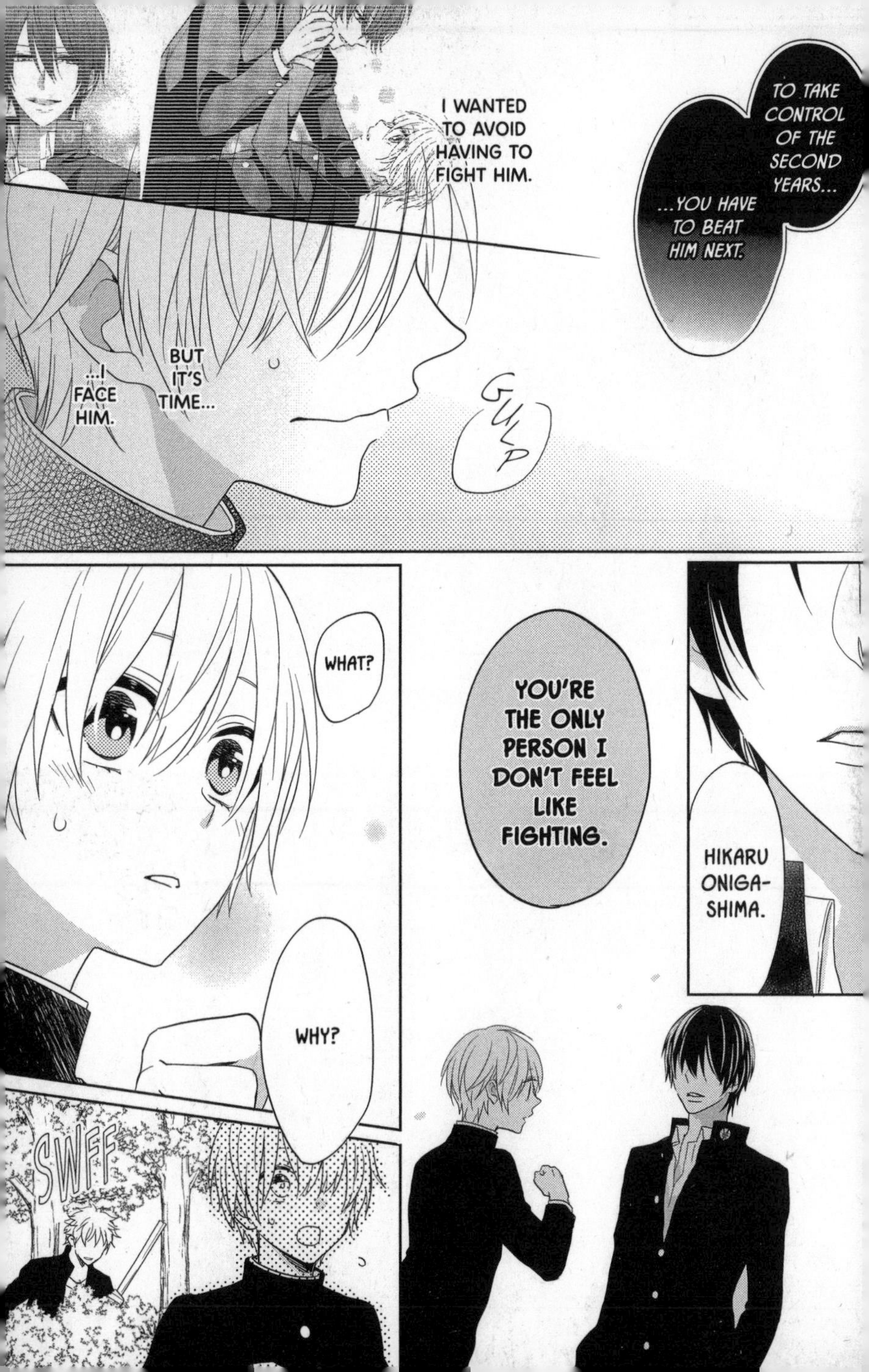
TO TAKE CONTROL OF THE SECOND YEARS...
...YOU HAVE TO BEAT HIM NEXT.
I WANTED TO AVOID HAVING TO FIGHT HIM.
BUT IT'S TIME...
...I FACE HIM.
GULP
HIKARU ONIGA-SHIMA.
YOU'RE THE ONLY PERSON I DON'T FEEL LIKE FIGHTING.
WHAT?
WHY?
SWFF

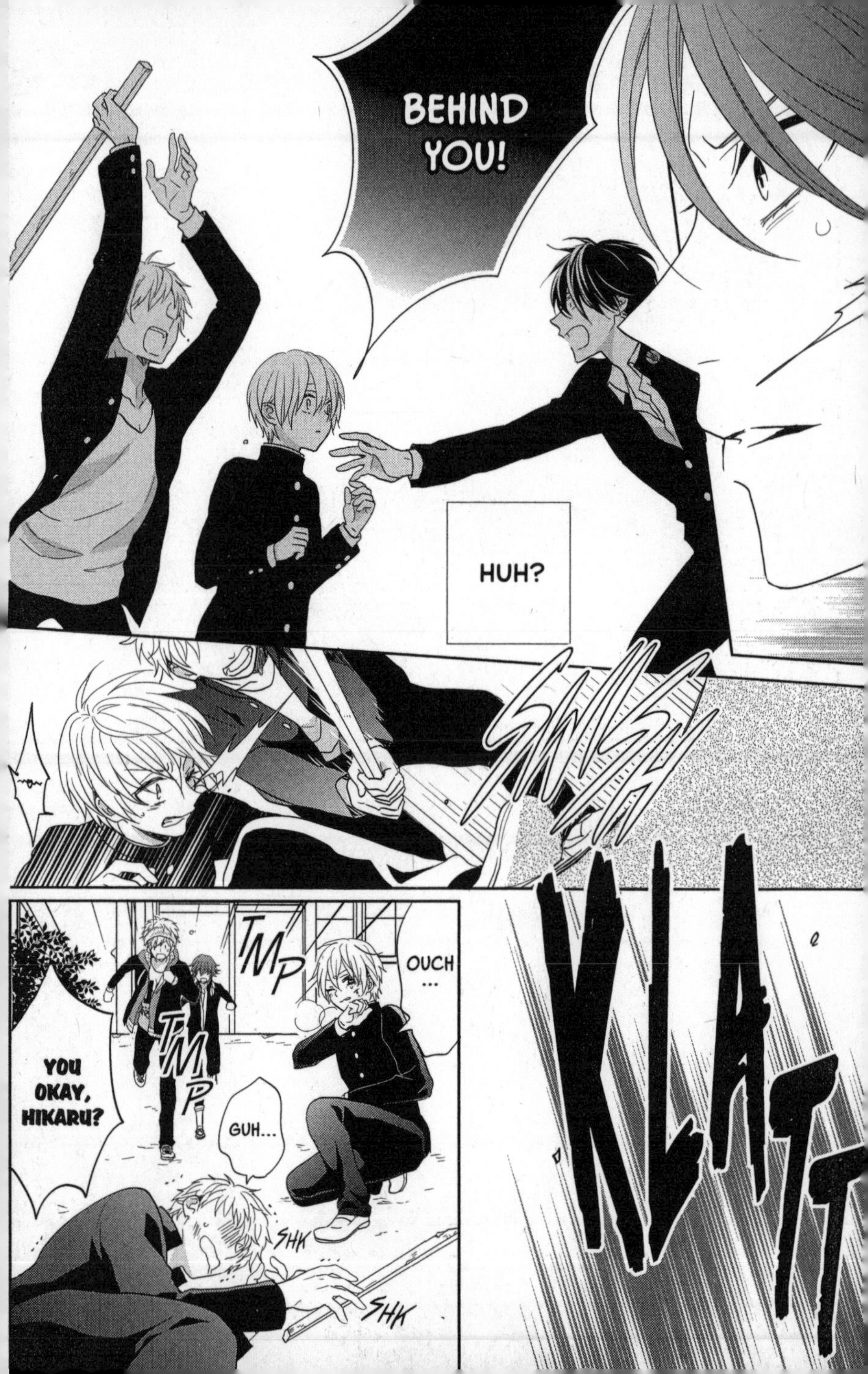
BEHIND YOU!
HUH?
SWISH
KLATT
OUCH...
TMP
TMP
YOU OKAY, HIKARU?
GUH...
SHK
SHK

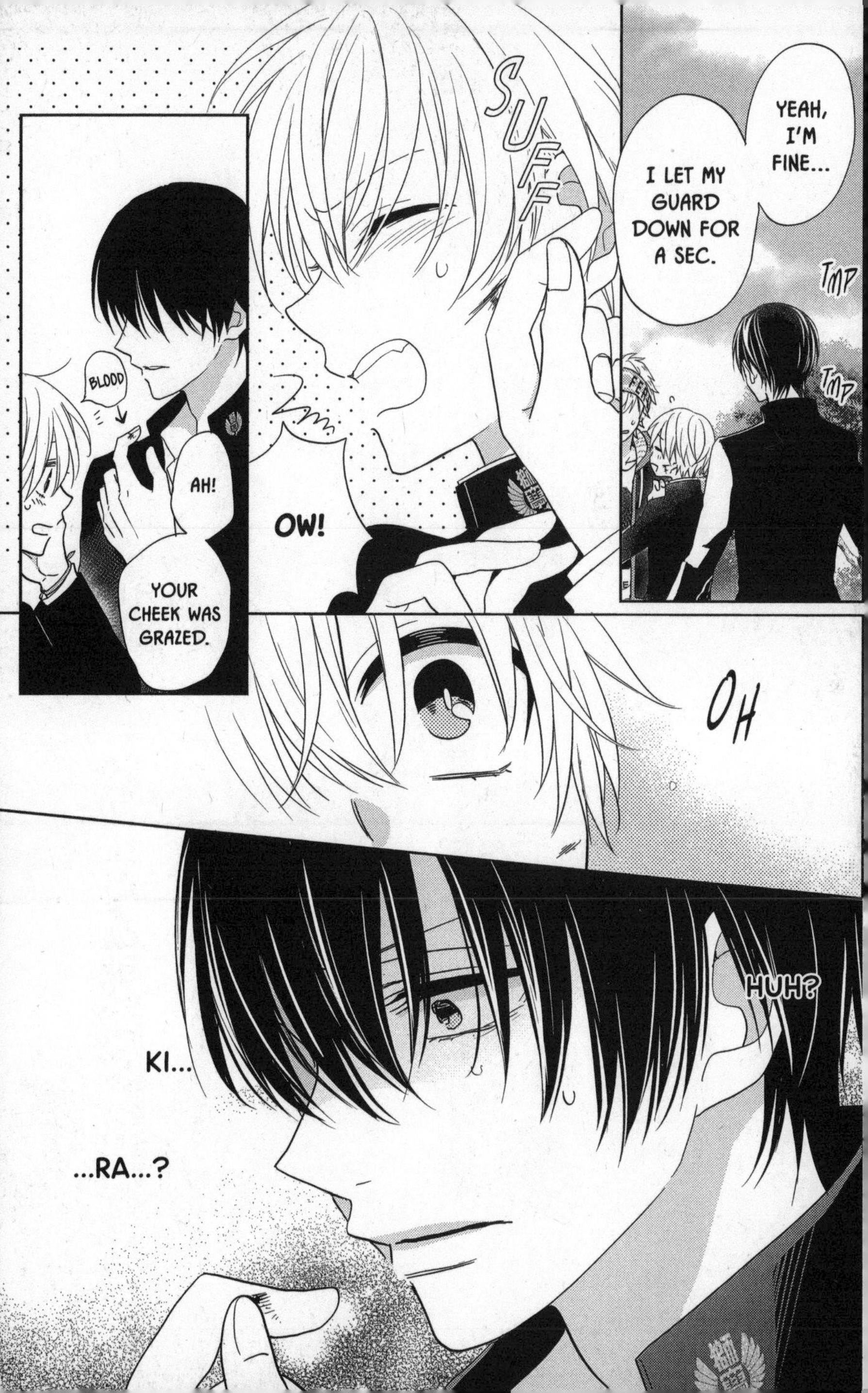
YEAH, I'M FINE...
I LET MY GUARD DOWN FOR A SEC.
TMP
TMP
SUFF
OW!
BLOOD
AH!
YOUR CHEEK WAS GRAZED.
OH
HUH?
KI...
...RA...?

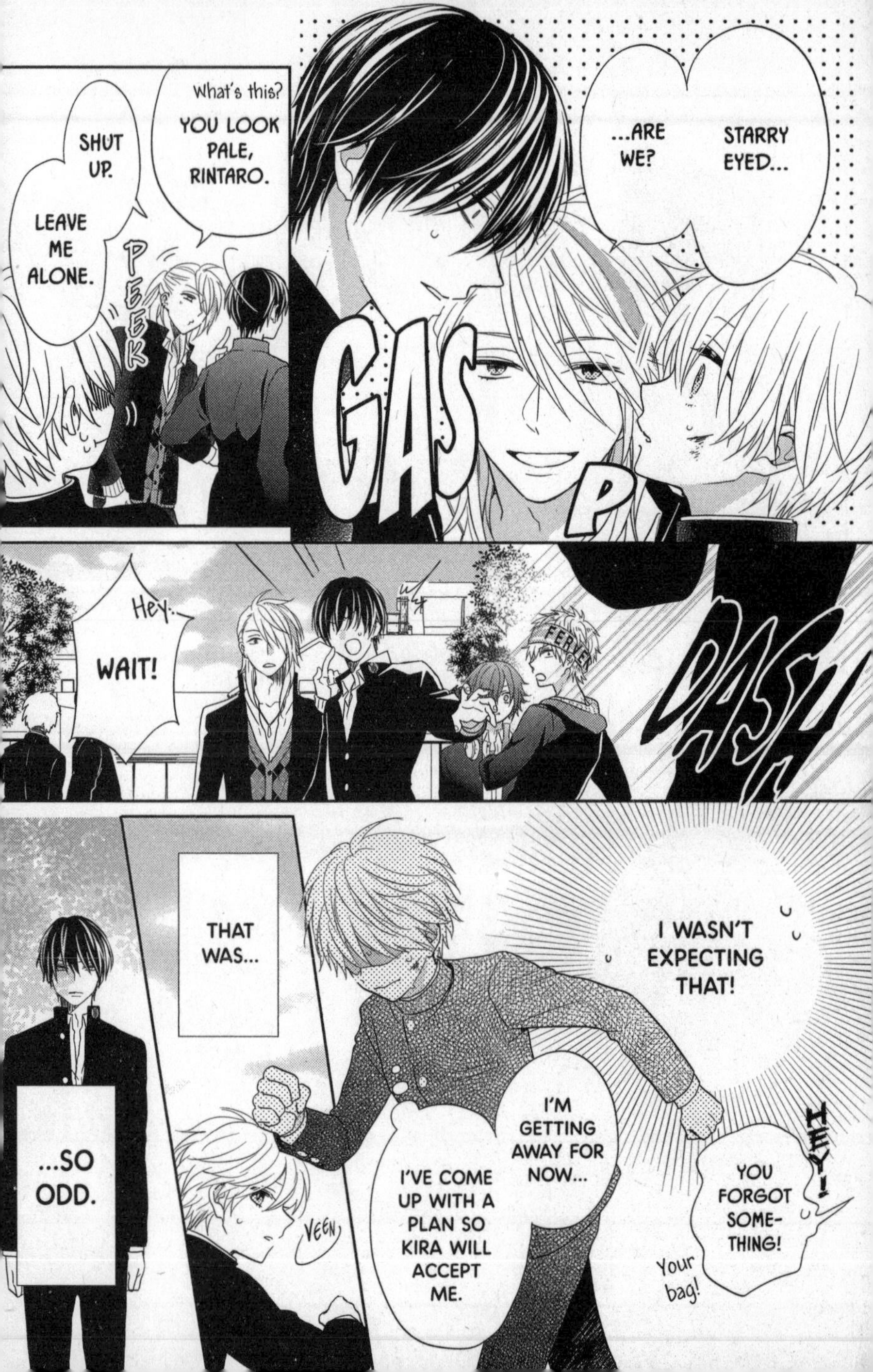
STARRY EYED... ...ARE WE?
GASP
What's this? YOU LOOK PALE, RINTARO.
PEEK
SHUT UP. LEAVE ME ALONE.
DASH
Hey...
WAIT!
I WASN'T EXPECTING THAT!
HEY!
YOU FORGOT SOME-THING!
Your bag!
I'M GETTING AWAY FOR NOW...
I'VE COME UP WITH A PLAN SO KIRA WILL ACCEPT ME.
VEEN
THAT WAS...
...SO ODD.

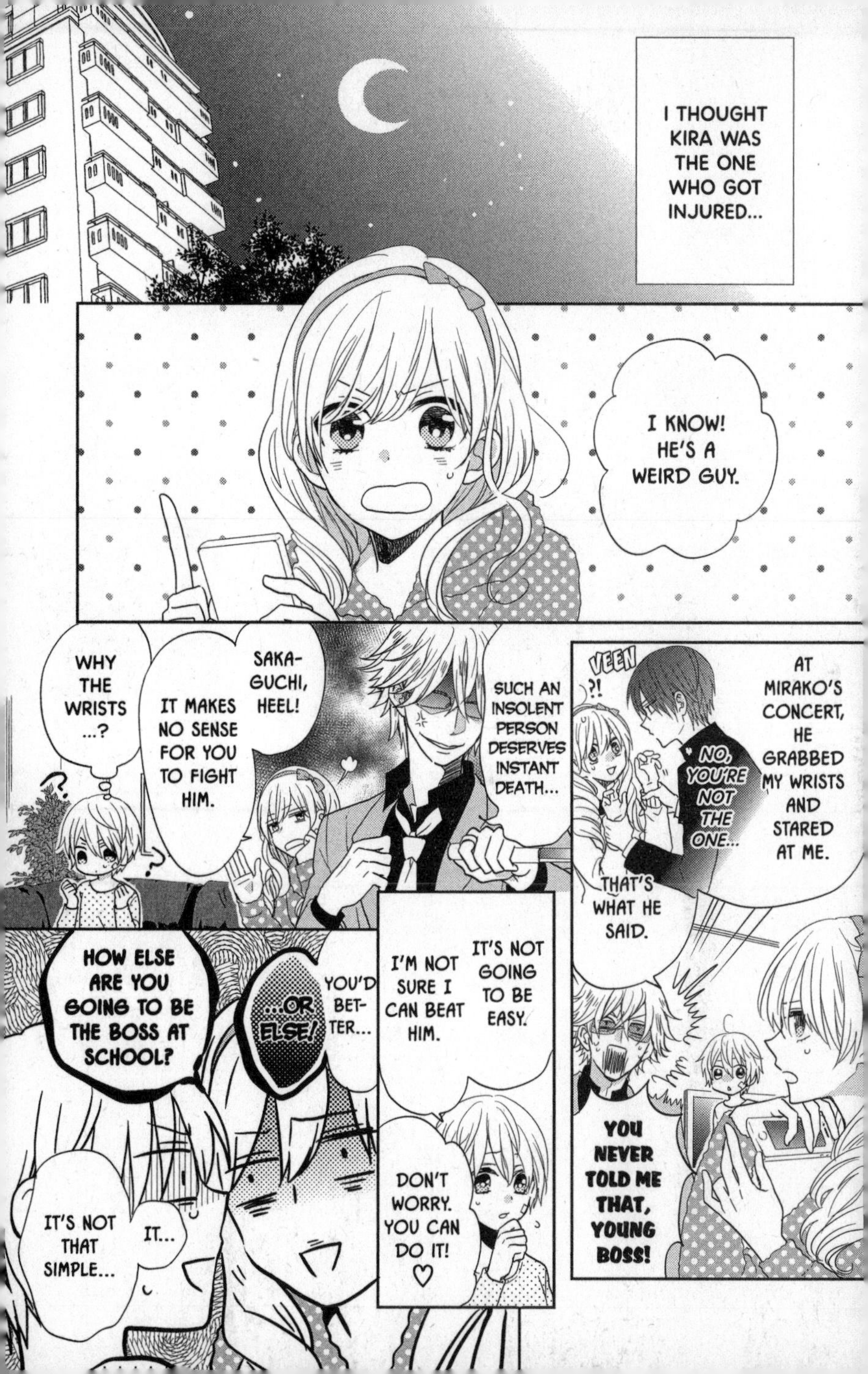
I THOUGHT KIRA WAS THE ONE WHO GOT INJURED...
I KNOW! HE'S A WEIRD GUY.
AT MIRAKO'S CONCERT, HE GRABBED MY WRISTS AND STARED AT ME.
VEEN
?!
NO, YOU'RE NOT THE ONE...
THAT'S WHAT HE SAID.
YOU NEVER TOLD ME THAT, YOUNG BOSS!
SUCH AN INSOLENT PERSON DESERVES INSTANT DEATH...
SAKAGUCHI, HEEL!
IT MAKES NO SENSE FOR YOU TO FIGHT HIM.
WHY THE WRISTS ...?
IT'S NOT GOING TO BE EASY.
I'M NOT SURE I CAN BEAT HIM.
DON'T WORRY. YOU CAN DO IT! ♡
YOU'D BETTER...
...OR ELSE!
HOW ELSE ARE YOU GOING TO BE THE BOSS AT SCHOOL?
IT...
IT'S NOT THAT SIMPLE...

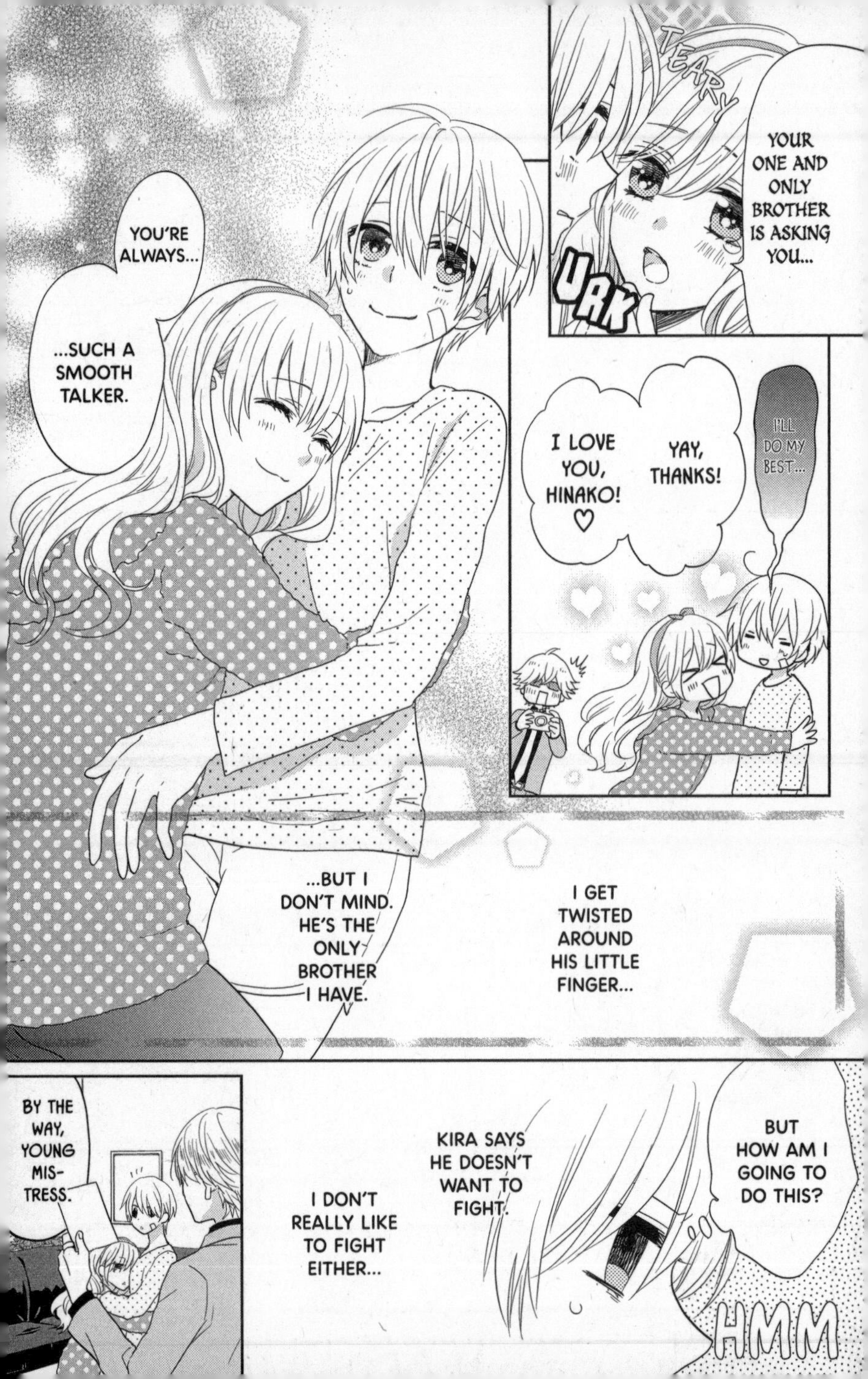
YOUR ONE AND ONLY BROTHER IS ASKING YOU...
TEARY
URK
I'LL DO MY BEST...
YAY, THANKS!
I LOVE YOU, HINAKO! ♡
YOU'RE ALWAYS...
...SUCH A SMOOTH TALKER.
I GET TWISTED AROUND HIS LITTLE FINGER...
...BUT I DON'T MIND. HE'S THE ONLY BROTHER I HAVE.
BUT HOW AM I GOING TO DO THIS?
HMM
KIRA SAYS HE DOESN'T WANT TO FIGHT.
I DON'T REALLY LIKE TO FIGHT EITHER...
BY THE WAY, YOUNG MIS-TRESS.

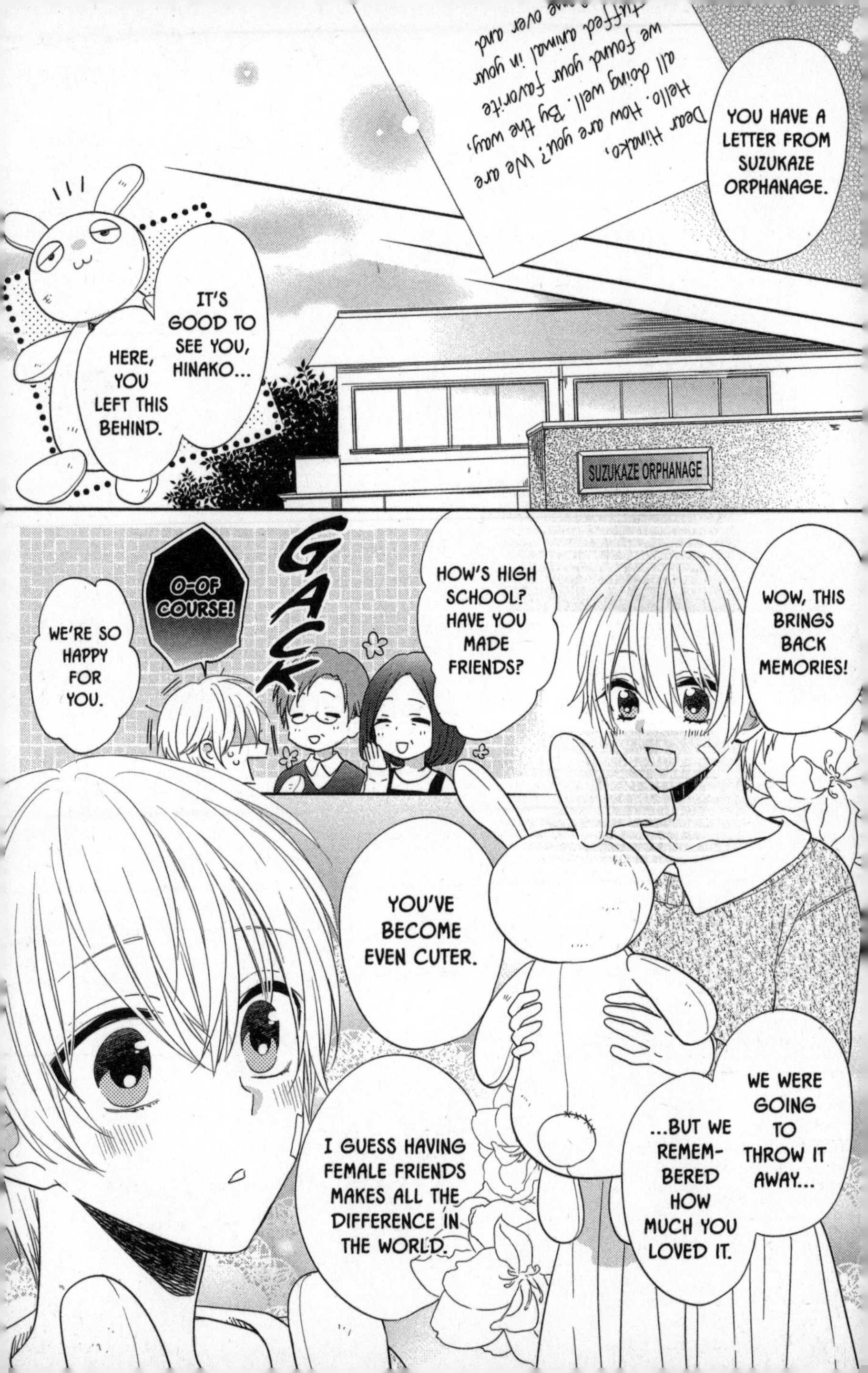
YOU HAVE A LETTER FROM SUZUKAZE ORPHANAGE.
Dear Hinako,
Hello. How are you? We are
all doing well. By the way,
we found your favorite
IT'S GOOD TO SEE YOU, HINAKO...
HERE, YOU LEFT THIS BEHIND.
SUZUKAZE ORPHANAGE
WOW, THIS BRINGS BACK MEMORIES!
HOW'S HIGH SCHOOL? HAVE YOU MADE FRIENDS?
GACK
O-OF COURSE!
WE'RE SO HAPPY FOR YOU.
WE WERE GOING TO THROW IT AWAY...
...BUT WE REMEM-BERED HOW MUCH YOU LOVED IT.
YOU'VE BECOME EVEN CUTER.
I GUESS HAVING FEMALE FRIENDS MAKES ALL THE DIFFERENCE IN THE WORLD.

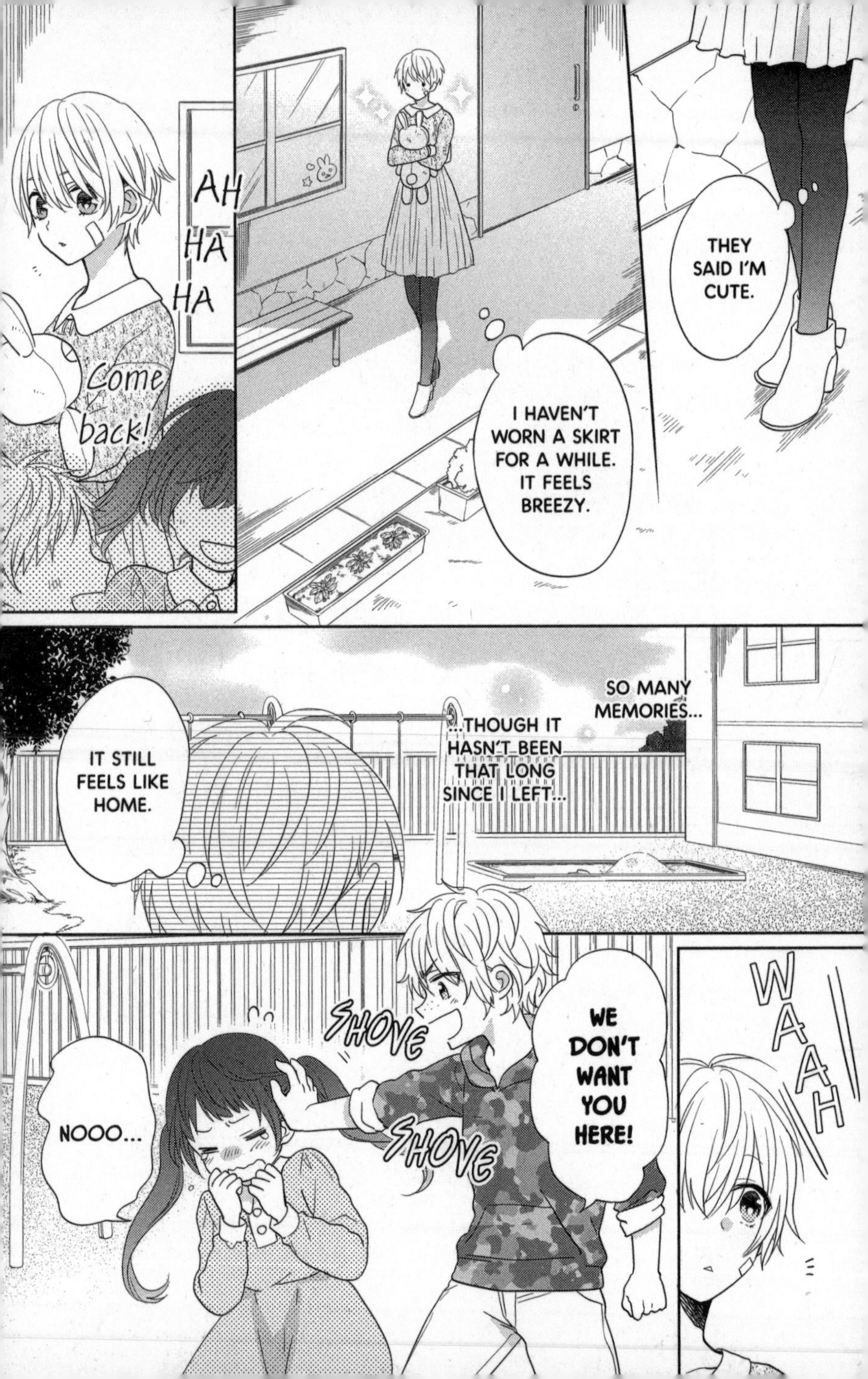
THEY SAID I'M CUTE.
I HAVEN'T WORN A SKIRT FOR A WHILE. IT FEELS BREEZY.
AH HA HA
Come back!
SO MANY MEMORIES...
...THOUGH IT HASN'T BEEN THAT LONG SINCE I LEFT...
IT STILL FEELS LIKE HOME.
WAAAH
WE DON'T WANT YOU HERE!
SHOVE
SHOVE
NOOO...

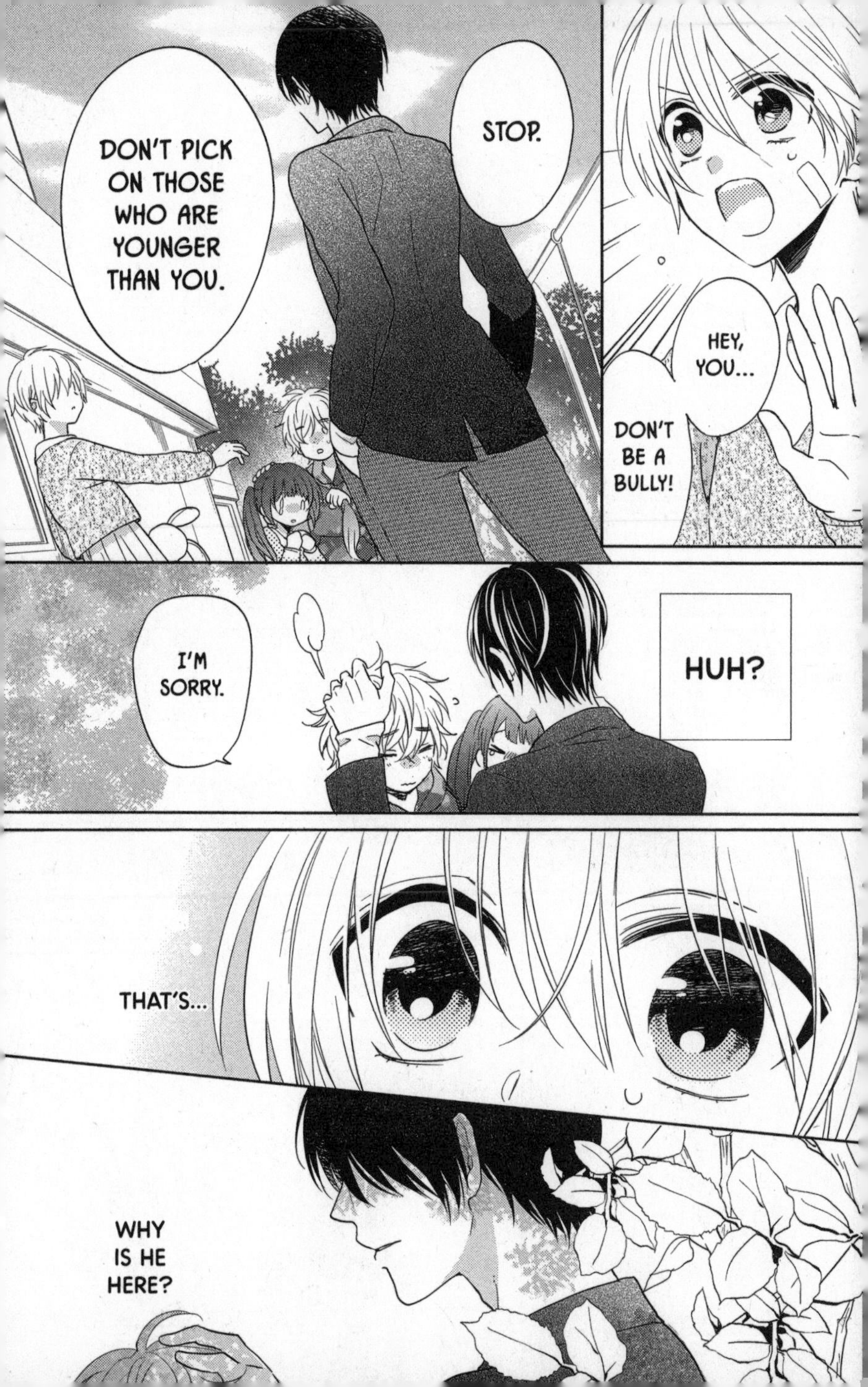
HEY, YOU...
DON'T BE A BULLY!
STOP.
DON'T PICK ON THOSE WHO ARE YOUNGER THAN YOU.
HUH?
I'M SORRY.
THAT'S...
WHY IS HE HERE?

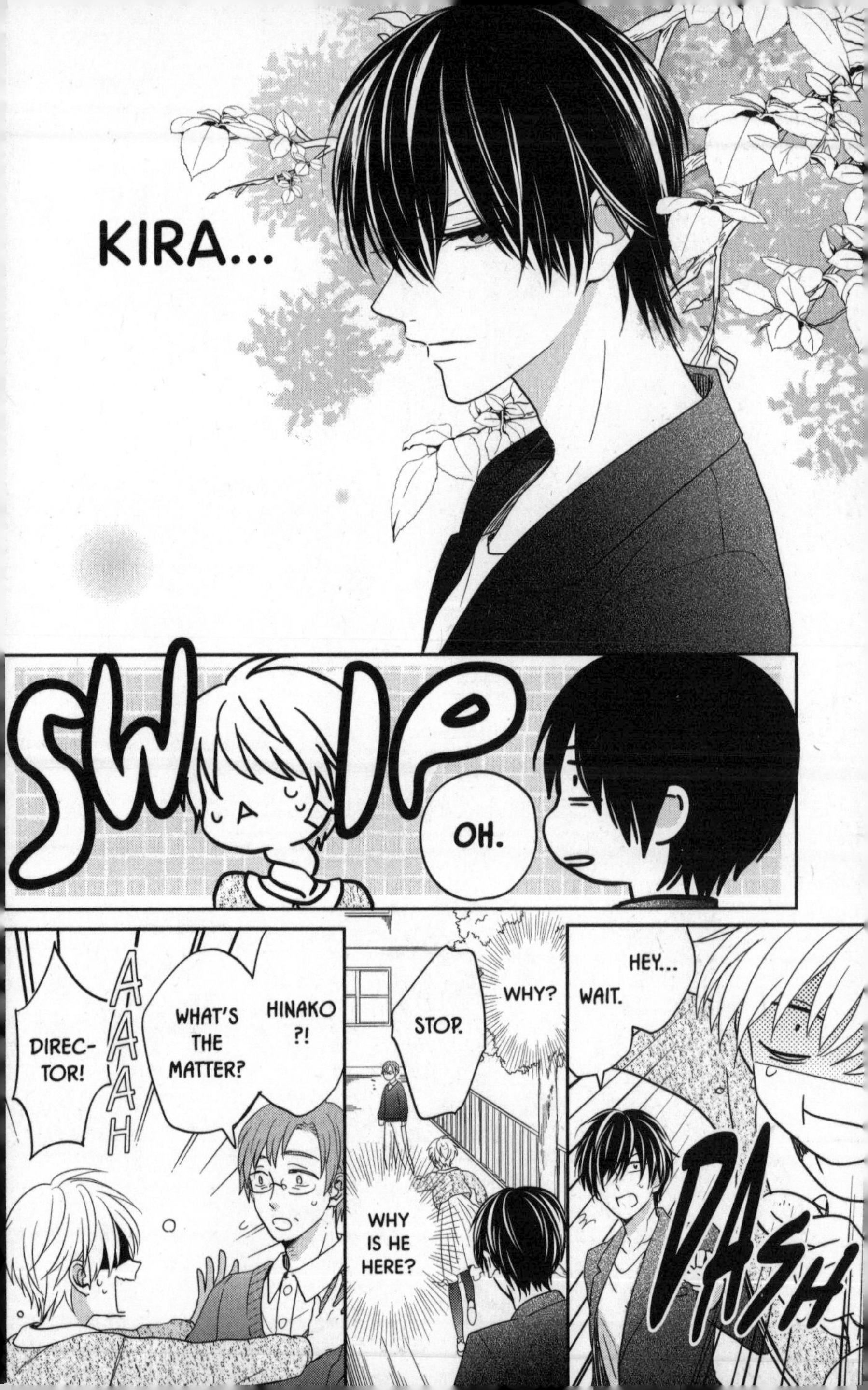
KIRA...
SWIP
OH.
HEY...
WAIT.
DASH
WHY?
STOP.
WHY IS HE HERE?
HINAKO ?!
WHAT'S THE MATTER?
AAAAH
DIREC-TOR!

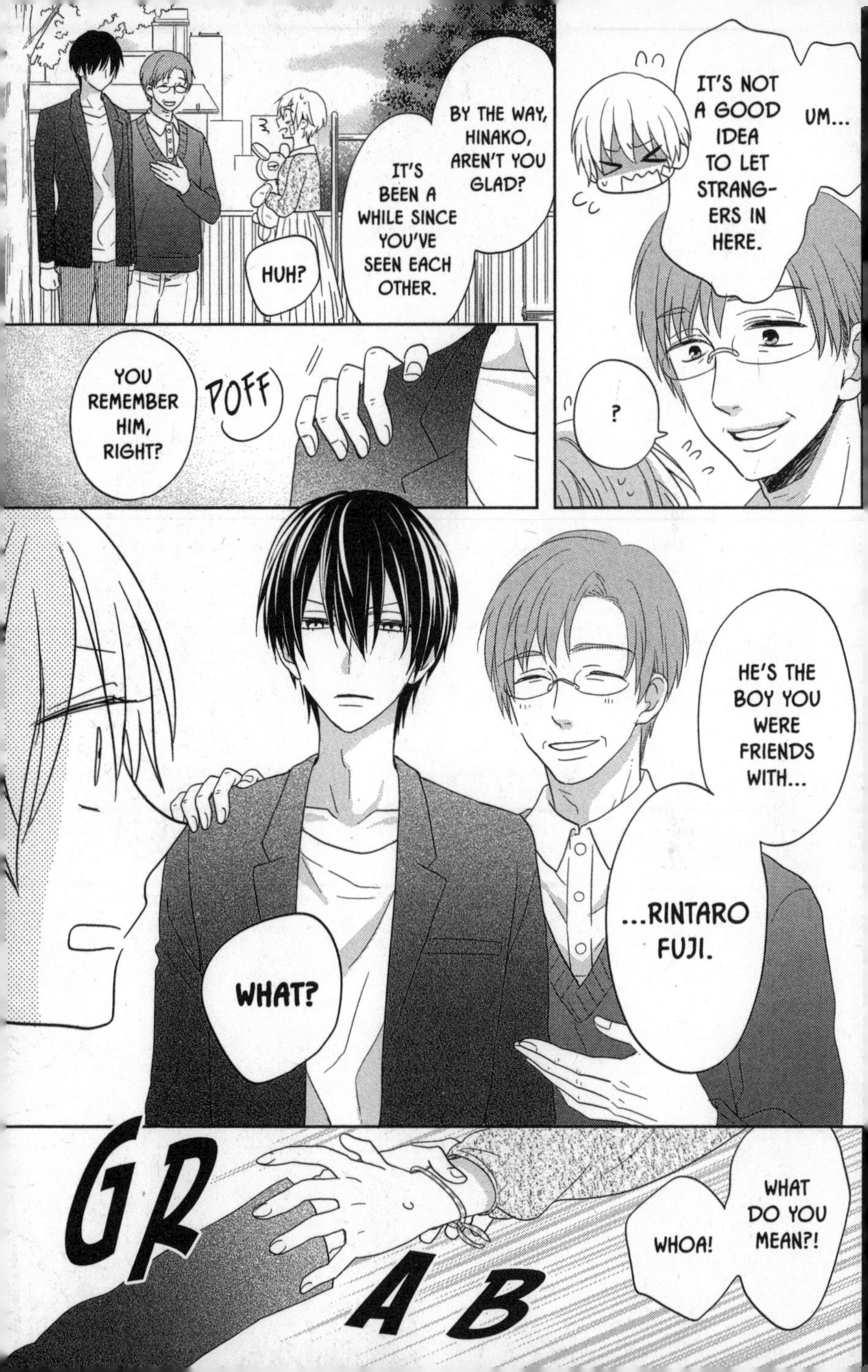
UM...
IT'S NOT A GOOD IDEA TO LET STRANGERS IN HERE.
?
BY THE WAY, HINAKO, AREN'T YOU GLAD?
IT'S BEEN A WHILE SINCE YOU'VE SEEN EACH OTHER.
HUH?
POFF
YOU REMEMBER HIM, RIGHT?
HE'S THE BOY YOU WERE FRIENDS WITH...
...RINTARO FUJI.
WHAT?
WHAT DO YOU MEAN?!
WHOA!
GRAB

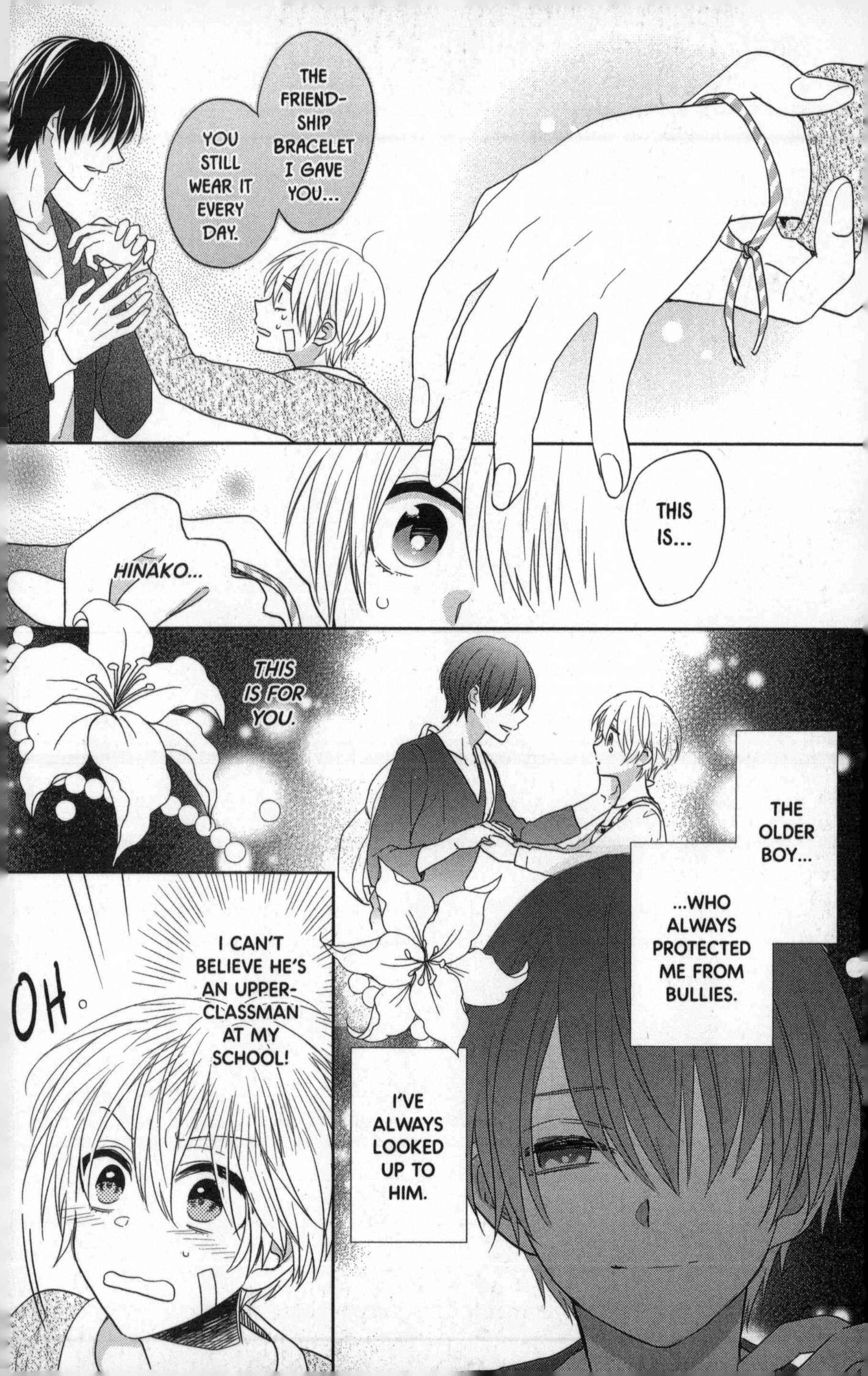
THE FRIEND-SHIP BRACELET I GAVE YOU...
YOU STILL WEAR IT EVERY DAY.
THIS IS...
HINAKO...
THIS IS FOR YOU.
THE OLDER BOY...
...WHO ALWAYS PROTECTED ME FROM BULLIES.
I'VE ALWAYS LOOKED UP TO HIM.
OH
I CAN'T BELIEVE HE'S AN UPPER-CLASSMAN AT MY SCHOOL!

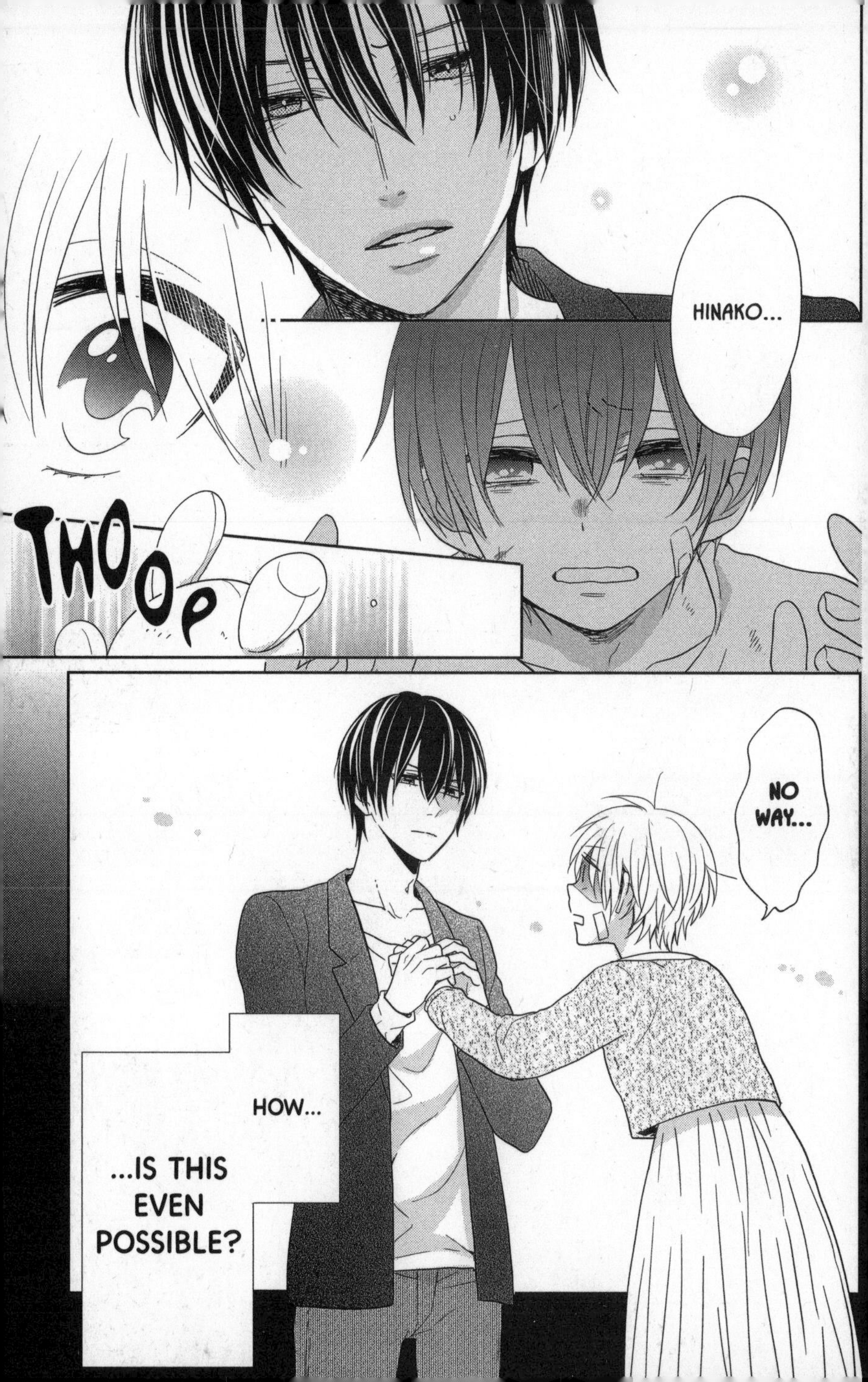
HINAKO...
THOOP
NO WAY...
HOW...
...IS THIS EVEN POSSIBLE?

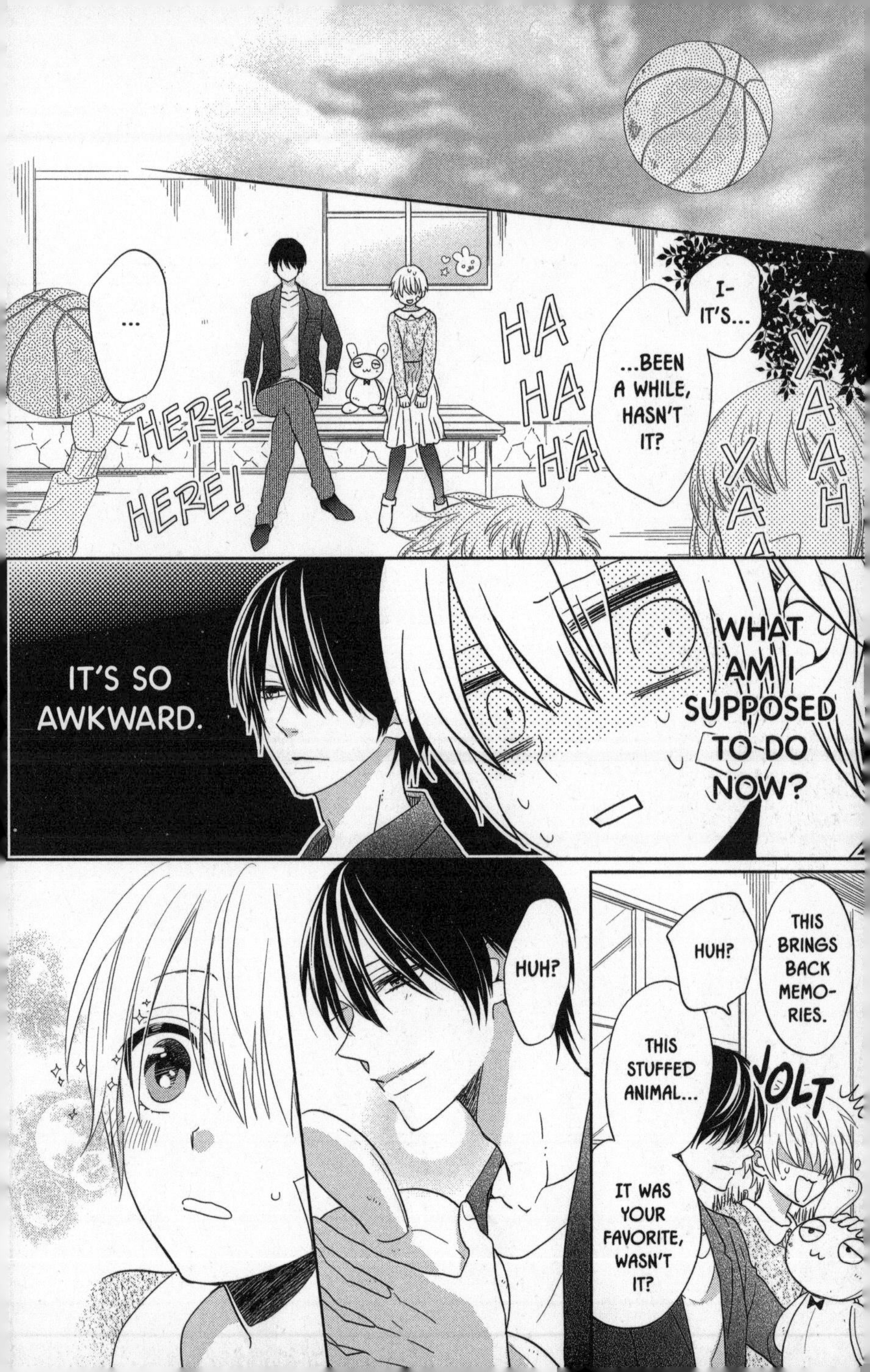
YAAH
YAA
I- IT'S...
...BEEN A WHILE, HASN'T IT?
HA HA HA
HERE! HERE!
...
WHAT AM I SUPPOSED TO DO NOW?
IT'S SO AWKWARD.
THIS BRINGS BACK MEMO-RIES.
HUH?
JOLT
THIS STUFFED ANIMAL...
IT WAS YOUR FAVORITE, WASN'T IT?
HUH?

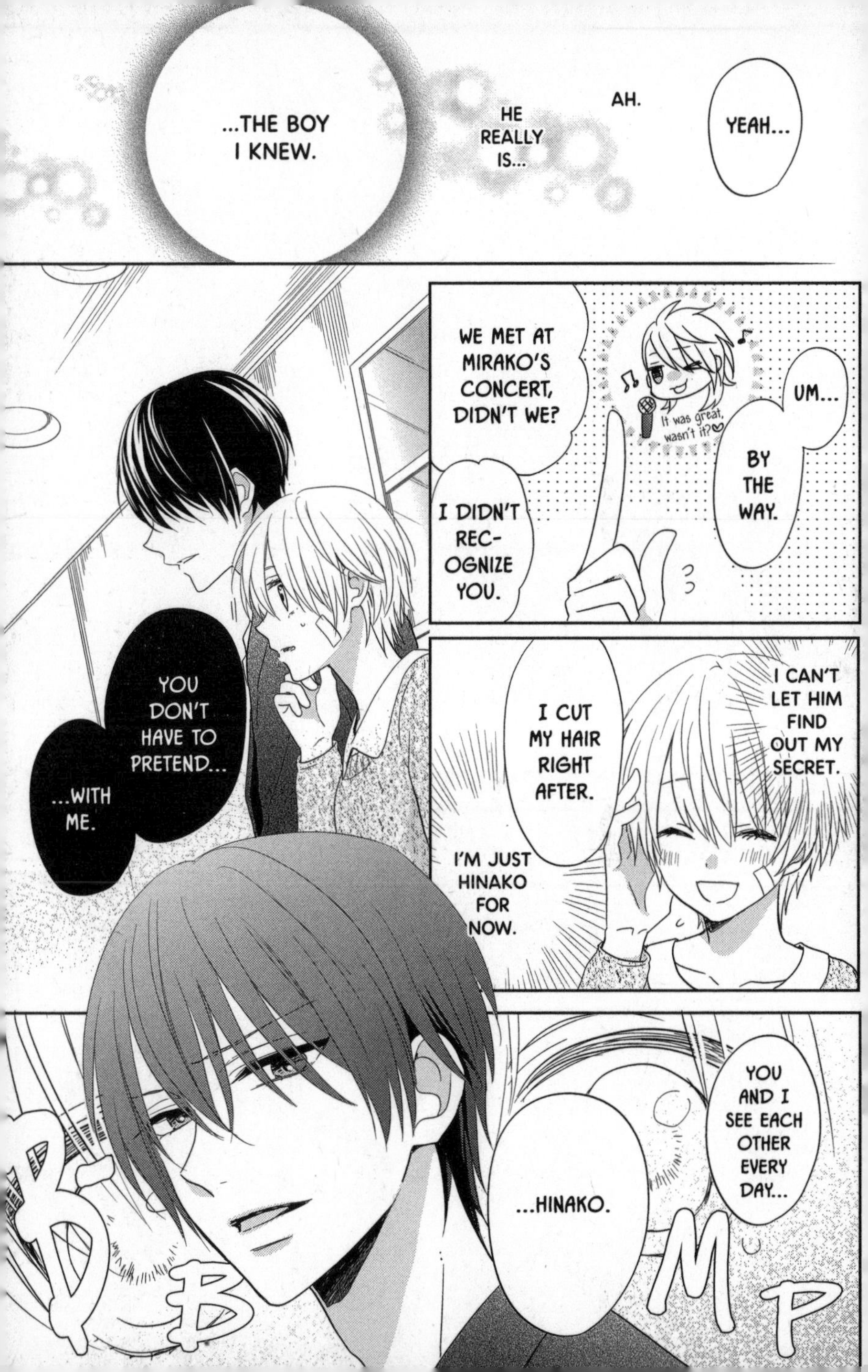
YEAH...
AH.
HE REALLY IS...
...THE BOY I KNEW.
UM... BY THE WAY.
WE MET AT MIRAKO'S CONCERT, DIDN'T WE?
It was great, wasn't it?
I DIDN'T RECOGNIZE YOU.
I CAN'T LET HIM FIND OUT MY SECRET.
I CUT MY HAIR RIGHT AFTER.
I'M JUST HINAKO FOR NOW.
YOU DON'T HAVE TO PRETEND...
...WITH ME.
YOU AND I SEE EACH OTHER EVERY DAY...
...HINAKO.
B B M P

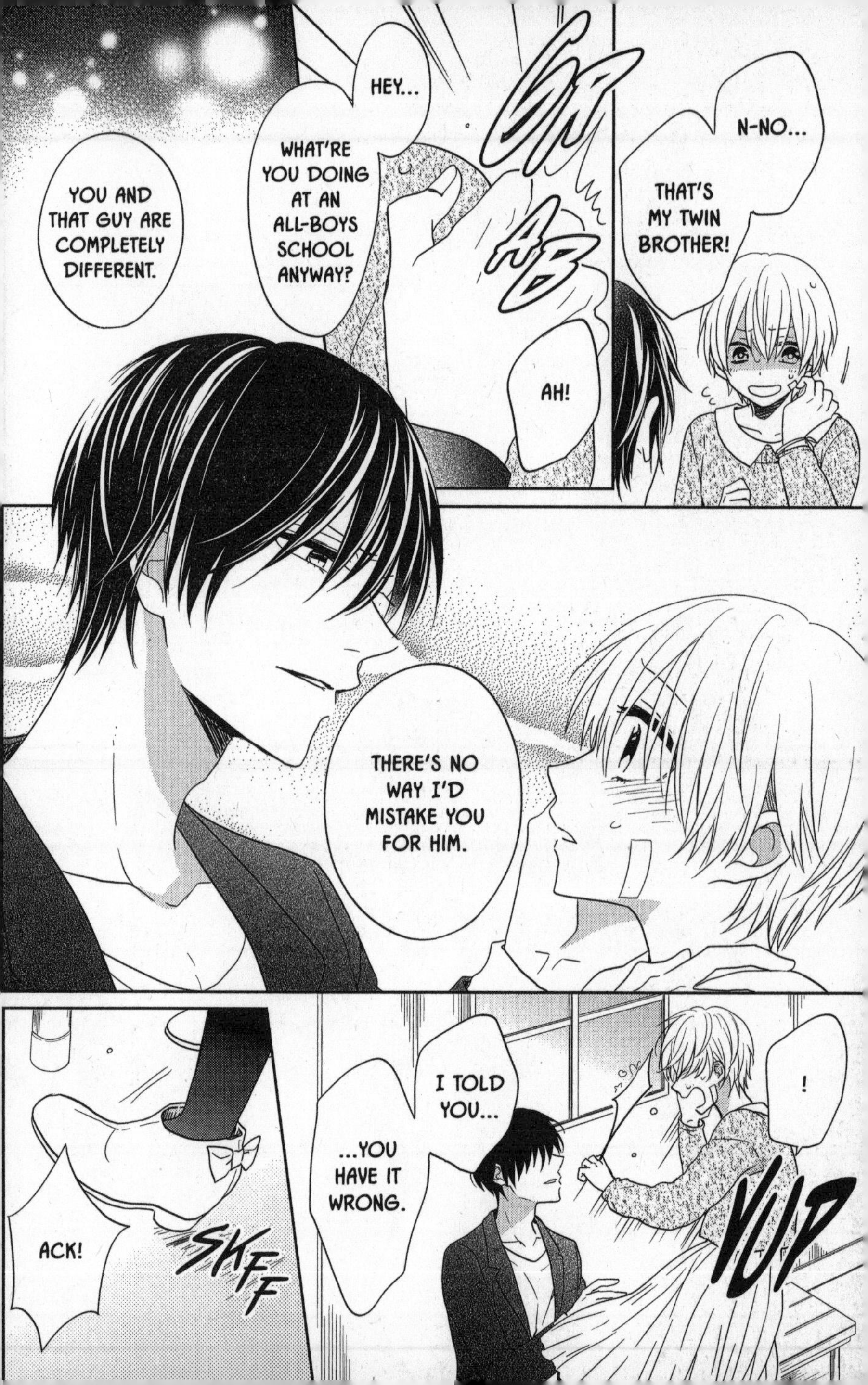
N-NO...
THAT'S MY TWIN BROTHER!
GRAB
AH!
HEY...
WHAT'RE YOU DOING AT AN ALL-BOYS SCHOOL ANYWAY?
YOU AND THAT GUY ARE COMPLETELY DIFFERENT.
THERE'S NO WAY I'D MISTAKE YOU FOR HIM.
!
YUP
I TOLD YOU...
...YOU HAVE IT WRONG.
SKFF
ACK!

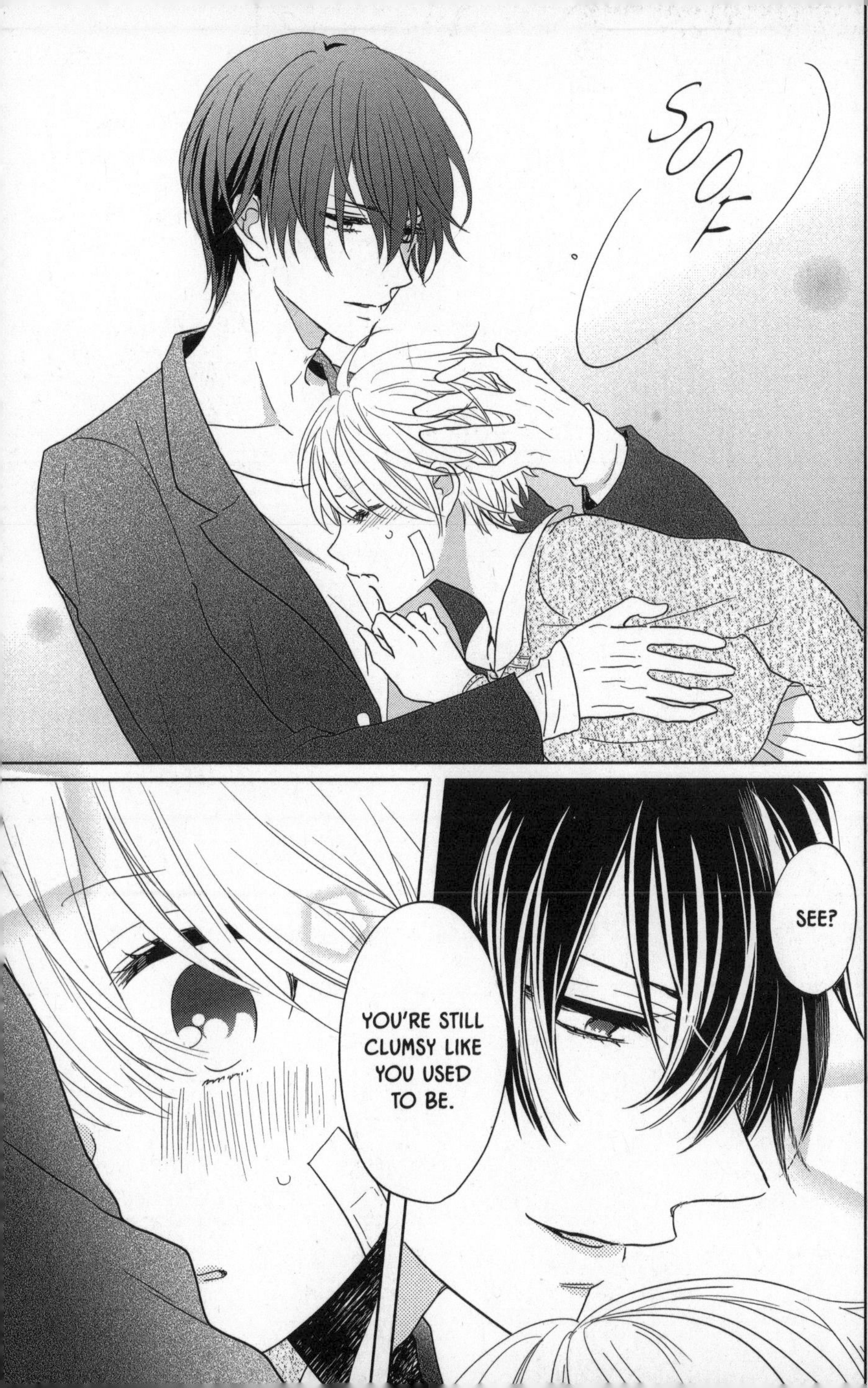
SOOF
SEE?
YOU'RE STILL CLUMSY LIKE YOU USED TO BE.

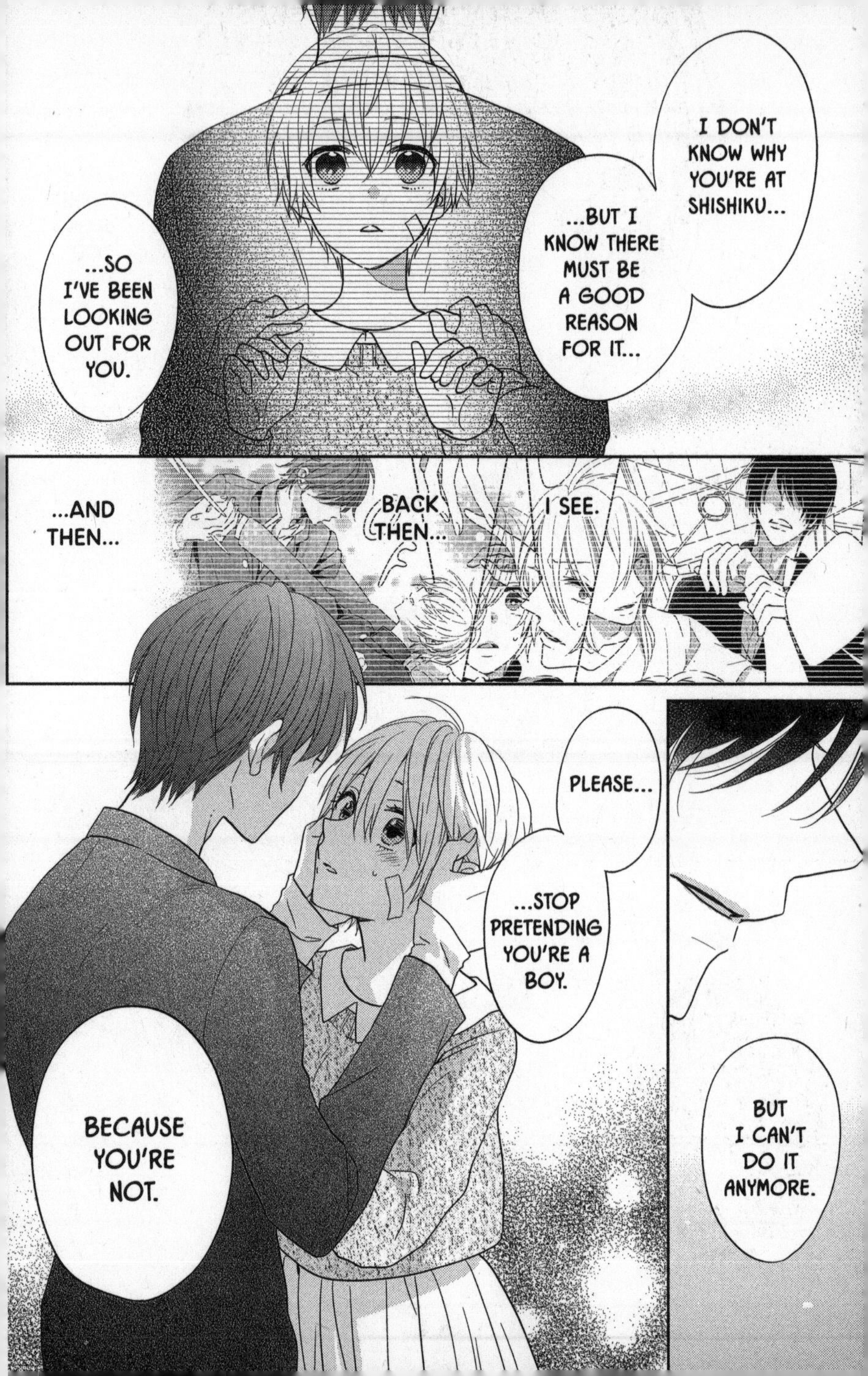
I DON'T KNOW WHY YOU'RE AT SHISHIKU...
...BUT I KNOW THERE MUST BE A GOOD REASON FOR IT...
...SO I'VE BEEN LOOKING OUT FOR YOU.
I SEE.
BACK THEN...
...AND THEN...
BUT I CAN'T DO IT ANYMORE.
PLEASE...
...STOP PRETENDING YOU'RE A BOY.
BECAUSE YOU'RE NOT.

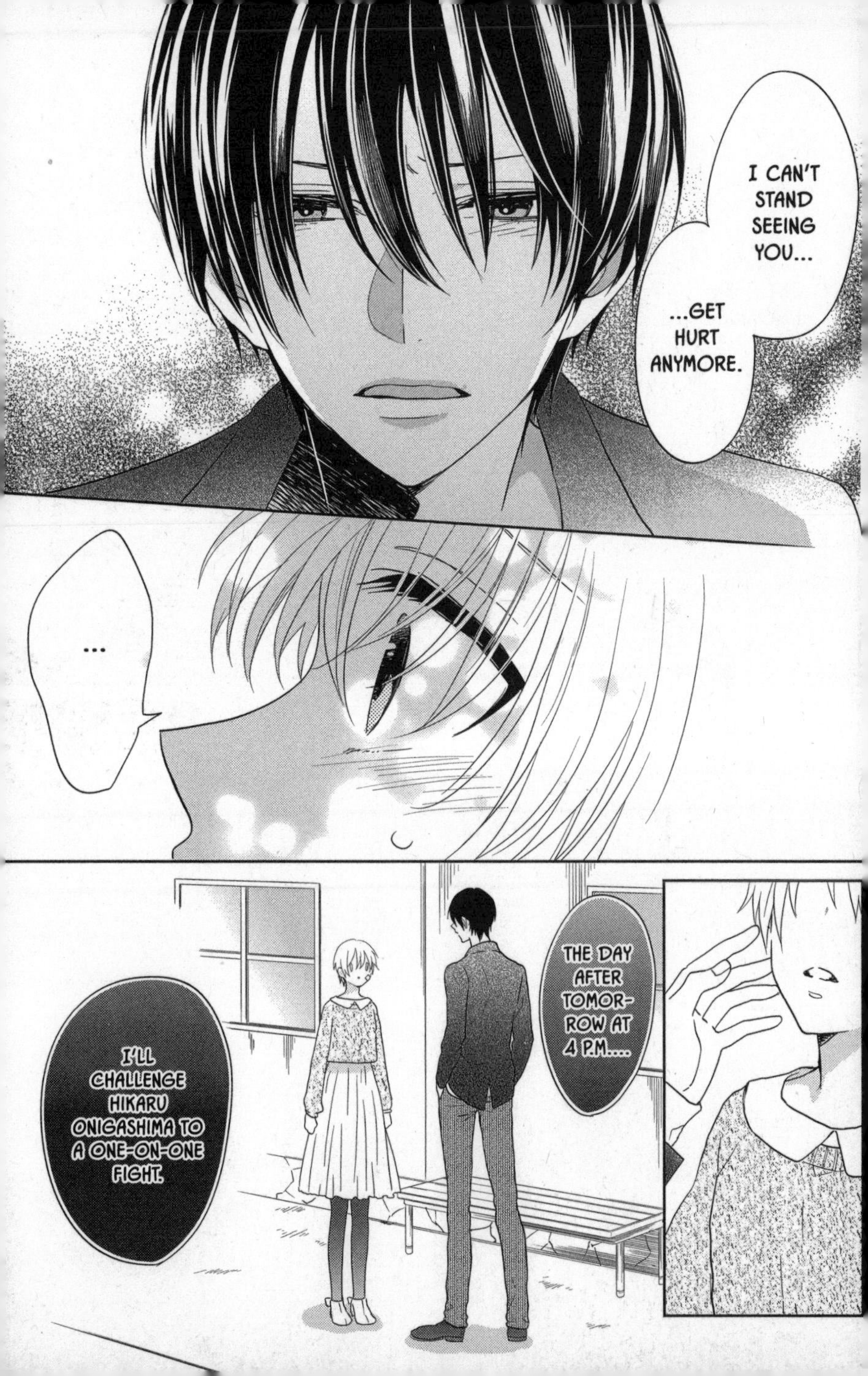
I CAN'T STAND SEEING YOU...
...GET HURT ANYMORE.
...
THE DAY AFTER TOMOR-ROW AT 4 P.M....
I'LL CHALLENGE HIKARU ONIGASHIMA TO A ONE-ON-ONE FIGHT.

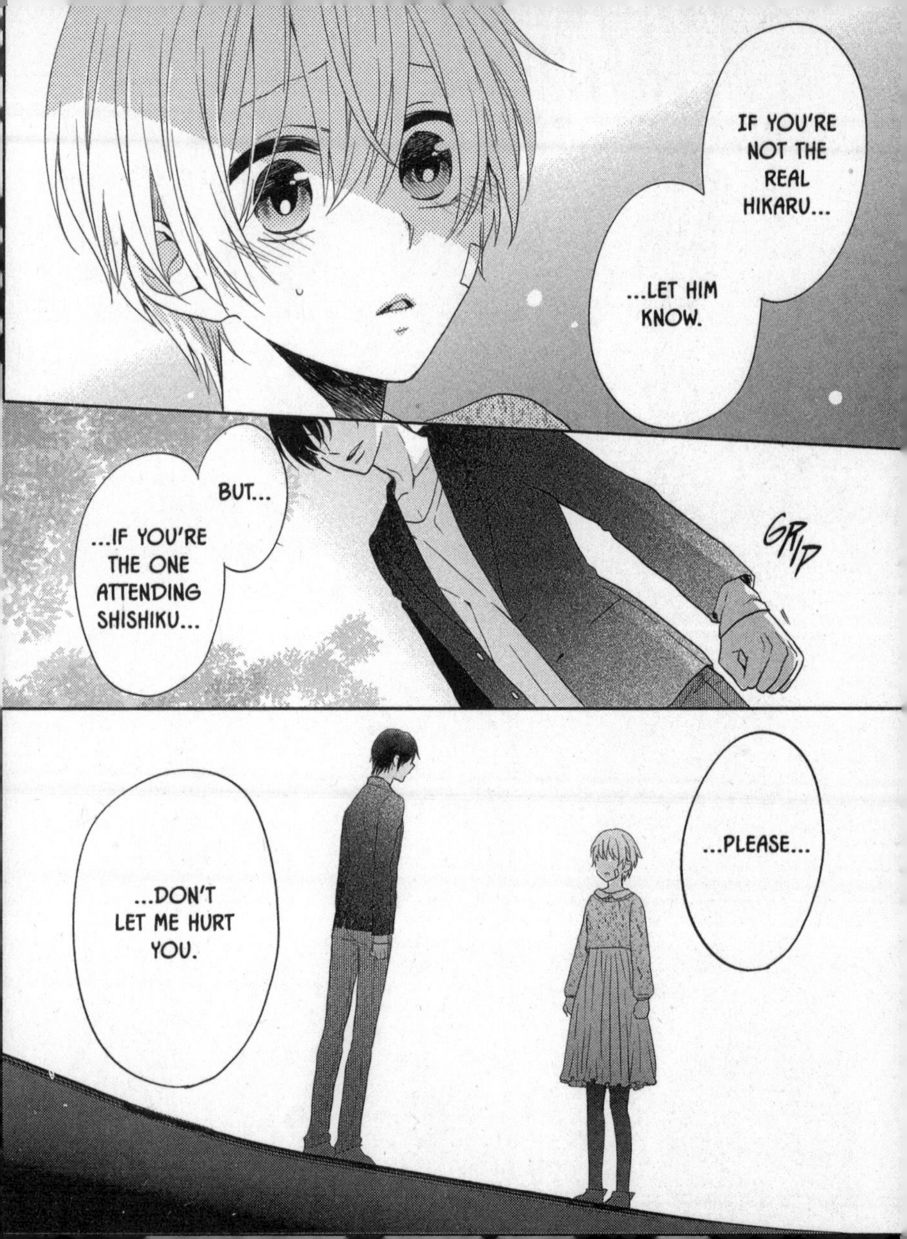
IF YOU'RE NOT THE REAL HIKARU...
...LET HIM KNOW.
BUT...
...IF YOU'RE THE ONE ATTENDING SHISHIKU...
GRIP
...PLEASE...
...DON'T LET ME HURT YOU.

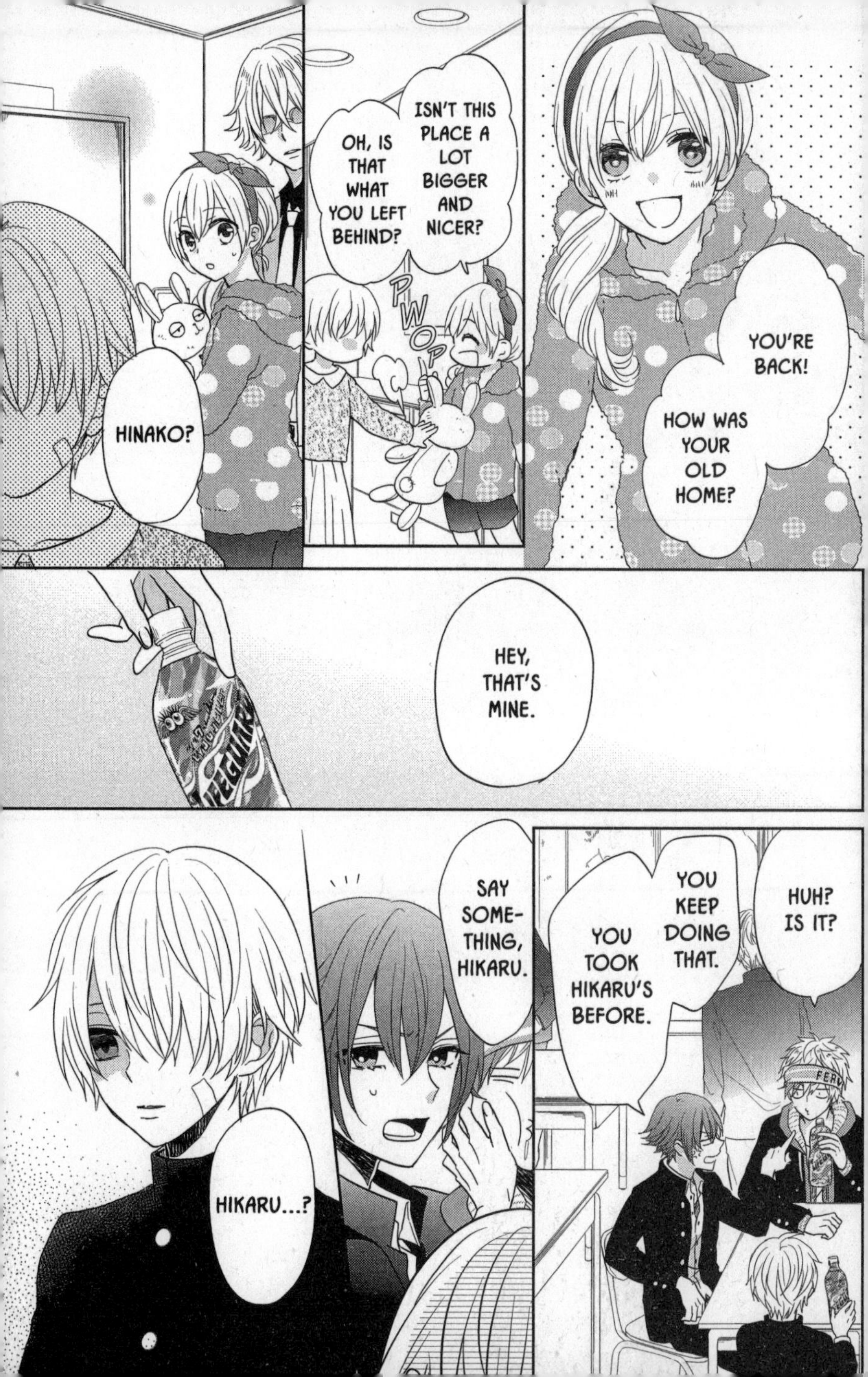
YOU'RE BACK!
HOW WAS YOUR OLD HOME?
ISN'T THIS PLACE A LOT BIGGER AND NICER?
OH, IS THAT WHAT YOU LEFT BEHIND?
PWOP
HINAKO?
HEY, THAT'S MINE.
HUH? IS IT?
YOU KEEP DOING THAT.
YOU TOOK HIKARU'S BEFORE.
SAY SOME-THING, HIKARU.
HIKARU...?

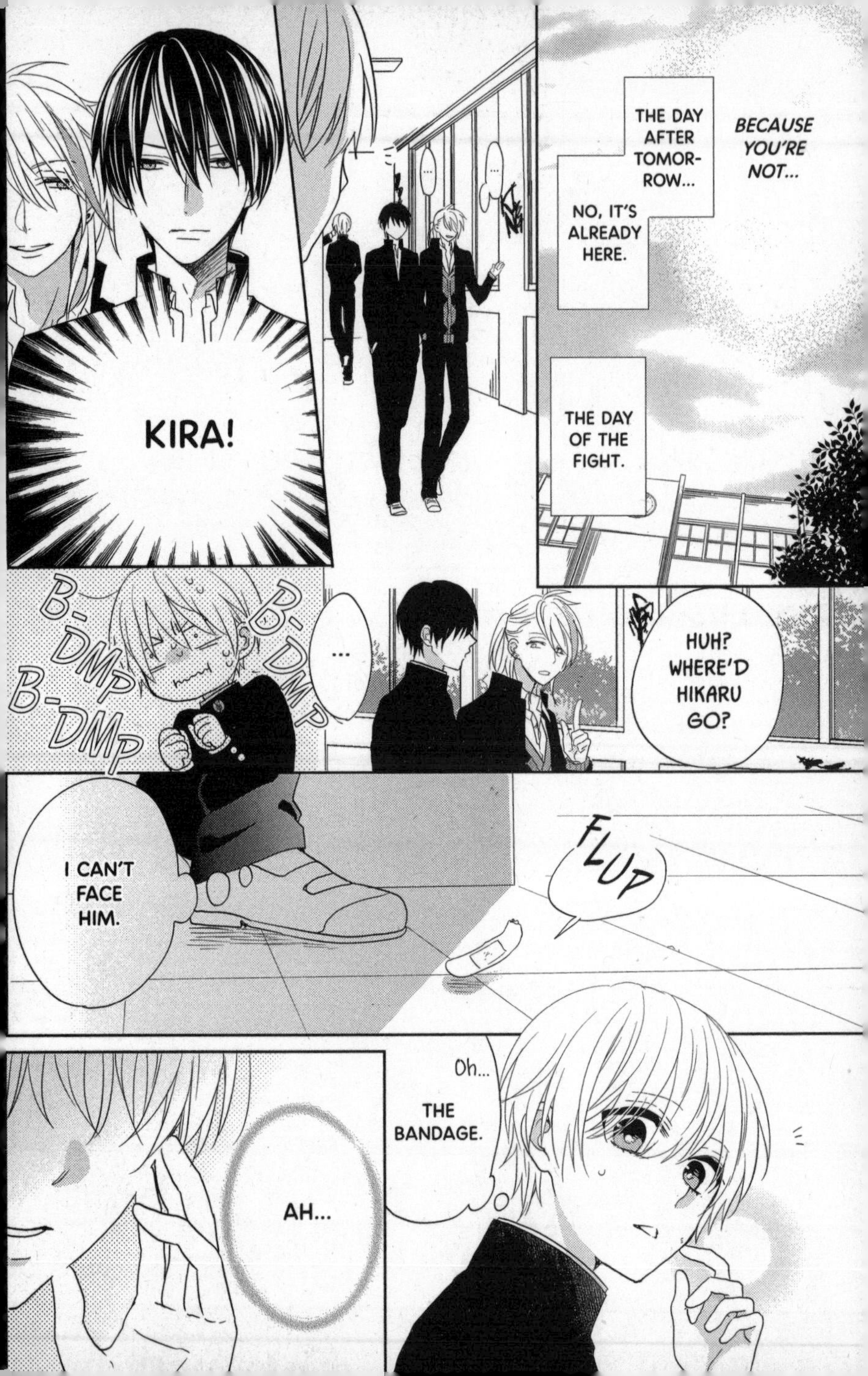
BECAUSE YOU'RE NOT...
THE DAY AFTER TOMOR-ROW...
NO, IT'S ALREADY HERE.
THE DAY OF THE FIGHT.
...
...
KIRA!
HUH? WHERE'D HIKARU GO?
...
B-DMP
B-DMP
B-DMP
FLUP
I CAN'T FACE HIM.
Oh...
THE BANDAGE.
AH...

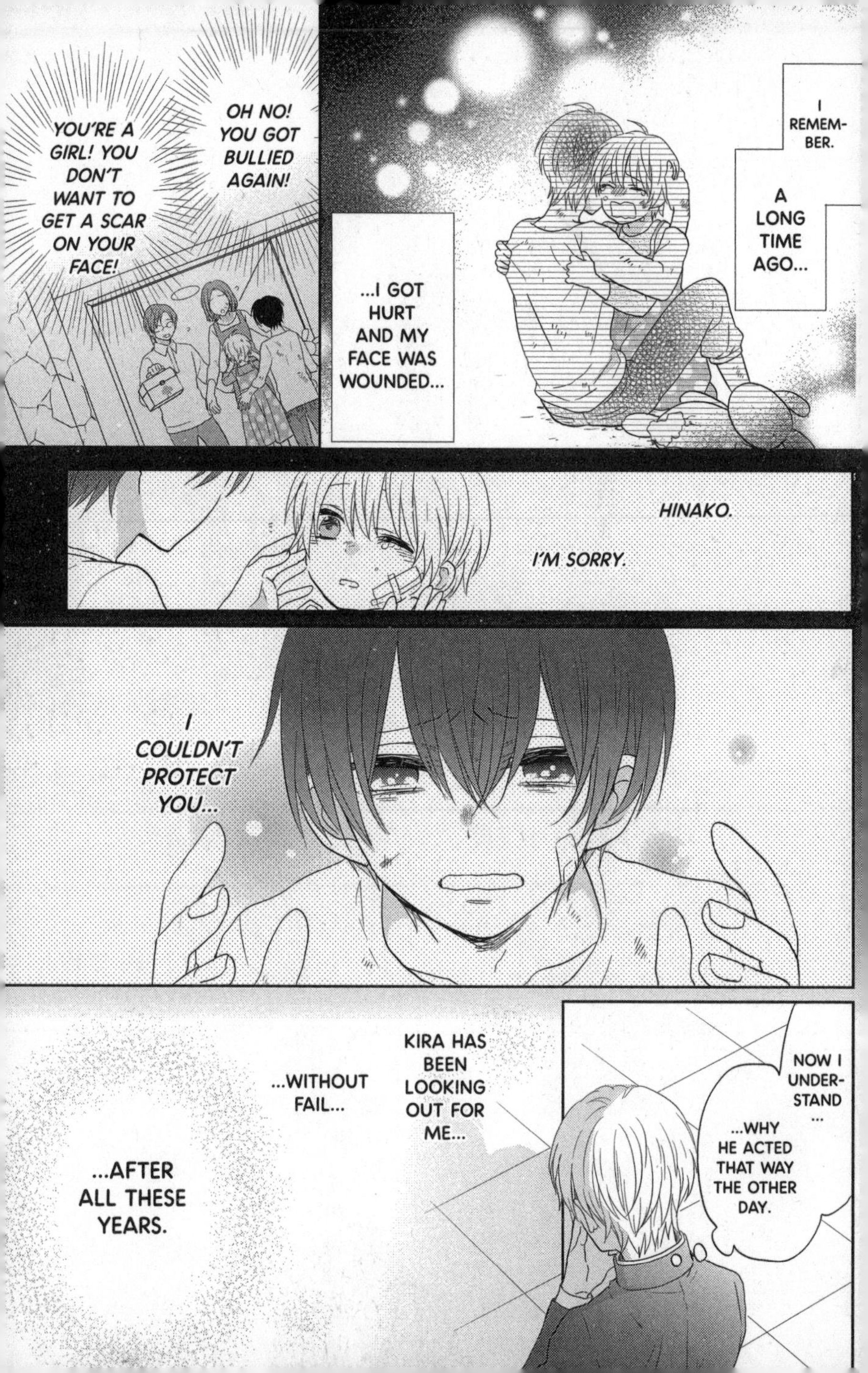
I REMEMBER.
A LONG TIME AGO...
...I GOT HURT AND MY FACE WAS WOUNDED...
OH NO! YOU GOT BULLIED AGAIN!
YOU'RE A GIRL! YOU DON'T WANT TO GET A SCAR ON YOUR FACE!
HINAKO.
I'M SORRY.
I COULDN'T PROTECT YOU...
NOW I UNDERSTAND...
...WHY HE ACTED THAT WAY THE OTHER DAY.
KIRA HAS BEEN LOOKING OUT FOR ME...
...WITHOUT FAIL...
...AFTER ALL THESE YEARS.

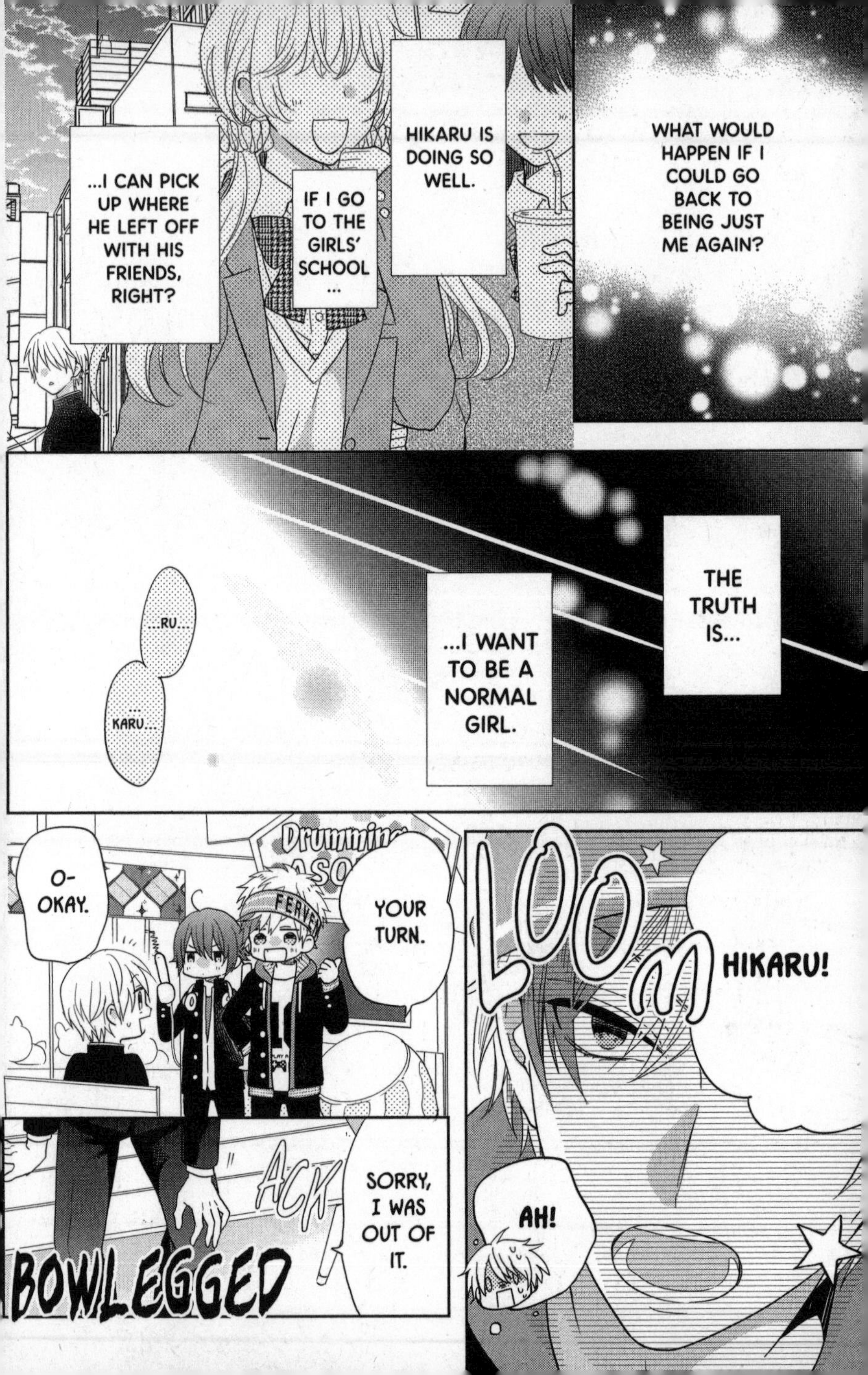
WHAT WOULD HAPPEN IF I COULD GO BACK TO BEING JUST ME AGAIN?
HIKARU IS DOING SO WELL.
IF I GO TO THE GIRLS' SCHOOL...
...I CAN PICK UP WHERE HE LEFT OFF WITH HIS FRIENDS, RIGHT?
THE TRUTH IS...
...I WANT TO BE A NORMAL GIRL.
...RU...
...KARU...
LOOM
HIKARU!
AH!
YOUR TURN.
O-OKAY.
ACK
SORRY, I WAS OUT OF IT.
BOWLEGGED

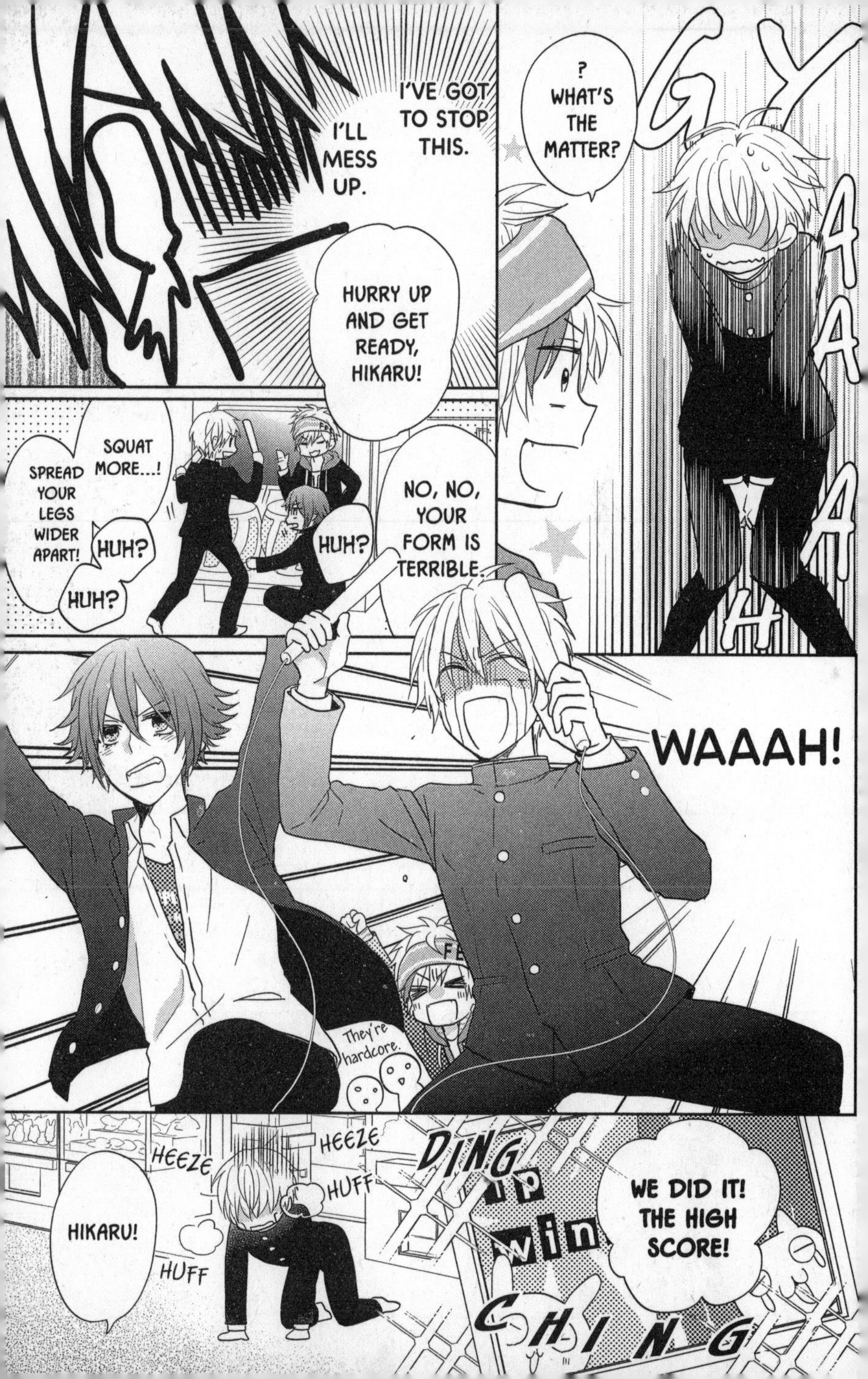
GYAAAAH
? WHAT'S THE MATTER?
I'VE GOT TO STOP THIS.
I'LL MESS UP.
HURRY UP AND GET READY, HIKARU!
NO, NO, YOUR FORM IS TERRIBLE.
HUH?
SQUAT MORE...!
SPREAD YOUR LEGS WIDER APART!
HUH?
HUH?
WAAAH!
They're hardcore.
WE DID IT! THE HIGH SCORE!
DING
1P win
CHING
HEEZE
HUFF
HEEZE
HUFF
HIKARU!
HUFF

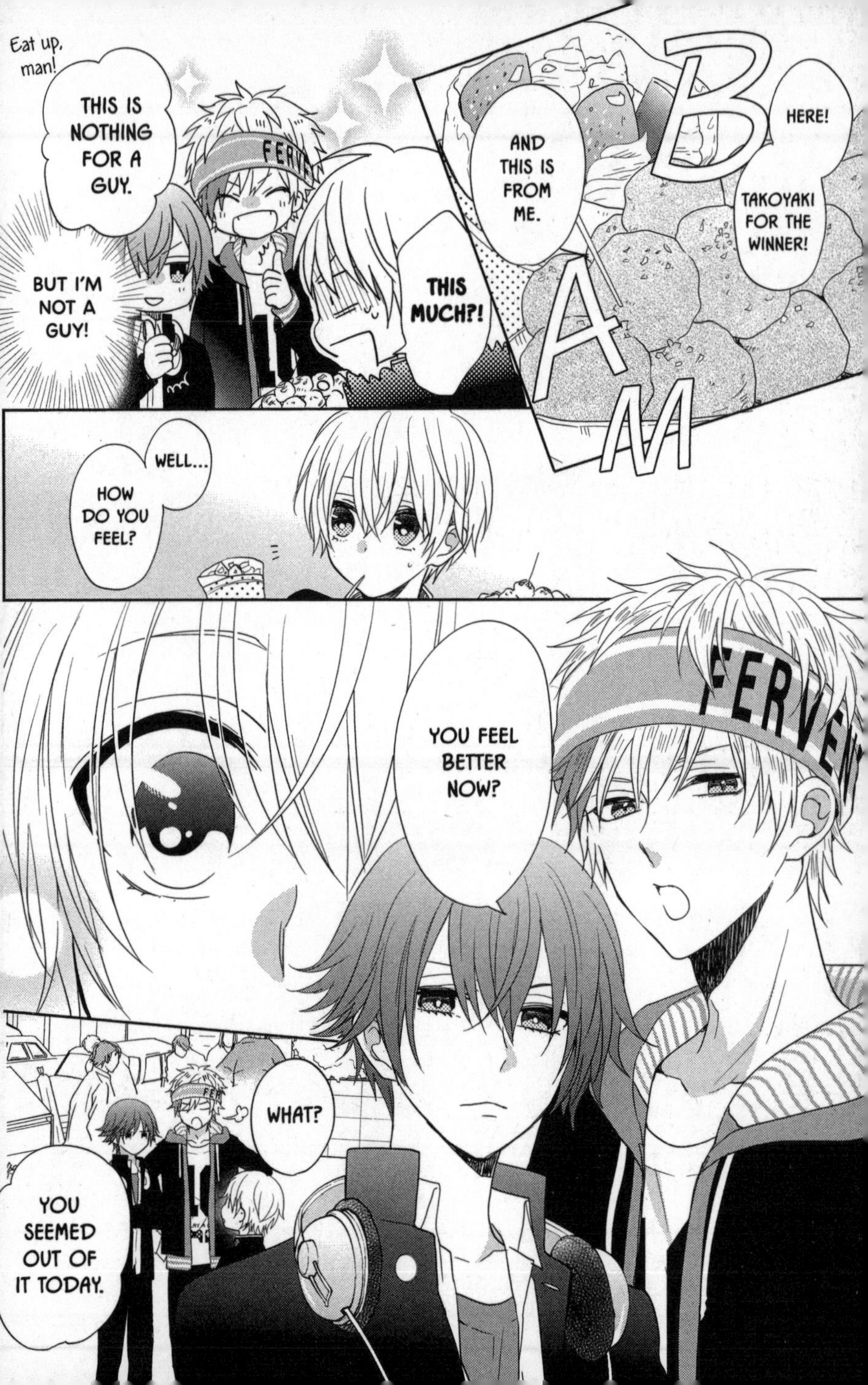
HERE!
TAKOYAKI FOR THE WINNER!
AND THIS IS FROM ME.
BAM
THIS MUCH?!
Eat up, man!
THIS IS NOTHING FOR A GUY.
BUT I'M NOT A GUY!
WELL...
HOW DO YOU FEEL?
FERVENT
YOU FEEL BETTER NOW?
WHAT?
YOU SEEMED OUT OF IT TODAY.

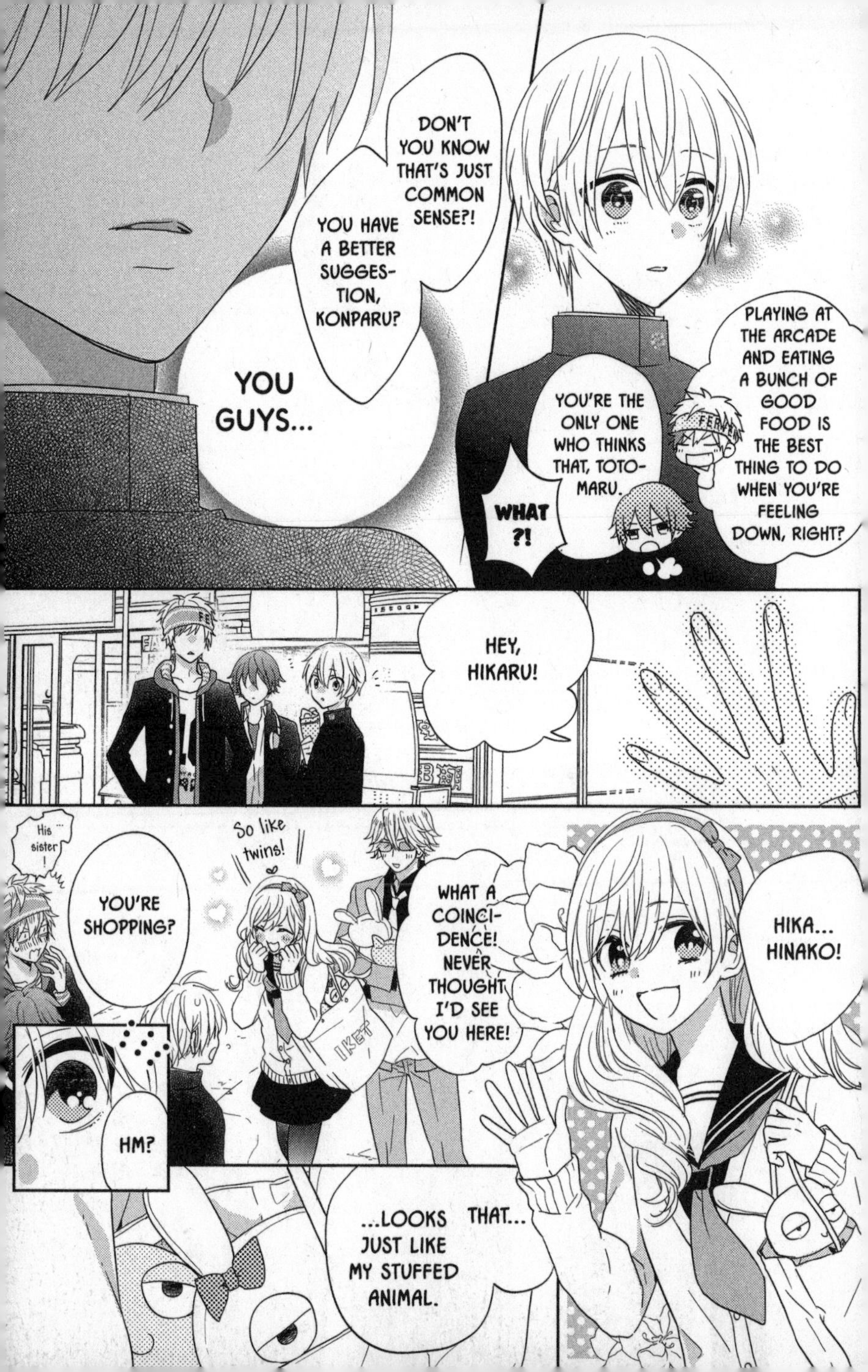
PLAYING AT THE ARCADE AND EATING A BUNCH OF GOOD FOOD IS THE BEST THING TO DO WHEN YOU'RE FEELING DOWN, RIGHT?
YOU'RE THE ONLY ONE WHO THINKS THAT, TOTOMARU.
WHAT ?!
DON'T YOU KNOW THAT'S JUST COMMON SENSE?!
YOU HAVE A BETTER SUGGESTION, KONPARU?
YOU GUYS...
HEY, HIKARU!
HIKA... HINAKO!
WHAT A COINCIDENCE! NEVER THOUGHT I'D SEE YOU HERE!
So like twins!
YOU'RE SHOPPING?
His ... sister!
HM?
THAT...
...LOOKS JUST LIKE MY STUFFED ANIMAL.

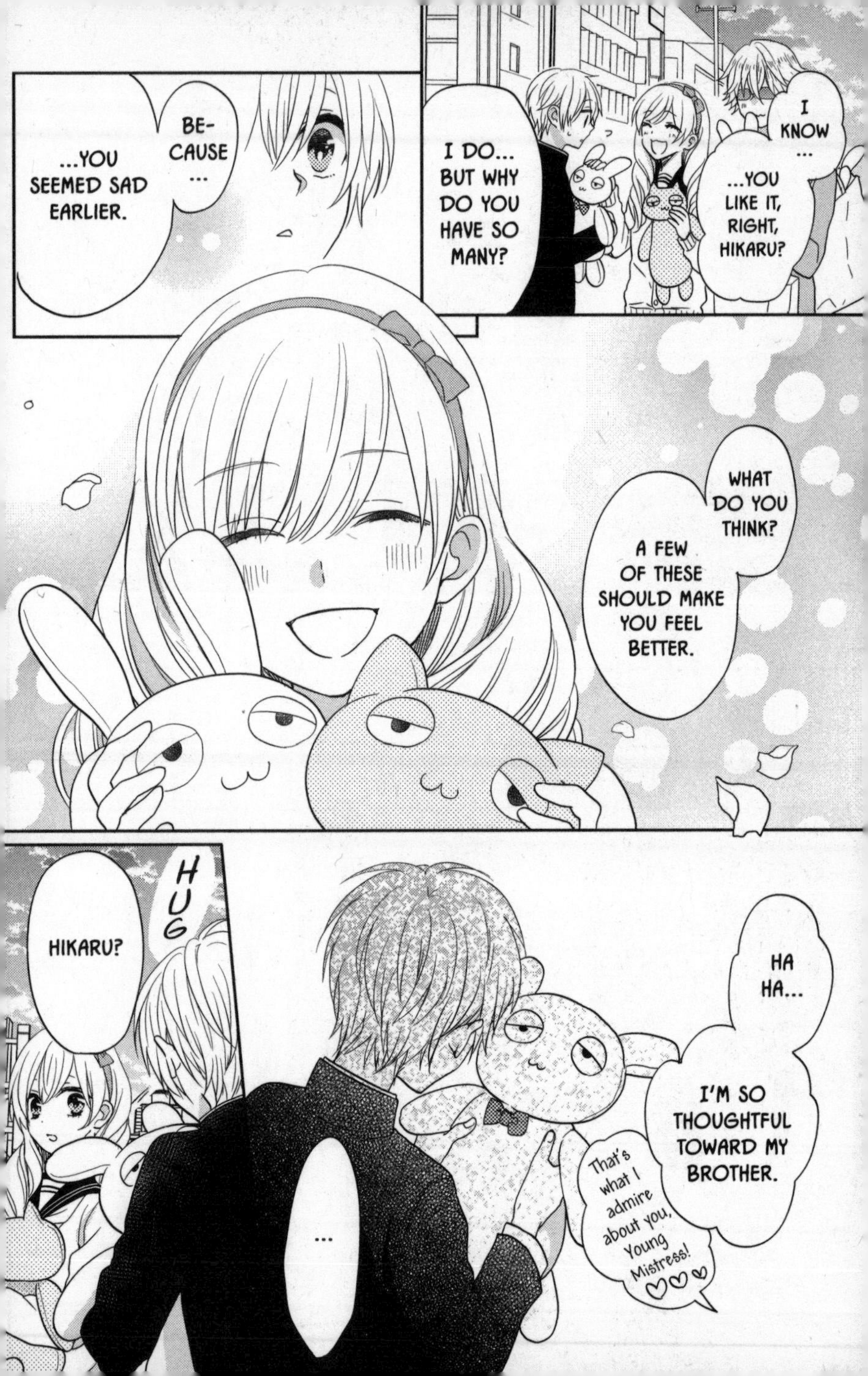
I KNOW ...
...YOU LIKE IT, RIGHT, HIKARU?
I DO... BUT WHY DO YOU HAVE SO MANY?
BE-CAUSE ...
...YOU SEEMED SAD EARLIER.
WHAT DO YOU THINK?
A FEW OF THESE SHOULD MAKE YOU FEEL BETTER.
HA HA...
I'M SO THOUGHTFUL TOWARD MY BROTHER.
That's what I admire about you, Young Mistress! ♡♡♡
HUG
HIKARU?
...

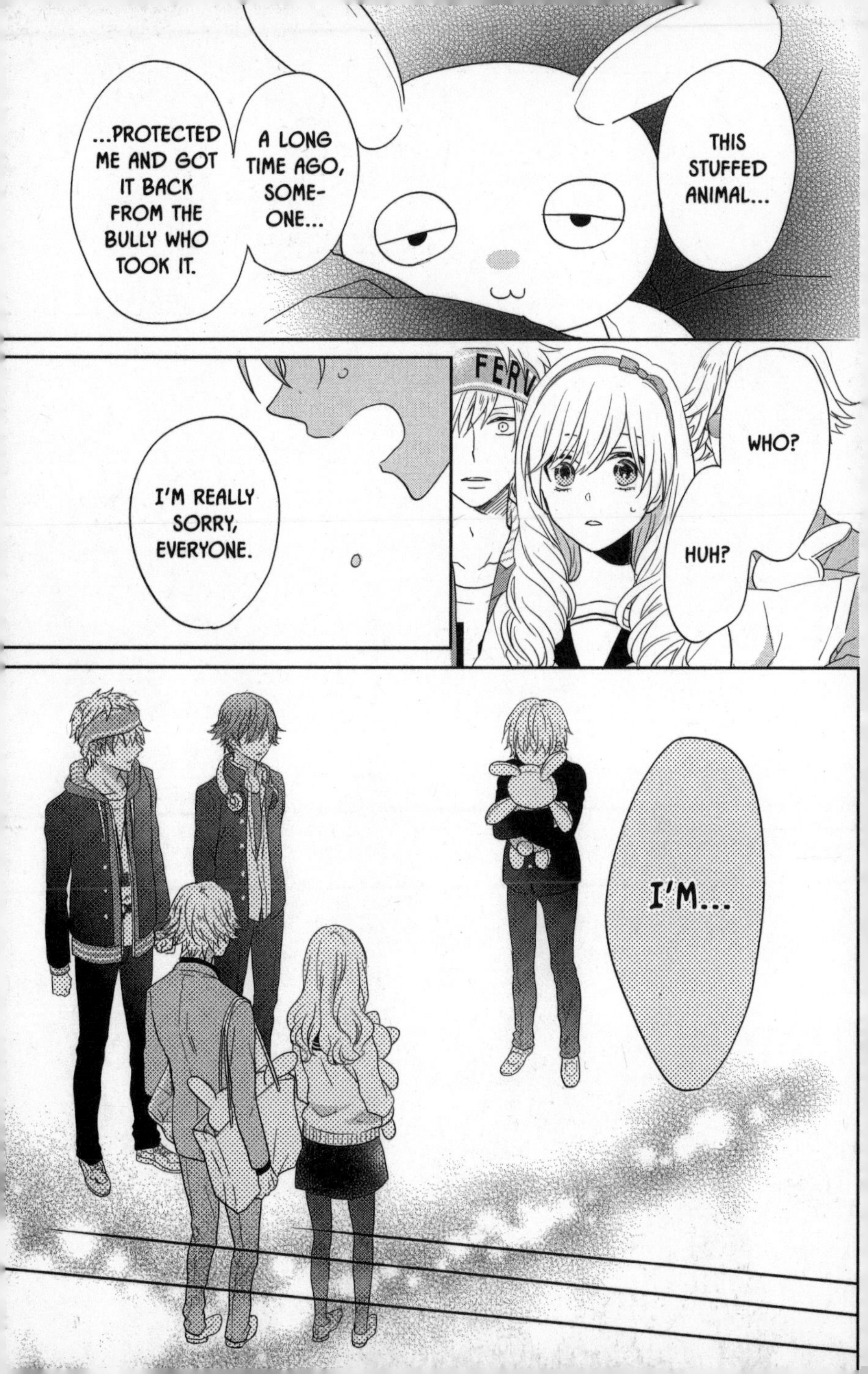
THIS STUFFED ANIMAL...
A LONG TIME AGO, SOME-ONE...
...PROTECTED ME AND GOT IT BACK FROM THE BULLY WHO TOOK IT.
WHO?
HUH?
I'M REALLY SORRY, EVERYONE.
I'M...

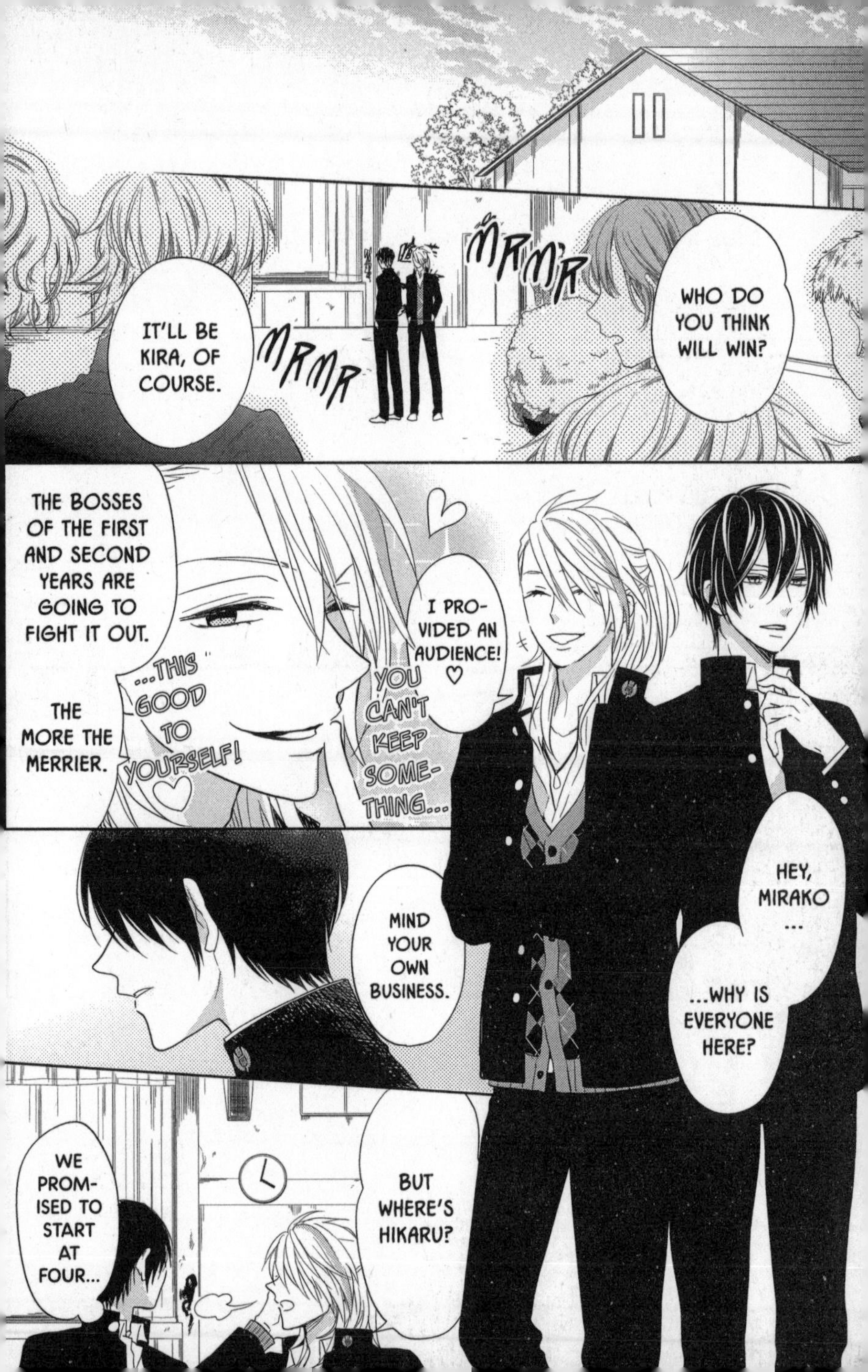

WHO DO YOU THINK WILL WIN?
MRMR
MRMR
IT'LL BE KIRA, OF COURSE.
MRMR
HEY, MIRAKO ...
...WHY IS EVERYONE HERE?
I PRO-VIDED AN AUDIENCE! ♡
YOU CAN'T KEEP SOME-THING...
...THIS GOOD TO YOURSELF! ♡
THE BOSSES OF THE FIRST AND SECOND YEARS ARE GOING TO FIGHT IT OUT.
THE MORE THE MERRIER.
MIND YOUR OWN BUSINESS.
BUT WHERE'S HIKARU?
WE PROM-ISED TO START AT FOUR...

IT'S BETTER THIS WAY.
SHE WASN'T MEANT TO BE HERE AT SHISHIKU.
THAT'S WHY...
ASTIR
TMP
SORRY TO KEEP YOU WAITING.

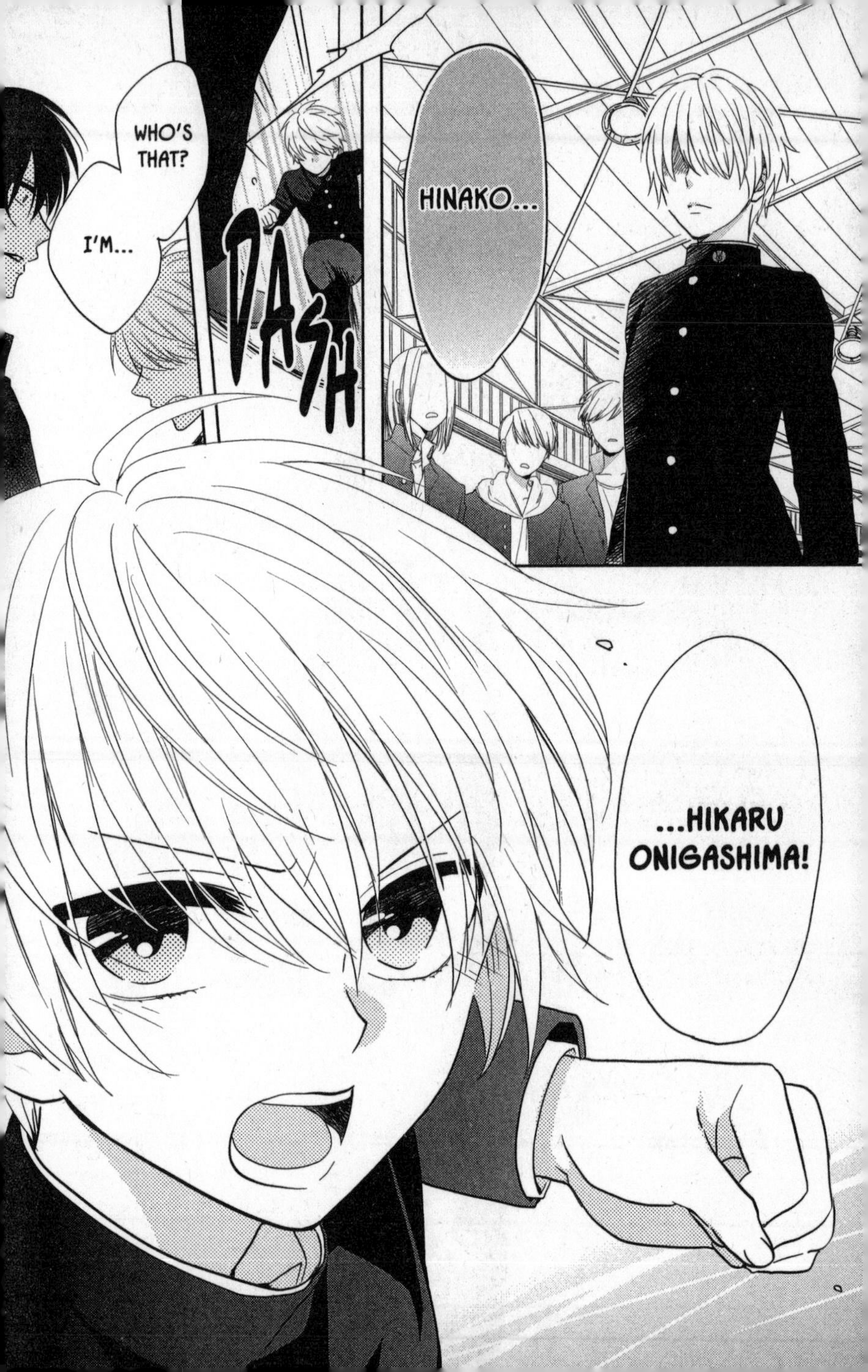
HINAKO...
DASH
WHO'S THAT?
I'M...
...HIKARU ONIGASHIMA!

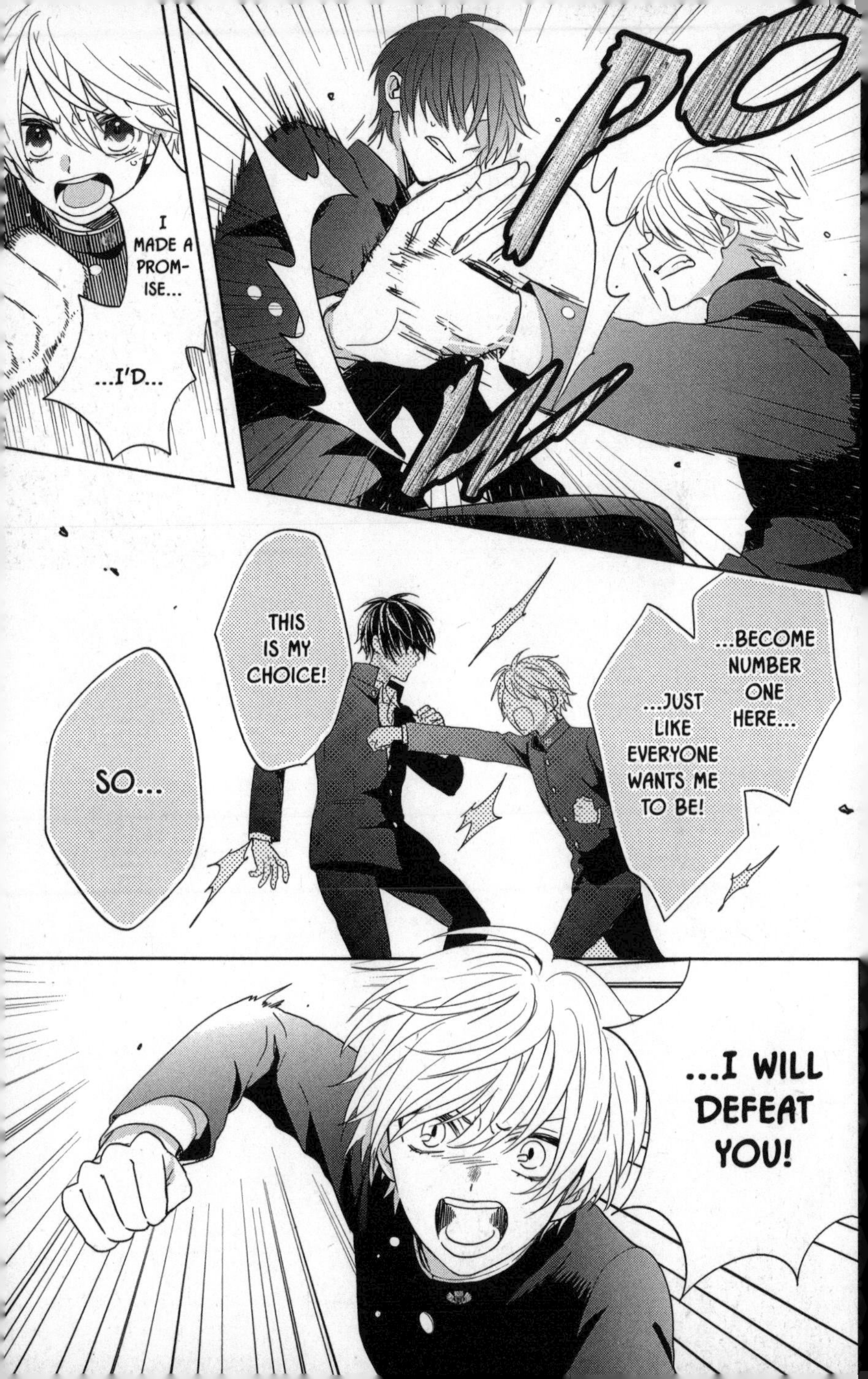
POW
I MADE A PROMISE...
...I'D...
...BECOME NUMBER ONE HERE...
...JUST LIKE EVERYONE WANTS ME TO BE!
THIS IS MY CHOICE!
SO...
...I WILL DEFEAT YOU!

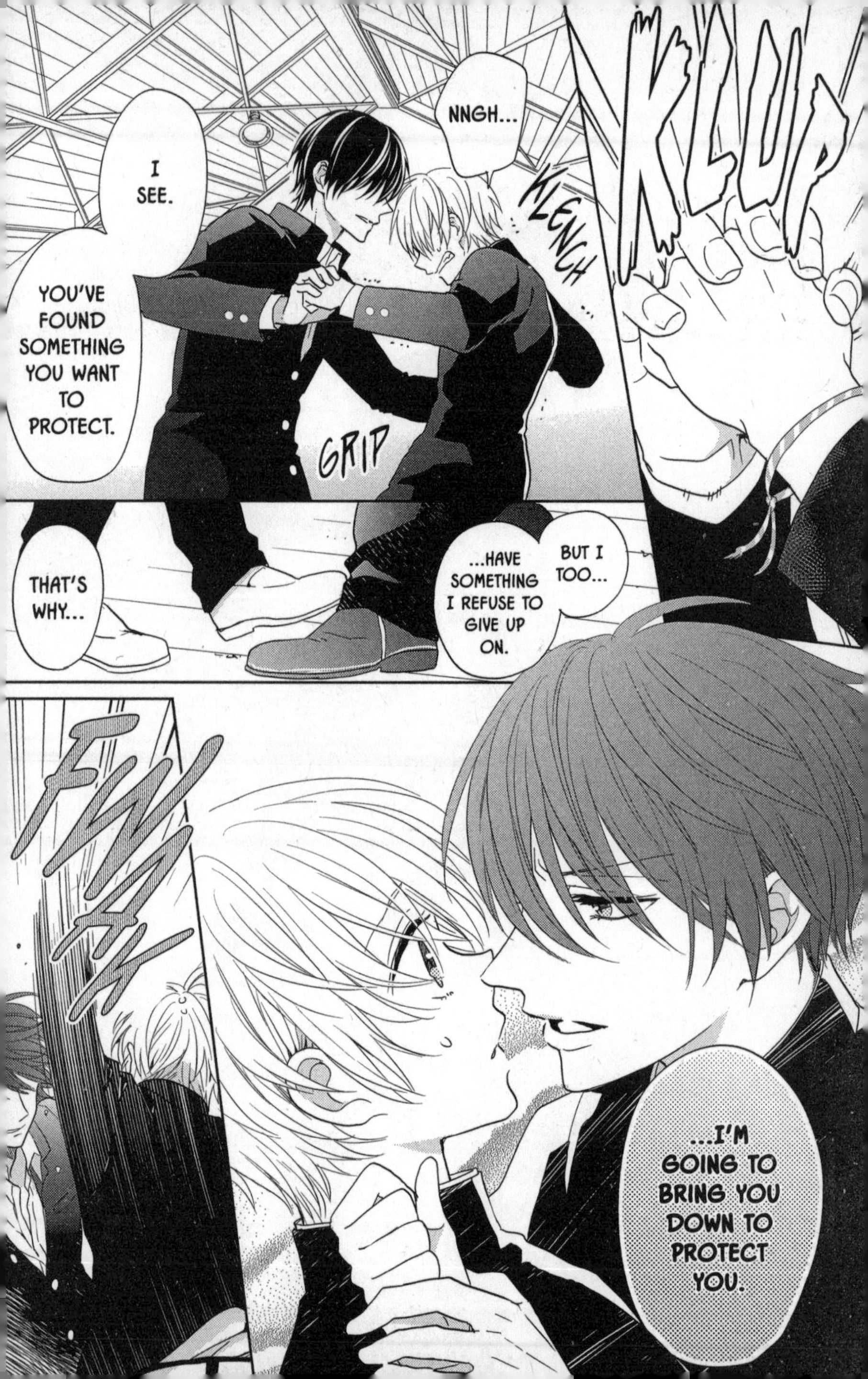
KLUP
NNGH...
KLENCH
I SEE.
YOU'VE FOUND SOMETHING YOU WANT TO PROTECT.
GRIP
BUT I TOO...
...HAVE SOMETHING I REFUSE TO GIVE UP ON.
THAT'S WHY...
FWAAH
...I'M GOING TO BRING YOU DOWN TO PROTECT YOU.

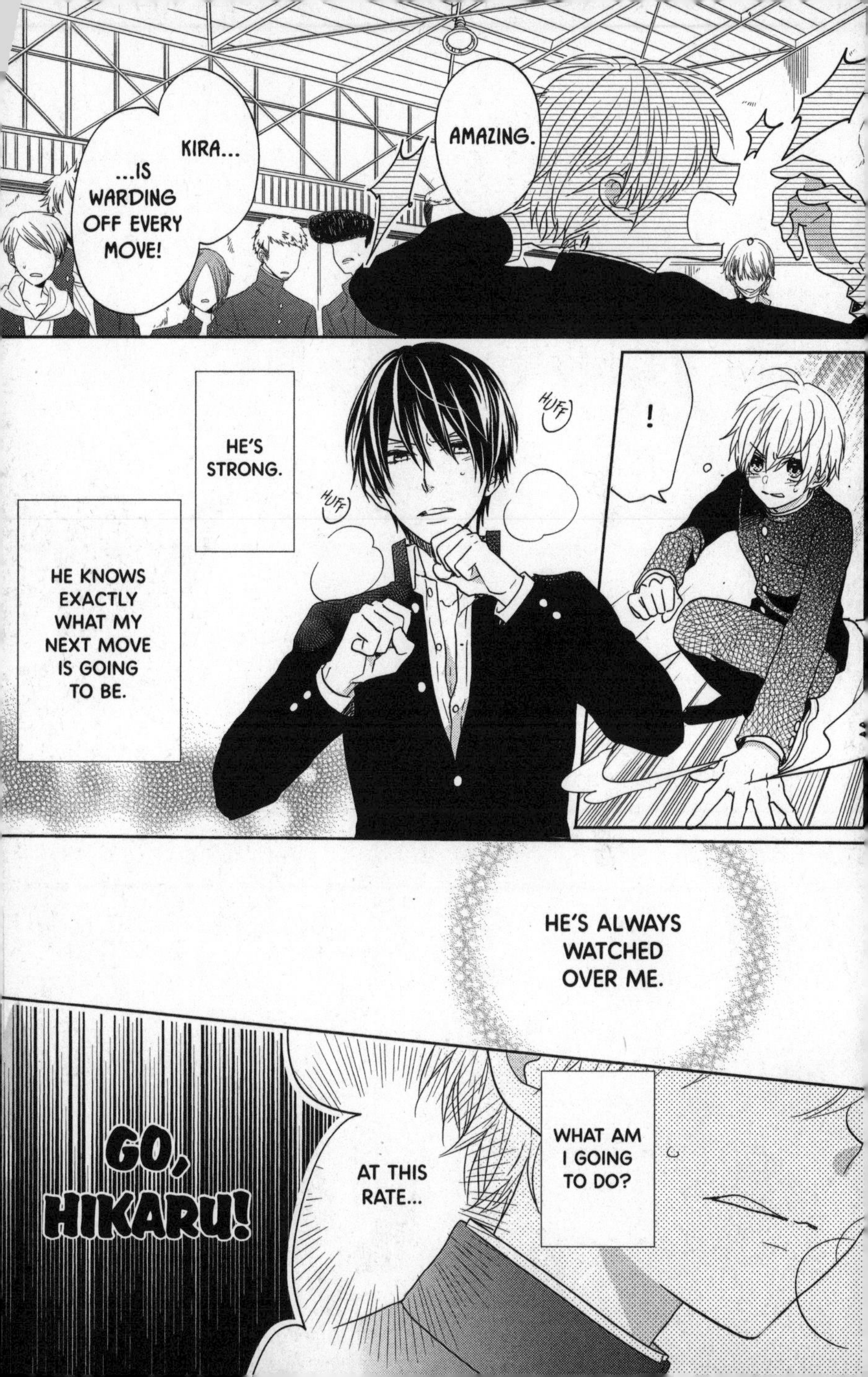
AMAZING.
KIRA... ...IS WARDING OFF EVERY MOVE!
!
HE'S STRONG.
HE KNOWS EXACTLY WHAT MY NEXT MOVE IS GOING TO BE.
HUFF
HUFF
HE'S ALWAYS WATCHED OVER ME.
WHAT AM I GOING TO DO?
AT THIS RATE...
GO, HIKARU!

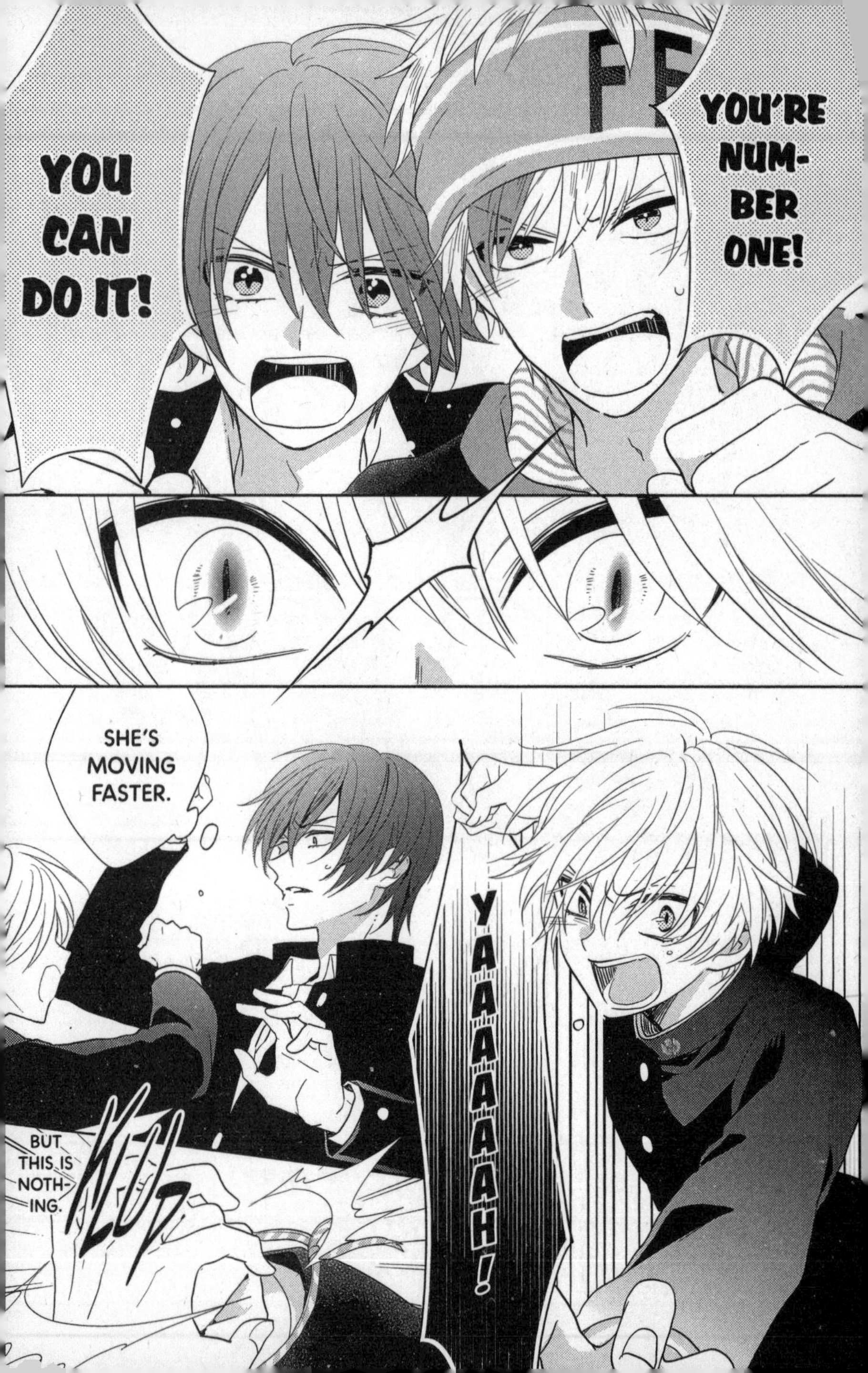
YOU'RE NUM-BER ONE!
YOU CAN DO IT!
YAAAAAAAAAH!
SHE'S MOVING FASTER.
BUT THIS IS NOTH-ING.

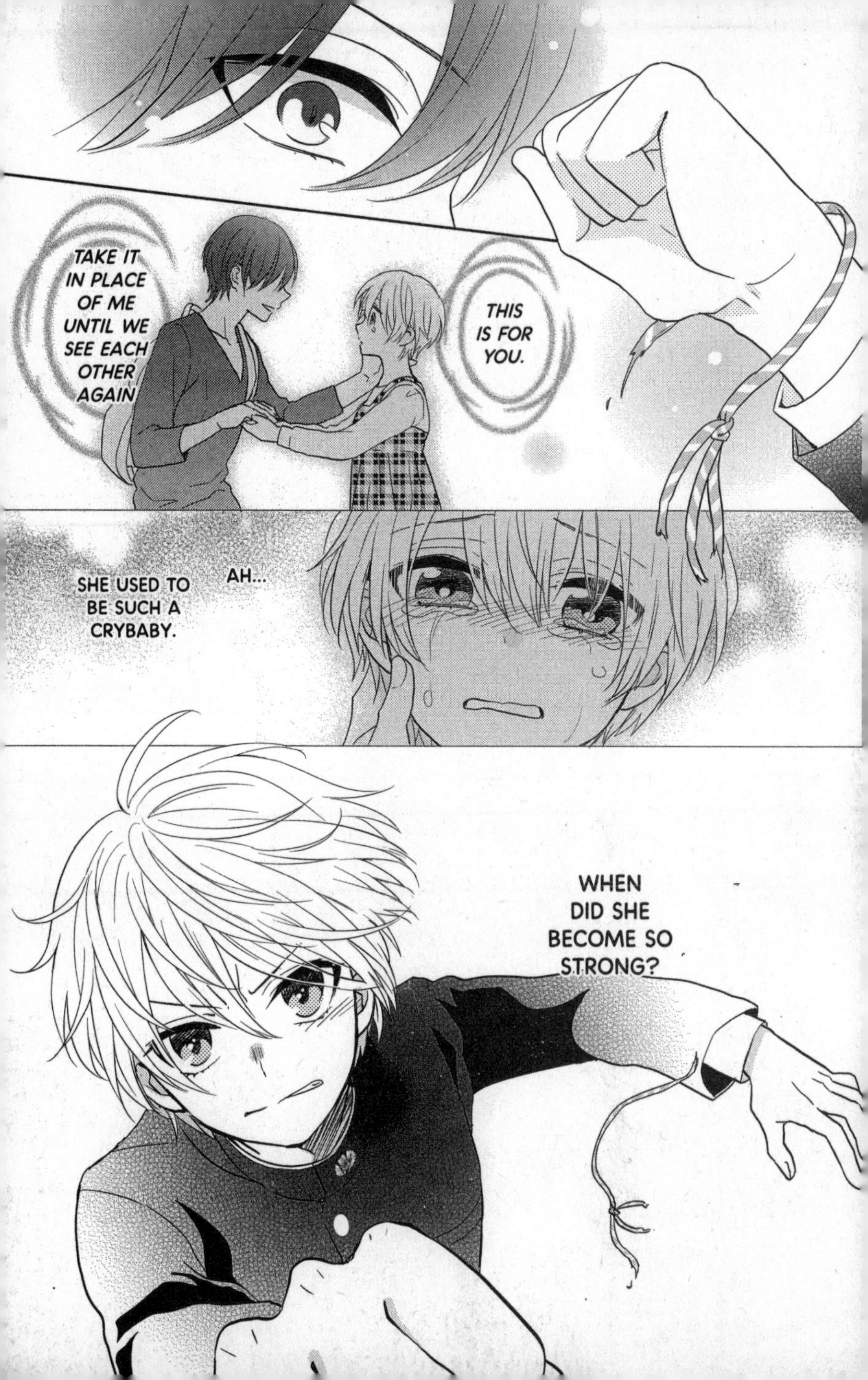
THIS IS FOR YOU.
TAKE IT IN PLACE OF ME UNTIL WE SEE EACH OTHER AGAIN.
AH...
SHE USED TO BE SUCH A CRYBABY.
WHEN DID SHE BECOME SO STRONG?

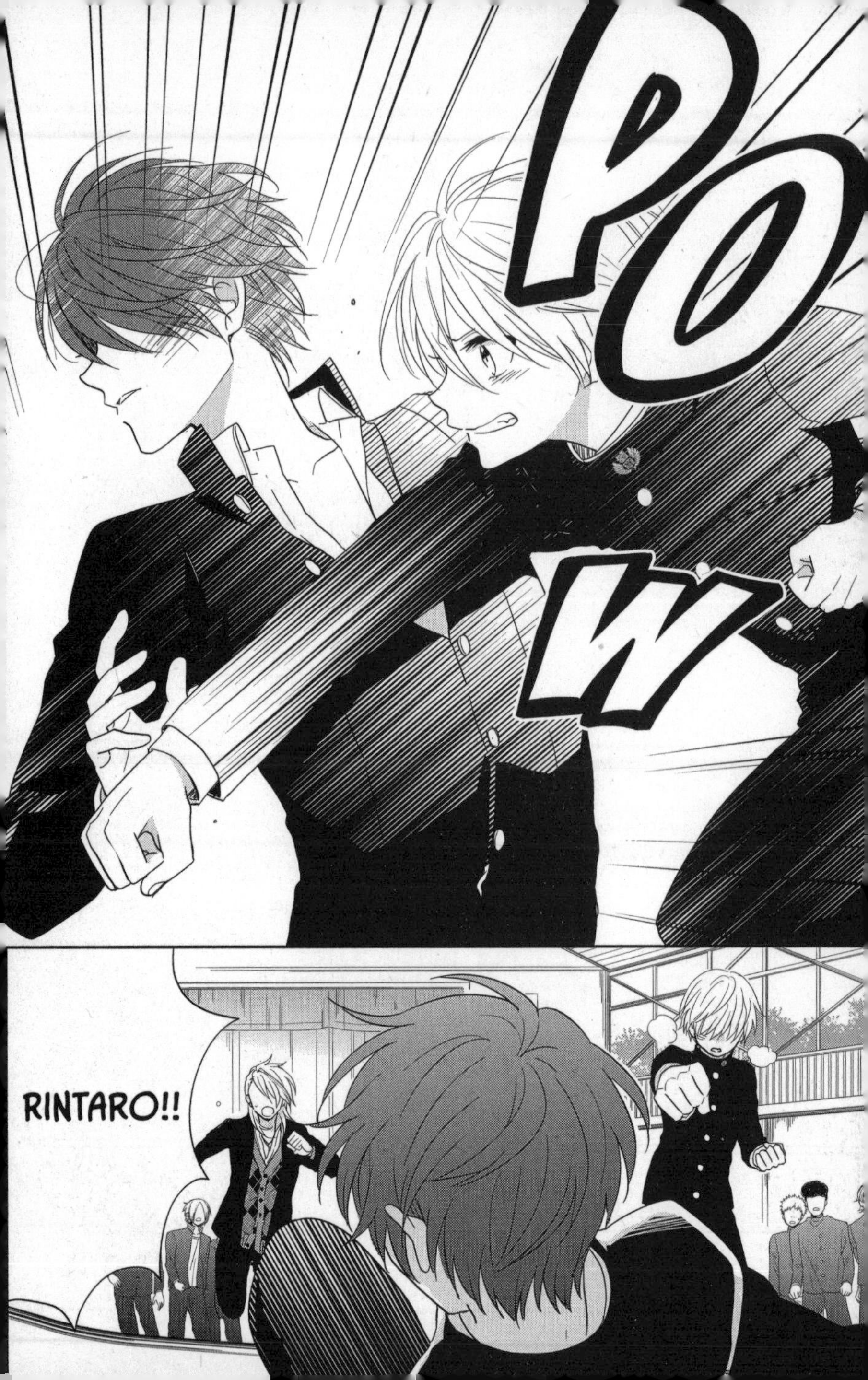
POW
RINTARO!!

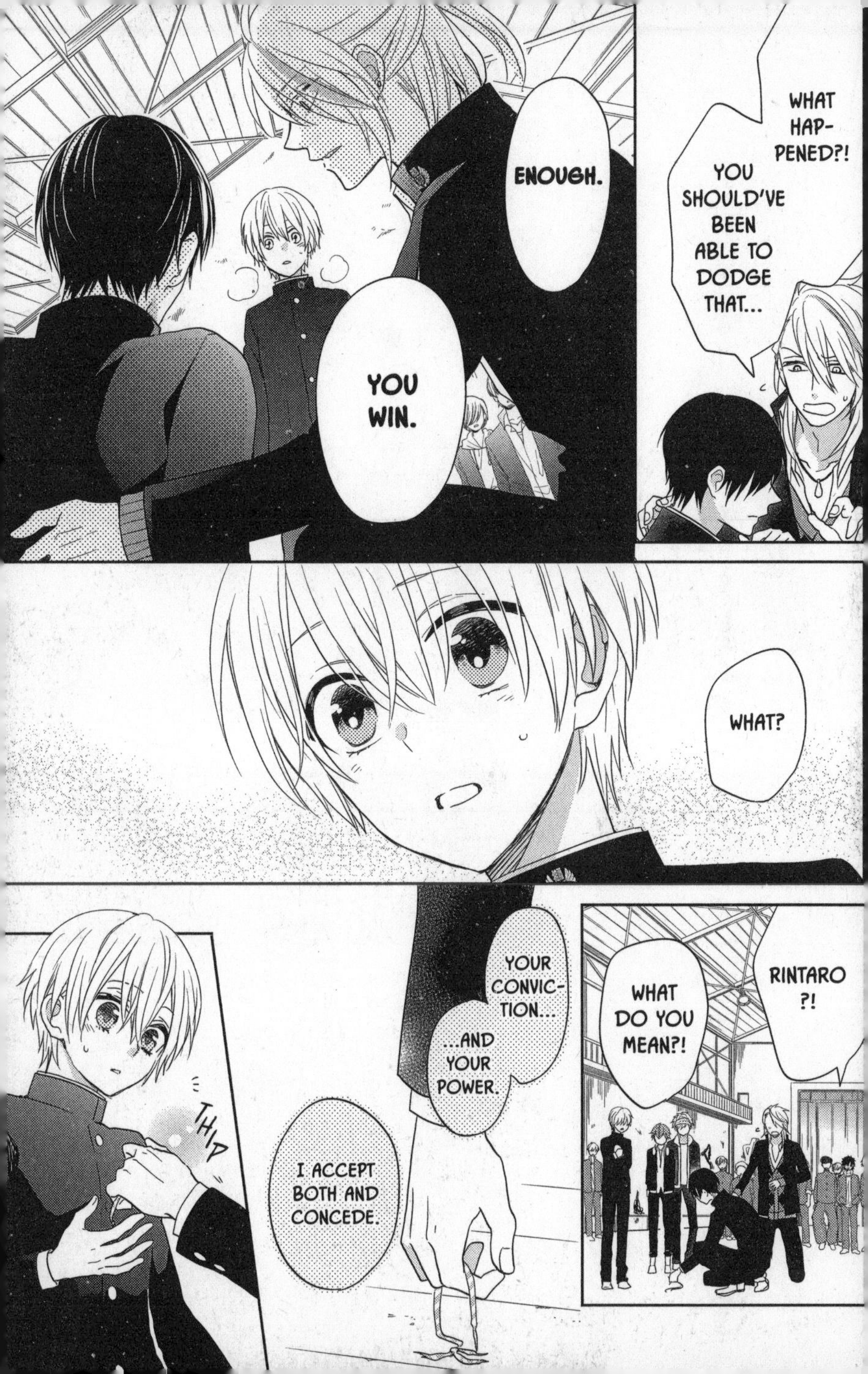
WHAT HAPPENED?!
YOU SHOULD'VE BEEN ABLE TO DODGE THAT...
ENOUGH.
YOU WIN.
WHAT?
RINTARO?!
WHAT DO YOU MEAN?!
YOUR CONVICTION...
...AND YOUR POWER.
I ACCEPT BOTH AND CONCEDE.
THIP

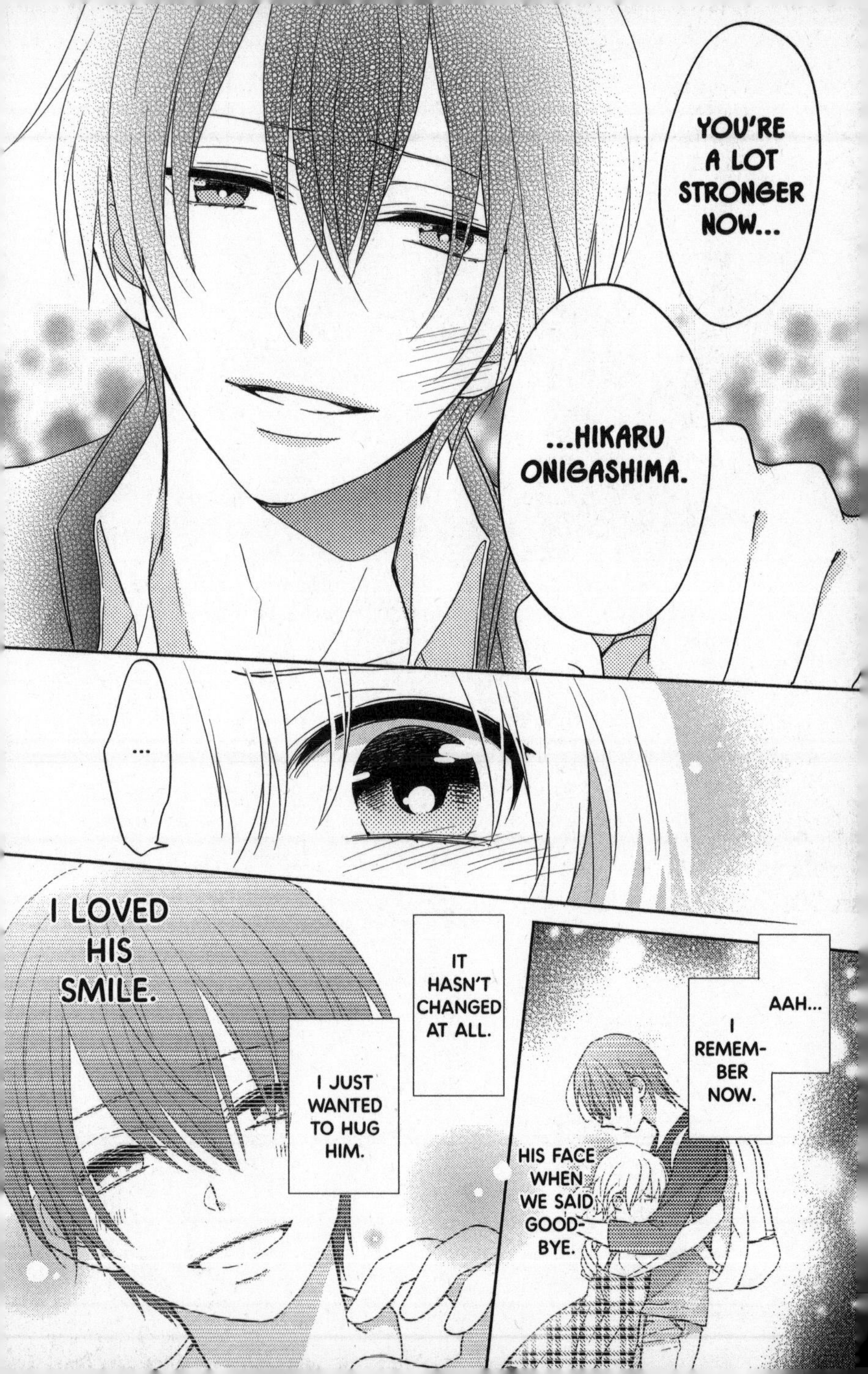
YOU'RE A LOT STRONGER NOW...
...HIKARU ONIGASHIMA.
...
AAH...
I REMEMBER NOW.
HIS FACE WHEN WE SAID GOOD-BYE.
IT HASN'T CHANGED AT ALL.
I LOVED HIS SMILE.
I JUST WANTED TO HUG HIM.

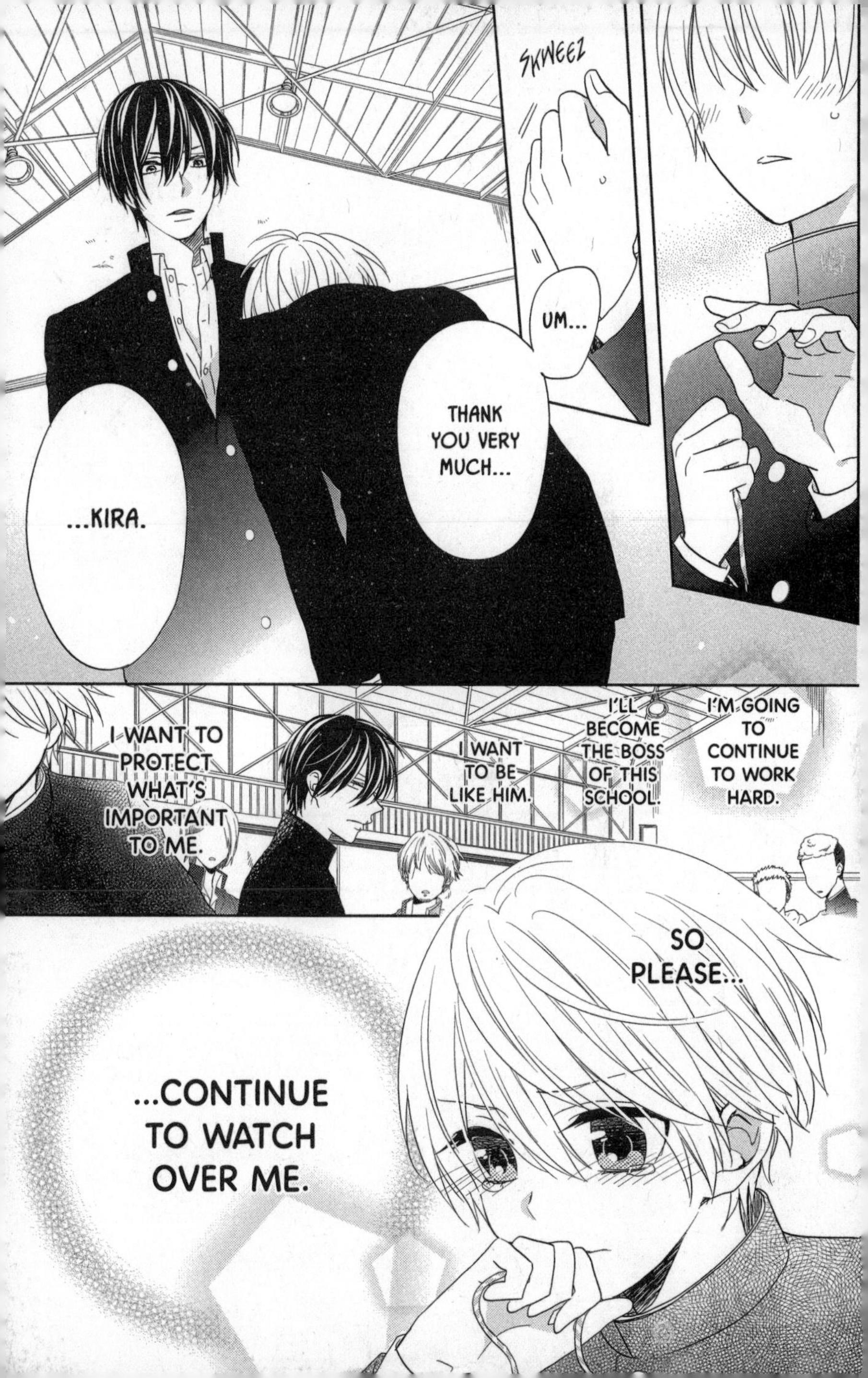
SKWEEZ
UM...
THANK YOU VERY MUCH...
...KIRA.
I'M GOING TO CONTINUE TO WORK HARD.
I'LL BECOME THE BOSS OF THIS SCHOOL.
I WANT TO BE LIKE HIM.
I WANT TO PROTECT WHAT'S IMPORTANT TO ME.
SO PLEASE...
...CONTINUE TO WATCH OVER ME.

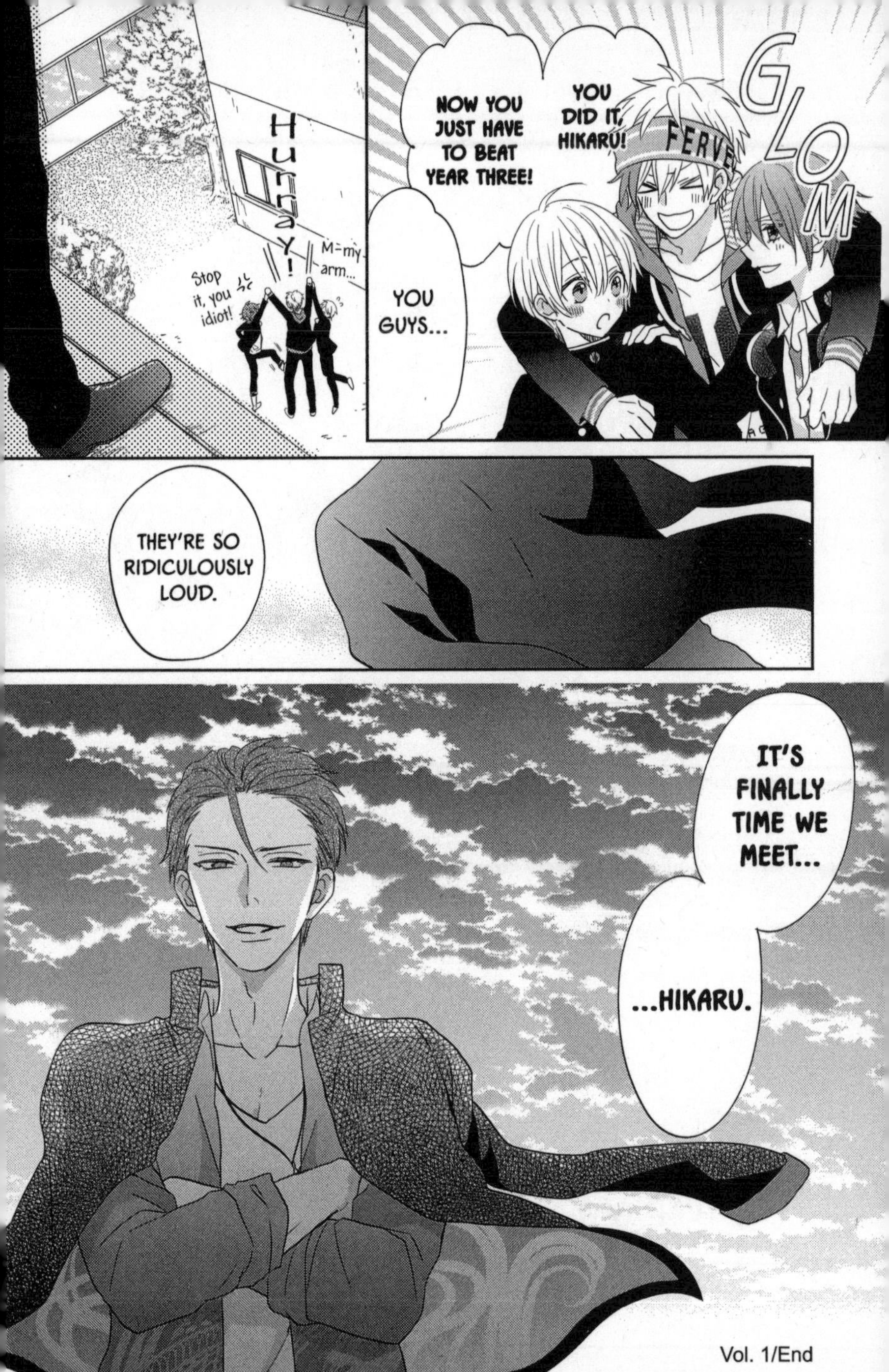
GLOM
YOU DID IT, HIKARU!
NOW YOU JUST HAVE TO BEAT YEAR THREE!
YOU GUYS...
Hurray!
M-my arm...
Stop it, you idiot!
THEY'RE SO RIDICULOUSLY LOUD.
IT'S FINALLY TIME WE MEET...
...HIKARU.

Vol. 1/End

KENKA BANCHO
Otome

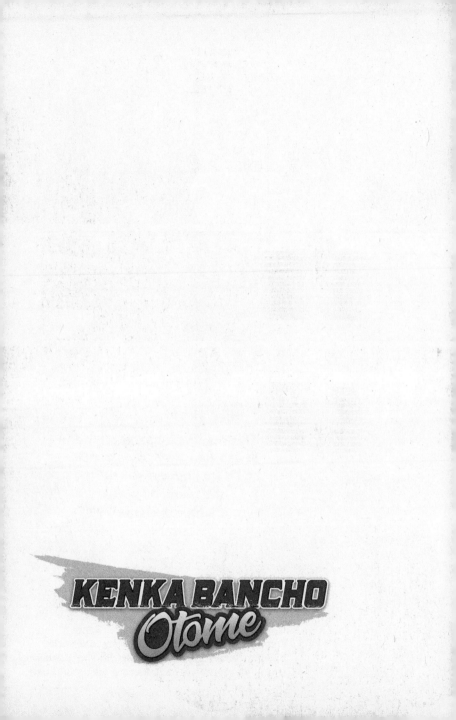

This manga is based off the *Kenka Bancho Otome* game, so I'd be happy if you played the game as well!

—CHIE SHIMADA

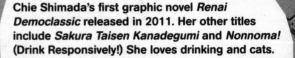

Chie Shimada's first graphic novel *Renai Democlassic* released in 2011. Her other titles include *Sakura Taisen Kanadegumi* and *Nonnoma!* (Drink Responsively!) She loves drinking and cats.

Kenka Bancho Otome:
Love's Battle Royale
Vol. 1

SHOJO BEAT MANGA EDITION

STORY AND ART BY
Chie Shimada

ORIGINAL CONCEPT BY
Spike Chunsoft

VIDEO GAME DEVELOPED BY
Red Entertainment

TRANSLATION **JN Productions**
TOUCH-UP ART & LETTERING **Inori Fukuda Trant**
GRAPHIC DESIGN **Alice Lewis**
EDITOR **Nancy Thistlethwaite**

KENKABANCHO OTOME -KOI NO BATTLE ROYALE-
by CHIE SHIMADA / SPIKE CHUNSOFT / RED ENTERTAINMENT
© Chie Shimada 2016
© Spike Chunsoft Co., Ltd. All Rights Reserved. Developed by RED.
All rights reserved.
First published in Japan in 2016 by HAKUSENSHA, Inc., Tokyo.
English language translation rights arranged with HAKUSENSHA, Inc., Tokyo.

Printed in the U.S.A.

Published by VIZ Media, LLC
P.O. Box 77010
San Francisco, CA 94107

10 9 8 7 6 5 4 3 2 1
First printing, April 2018

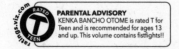

viz.com   shojobeat.com

Nino Arisugawa, a girl who loves to sing, experiences her first heart-wrenching goodbye when her beloved childhood friend, Momo, moves away. And after Nino befriends Yuzu, a music composer, she experiences another sad parting! With music as their common ground and only outlet, how will everyone's unrequited loves play out?

ANONYMOUS NOISE

Story & Art by
Ryoko Fukuyama

Behind the Scenes!!

STORY AND ART BY **BISCO HATORI**

From the creator of Ouran High School Host Club

Behind the Scenes!!
01
Behind the Scenes!!
01
BISCO HATORI
STORY AND ART BY
BISCO HATORI

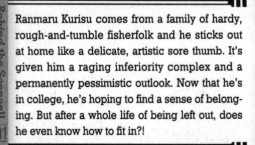

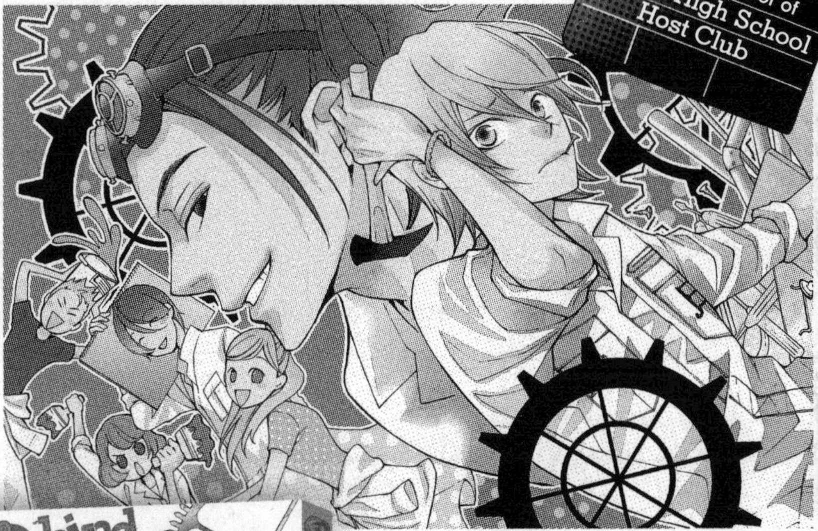

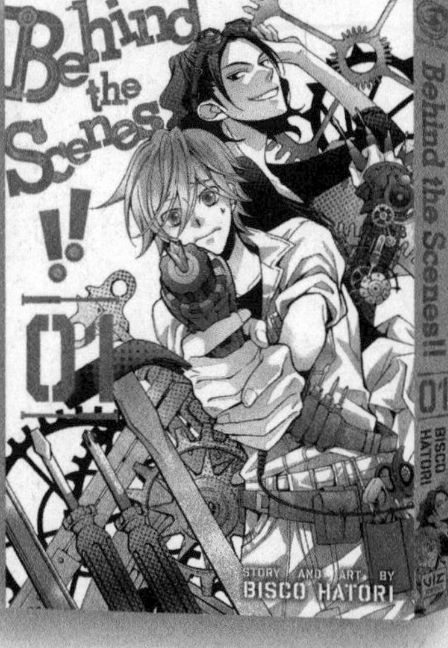

Ranmaru Kurisu comes from a family of hardy, rough-and-tumble fisherfolk and he sticks out at home like a delicate, artistic sore thumb. It's given him a raging inferiority complex and a permanently pessimistic outlook. Now that he's in college, he's hoping to find a sense of belonging. But after a whole life of being left out, does he even know how to fit in?!

RATED T FOR TEEN
ratings.viz.com

VIZ MEDIA
www.viz.com

Shojo Beat

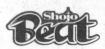

IDOL *dreams*

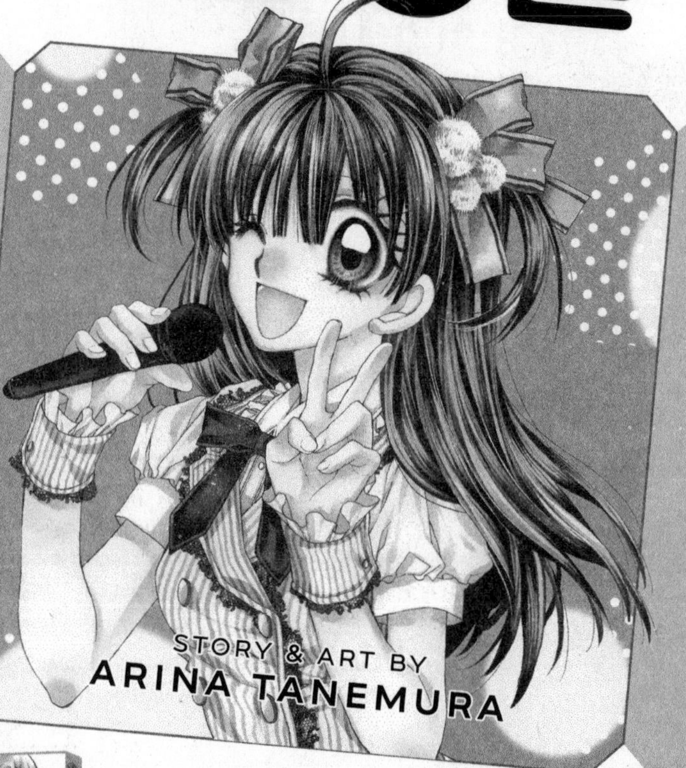

STORY & ART BY
ARINA TANEMURA

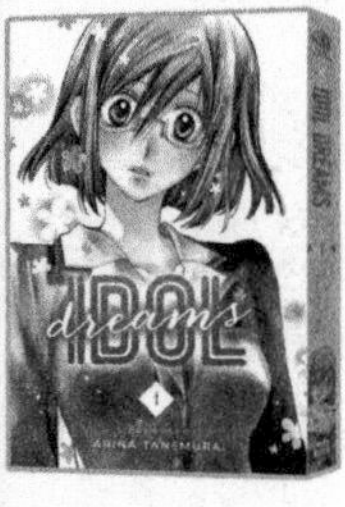
IDOL
dreams
ARINA TANEMURA

At age 31, office worker Chikage Deguchi feels she missed her chances at love and success. When word gets out that she's a virgin, Chikage is humiliated and wishes she could turn back time to when she was still young and popular. She takes an experimental drug that changes her appearance back to when she was 15. Now Chikage is determined to pursue everything she missed out on all those years ago—including becoming a star!

Shojo Beat · VIZ media · www.viz.com · RATED T FOR TEEN · ratings.viz.com

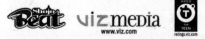

Shuriken
and Pleats

When the master she has sworn to protect is killed, Mikage Kirio, a skilled ninja, travels to Japan to start a new, peaceful life for herself. But as soon as she arrives, she finds herself fighting to protect the life of Mahito Wakashimatsu, a man who is under attack by a band of ninja. From that time on, Mikage is drawn deeper into the machinations of his powerful family.

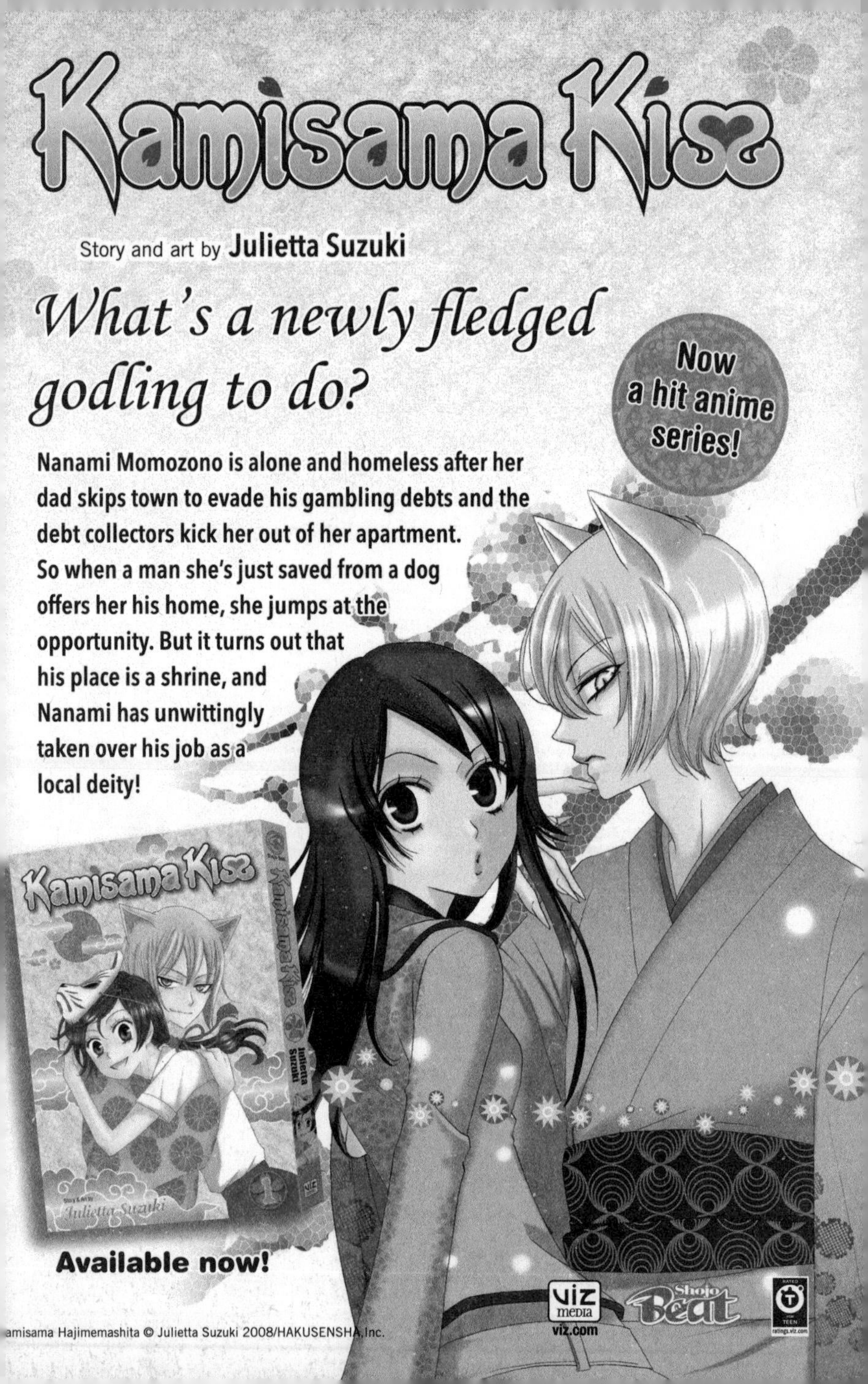
Kamisama Kiss
Story and art by Julietta Suzuki
What's a newly fledged godling to do?
Now a hit anime series!
Nanami Momozono is alone and homeless after her dad skips town to evade his gambling debts and the debt collectors kick her out of her apartment. So when a man she's just saved from a dog offers her his home, she jumps at the opportunity. But it turns out that his place is a shrine, and Nanami has unwittingly taken over his job as a local deity!
Kamisama Kiss
1
Julietta Suzuki
Available now!
amisama Hajimemashita © Julietta Suzuki 2008/HAKUSENSHA, Inc.
VIZ MEDIA
viz.com
Shojo Beat
T
TEEN
ratings.viz.com

STOP!

You may be reading the wrong way!

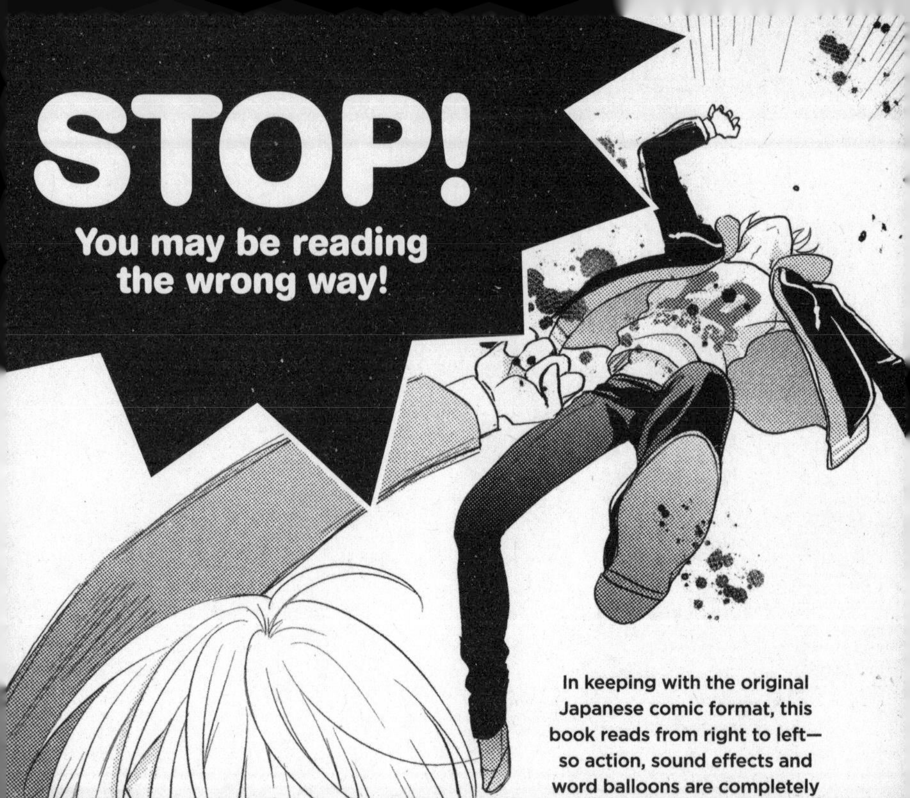

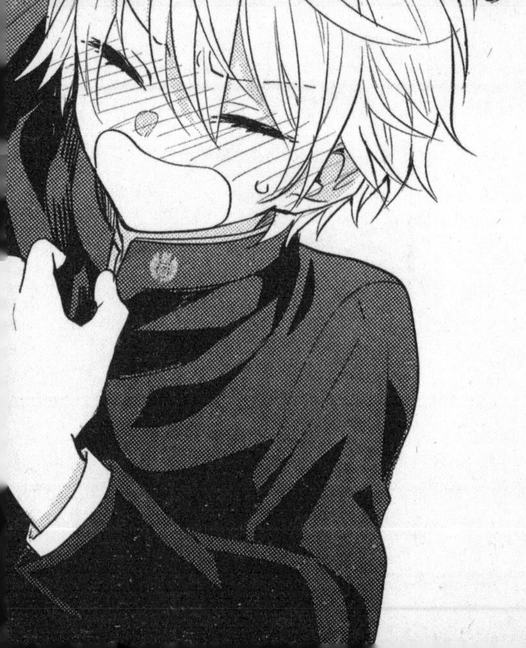

In keeping with the original Japanese comic format, this book reads from right to left—so action, sound effects and word balloons are completely reversed to preserve the orientation of the original artwork.

Check out the diagram shown here to get the hang of things, and then turn to the other side of the book to get started!

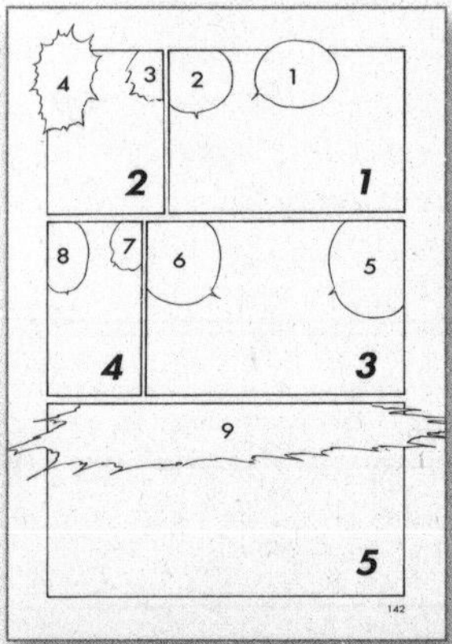
1
2
3
4
1
2
5
6
7
8
3
4
9
5
142